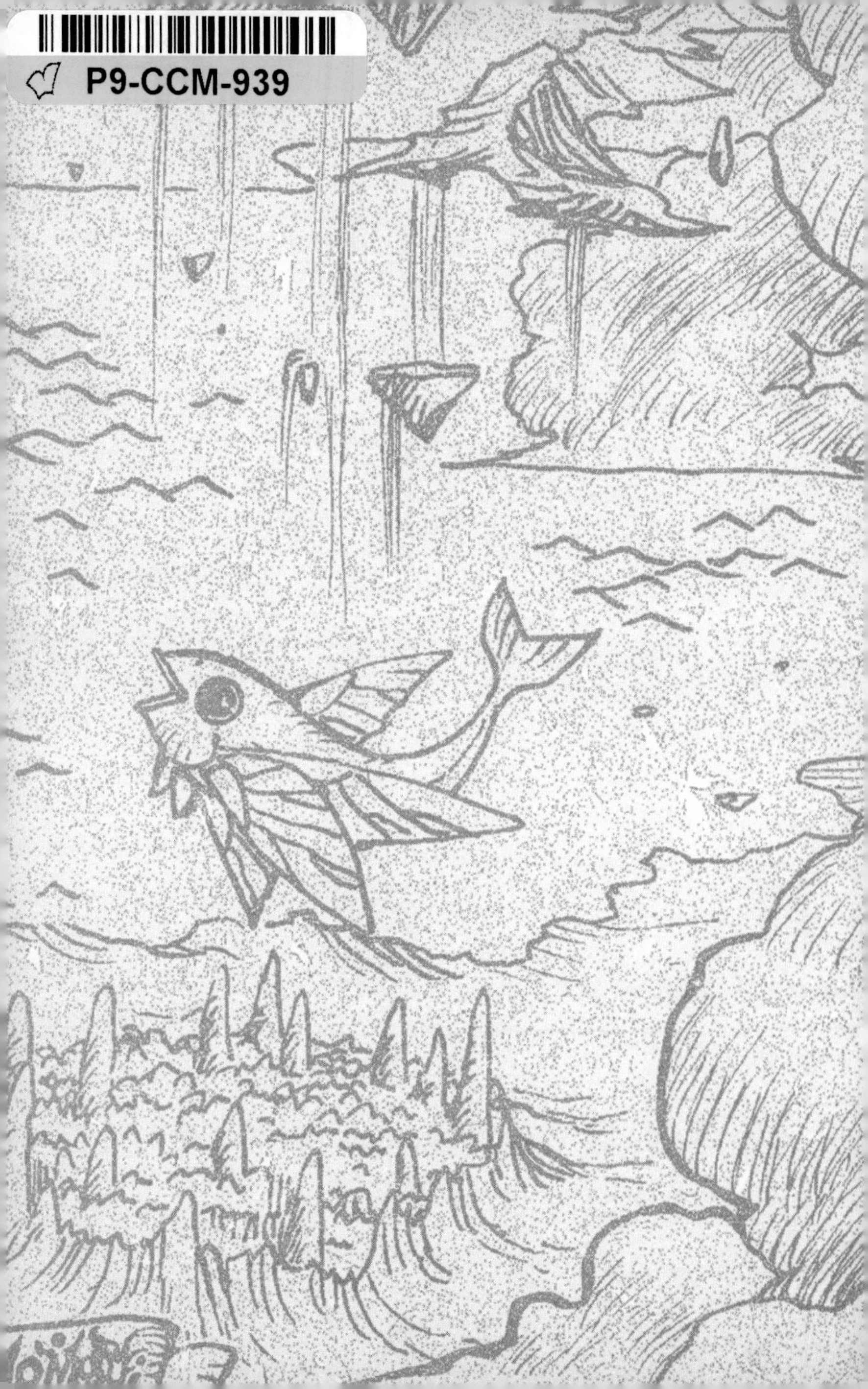

ALSO AVAILABLE FROM TOKYOPOP®

MANGA

.HACK//LEGEND OF THE TWILIGHT (September 2003)
@LARGE (COMING SOON)
ANGELIC LAYER*
BABY BIRTH* (September 2003)
BATTLE ROYALE*
BRAIN POWERED*
BRIGADOON* (August 2003)
CARDCAPTOR SAKURA
CARDCAPTOR SAKURA: MASTER OF THE CLOW*
CHOBITS*
CHRONICLES OF THE CURSED SWORD
CLAMP SCHOOL DETECTIVES*
CLOVER
CONFIDENTIAL CONFESSIONS*
CORRECTOR YUI
COWBOY BEBOP*
COWBOY BEBOP: SHOOTING STAR*
DEMON DIARY
DIGIMON*
DRAGON HUNTER
DRAGON KNIGHTS*
DUKLYON: CLAMP SCHOOL DEFENDERS*
ERICA SAKURAZAWA*
FAKE*
FLCL* (September 2003)
FORBIDDEN DANCE* (August 2003)
GATE KEEPERS*
G GUNDAM*
GRAVITATION*
GTO*
GUNDAM WING
GUNDAM WING: BATTLEFIELD OF PACIFISTS
GUNDAM WING: ENDLESS WALTZ*
GUNDAM WING: THE LAST OUTPOST*
HAPPY MANIA*
HARLEM BEAT
I.N.V.U.
INITIAL D*
ISLAND
JING: KING OF BANDITS*
JULINE
KARE KANO*
KINDAICHI CASE FILES, THE*
KING OF HELL
KODOCHA: SANA'S STAGE*
LOVE HINA*
LUPIN III*
MAGIC KNIGHT RAYEARTH* (August 2003)
MAGIC KNIGHT RAYEARTH II* (COMING SOON)

MAN OF MANY FACES*
MARMALADE BOY*
MARS*
MIRACLE GIRLS
MIYUKI-CHAN IN WONDERLAND* (October 2003)
MONSTERS, INC.
PARADISE KISS*
PARASYTE
PEACH GIRL
PEACH GIRL: CHANGE OF HEART*
PET SHOP OF HORRORS*
PLANET LADDER*
PLANETES* (October 2003)
PRIEST
RAGNAROK
RAVE MASTER*
REALITY CHECK
REBIRTH
REBOUND*
RISING STARS OF MANGA
SABER MARIONETTE J*
SAILOR MOON
SAINT TAIL
SAMURAI DEEPER KYO*
SAMURAI GIRL: REAL BOUT HIGH SCHOOL*
SCRYED*
SHAOLIN SISTERS*
SHIRAHIME-SYO: SNOW GODDESS TALES* (Dec. 2003)
SHUTTERBOX (November 2003)
SORCERER HUNTERS
THE SKULL MAN*
THE VISION OF ESCAFLOWNE
TOKYO MEW MEW*
UNDER THE GLASS MOON
VAMPIRE GAME*
WILD ACT*
WISH*
WORLD OF HARTZ (COMING SOON)
X-DAY* (August 2003)
ZODIAC P.I. *

For more information visit www.TOKYOPOP.com

*INDICATES 100% AUTHENTIC MANGA (RIGHT-TO-LEFT FORMAT)

CINE-MANGA™

CARDCAPTORS
JACKIE CHAN ADVENTURES (COMING SOON)
JIMMY NEUTRON (September 2003)
KIM POSSIBLE
LIZZIE MCGUIRE
POWER RANGERS: NINJA STORM (August 2003)
SPONGEBOB SQUAREPANTS (September 2003)
SPY KIDS 2

NOVELS

KARMA CLUB (April 2004)
SAILOR MOON

TOKYOPOP KIDS

STRAY SHEEP (September 2003)

ART BOOKS

CARDCAPTOR SAKURA*
MAGIC KNIGHT RAYEARTH*

ANIME GUIDES

COWBOY BEBOP ANIME GUIDES
GUNDAM TECHNICAL MANUALS
SAILOR MOON SCOUT GUIDES

6-5-03

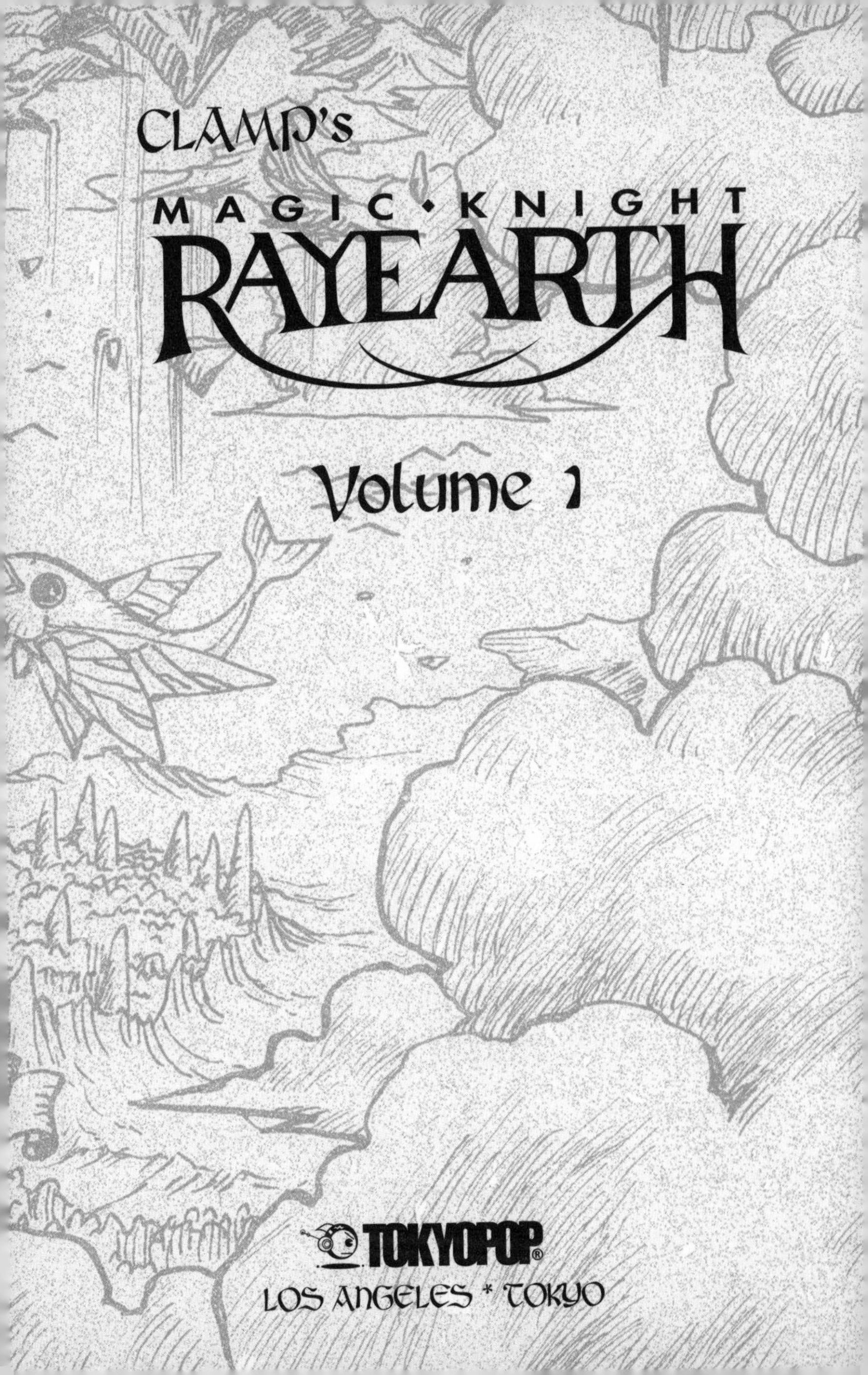

CLAMP's

MAGIC • KNIGHT RAYEARTH

Volume 1

TOKYOPOP®

LOS ANGELES * TOKYO

Translator - Anita Sengupta
English Adaptation - Jamie S. Rich
Editor - Jake Forbes
Retouch and Lettering - Anna Kernbaum
Cover Artist - Patrick Hook

Editor - Jake Forbes
Managing Editor - Jill Freshney
Production Coordinator - Antonio DePietro
Production Manager - Jennifer Miller
Art Director - Matt Alford
Editorial Director - Jeremy Ross
VP of Production - Ron Klamert
President & C.O.O. - John Parker
Publisher & C.E.O. - Stuart Levy

Email: editor@TOKYOPOP.com
Come visit us online at www.TOKYOPOP.com

A 🐱 **TOKYOPOP**® Manga
TOKYOPOP® is an imprint of Mixx Entertainment, Inc.
5900 Wilshire Blvd. Suite 2000, Los Angeles, CA 90036

ISBN: 1-59182-082-0

First TOKYOPOP® printing: November 2002

10 9 8 7 6 5 4 3 2 1

Printed in Canada

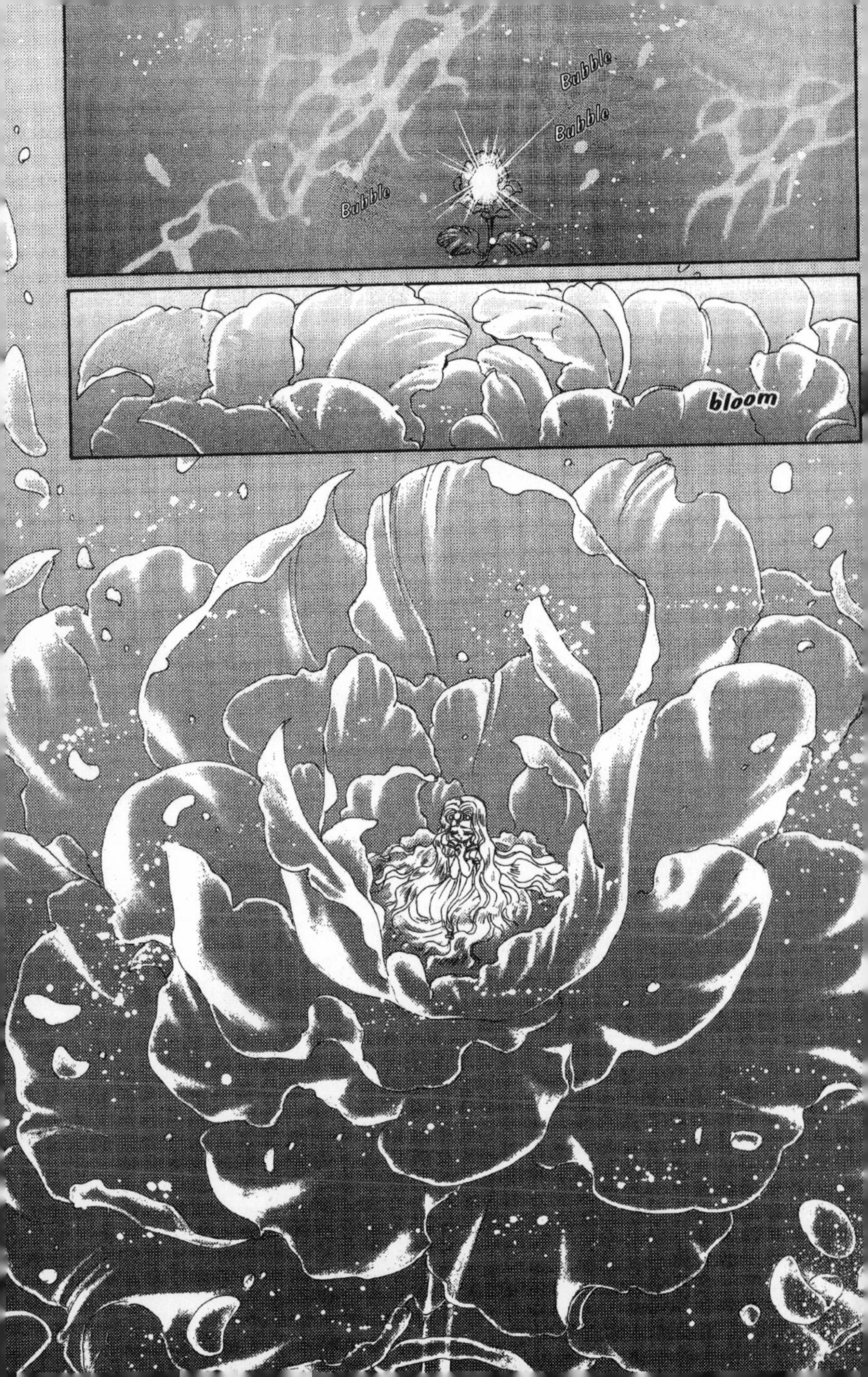
Bubble
Bubble
Bubble
bloom

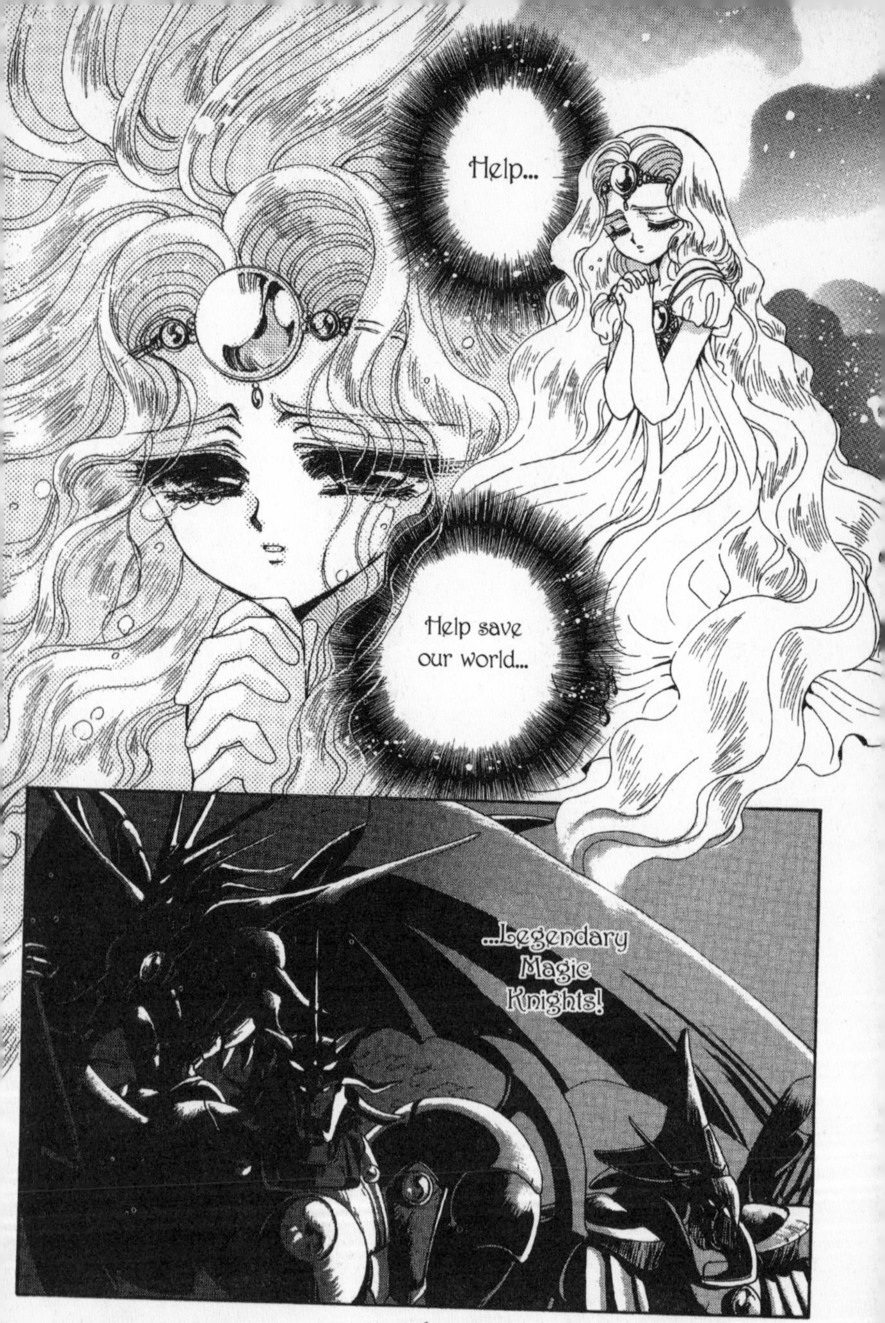
Help...
Help save our world...
...Legendary Magic Knights!

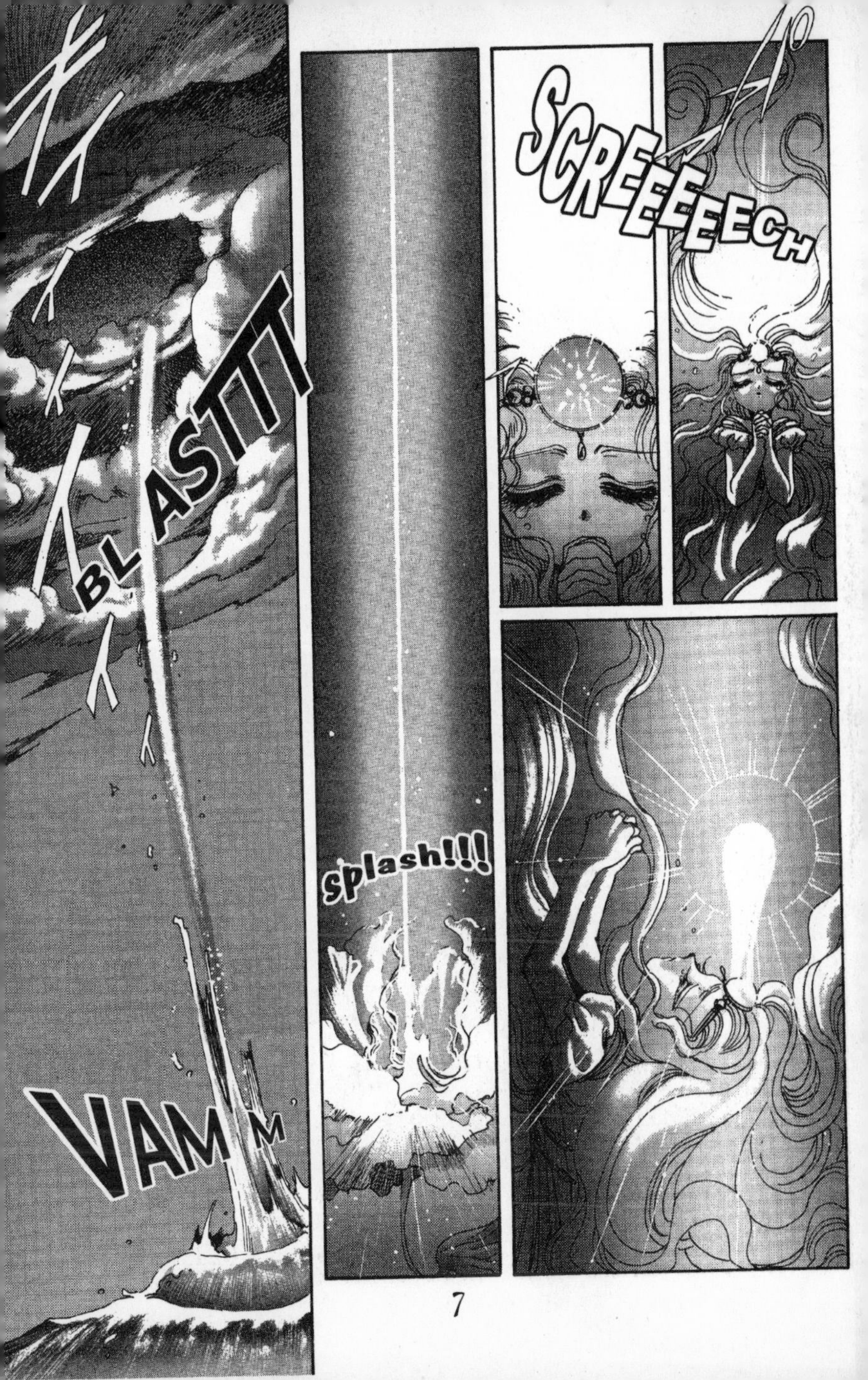
SCREEEEEECH
splash!!!
BLASTTT
VAMMM

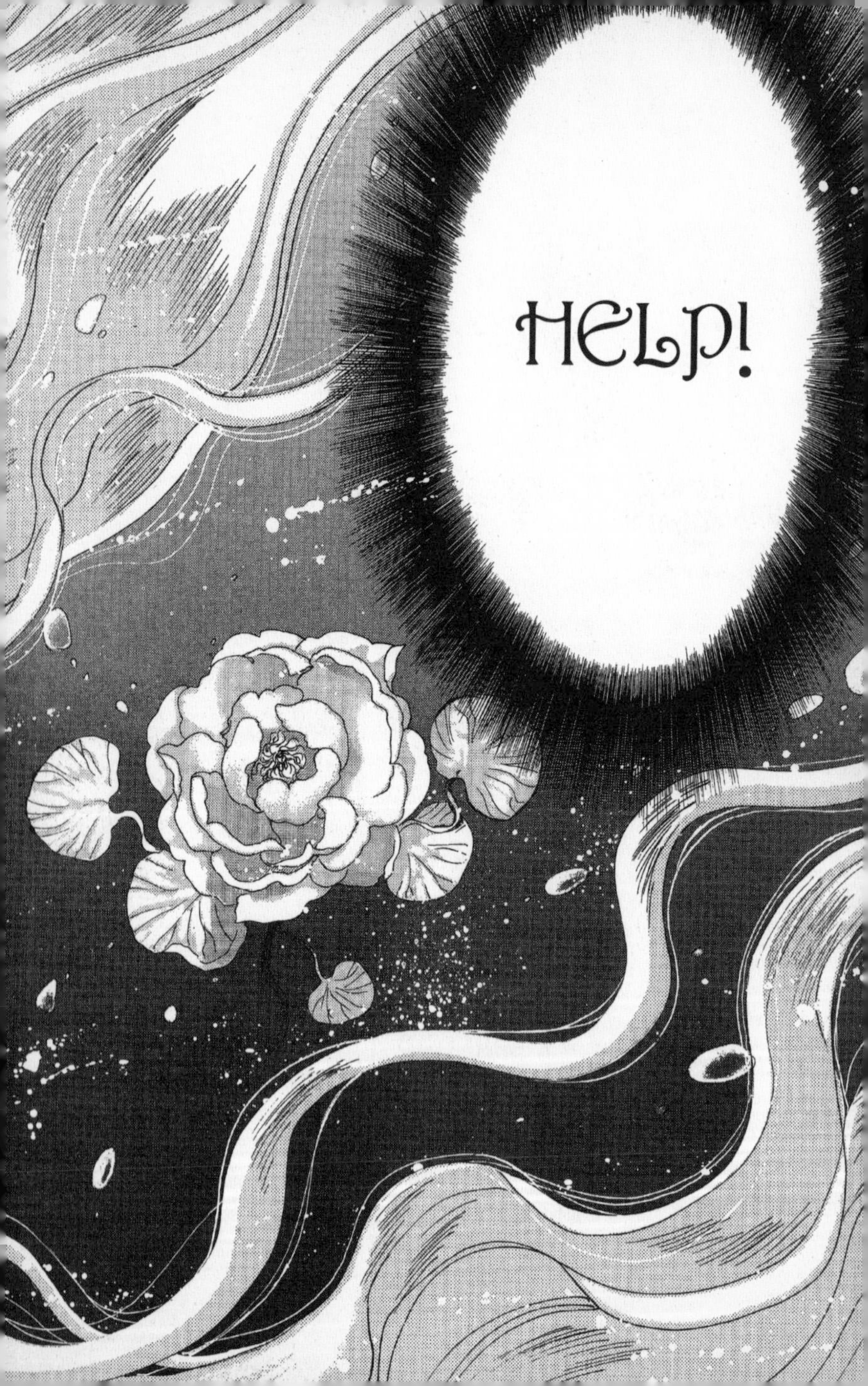
HELP!

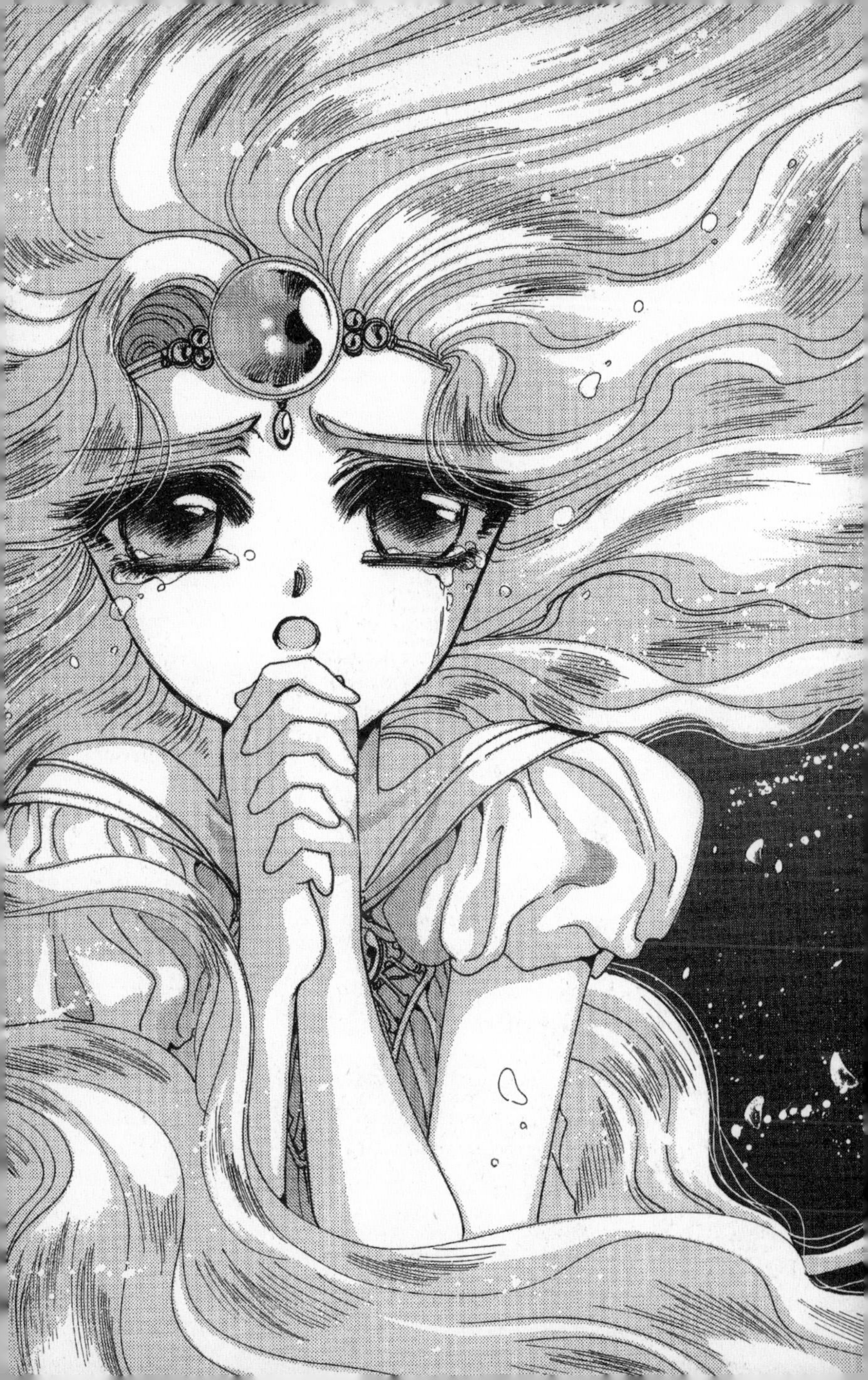

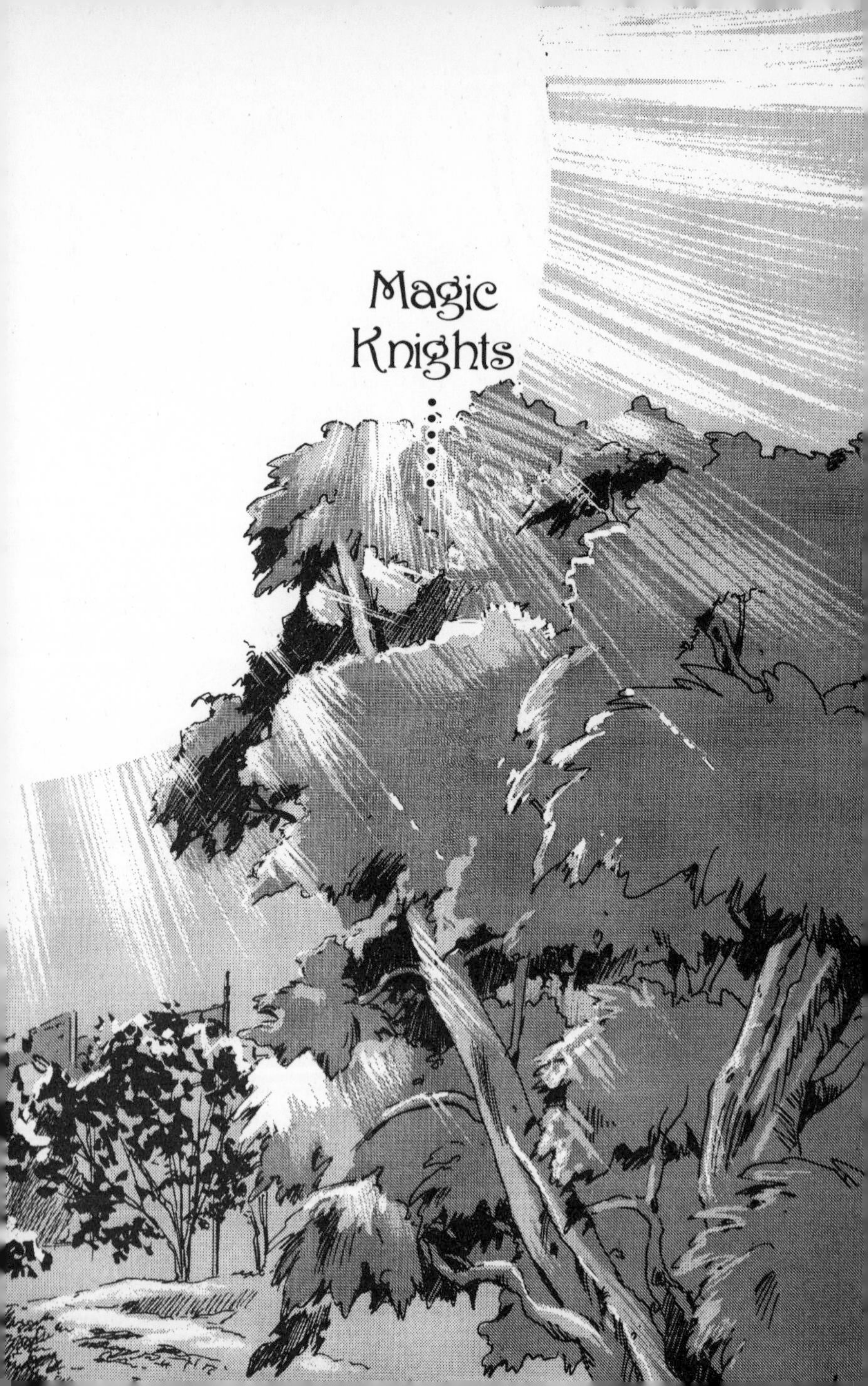
Magic
Knights

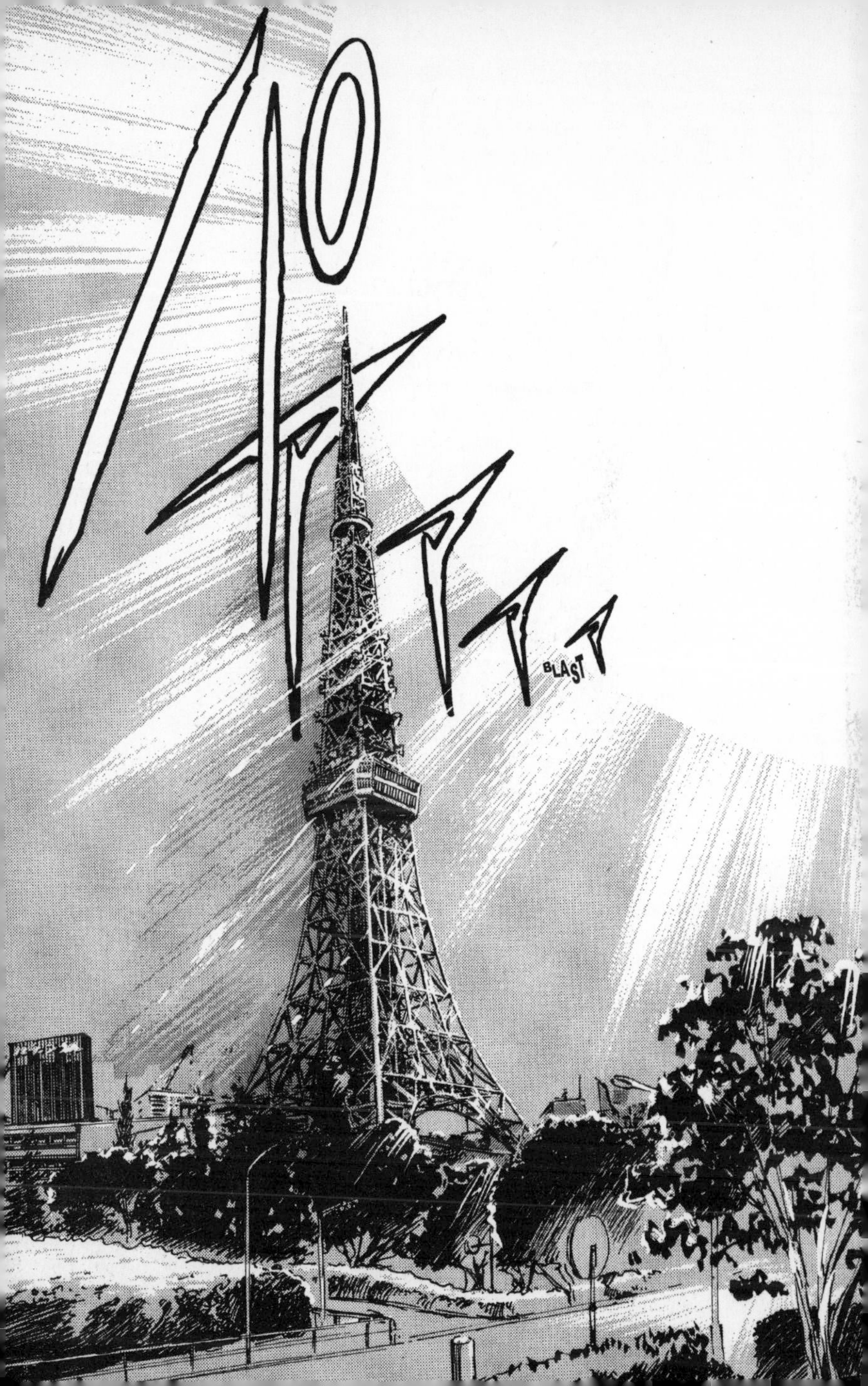
BLAST

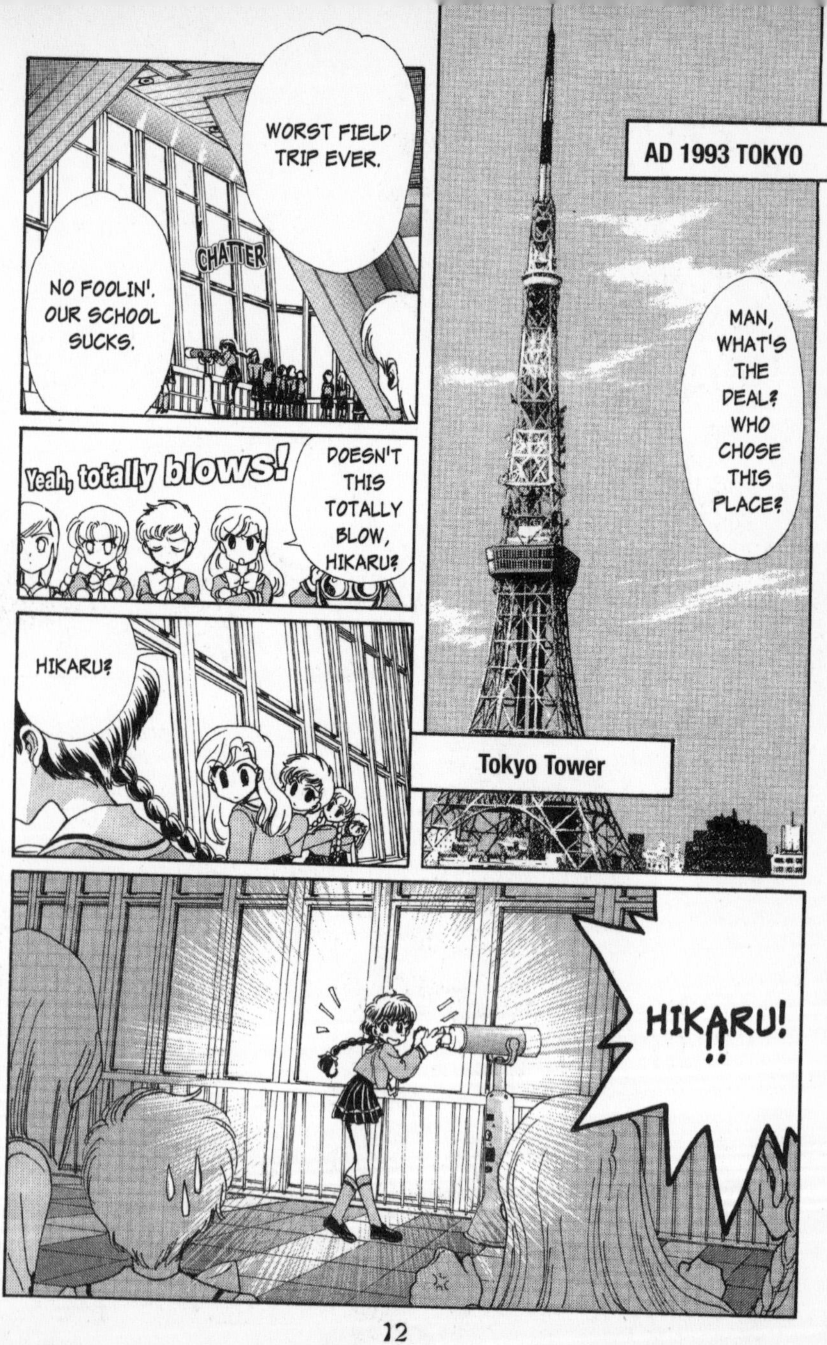
AD 1993 TOKYO
MAN, WHAT'S THE DEAL? WHO CHOSE THIS PLACE?
Tokyo Tower
WORST FIELD TRIP EVER.
CHATTER
NO FOOLIN'. OUR SCHOOL SUCKS.
DOESN'T THIS TOTALLY BLOW, HIKARU?
Yeah, totally blows!
HIKARU?
HIKARU!
!!

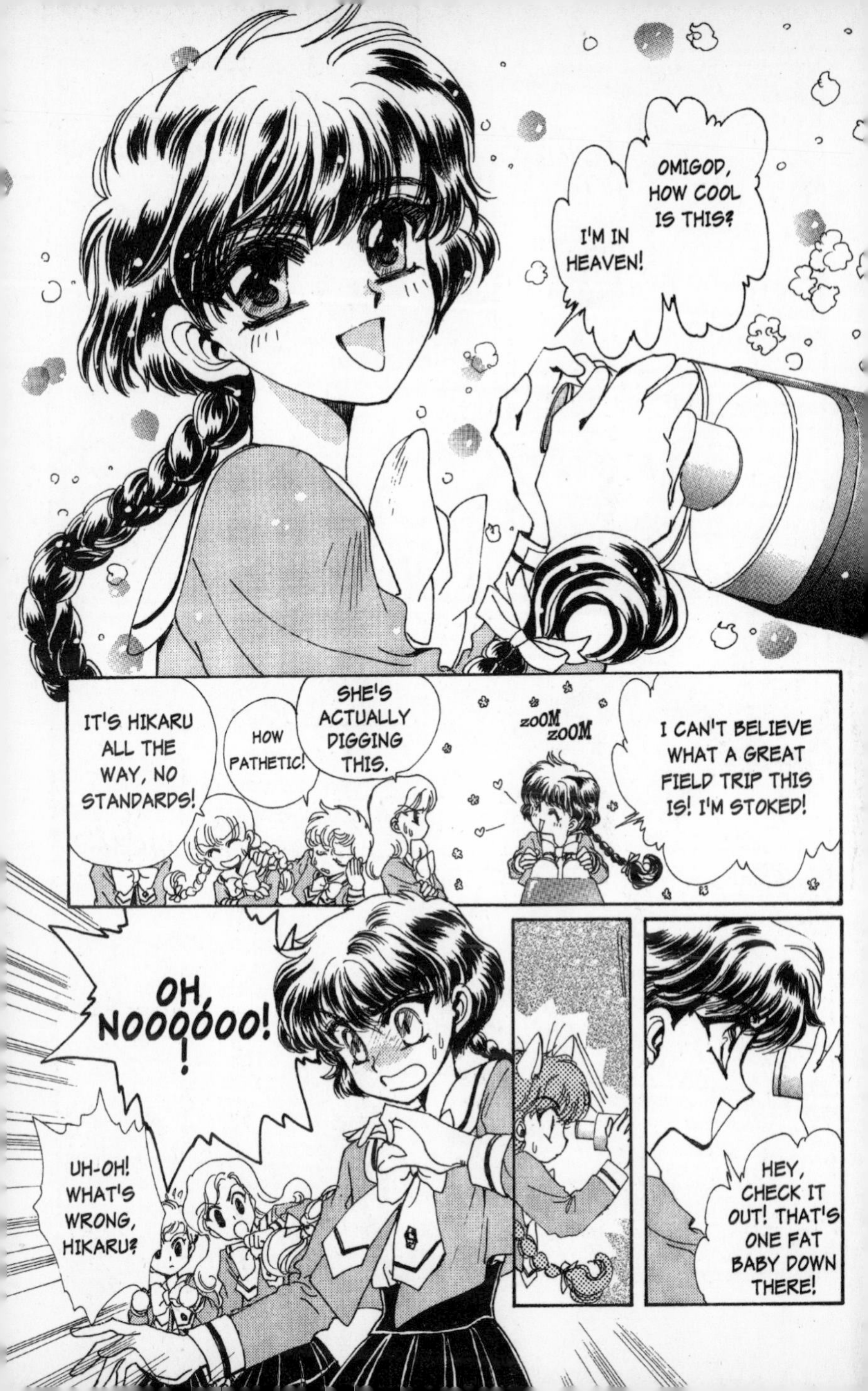
OMIGOD, HOW COOL IS THIS?
I'M IN HEAVEN!
I CAN'T BELIEVE WHAT A GREAT FIELD TRIP THIS IS! I'M STOKED!
ZOOM ZOOM
SHE'S ACTUALLY DIGGING THIS.
HOW PATHETIC!
IT'S HIKARU ALL THE WAY, NO STANDARDS!
HEY, CHECK IT OUT! THAT'S ONE FAT BABY DOWN THERE!
OH, NOOOOOO!!
UH-OH! WHAT'S WRONG, HIKARU?

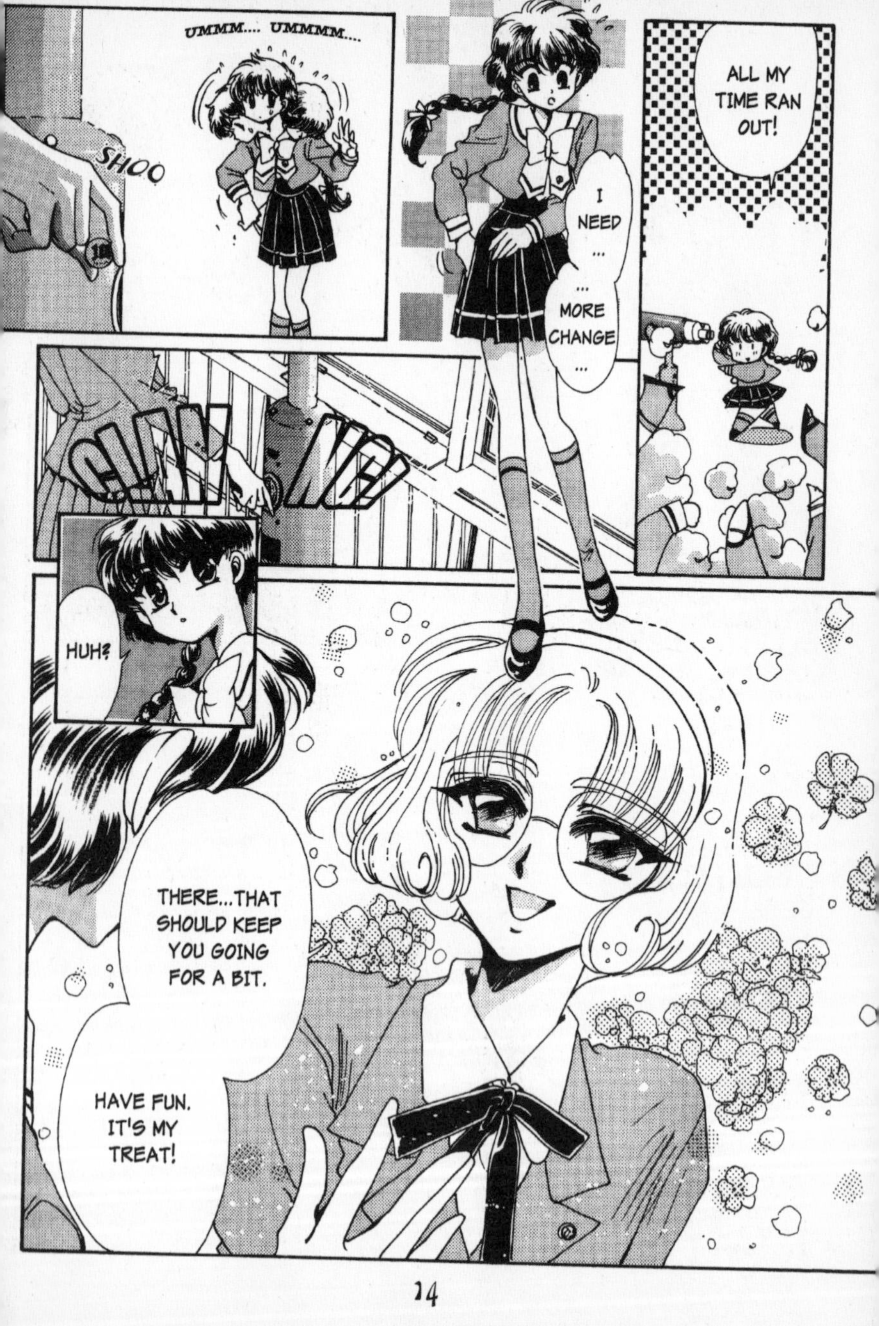
ALL MY TIME RAN OUT!
I NEED ... ... MORE CHANGE ...
UMMM.... UMMMM....
SHOO
HUH?
THERE...THAT SHOULD KEEP YOU GOING FOR A BIT.
HAVE FUN. IT'S MY TREAT!

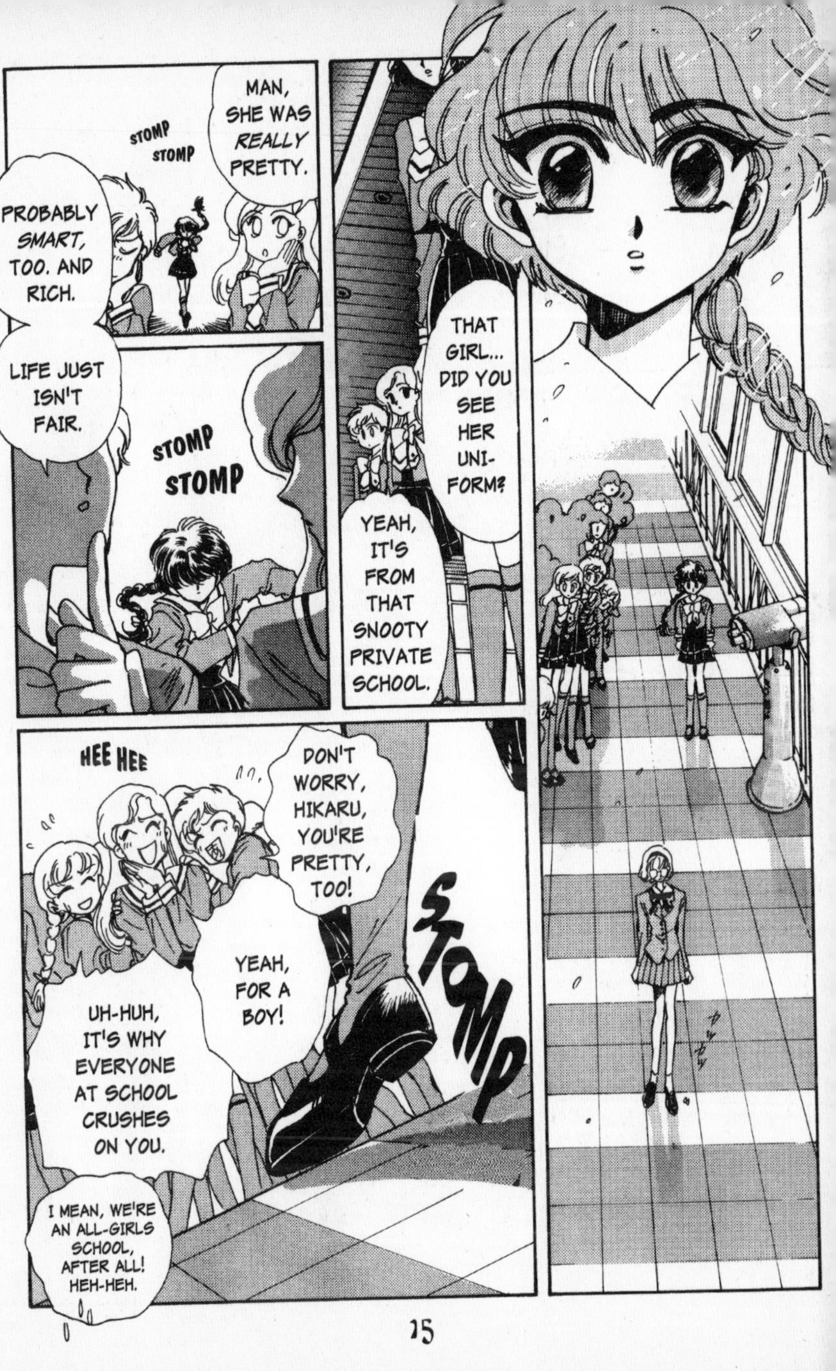

THAT GIRL... DID YOU SEE HER UNI-FORM?
YEAH, IT'S FROM THAT SNOOTY PRIVATE SCHOOL.
MAN, SHE WAS *REALLY* PRETTY.
STOMP STOMP
PROBABLY *SMART*, TOO. AND RICH.
LIFE JUST ISN'T FAIR.
STOMP STOMP
HEE HEE
DON'T WORRY, HIKARU, YOU'RE PRETTY, TOO!
YEAH, FOR A BOY!
STOMP
UH-HUH, IT'S WHY EVERYONE AT SCHOOL CRUSHES ON YOU.
I MEAN, WE'RE AN ALL-GIRLS SCHOOL, AFTER ALL! HEH-HEH.

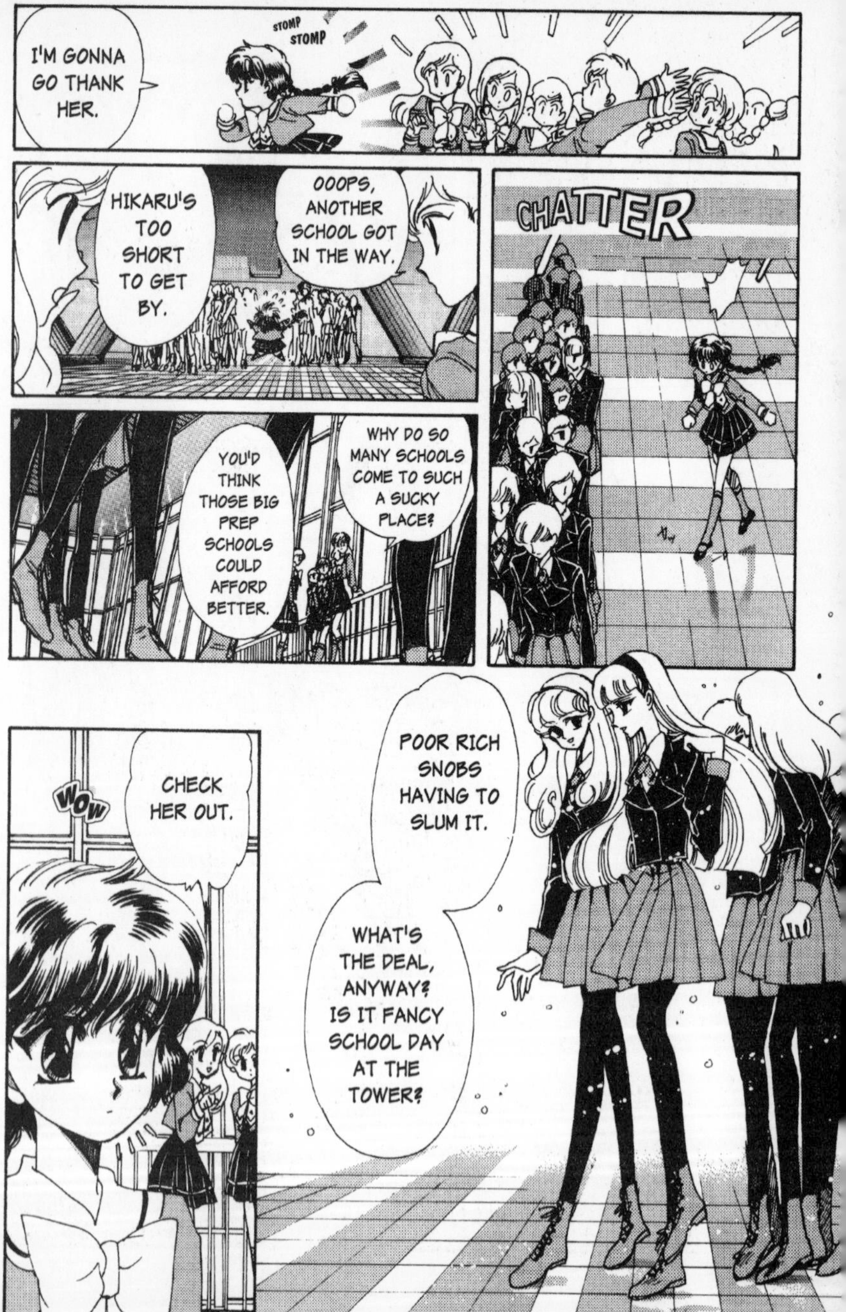
STOMP
STOMP
I'M GONNA GO THANK HER.
CHATTER
OOOPS, ANOTHER SCHOOL GOT IN THE WAY.
HIKARU'S TOO SHORT TO GET BY.
WHY DO SO MANY SCHOOLS COME TO SUCH A SUCKY PLACE?
YOU'D THINK THOSE BIG PREP SCHOOLS COULD AFFORD BETTER.
POOR RICH SNOBS HAVING TO SLUM IT.
WHAT'S THE DEAL, ANYWAY? IS IT FANCY SCHOOL DAY AT THE TOWER?
WOW
CHECK HER OUT.

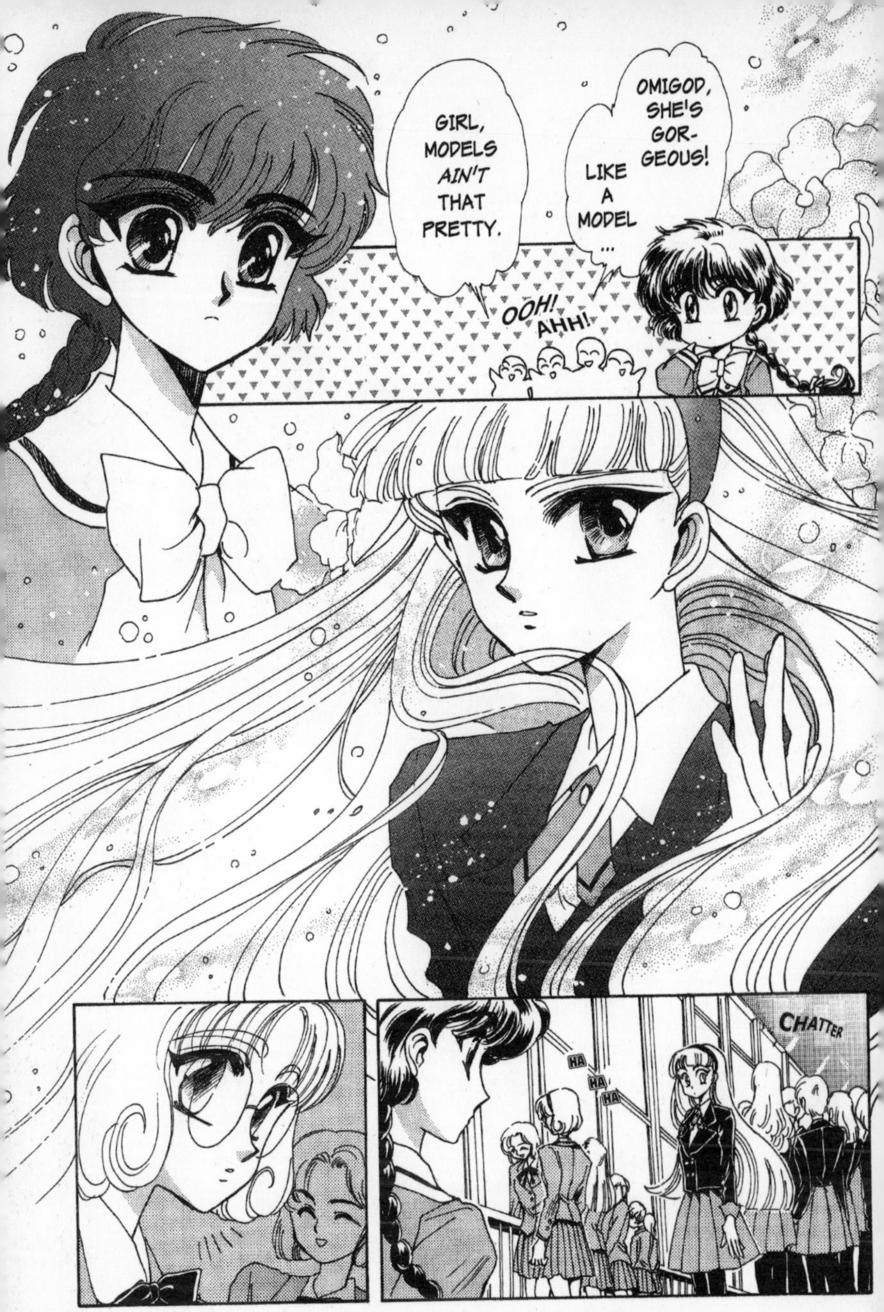
OMIGOD, SHE'S GOR-GEOUS!
LIKE A MODEL ...
GIRL, MODELS AIN'T THAT PRETTY.
OOH! AHH!
CHATTER
HA HA HA

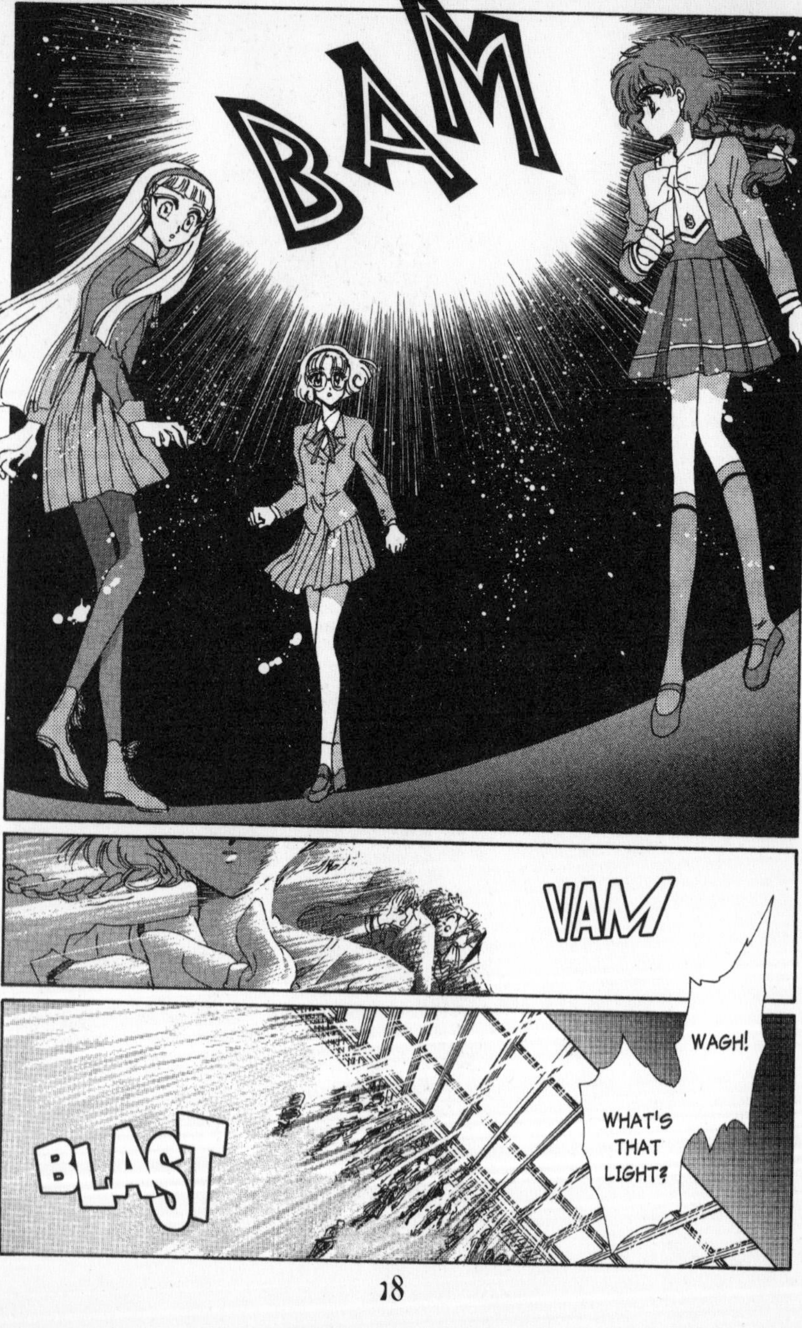
BAM
VAM
WAGH!
WHAT'S THAT LIGHT?
BLAST

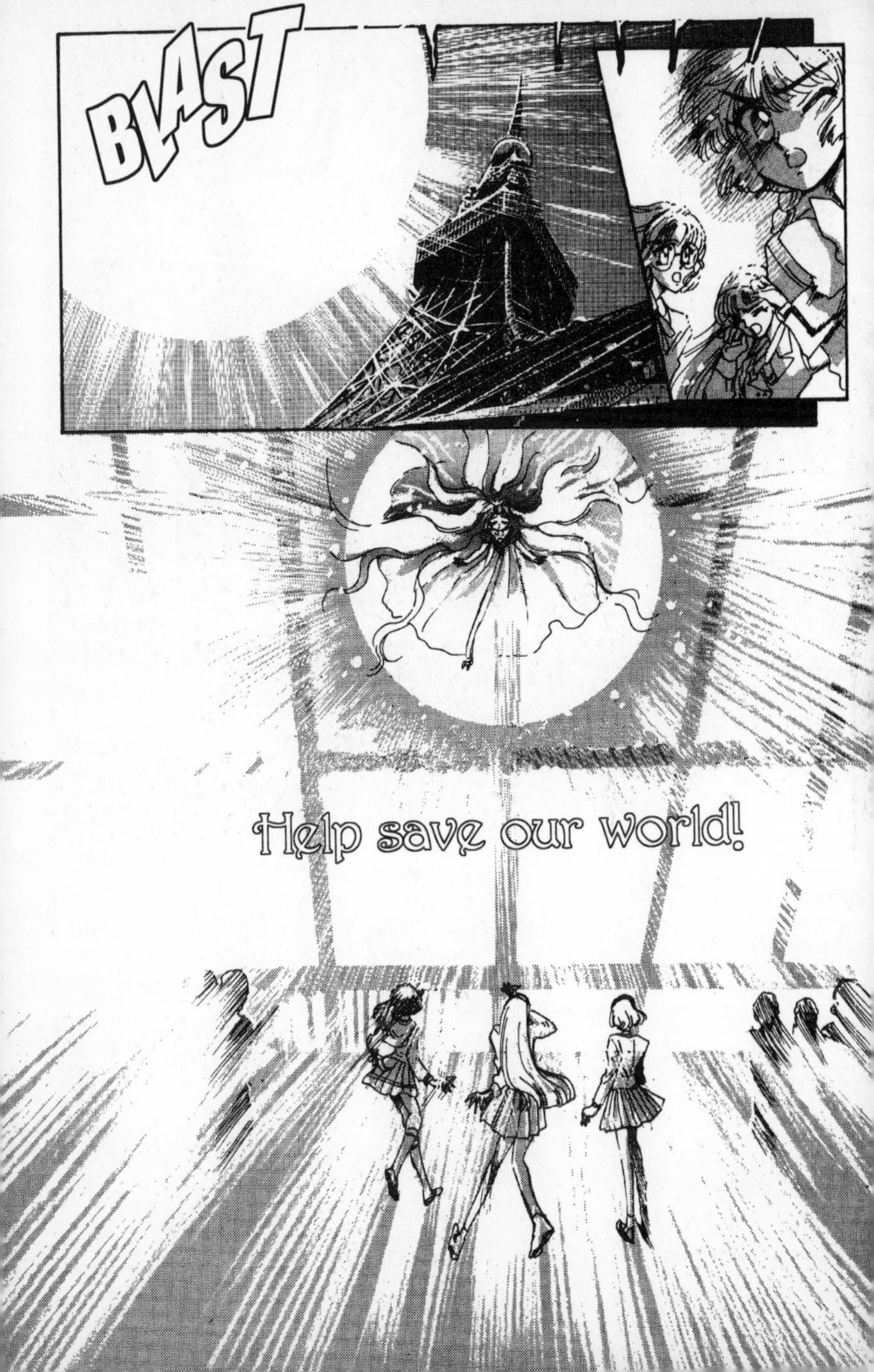
BLAST
Help save our world!

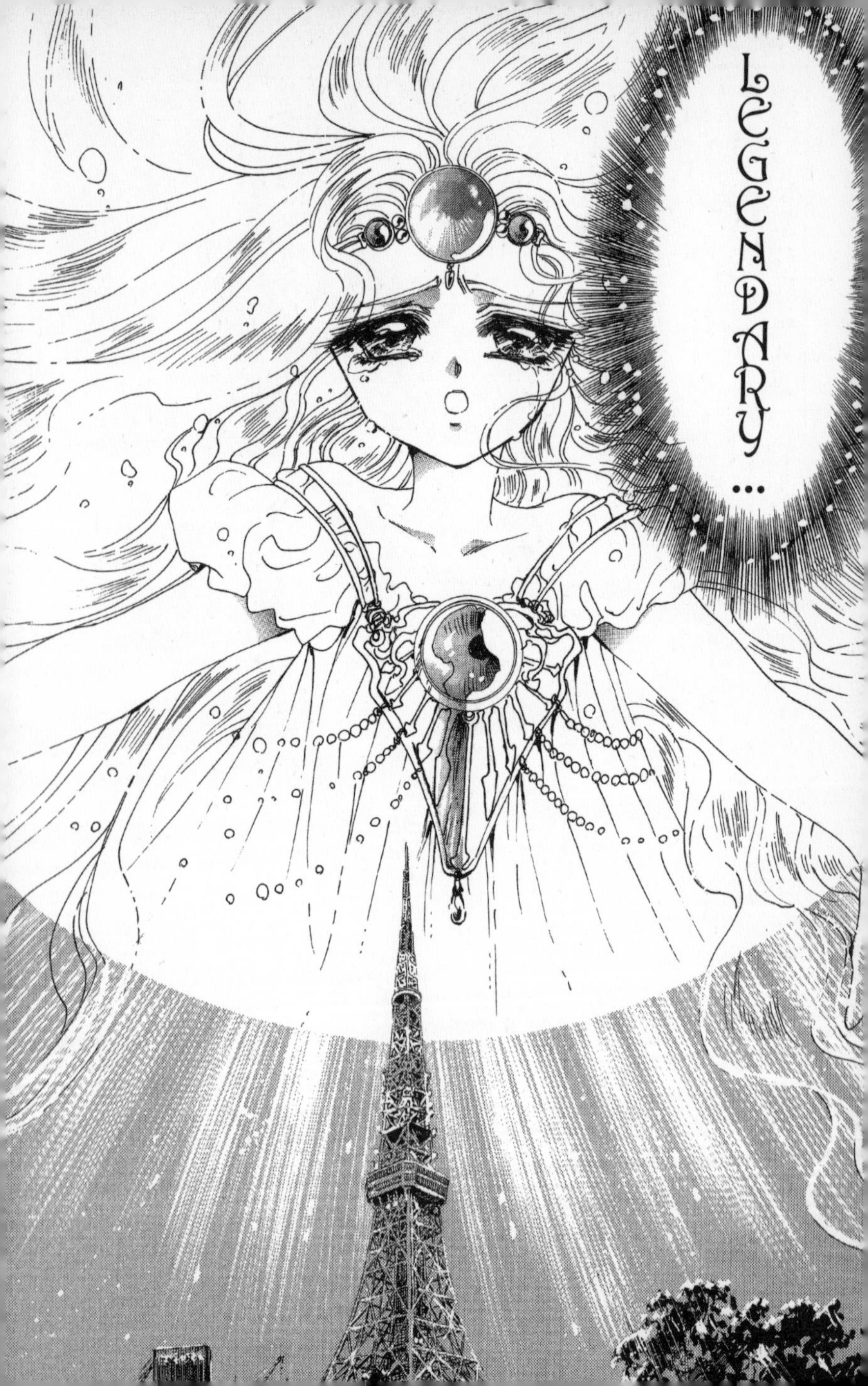
LEGENDARY...

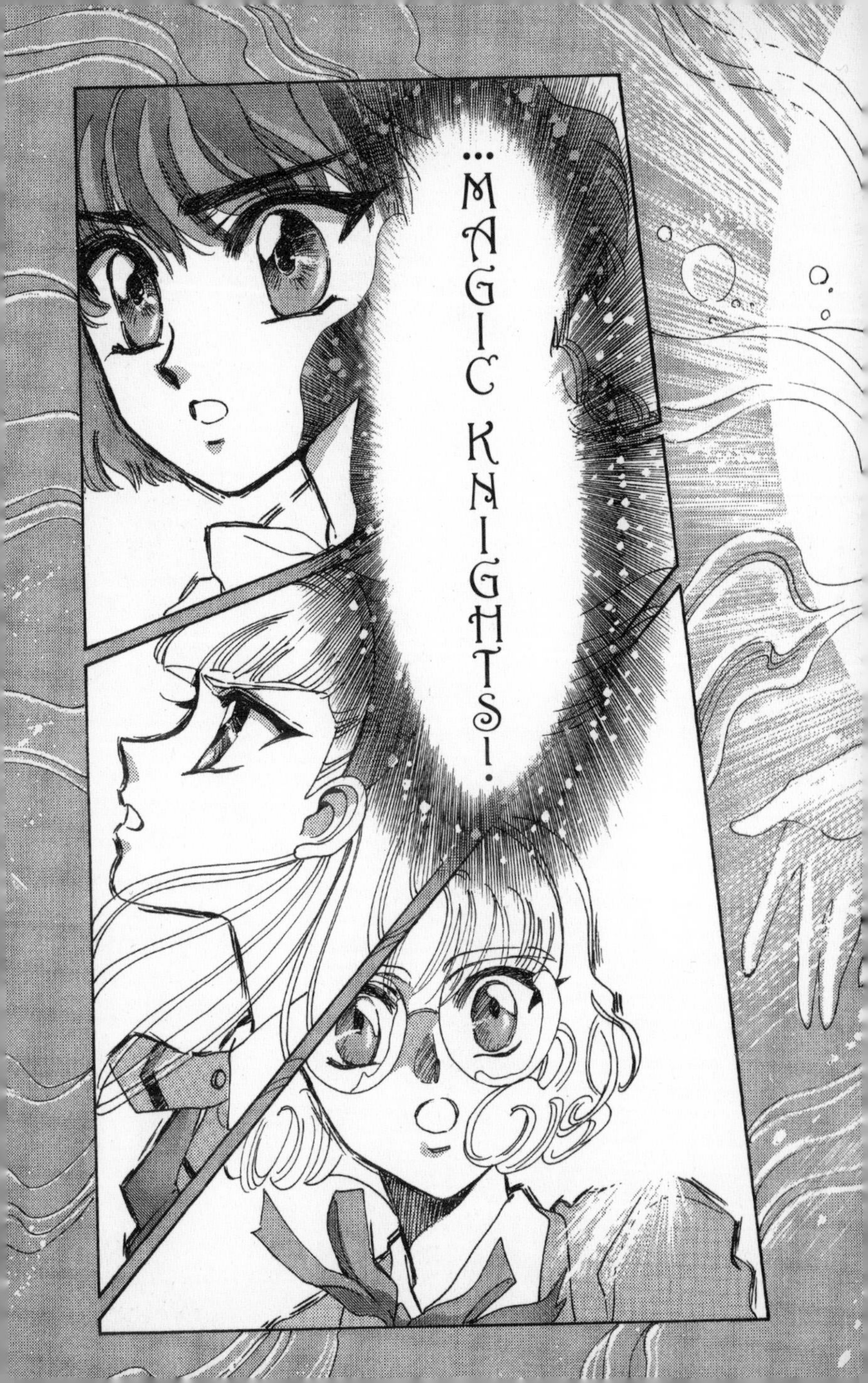
...MAGIC KNIGHTS!

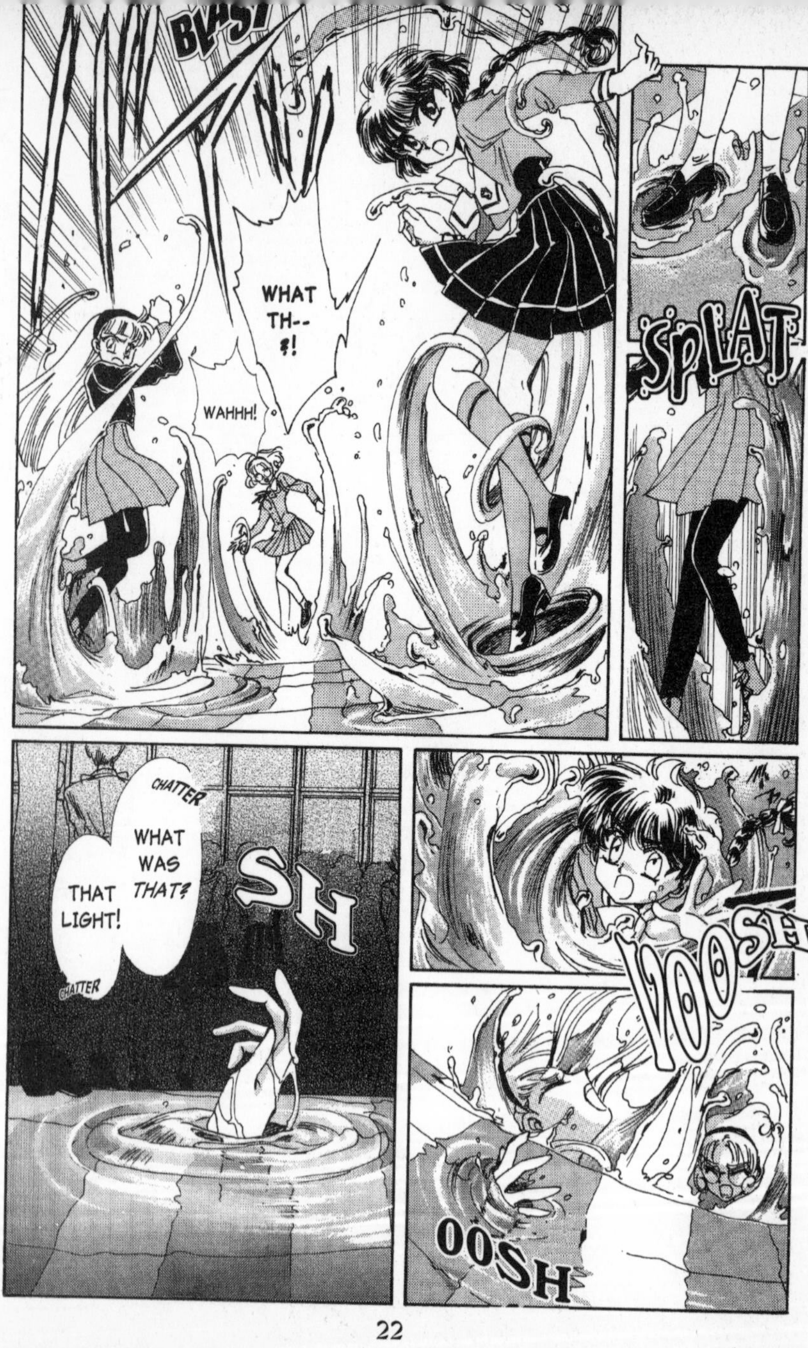
SPLAT
BLAST
WHAT TH-- ?!
WAHHH!
WOOSH
OOSH
SH
CHATTER
WHAT WAS THAT?
THAT LIGHT!
CHATTER

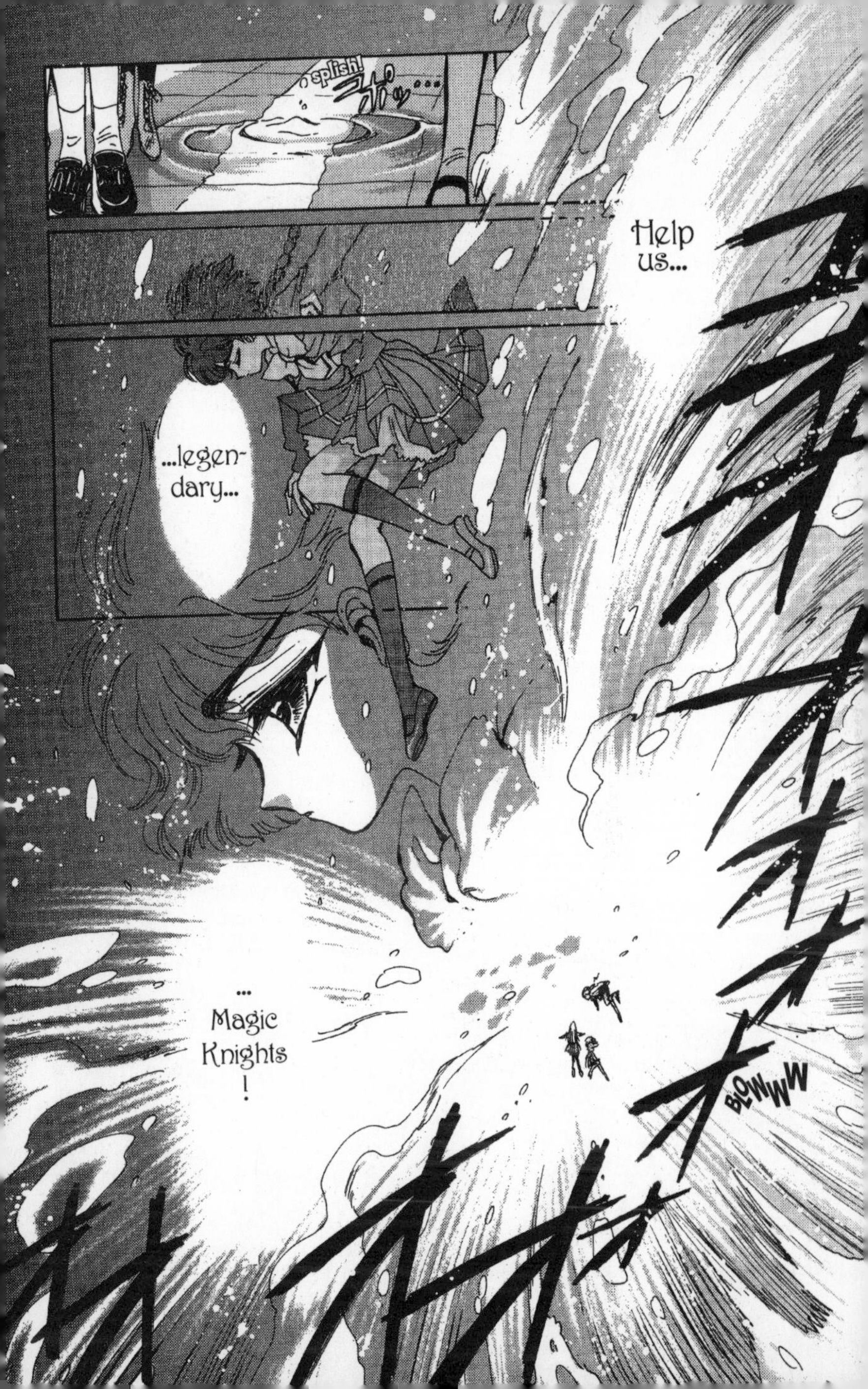
splish!
Help us...
...legendary...
...Magic Knights!
BLOWWW

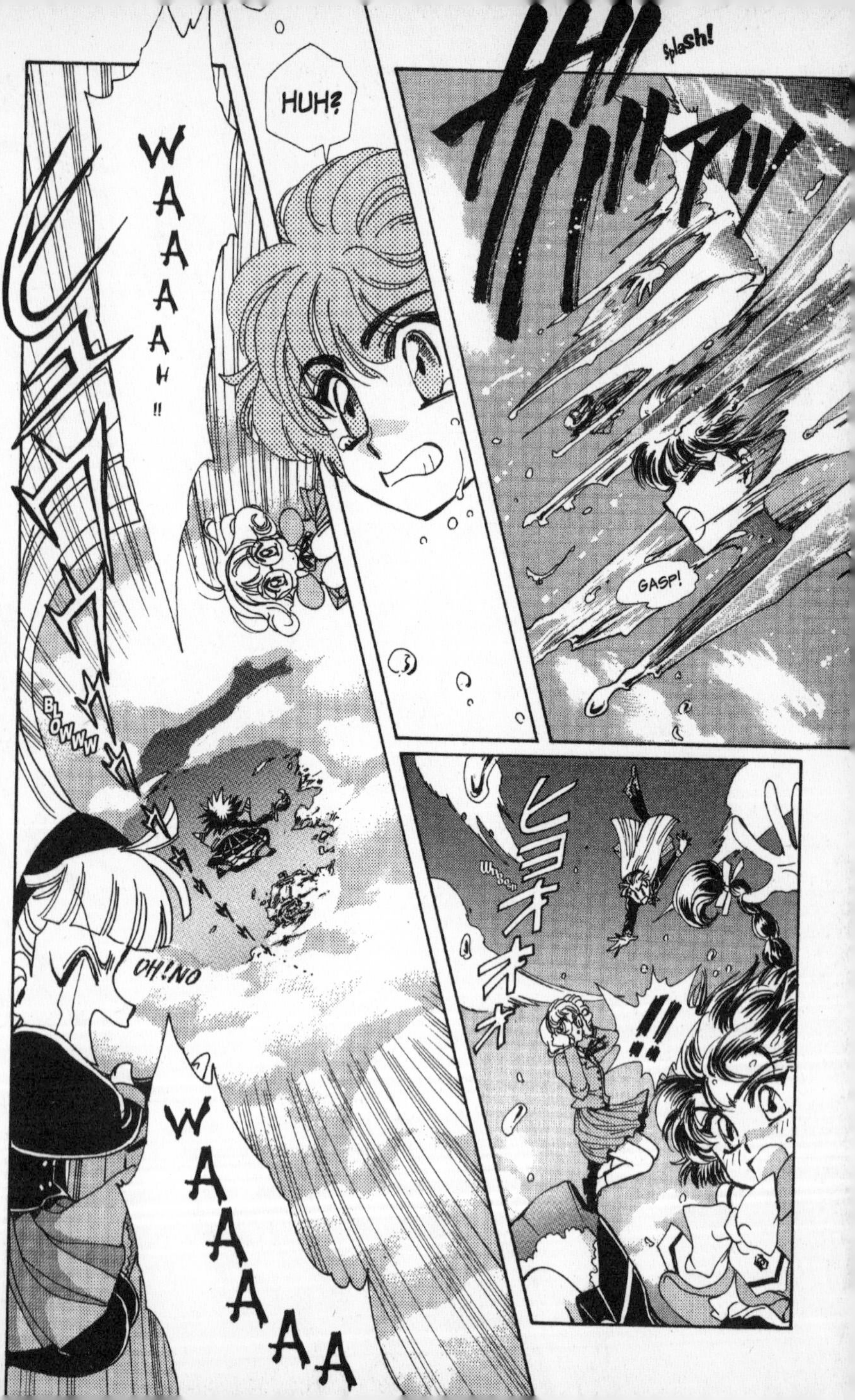
Splash!
GASP!
!!
HUH?
WAAAAAH!!
BLOWWW
OH!NO
WAAAAAA

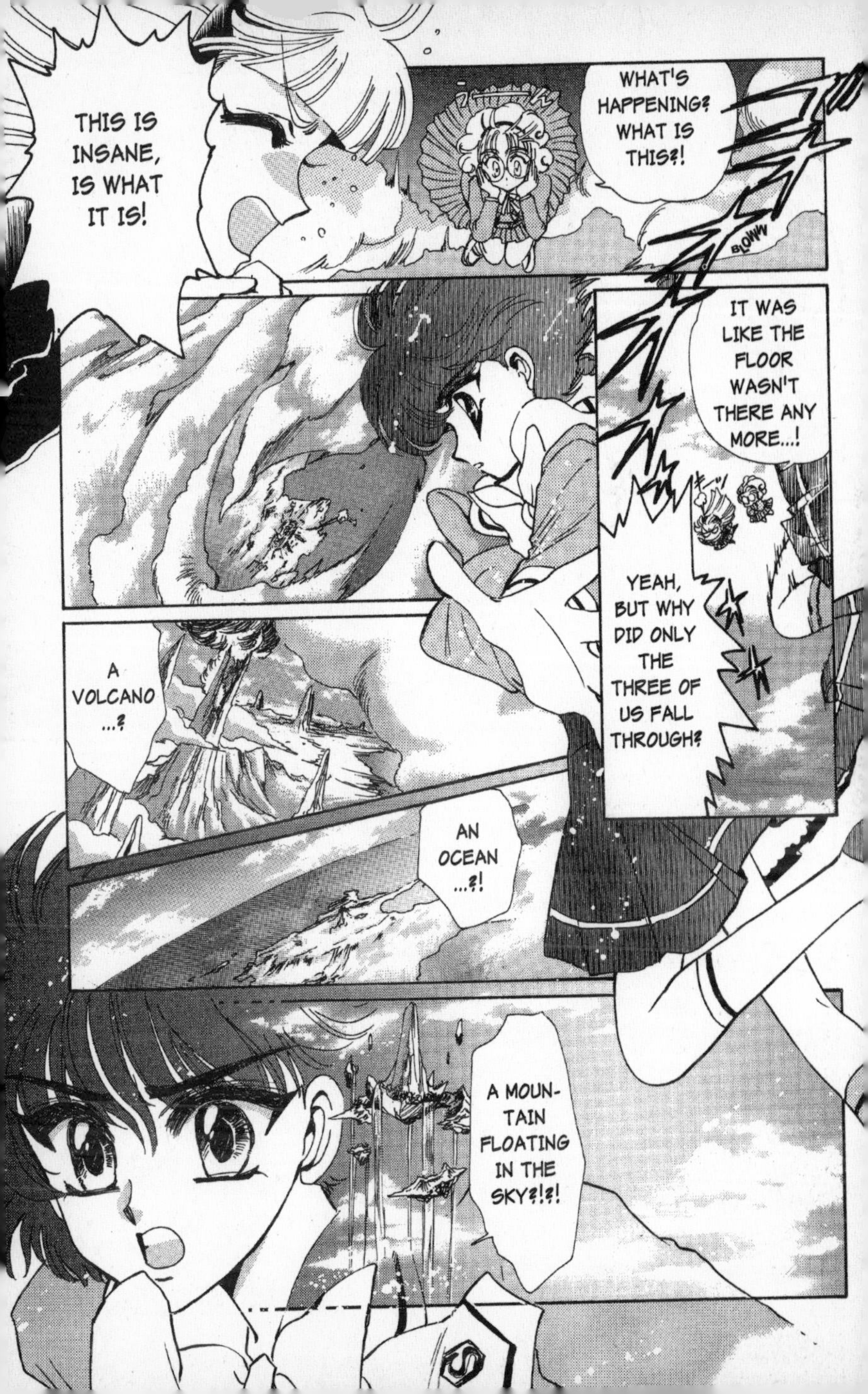
WHAT'S HAPPENING? WHAT IS THIS?!
THIS IS INSANE, IS WHAT IT IS!
BLOWW
IT WAS LIKE THE FLOOR WASN'T THERE ANY MORE...!
YEAH, BUT WHY DID ONLY THE THREE OF US FALL THROUGH?
A VOLCANO ...?
AN OCEAN ...?!
A MOUN-TAIN FLOATING IN THE SKY?!?!

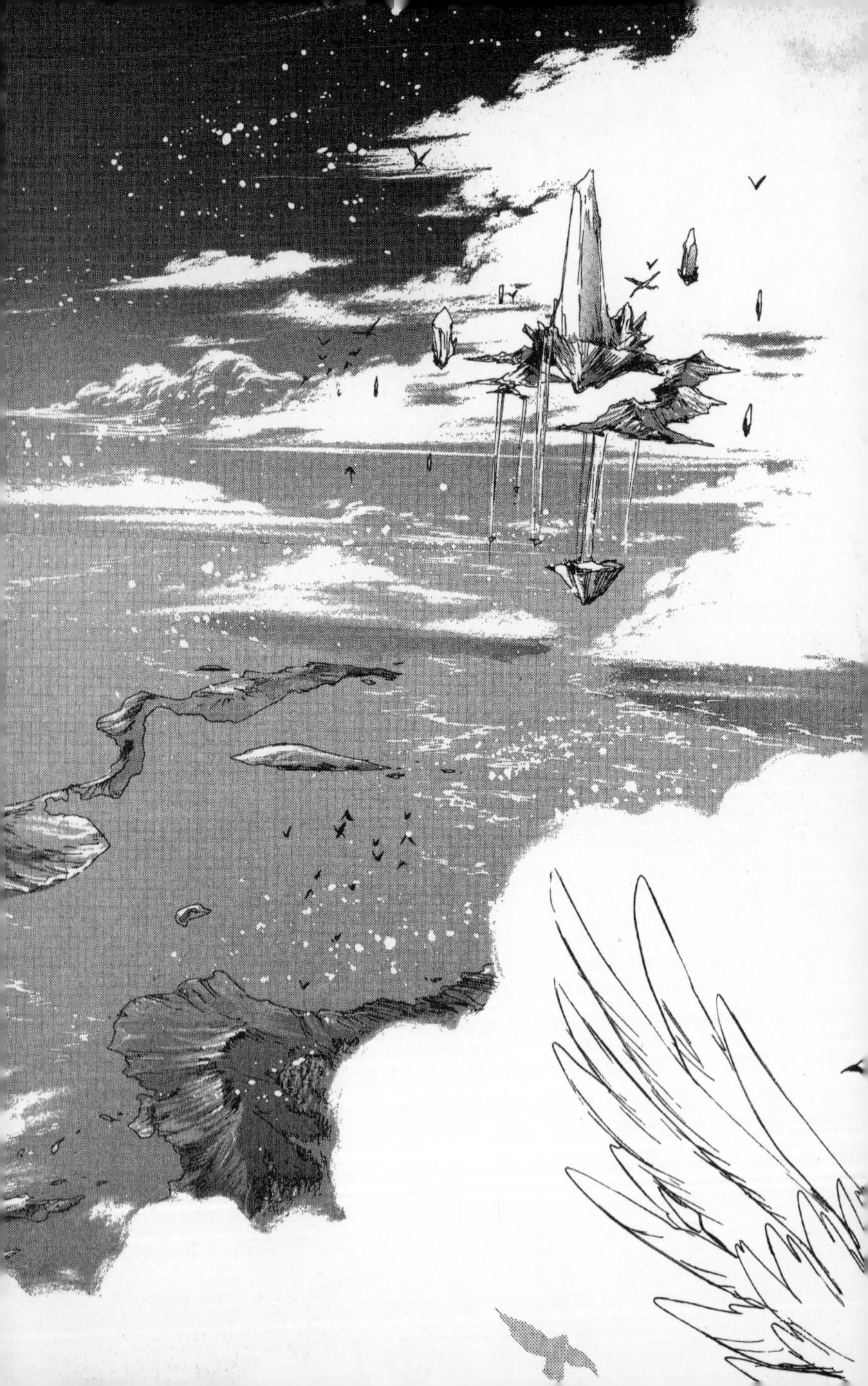

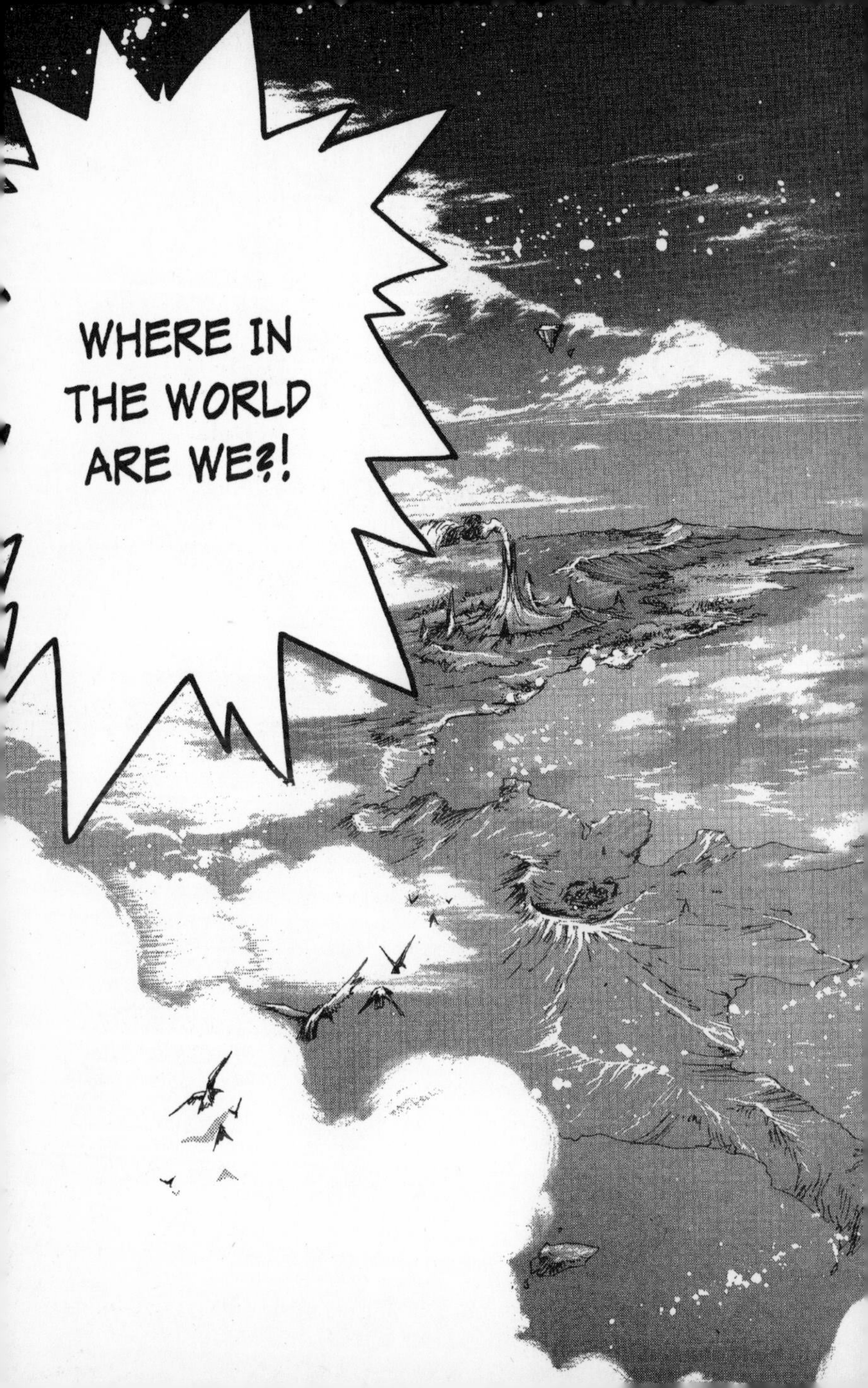
WHERE IN THE WORLD ARE WE?!

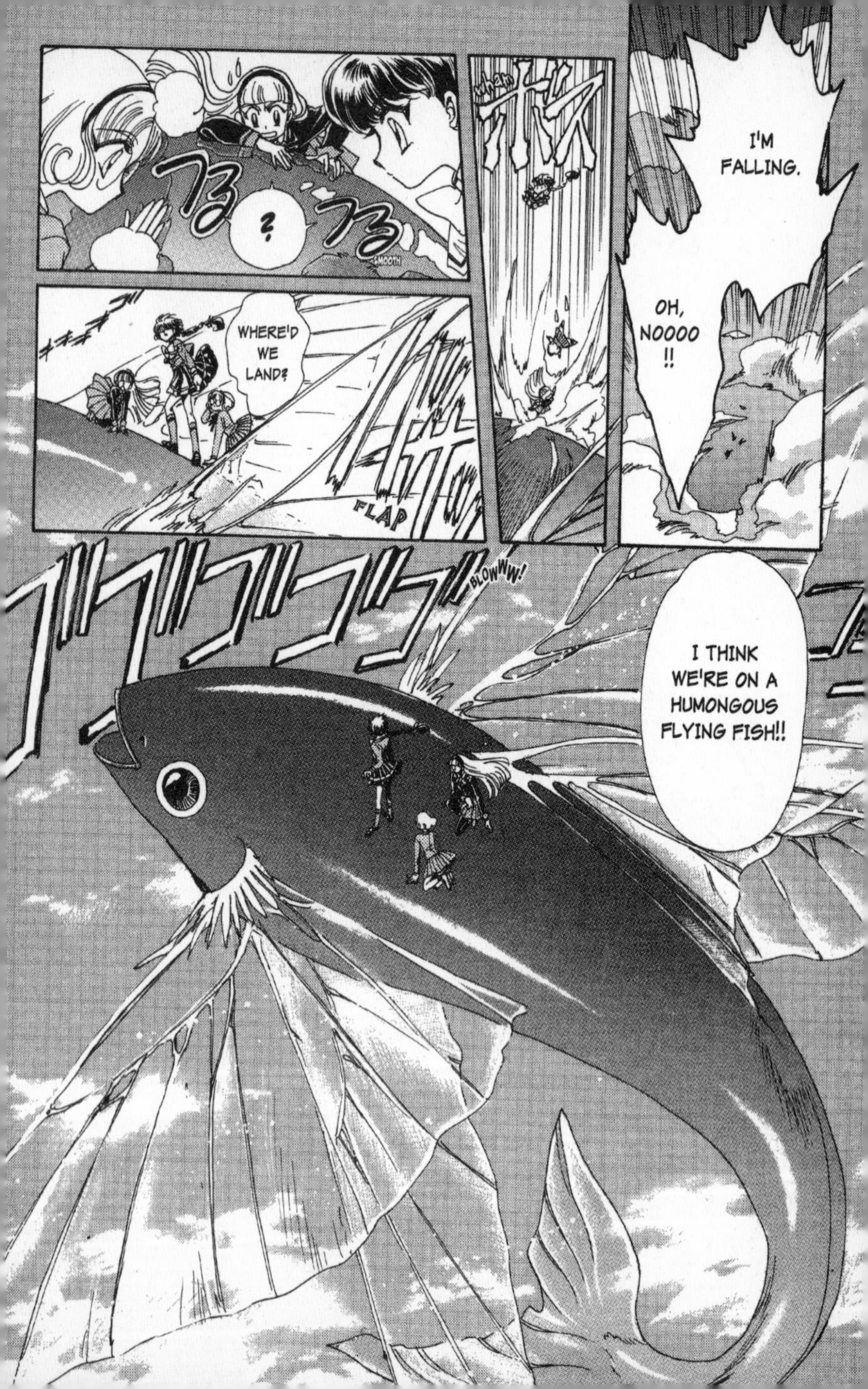
I'M FALLING.
OH, NOOOO!!
wham
?
SMOOTH
WHERE'D WE LAND?
FLAP
BLOWWW!
I THINK WE'RE ON A HUMONGOUS FLYING FISH!!

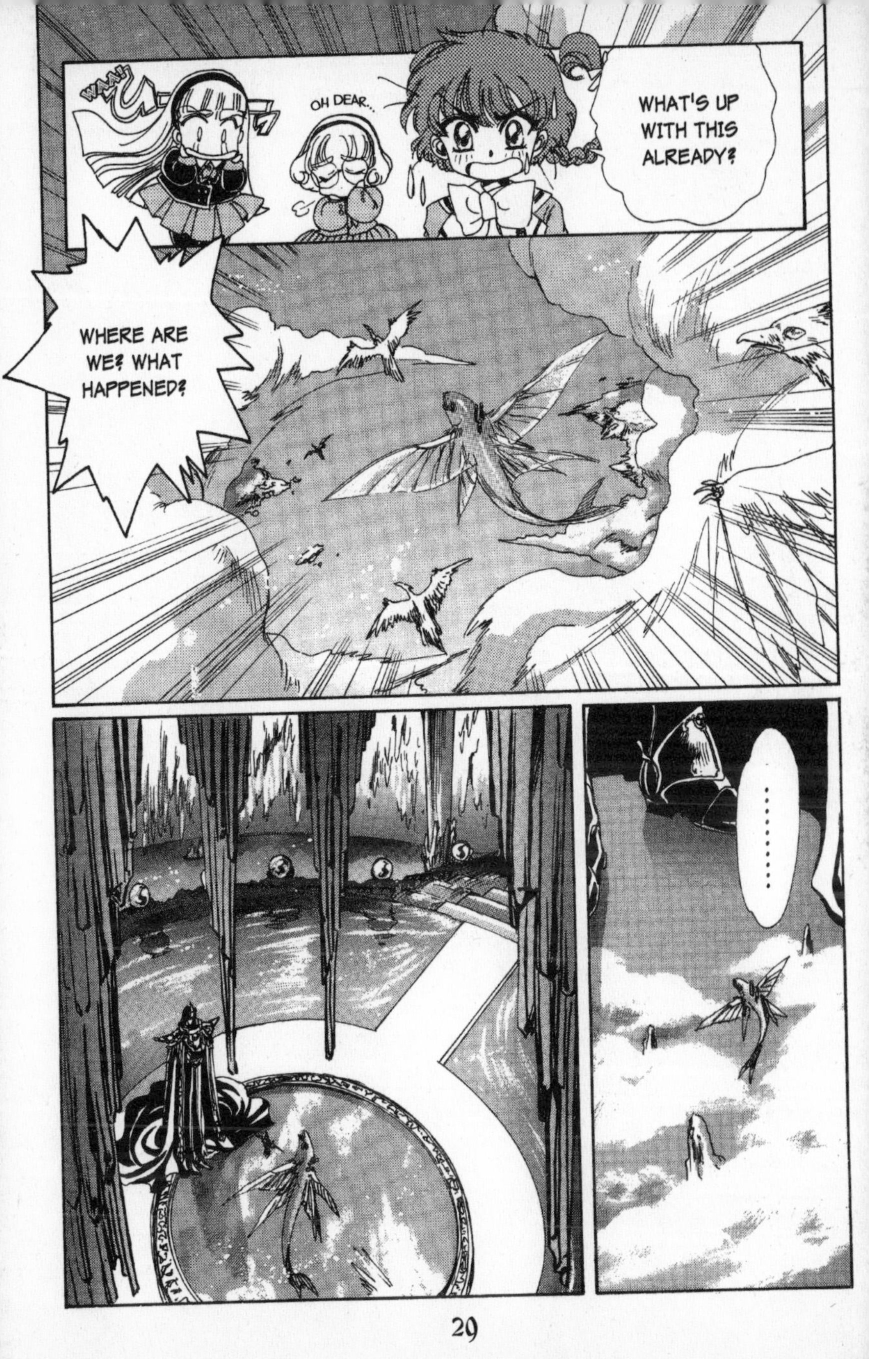
WHAT'S UP WITH THIS ALREADY?
OH DEAR...
WAAAH
WHERE ARE WE? WHAT HAPPENED?
....

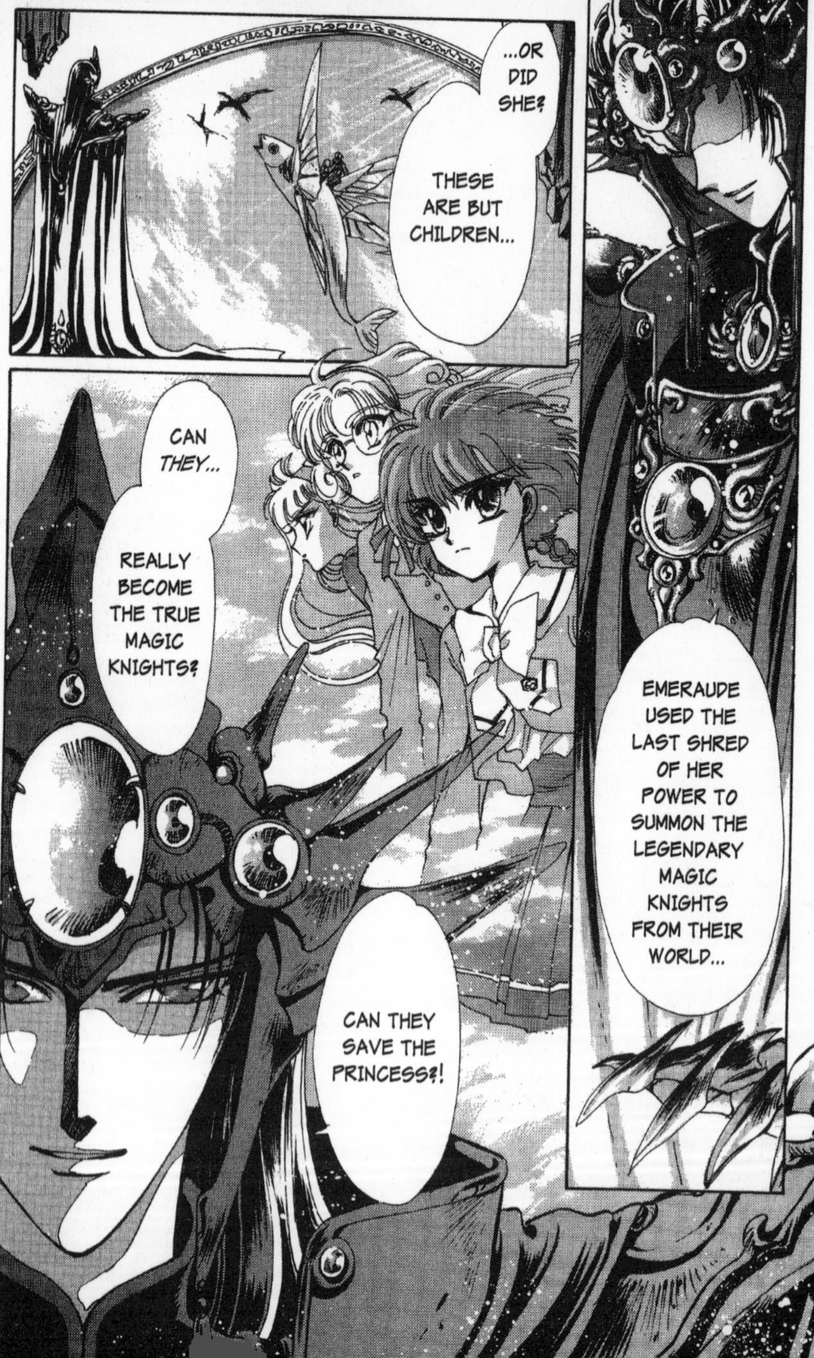
EMERAUDE USED THE LAST SHRED OF HER POWER TO SUMMON THE LEGENDARY MAGIC KNIGHTS FROM THEIR WORLD...
...OR DID SHE?
THESE ARE BUT CHILDREN...
CAN *THEY*...
REALLY BECOME THE TRUE MAGIC KNIGHTS?
CAN THEY SAVE THE PRINCESS?!

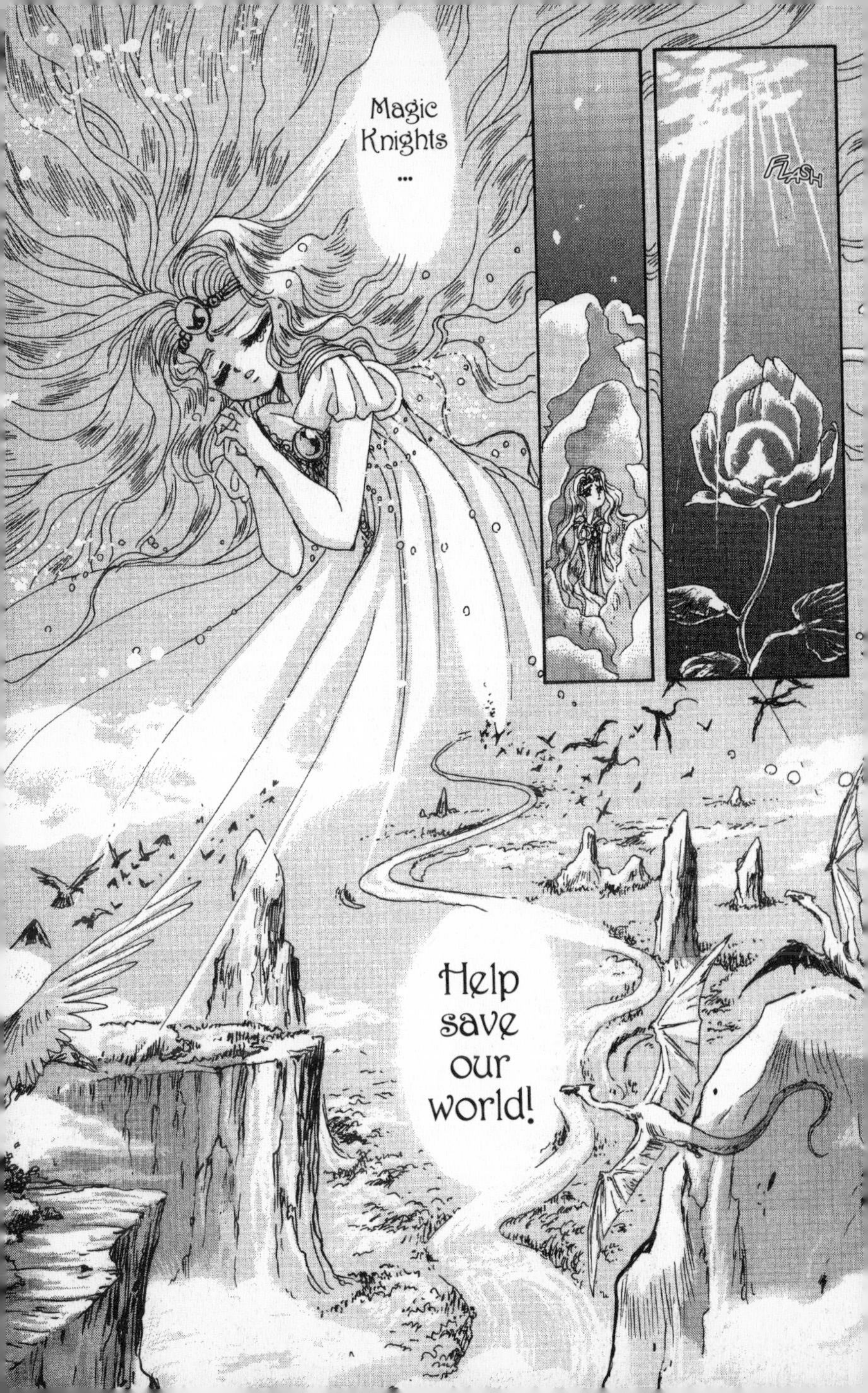
FLASH
Magic Knights ...
Help save our world!

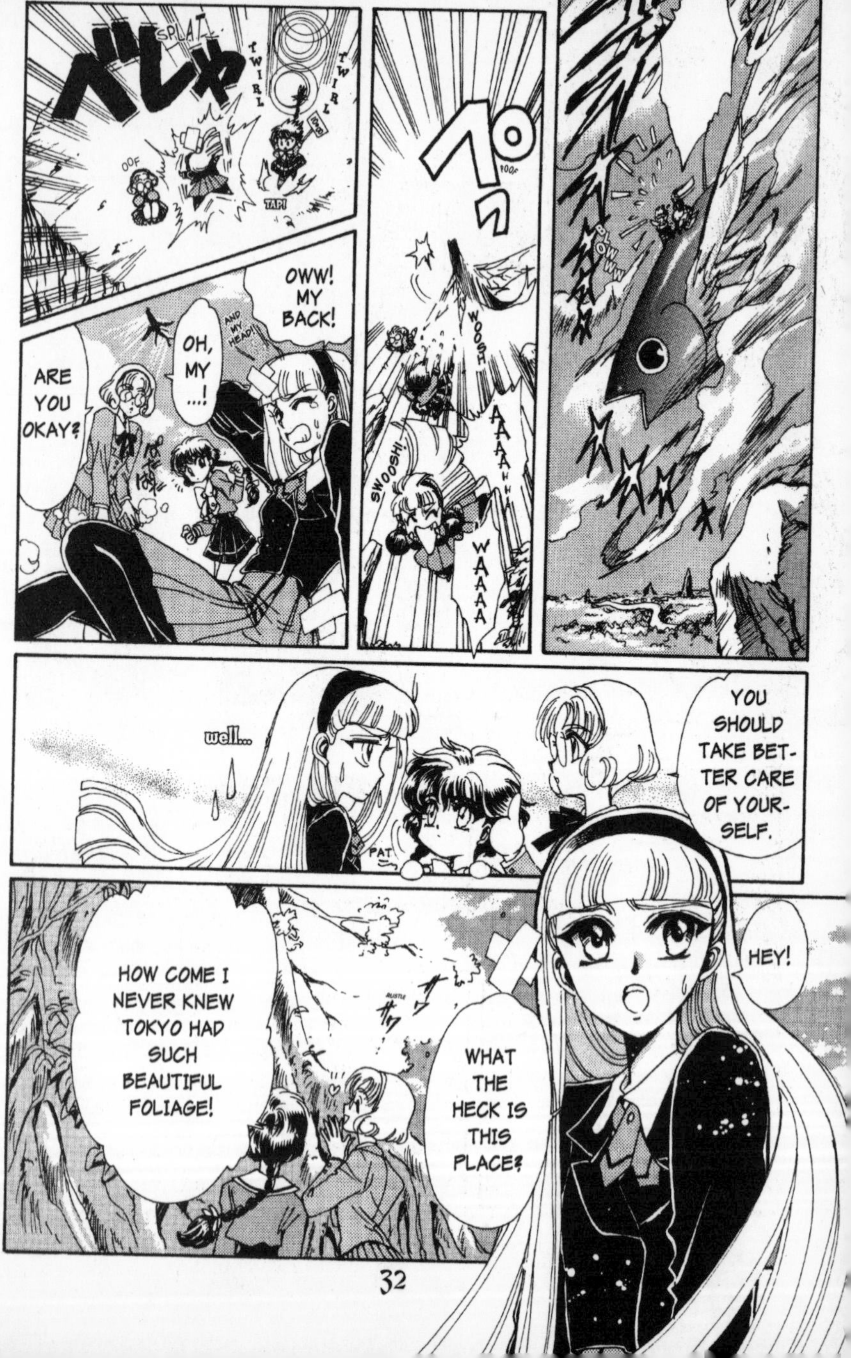
BLOWWW
POOF
WOOSH
AAAAAHH
SWOOSH!
WAAAAA
SPLAT!
TWIRL
TWIRL
OOF
TAP!
OWW! MY BACK!
AND MY HEAD!!
OH, MY ...!
ARE YOU OKAY?
YOU SHOULD TAKE BETTER CARE OF YOURSELF.
well...
PAT
HEY!
WHAT THE HECK IS THIS PLACE?
RUSTLE
HOW COME I NEVER KNEW TOKYO HAD SUCH BEAUTIFUL FOLIAGE!

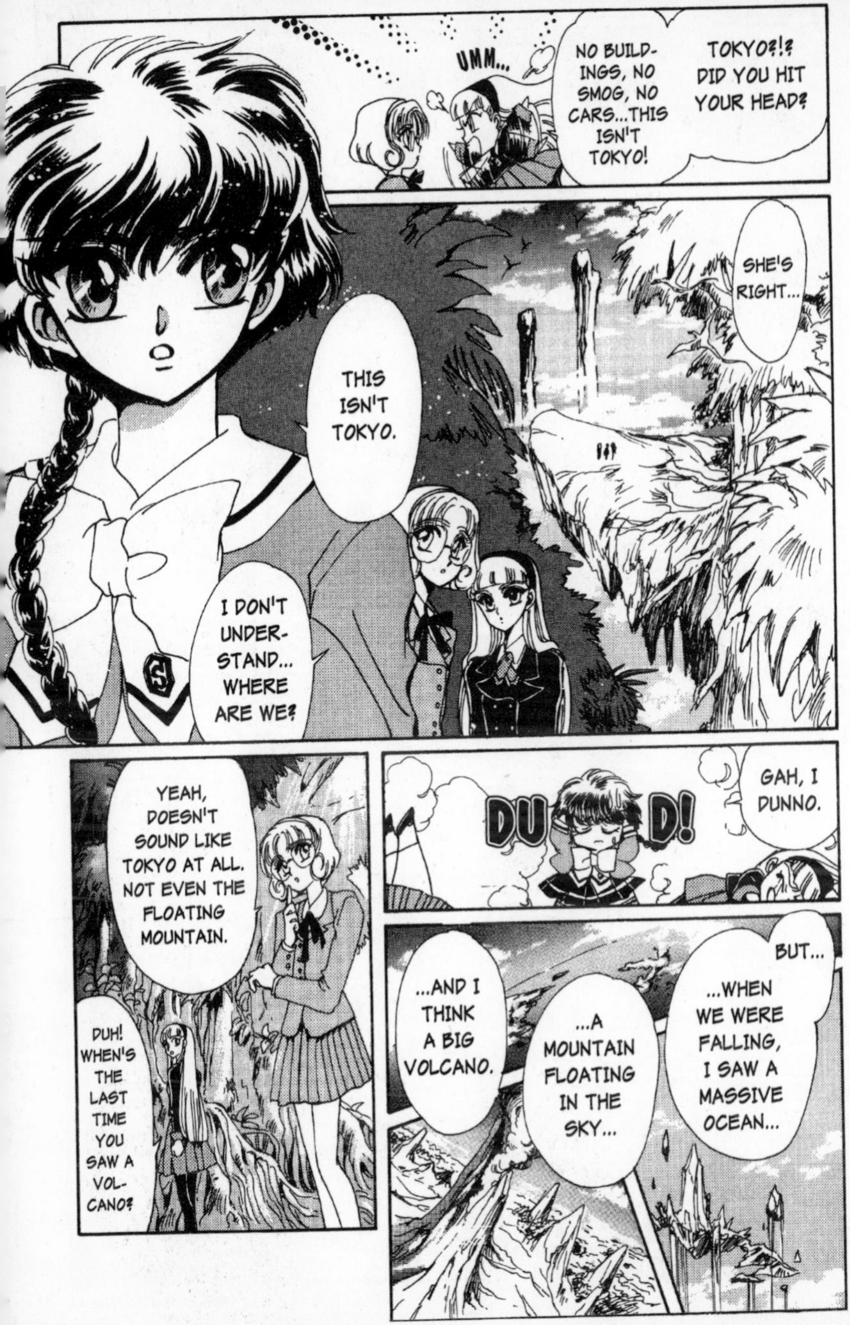
TOKYO?!? DID YOU HIT YOUR HEAD?
NO BUILD-INGS, NO SMOG, NO CARS...THIS ISN'T TOKYO!
UMM...
SHE'S RIGHT...
THIS ISN'T TOKYO.
I DON'T UNDER-STAND... WHERE ARE WE?
GAH, I DUNNO.
DU D!
BUT...
...WHEN WE WERE FALLING, I SAW A MASSIVE OCEAN...
...A MOUNTAIN FLOATING IN THE SKY...
...AND I THINK A BIG VOLCANO.
YEAH, DOESN'T SOUND LIKE TOKYO AT ALL. NOT EVEN THE FLOATING MOUNTAIN.
DUH! WHEN'S THE LAST TIME YOU SAW A VOL-CANO?

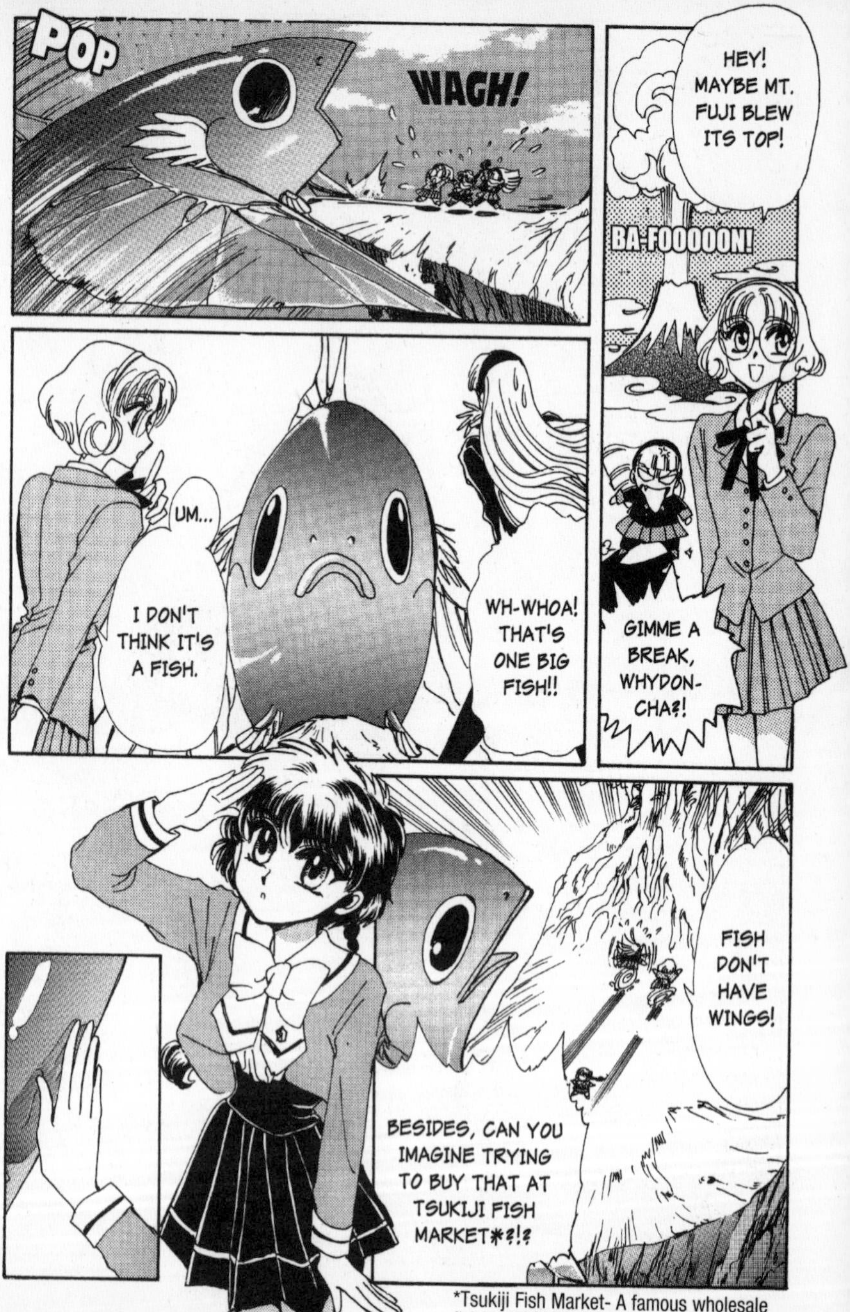
HEY! MAYBE MT. FUJI BLEW ITS TOP!
BA-FOOOOON!
GIMME A BREAK, WHYDON-CHA?!
POP
WAGH!
WH-WHOA! THAT'S ONE BIG FISH!!
UM...
I DON'T THINK IT'S A FISH.
FISH DON'T HAVE WINGS!
BESIDES, CAN YOU IMAGINE TRYING TO BUY THAT AT TSUKIJI FISH MARKET*?!?

*Tsukiji Fish Market- A famous wholesale fish market in Tokyo, the largest in the area.

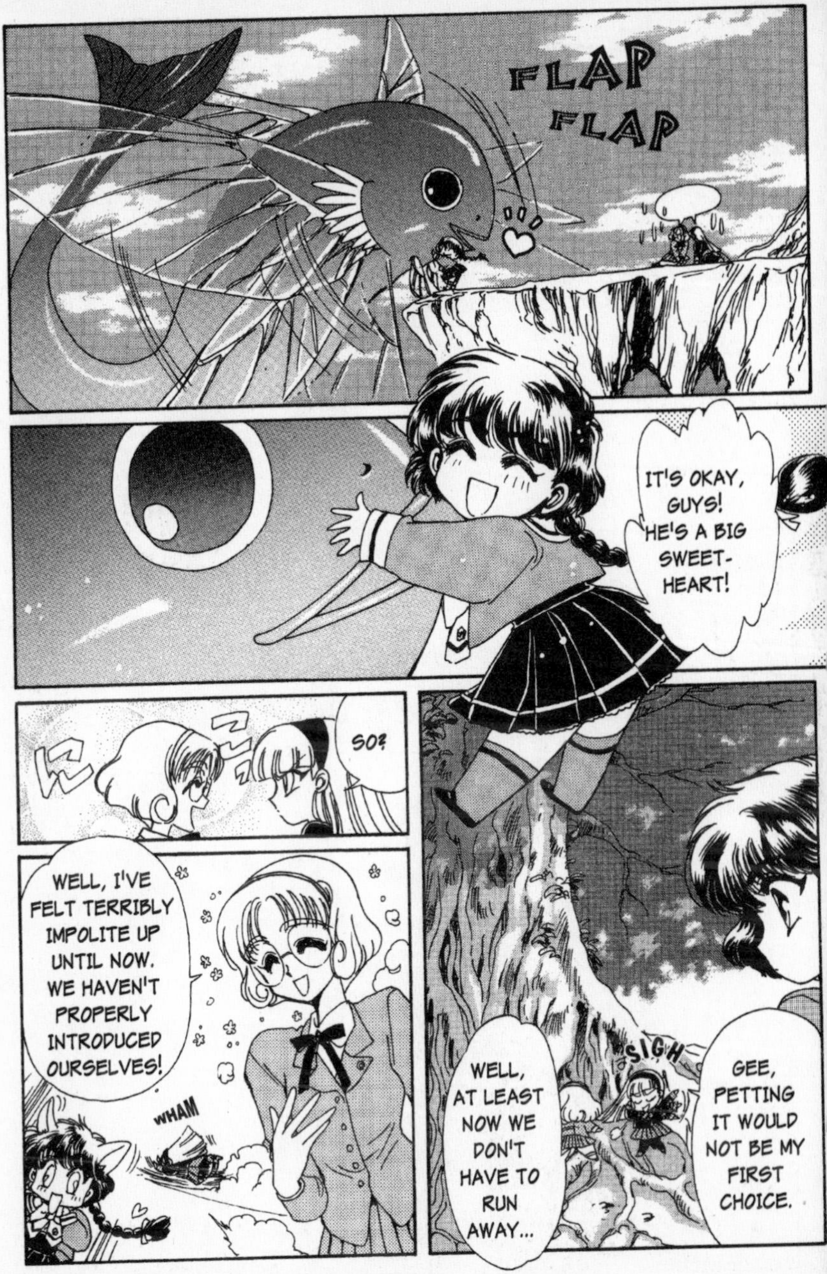
FLAP
FLAP
IT'S OKAY, GUYS! HE'S A BIG SWEET-HEART!
GEE, PETTING IT WOULD NOT BE MY FIRST CHOICE.
SIGH
WELL, AT LEAST NOW WE DON'T HAVE TO RUN AWAY...
SO?
WELL, I'VE FELT TERRIBLY IMPOLITE UP UNTIL NOW. WE HAVEN'T PROPERLY INTRODUCED OURSELVES!
WHAM

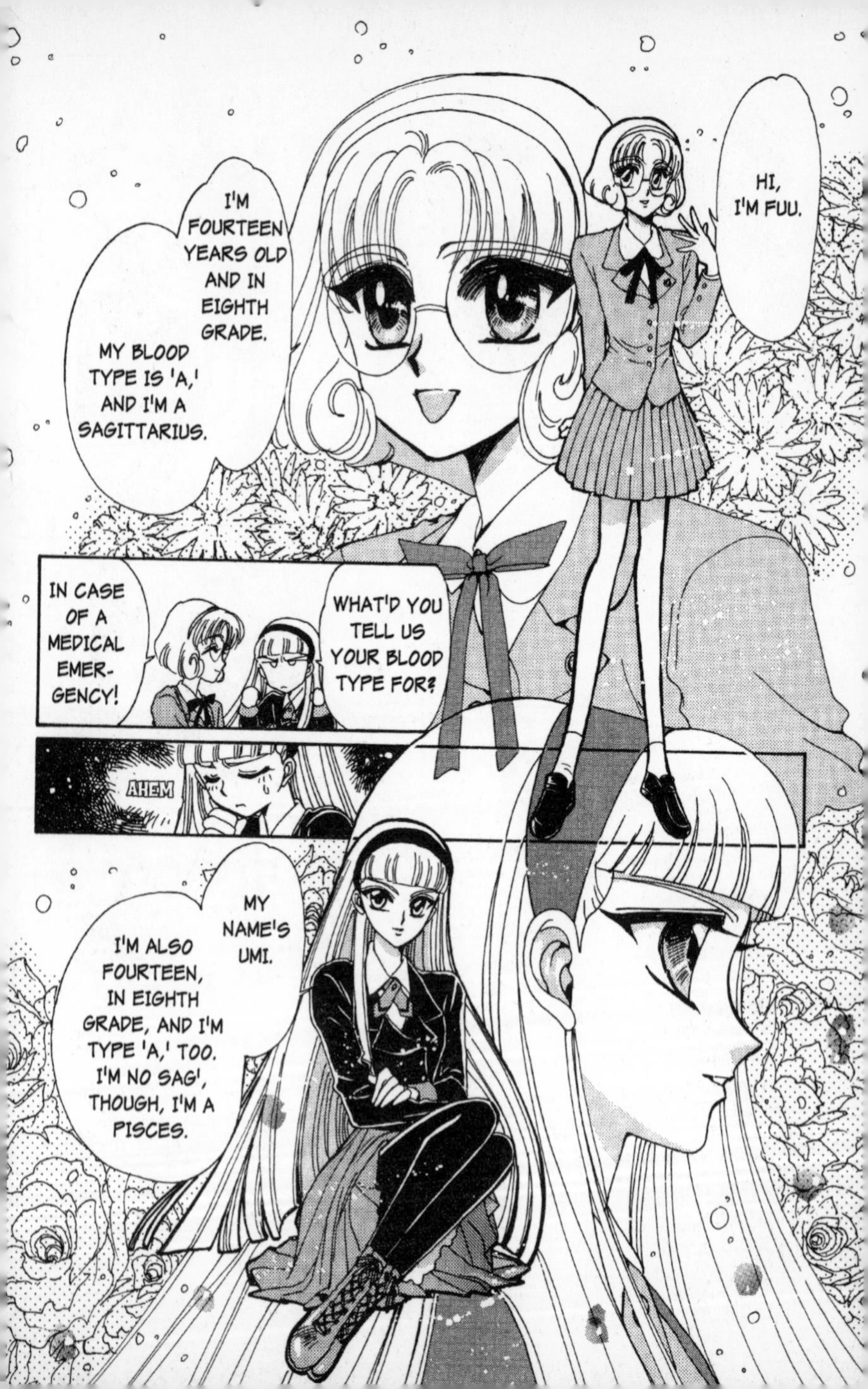
HI, I'M FUU.
I'M FOURTEEN YEARS OLD AND IN EIGHTH GRADE.
MY BLOOD TYPE IS 'A,' AND I'M A SAGITTARIUS.
WHAT'D YOU TELL US YOUR BLOOD TYPE FOR?
IN CASE OF A MEDICAL EMER-GENCY!
AHEM
MY NAME'S UMI.
I'M ALSO FOURTEEN, IN EIGHTH GRADE, AND I'M TYPE 'A,' TOO. I'M NO SAG', THOUGH, I'M A PISCES.

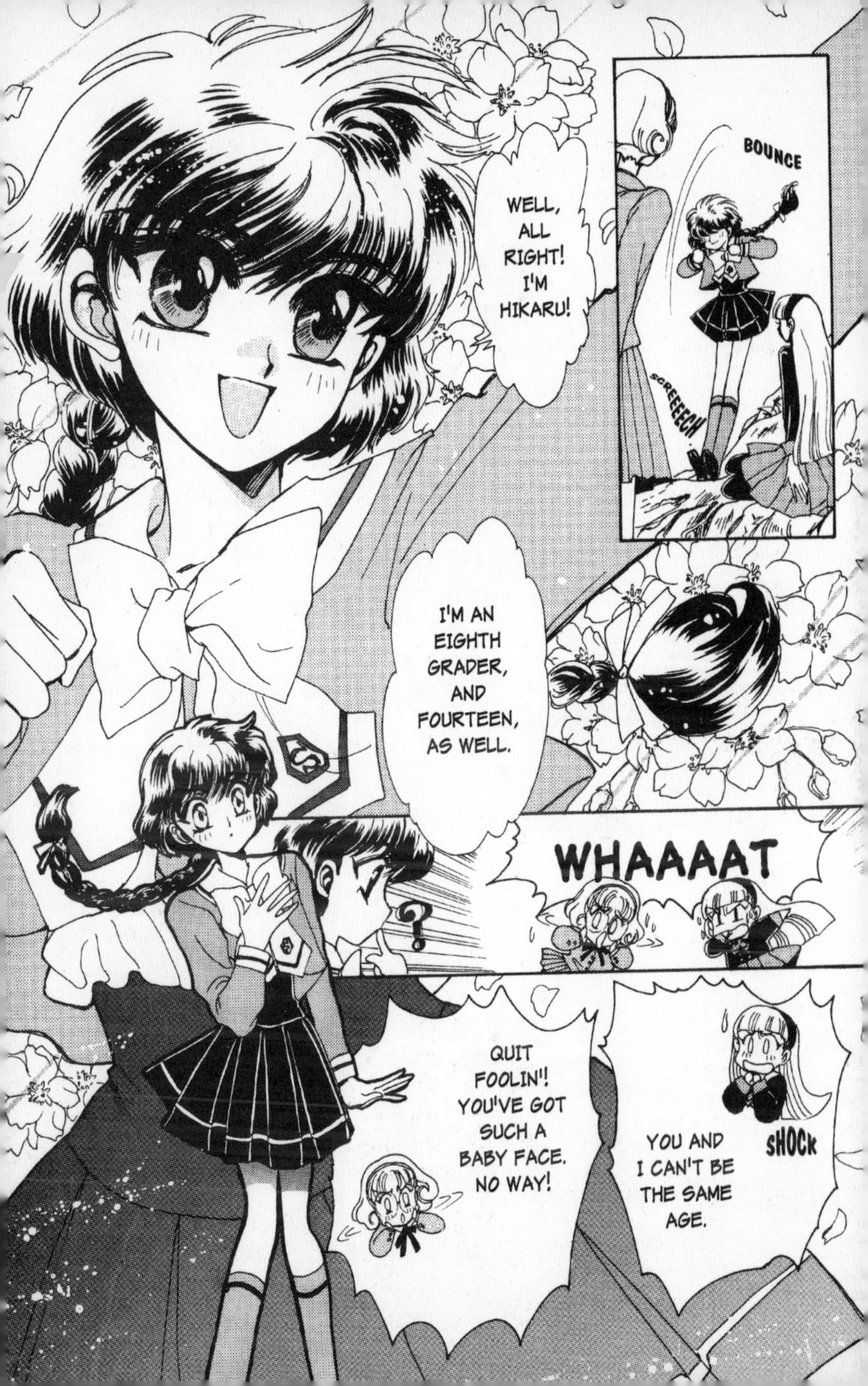
BOUNCE
SCREEEECH
WELL, ALL RIGHT! I'M HIKARU!
I'M AN EIGHTH GRADER, AND FOURTEEN, AS WELL.
WHAAAAT
YOU AND I CAN'T BE THE SAME AGE.
SHOCK
QUIT FOOLIN'! YOU'VE GOT SUCH A BABY FACE. NO WAY!

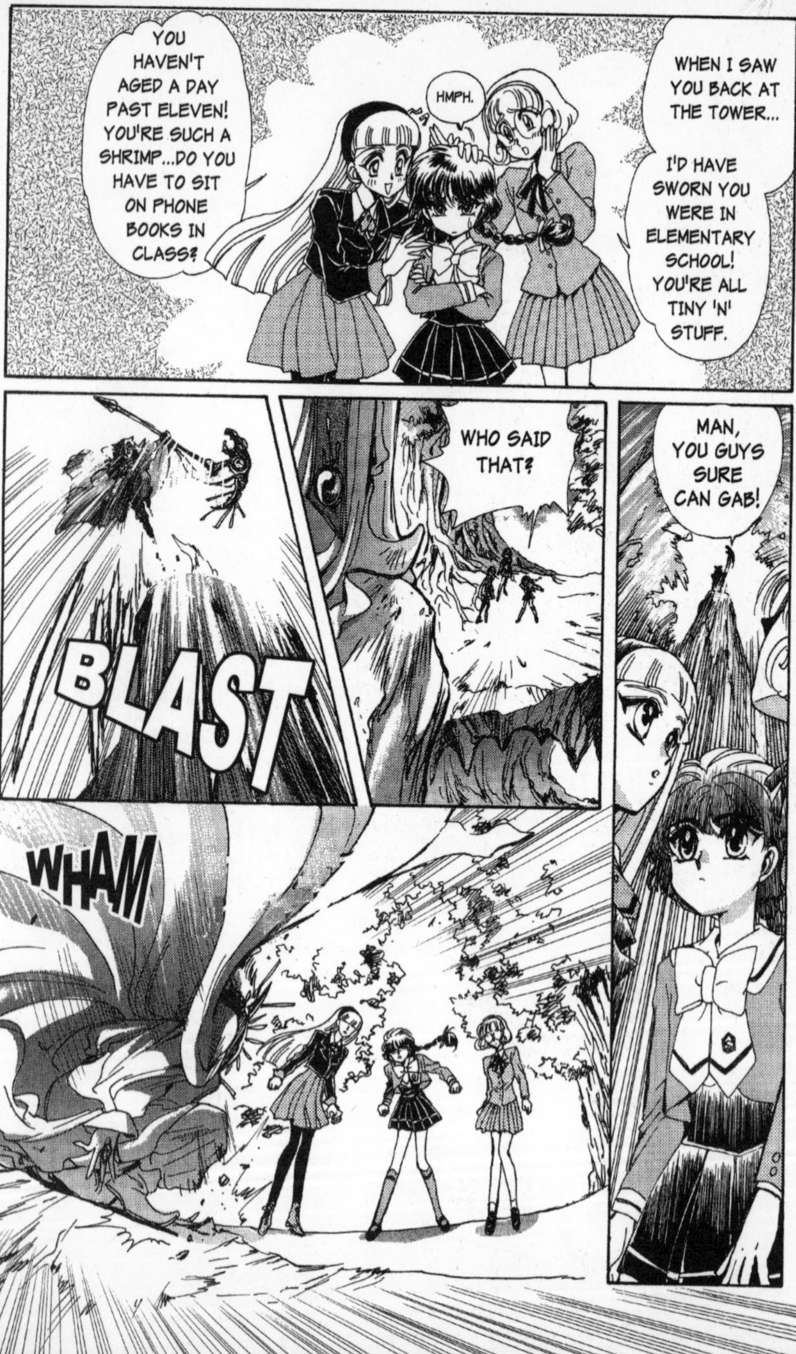
WHEN I SAW YOU BACK AT THE TOWER...
I'D HAVE SWORN YOU WERE IN ELEMENTARY SCHOOL! YOU'RE ALL TINY 'N' STUFF.
HMPH.
YOU HAVEN'T AGED A DAY PAST ELEVEN! YOU'RE SUCH A SHRIMP...DO YOU HAVE TO SIT ON PHONE BOOKS IN CLASS?
MAN, YOU GUYS SURE CAN GAB!
WHO SAID THAT?
BLAST
WHAM

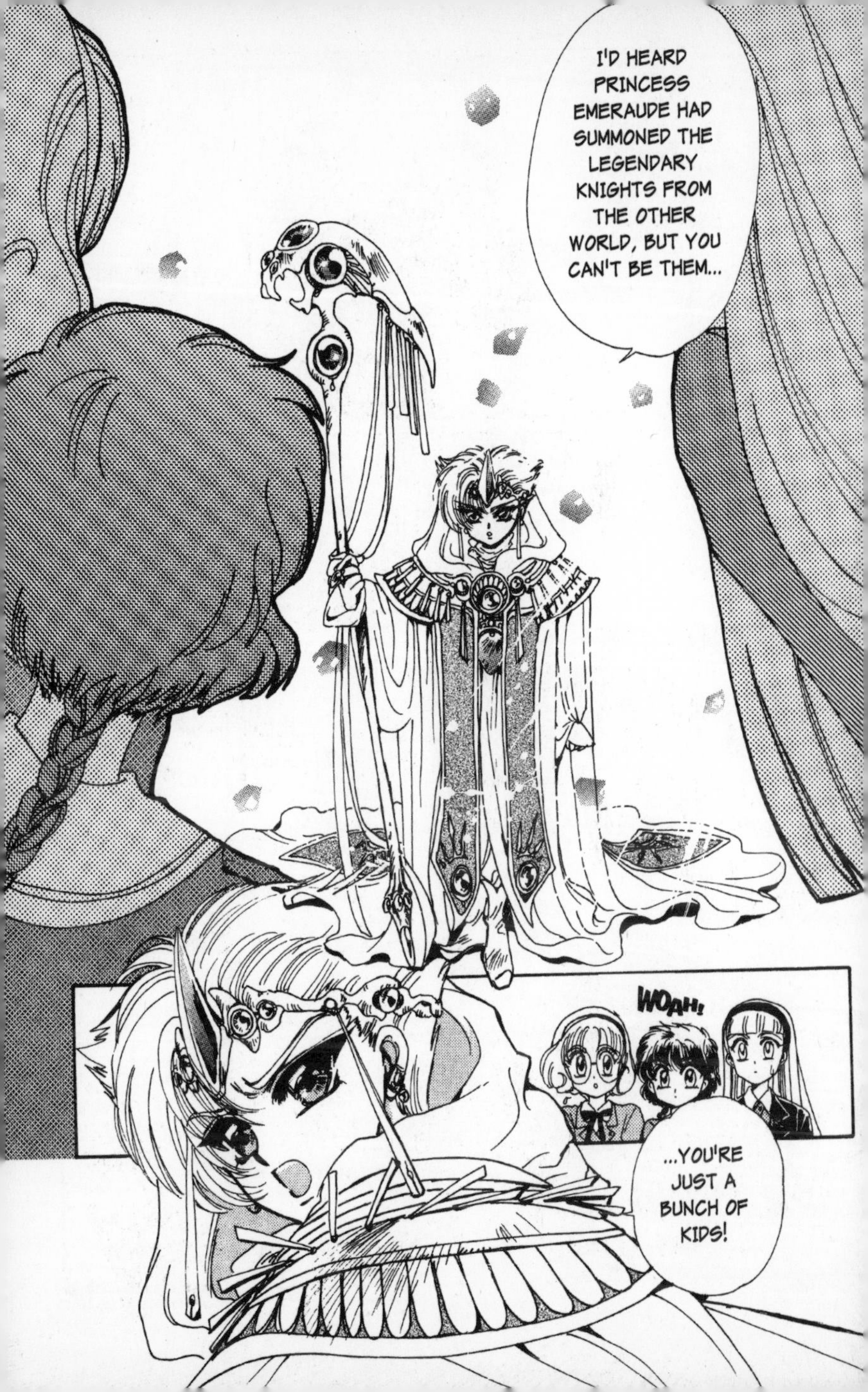
I'D HEARD PRINCESS EMERAUDE HAD SUMMONED THE LEGENDARY KNIGHTS FROM THE OTHER WORLD, BUT YOU CAN'T BE THEM...
WOAH!
...YOU'RE JUST A BUNCH OF KIDS!

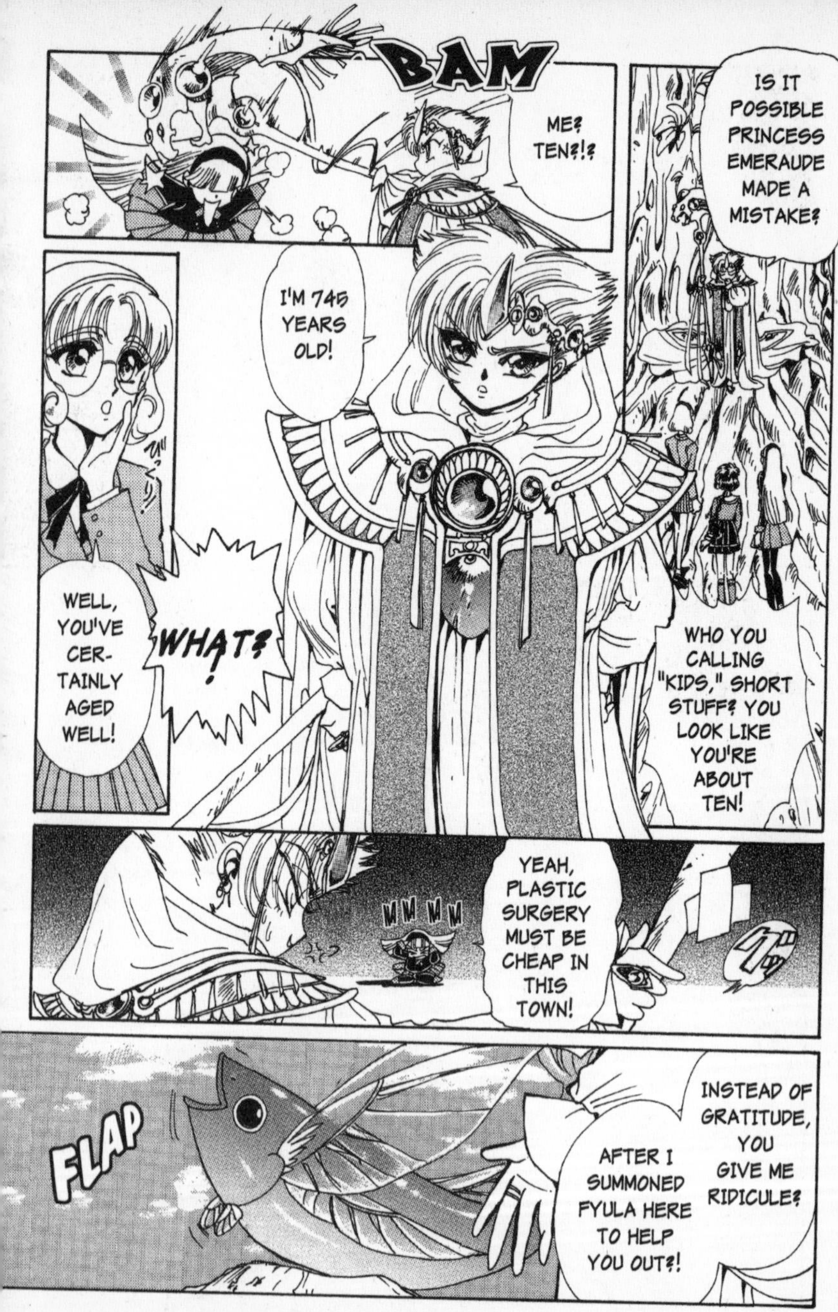
IS IT POSSIBLE PRINCESS EMERAUDE MADE A MISTAKE?
WHO YOU CALLING "KIDS," SHORT STUFF? YOU LOOK LIKE YOU'RE ABOUT TEN!
BAM
ME? TEN?!?
I'M 745 YEARS OLD!
WHAT?!
WELL, YOU'VE CER-TAINLY AGED WELL!
YEAH, PLASTIC SURGERY MUST BE CHEAP IN THIS TOWN!
INSTEAD OF GRATITUDE, YOU GIVE ME RIDICULE?
AFTER I SUMMONED FYULA HERE TO HELP YOU OUT?!
FLAP

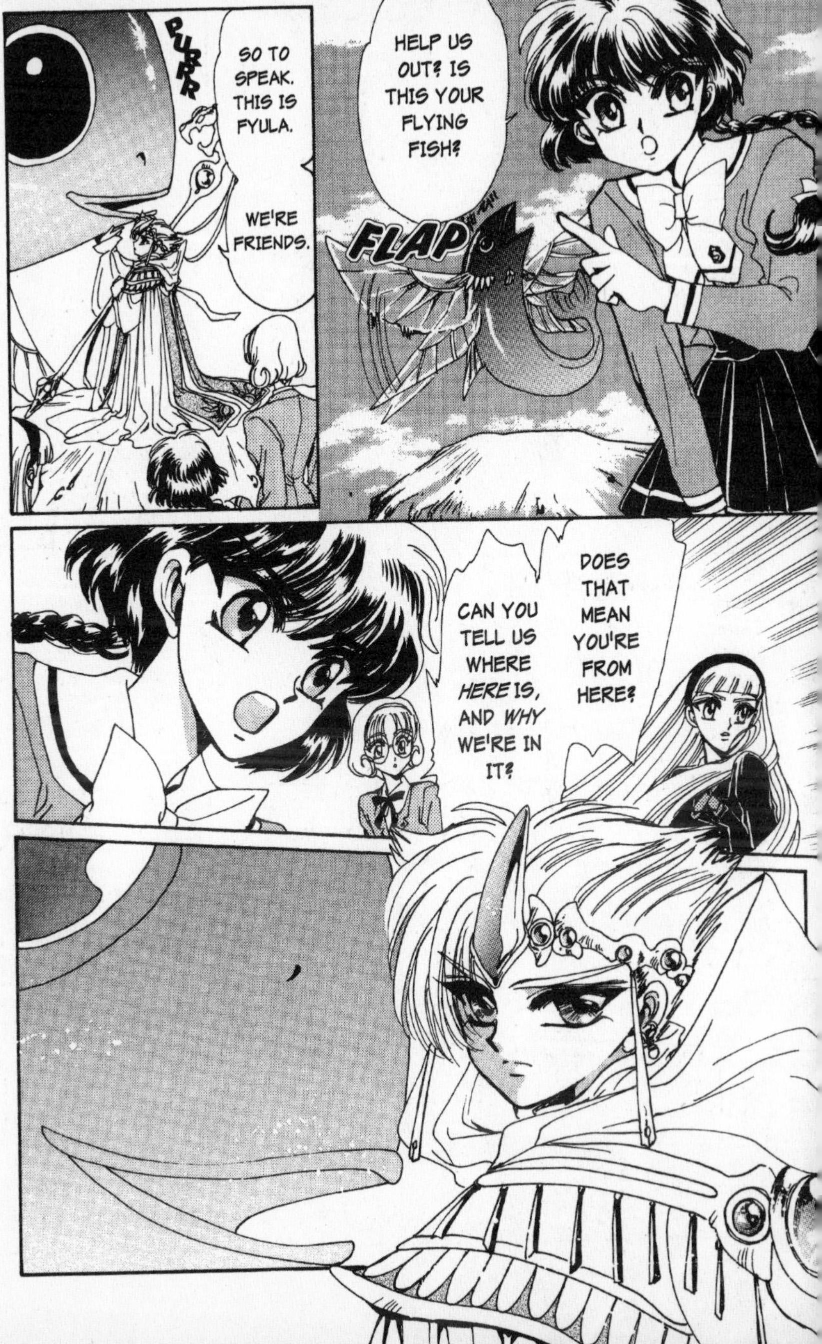
HELP US OUT? IS THIS YOUR FLYING FISH?
FLAP
PURRR
SO TO SPEAK. THIS IS FYULA.
WE'RE FRIENDS.
DOES THAT MEAN YOU'RE FROM HERE?
CAN YOU TELL US WHERE *HERE* IS, AND *WHY* WE'RE IN IT?

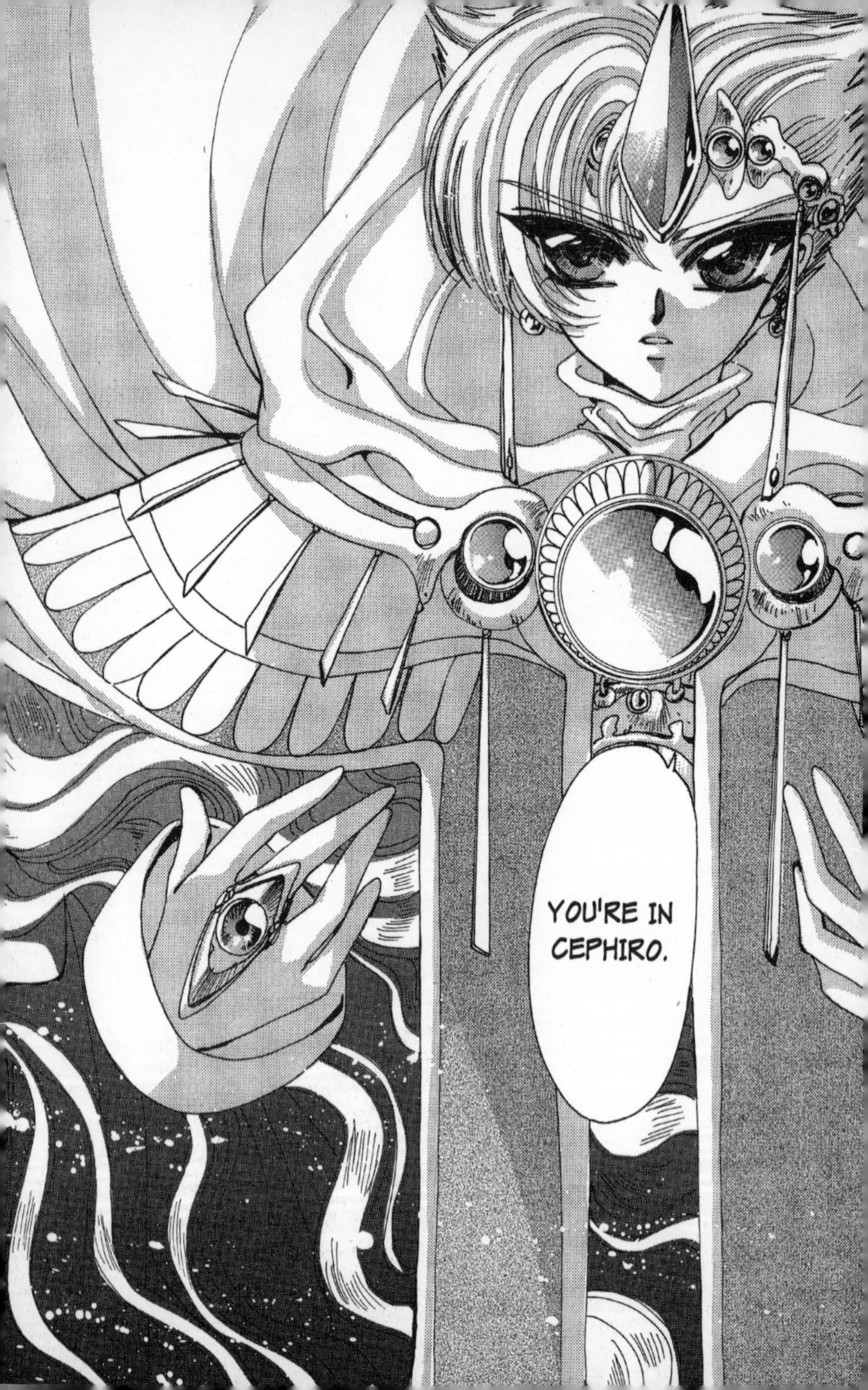
YOU'RE IN CEPHIRO.

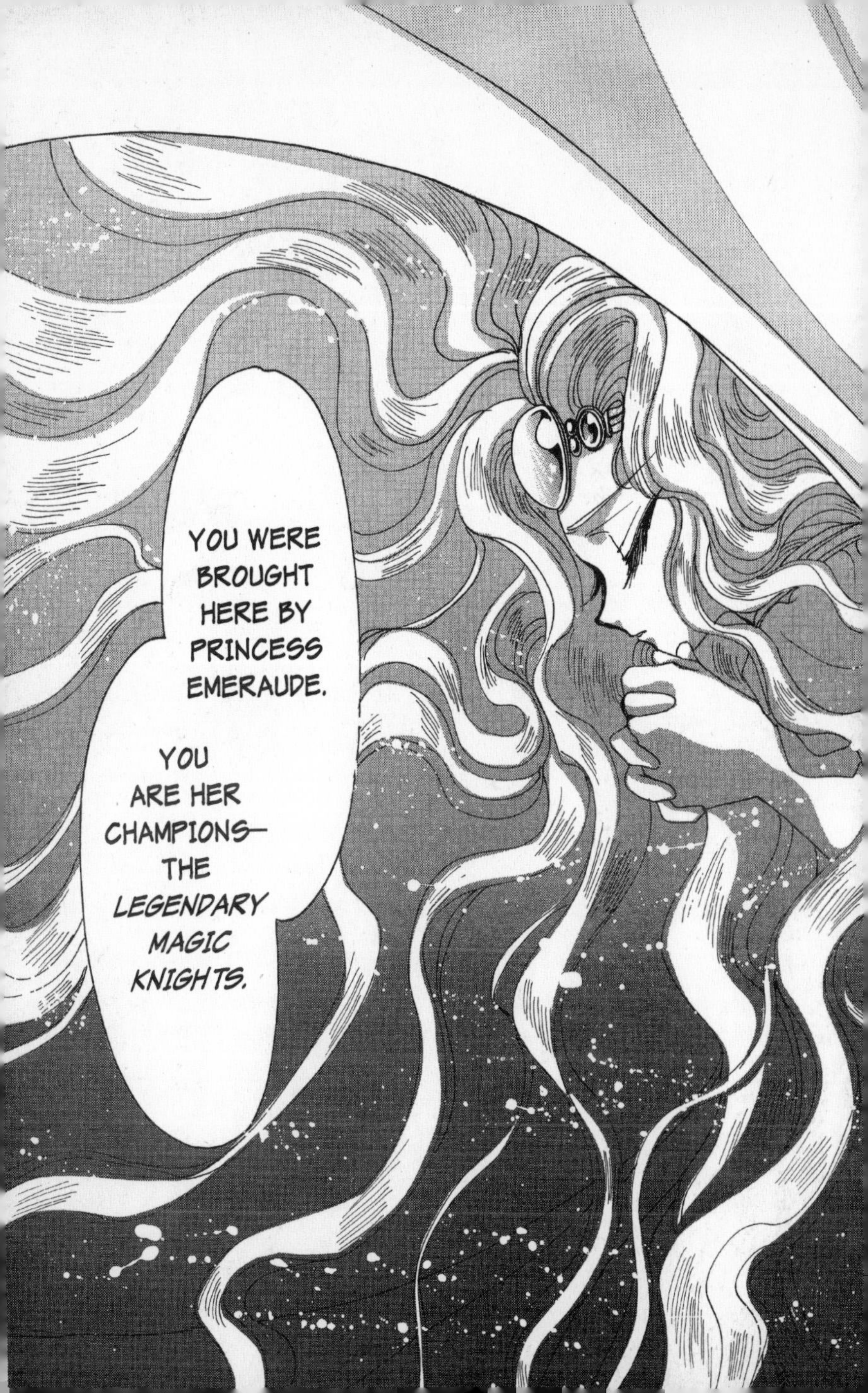
YOU WERE BROUGHT HERE BY PRINCESS EMERAUDE.
YOU ARE HER CHAMPIONS— THE LEGENDARY MAGIC KNIGHTS.

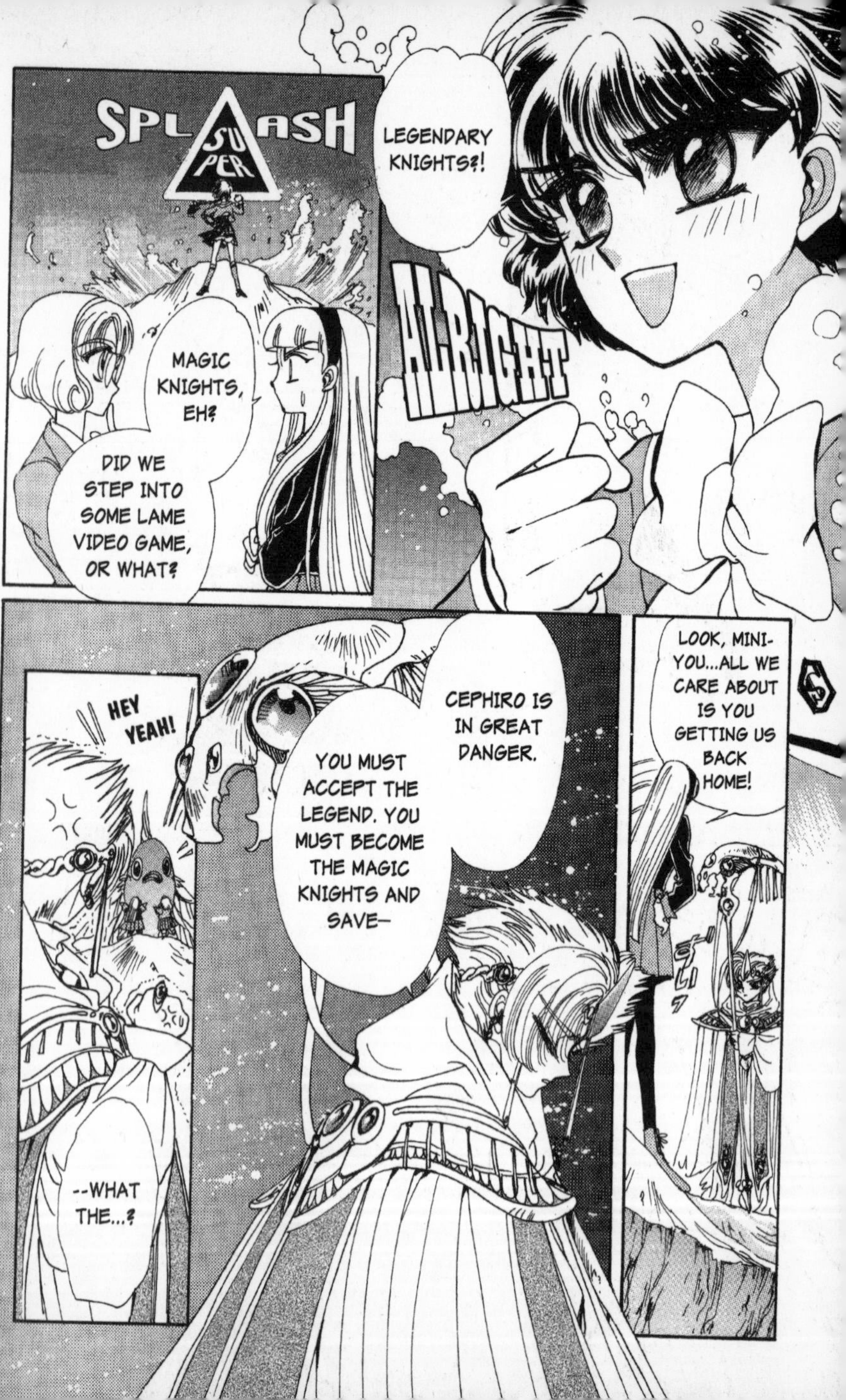
LEGENDARY KNIGHTS?!
ALRIGHT
SPLASH SUPER
MAGIC KNIGHTS, EH?
DID WE STEP INTO SOME LAME VIDEO GAME, OR WHAT?
LOOK, MINI-YOU...ALL WE CARE ABOUT IS YOU GETTING US BACK HOME!
CEPHIRO IS IN GREAT DANGER.
YOU MUST ACCEPT THE LEGEND. YOU MUST BECOME THE MAGIC KNIGHTS AND SAVE–
HEY YEAH!
--WHAT THE...?

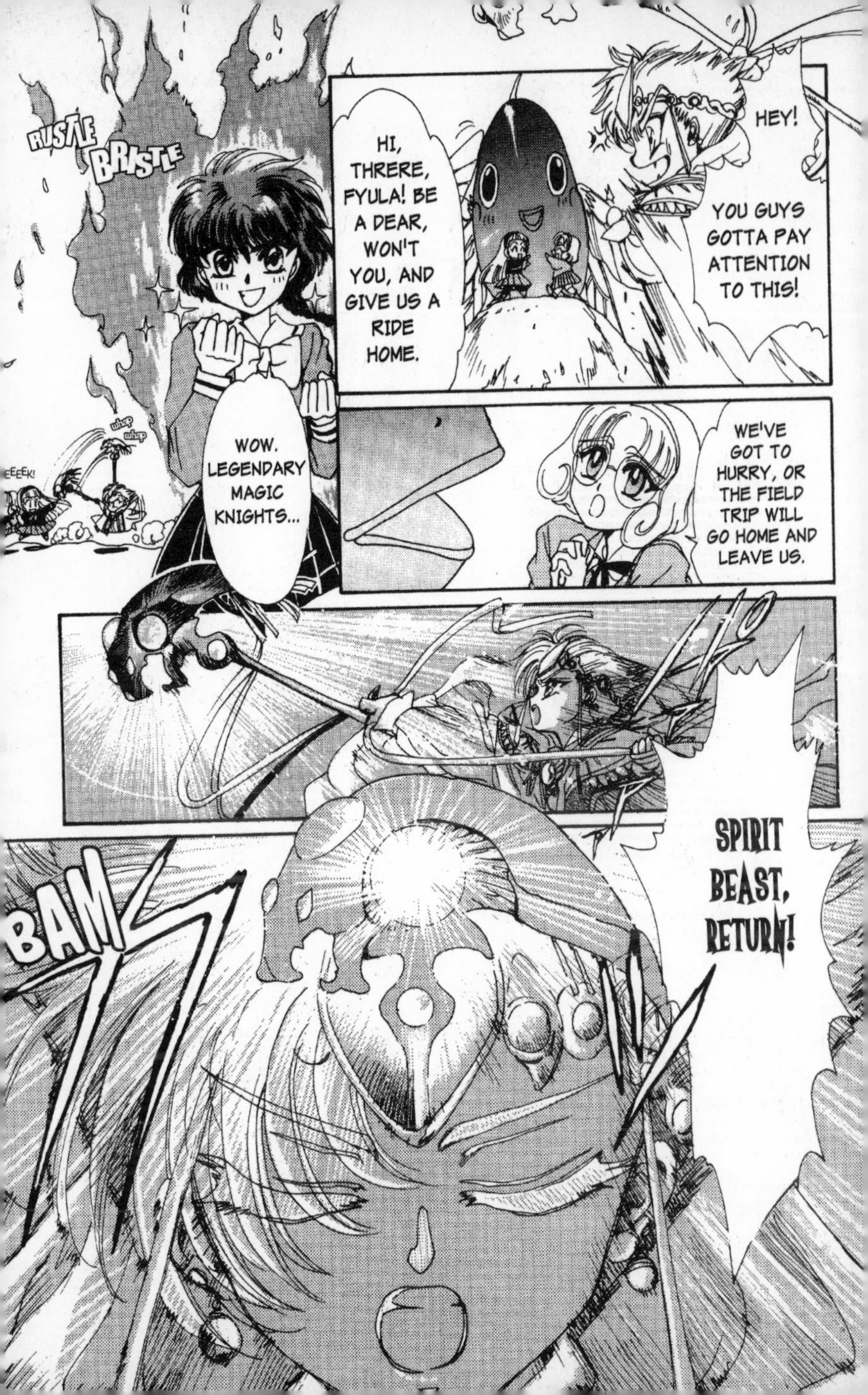
HEY!
YOU GUYS GOTTA PAY ATTENTION TO THIS!
HI, THRERE, FYULA! BE A DEAR, WON'T YOU, AND GIVE US A RIDE HOME.
WE'VE GOT TO HURRY, OR THE FIELD TRIP WILL GO HOME AND LEAVE US.
RUSTLE BRISTLE
WOW. LEGENDARY MAGIC KNIGHTS...
whap whap
EEEEK!
SPIRIT BEAST, RETURN!
BAM

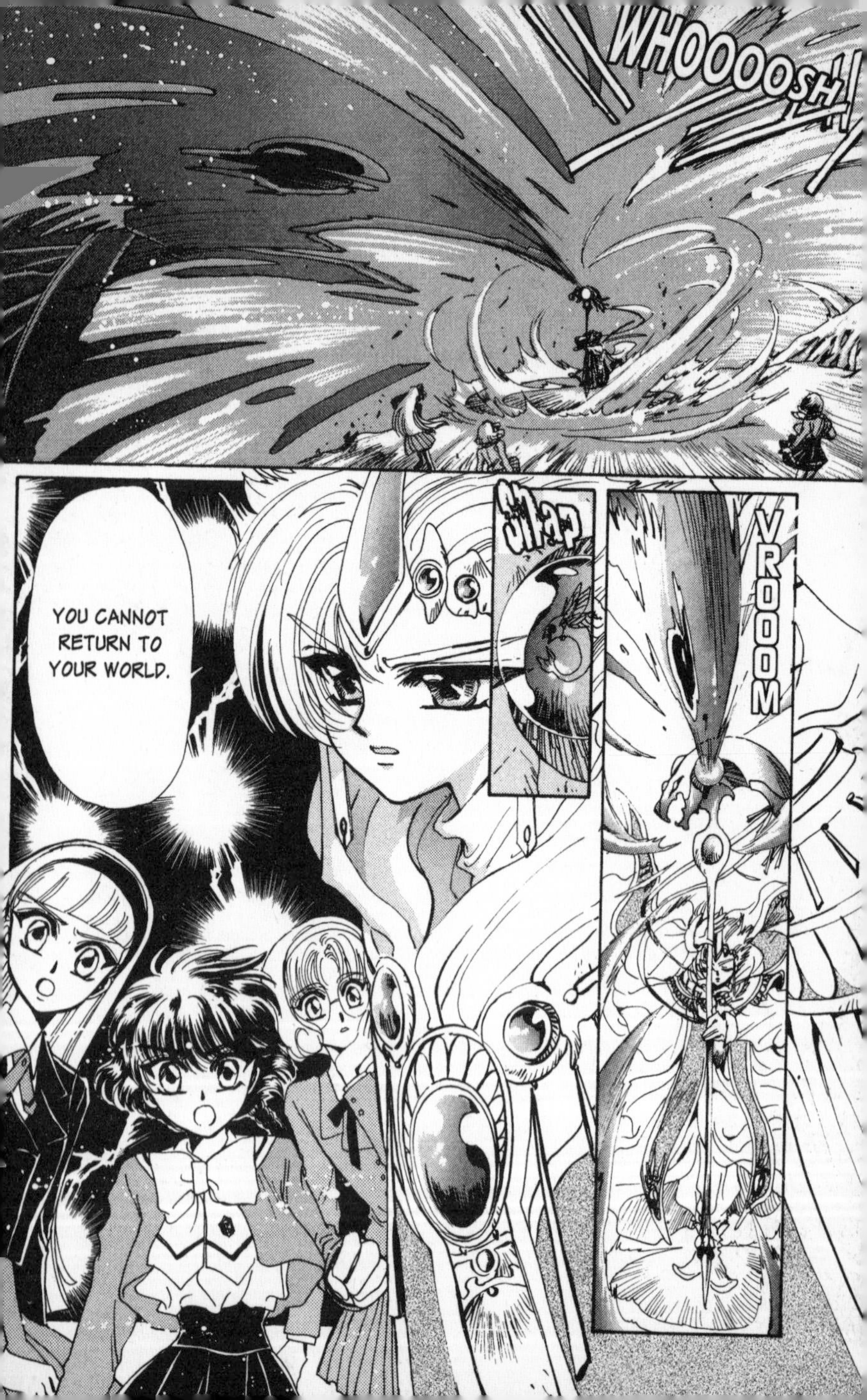
WHOOOOSH
VROOOM
SNAP
YOU CANNOT RETURN TO YOUR WORLD.

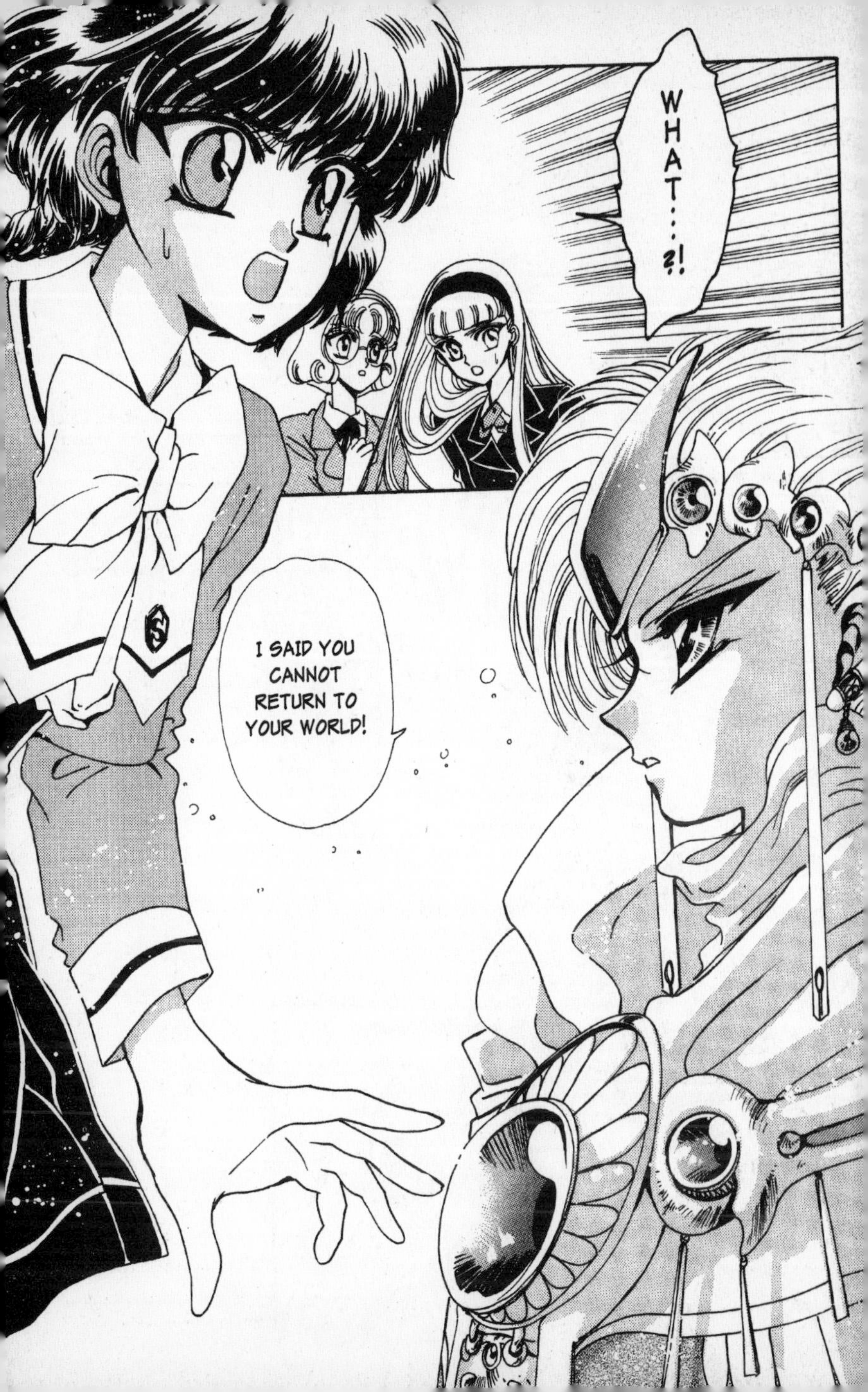
WHAT...?!
I SAID YOU CANNOT RETURN TO YOUR WORLD!

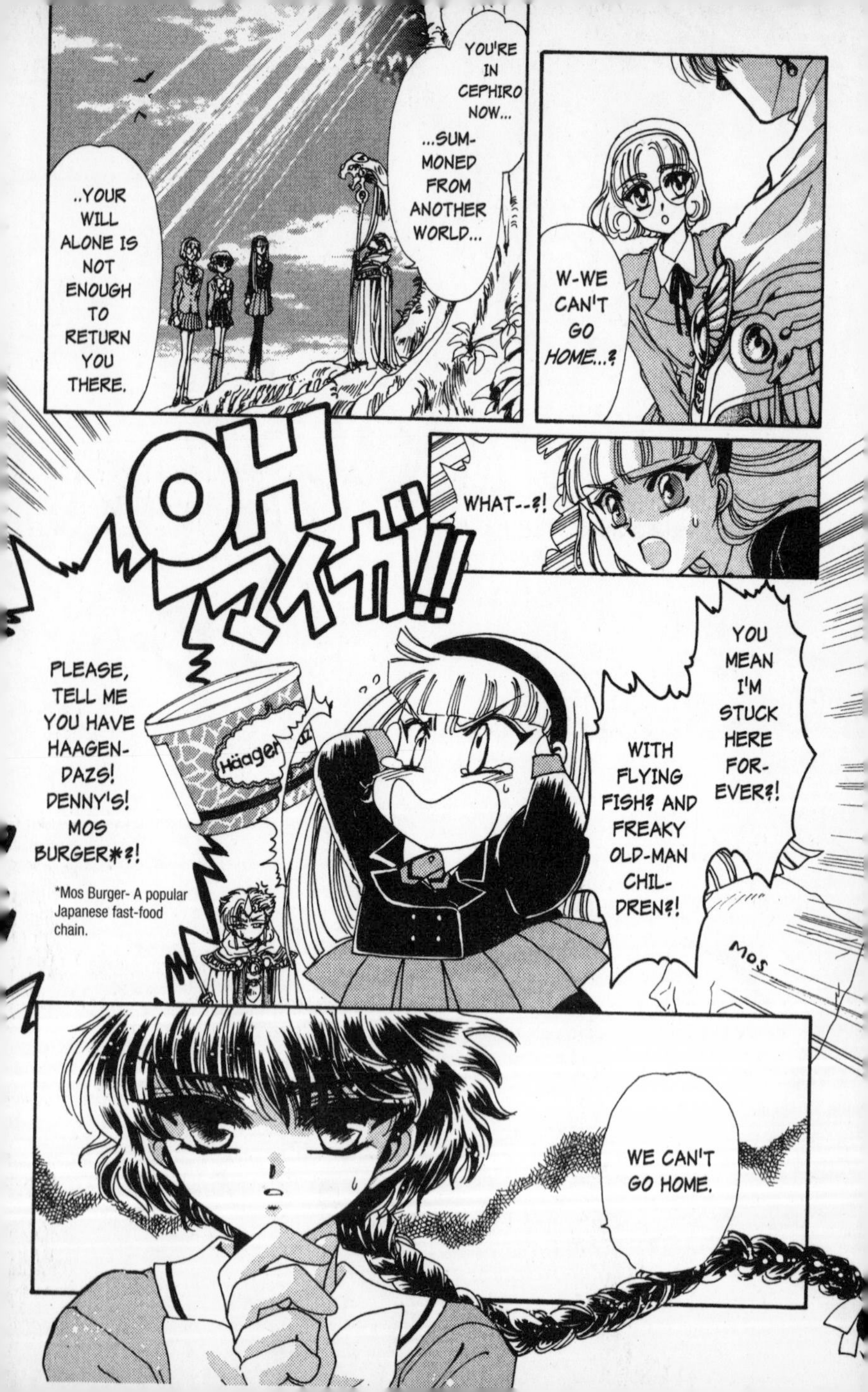
W-WE CAN'T GO HOME...?
YOU'RE IN CEPHIRO NOW...
...SUM-MONED FROM ANOTHER WORLD...
..YOUR WILL ALONE IS NOT ENOUGH TO RETURN YOU THERE.
WHAT--?!
OH マイガ!!
YOU MEAN I'M STUCK HERE FOR-EVER?!
WITH FLYING FISH? AND FREAKY OLD-MAN CHIL-DREN?!
PLEASE, TELL ME YOU HAVE HAAGEN-DAZS! DENNY'S! MOS BURGER*?!
Häagen-Dazs
MOS
WE CAN'T GO HOME.

*Mos Burger- A popular Japanese fast-food chain.

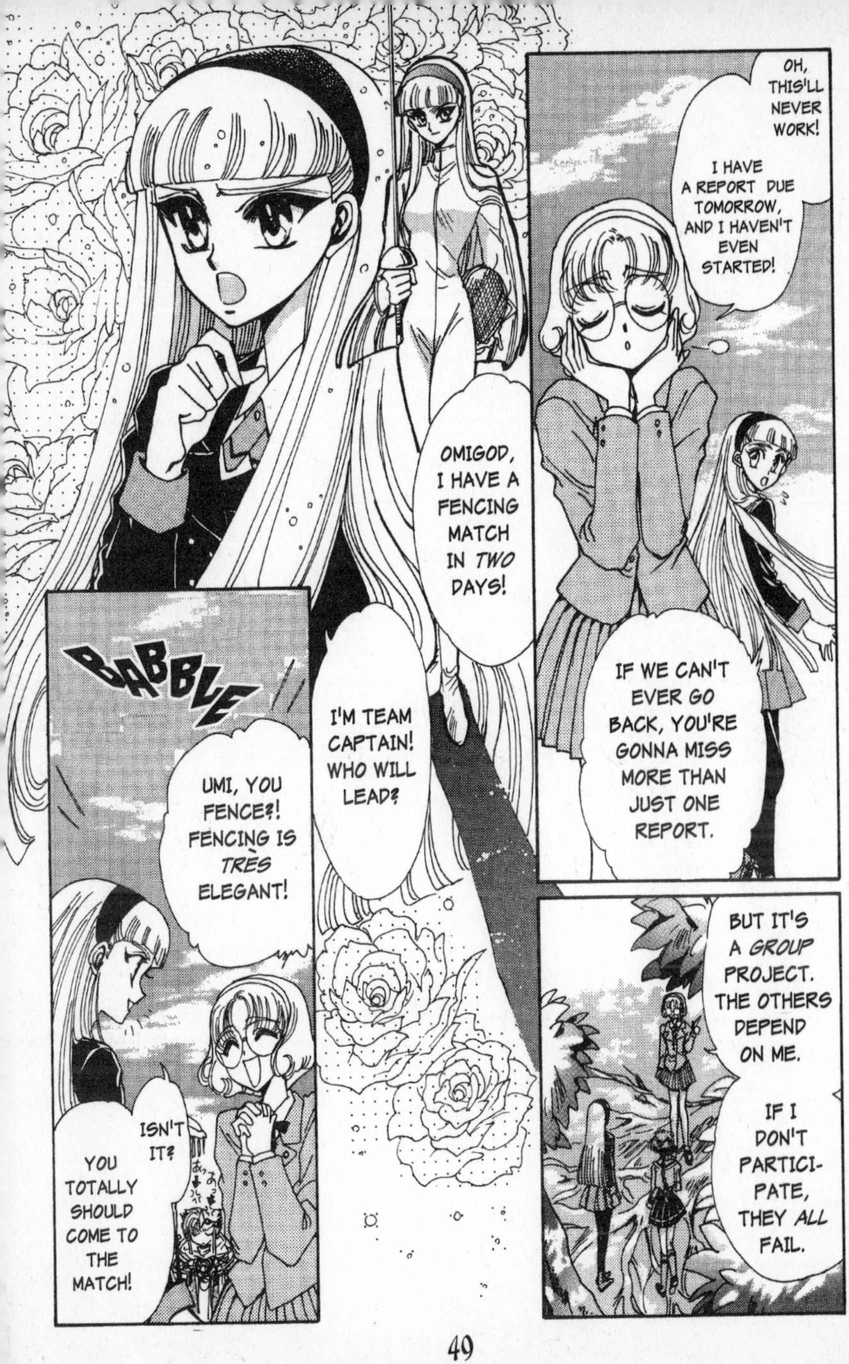

OH, THIS'LL NEVER WORK!
I HAVE A REPORT DUE TOMORROW, AND I HAVEN'T EVEN STARTED!
IF WE CAN'T EVER GO BACK, YOU'RE GONNA MISS MORE THAN JUST ONE REPORT.
OMIGOD, I HAVE A FENCING MATCH IN *TWO* DAYS!
I'M TEAM CAPTAIN! WHO WILL LEAD?
BUT IT'S A *GROUP* PROJECT. THE OTHERS DEPEND ON ME.
IF I DON'T PARTICI-PATE, THEY *ALL* FAIL.
BABBLE
UMI, YOU FENCE?! FENCING IS *TRÈS* ELEGANT!
ISN'T IT?
YOU TOTALLY SHOULD COME TO THE MATCH!

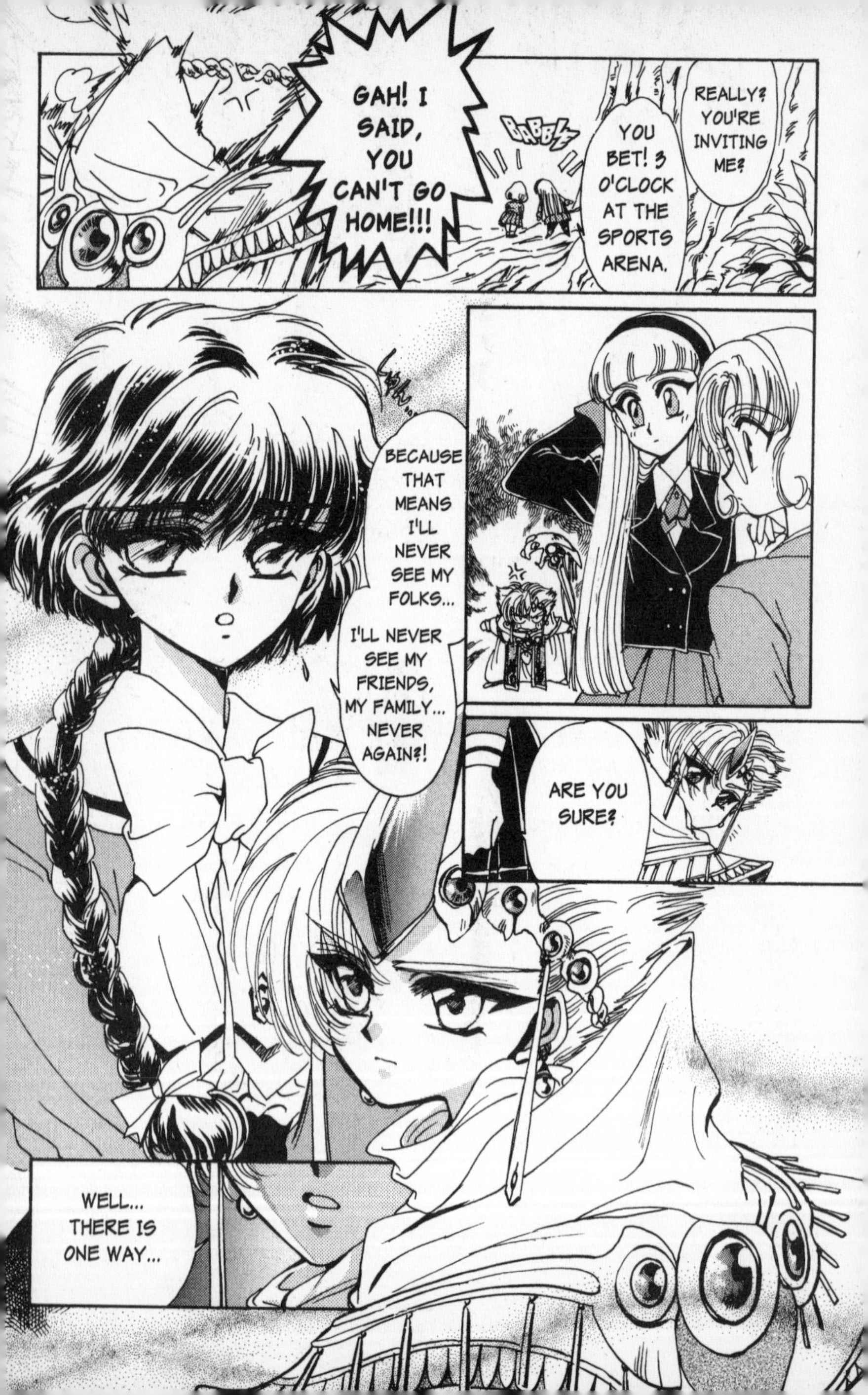
REALLY? YOU'RE INVITING ME?
YOU BET! 3 O'CLOCK AT THE SPORTS ARENA.
BABBLE
GAH! I SAID, YOU CAN'T GO HOME!!!
BECAUSE THAT MEANS I'LL NEVER SEE MY FOLKS...
I'LL NEVER SEE MY FRIENDS, MY FAMILY... NEVER AGAIN?!
ARE YOU SURE?
WELL... THERE IS ONE WAY...

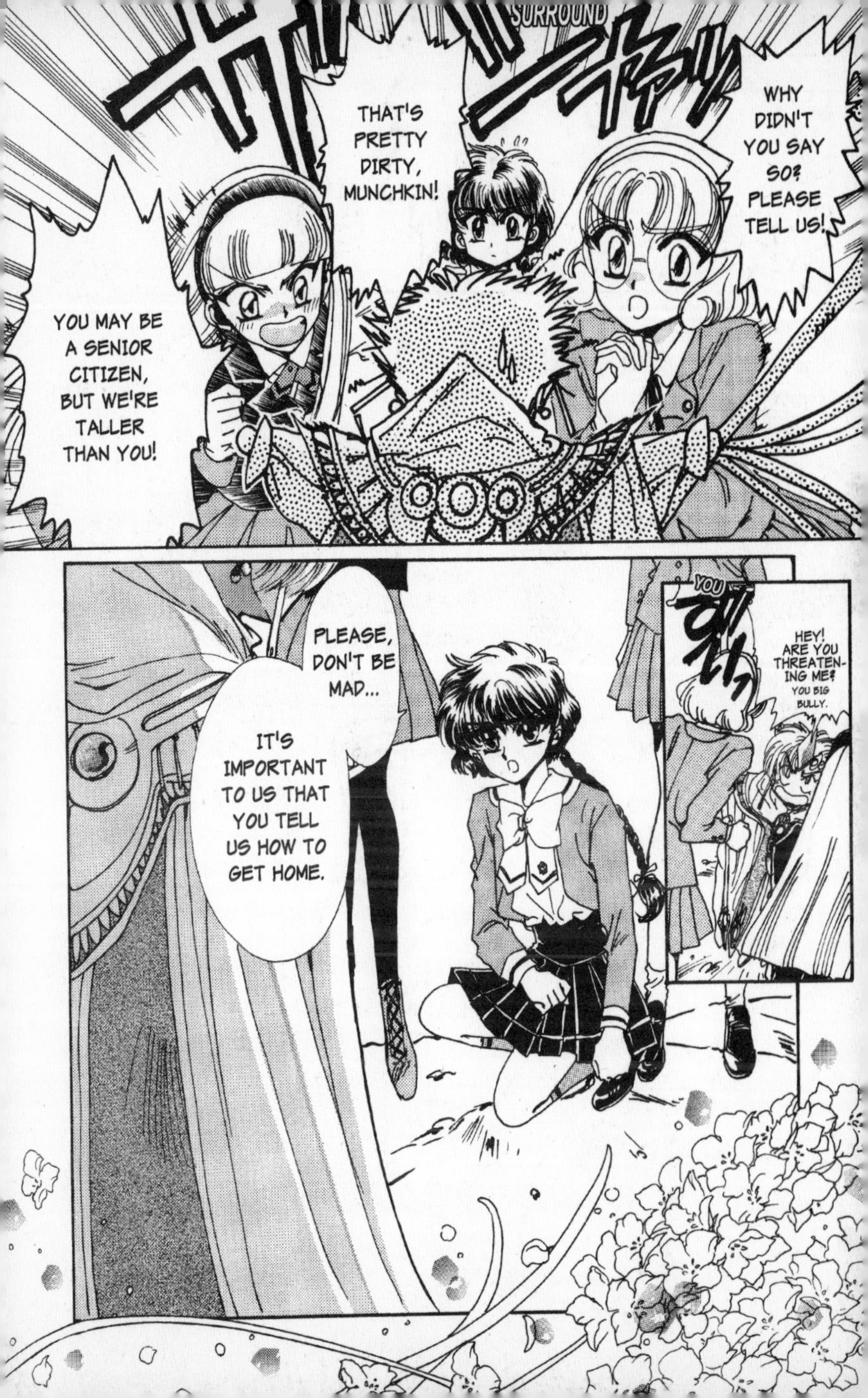
SURROUND
WHY DIDN'T YOU SAY SO? PLEASE TELL US!
THAT'S PRETTY DIRTY, MUNCHKIN!
YOU MAY BE A SENIOR CITIZEN, BUT WE'RE TALLER THAN YOU!
YOU
HEY! ARE YOU THREATEN-ING ME? YOU BIG BULLY.
PLEASE, DON'T BE MAD...
IT'S IMPORTANT TO US THAT YOU TELL US HOW TO GET HOME.

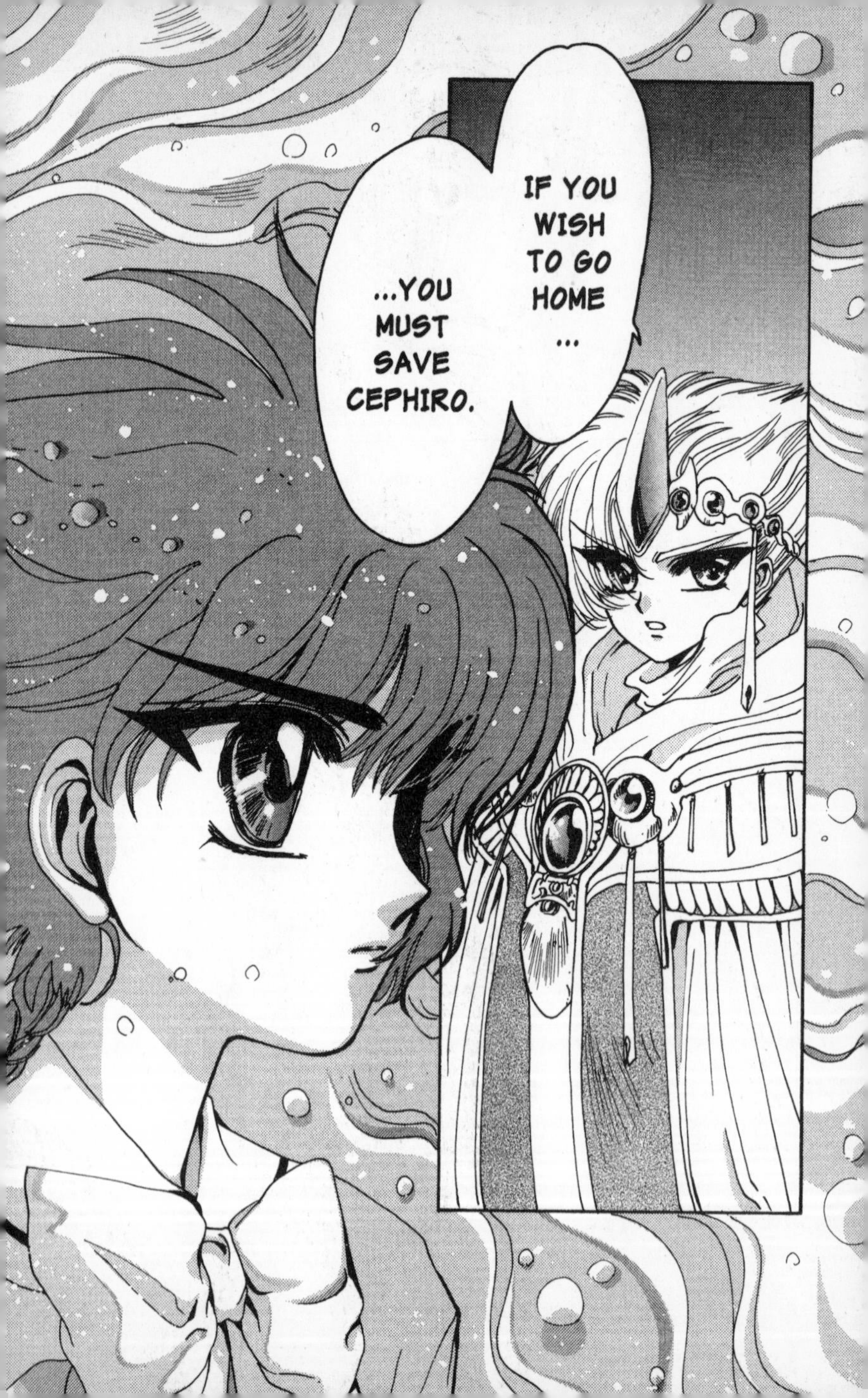
IF YOU WISH TO GO HOME ...
...YOU MUST SAVE CEPHIRO.

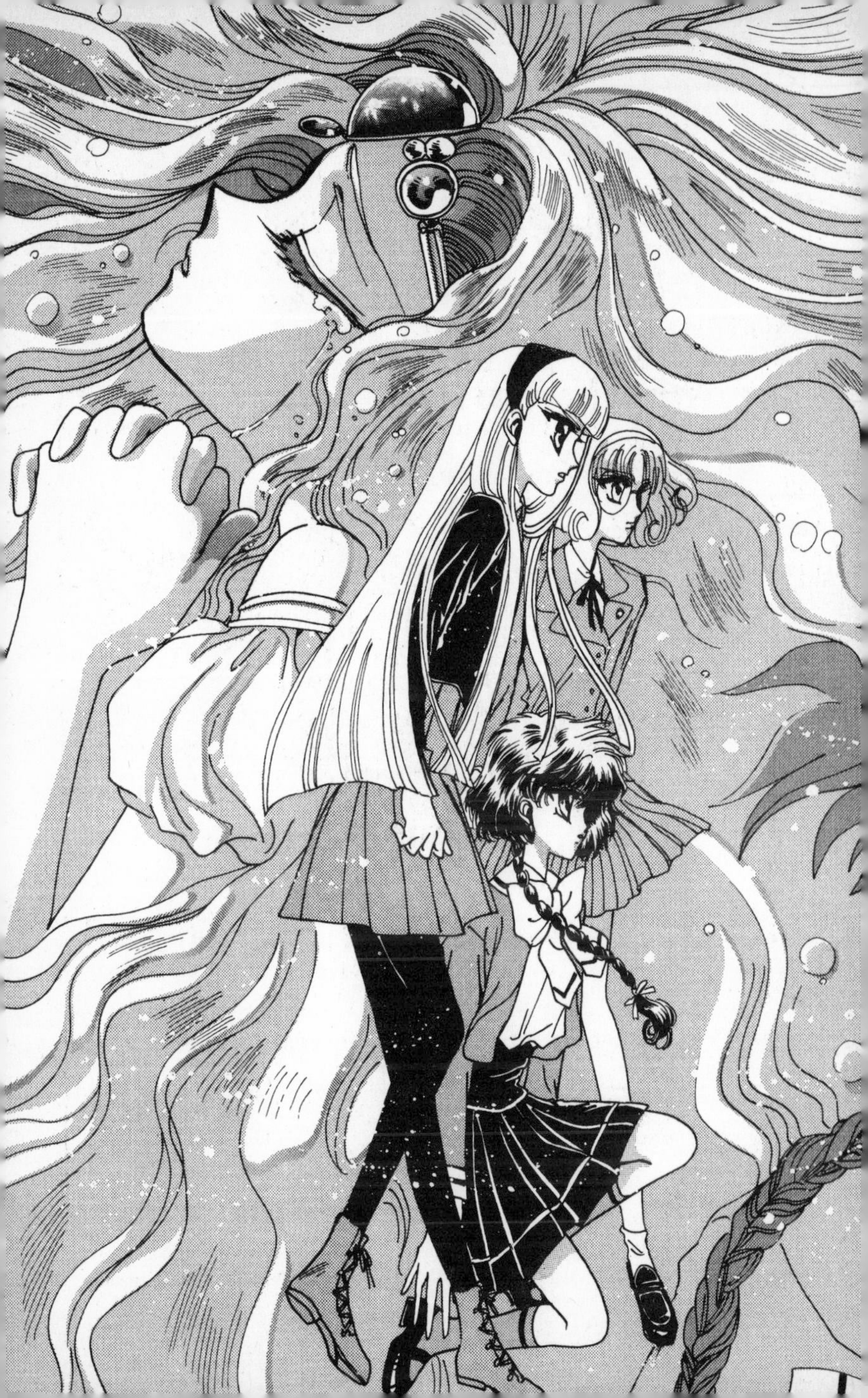

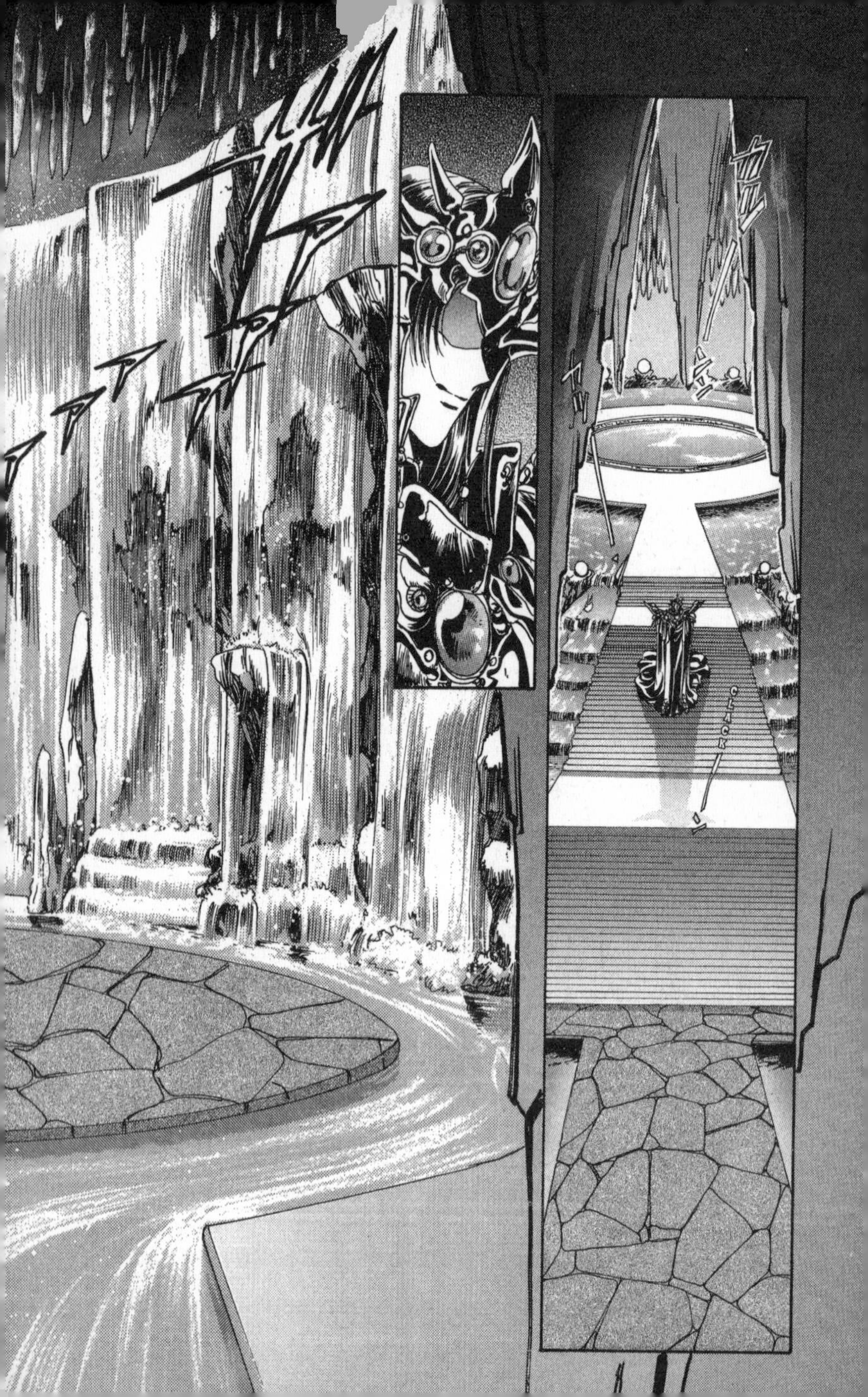
CLACK!

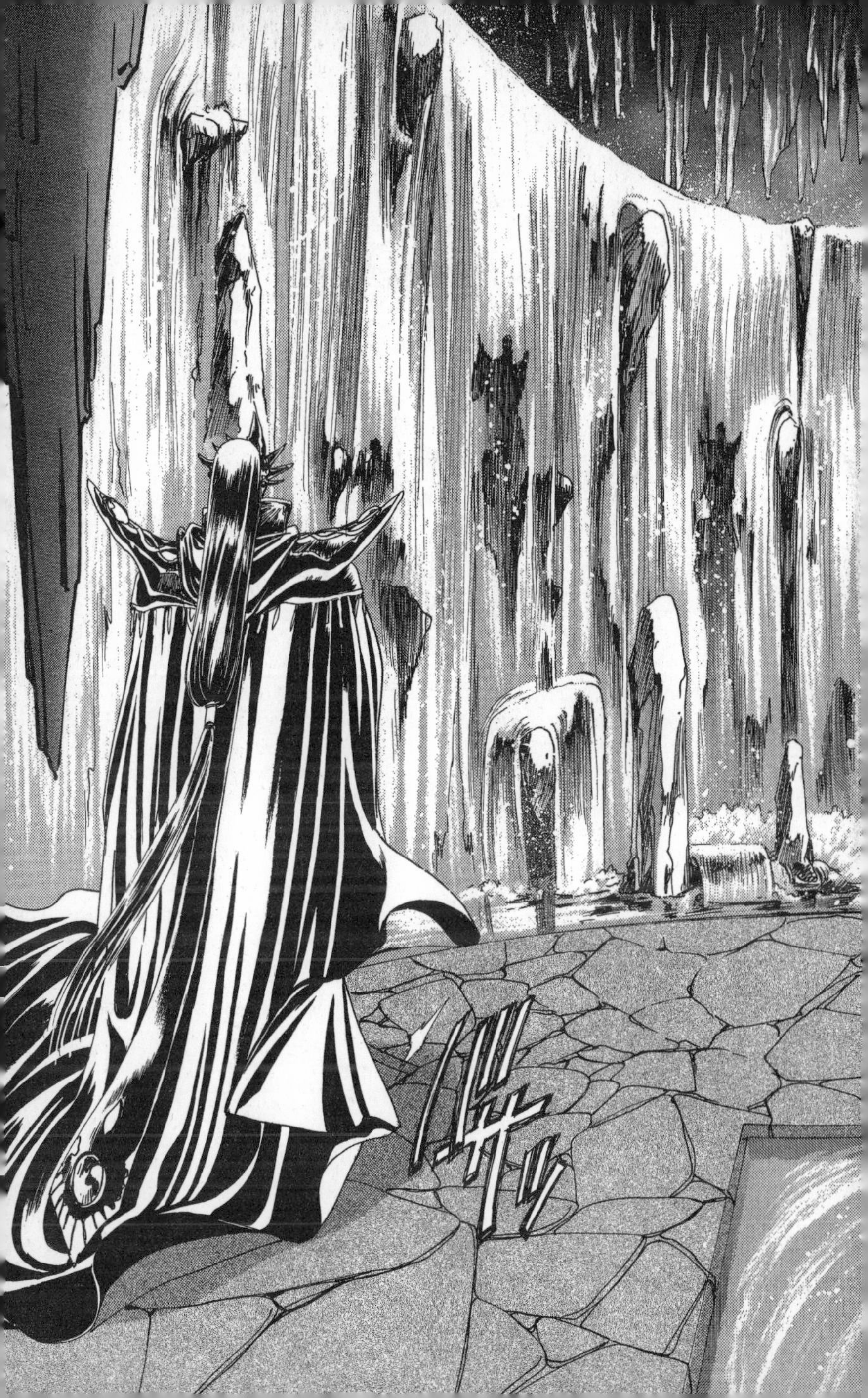
バサッ

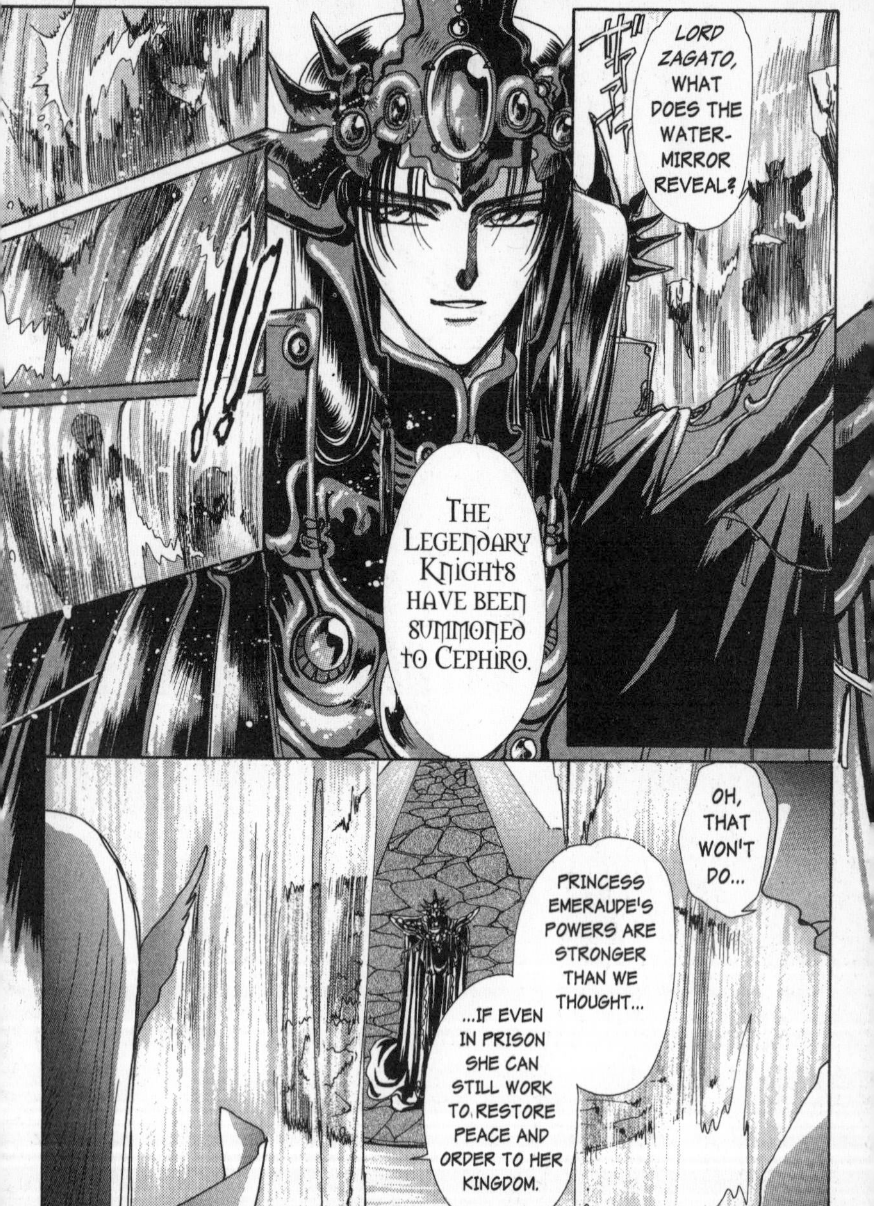
LORD ZAGATO, WHAT DOES THE WATER-MIRROR REVEAL?
THE LEGENDARY KNIGHTS HAVE BEEN SUMMONED TO CEPHIRO.
OH, THAT WON'T DO...
PRINCESS EMERAUDE'S POWERS ARE STRONGER THAN WE THOUGHT...
...IF EVEN IN PRISON SHE CAN STILL WORK TO RESTORE PEACE AND ORDER TO HER KINGDOM.

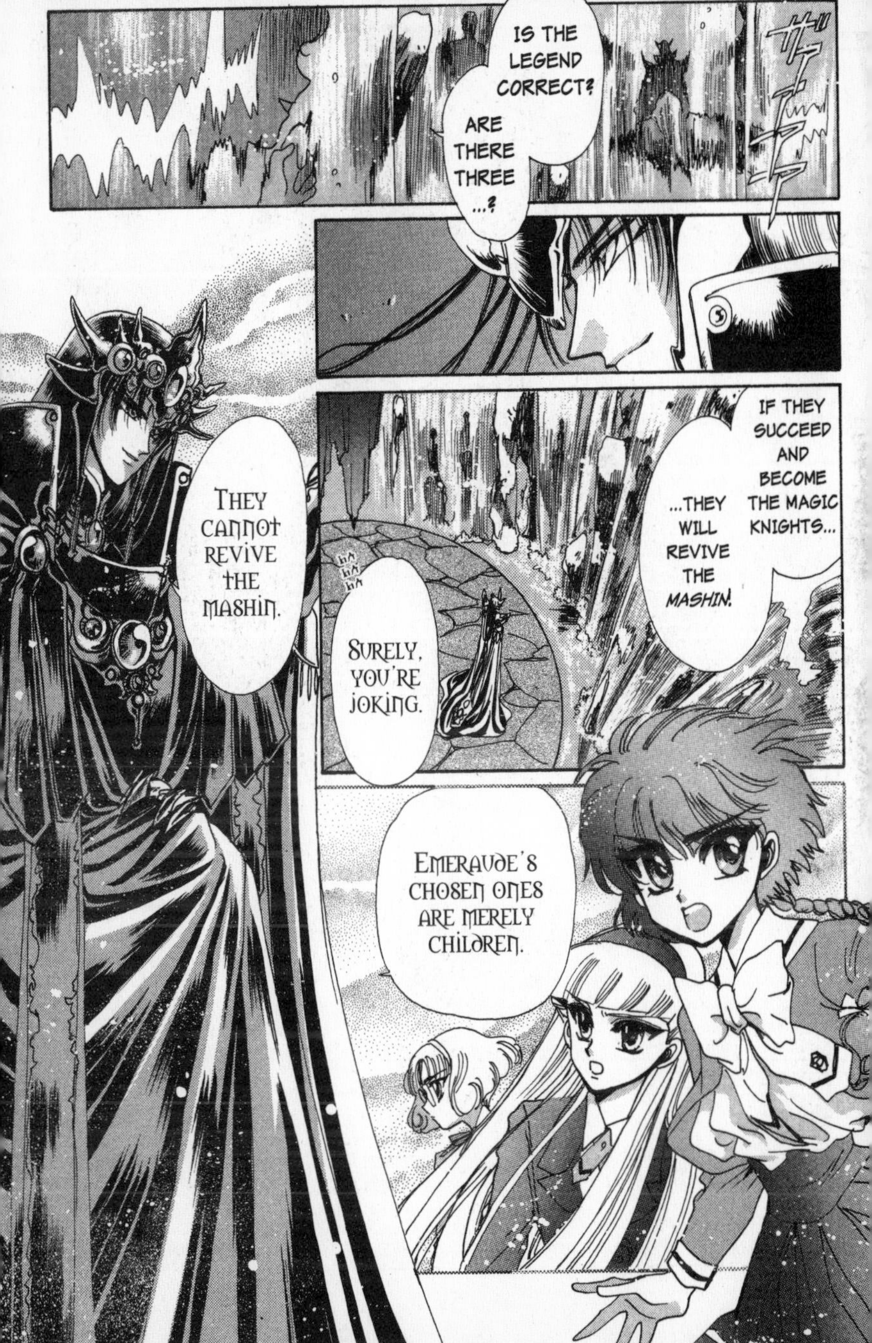
IS THE LEGEND CORRECT?
ARE THERE THREE ...?
IF THEY SUCCEED AND BECOME THE MAGIC KNIGHTS...
...THEY WILL REVIVE THE MASHIN!
SURELY, YOU'RE JOKING.
EMERAUDE'S CHOSEN ONES ARE MERELY CHILDREN.
THEY CANNOT REVIVE THE MASHIN.

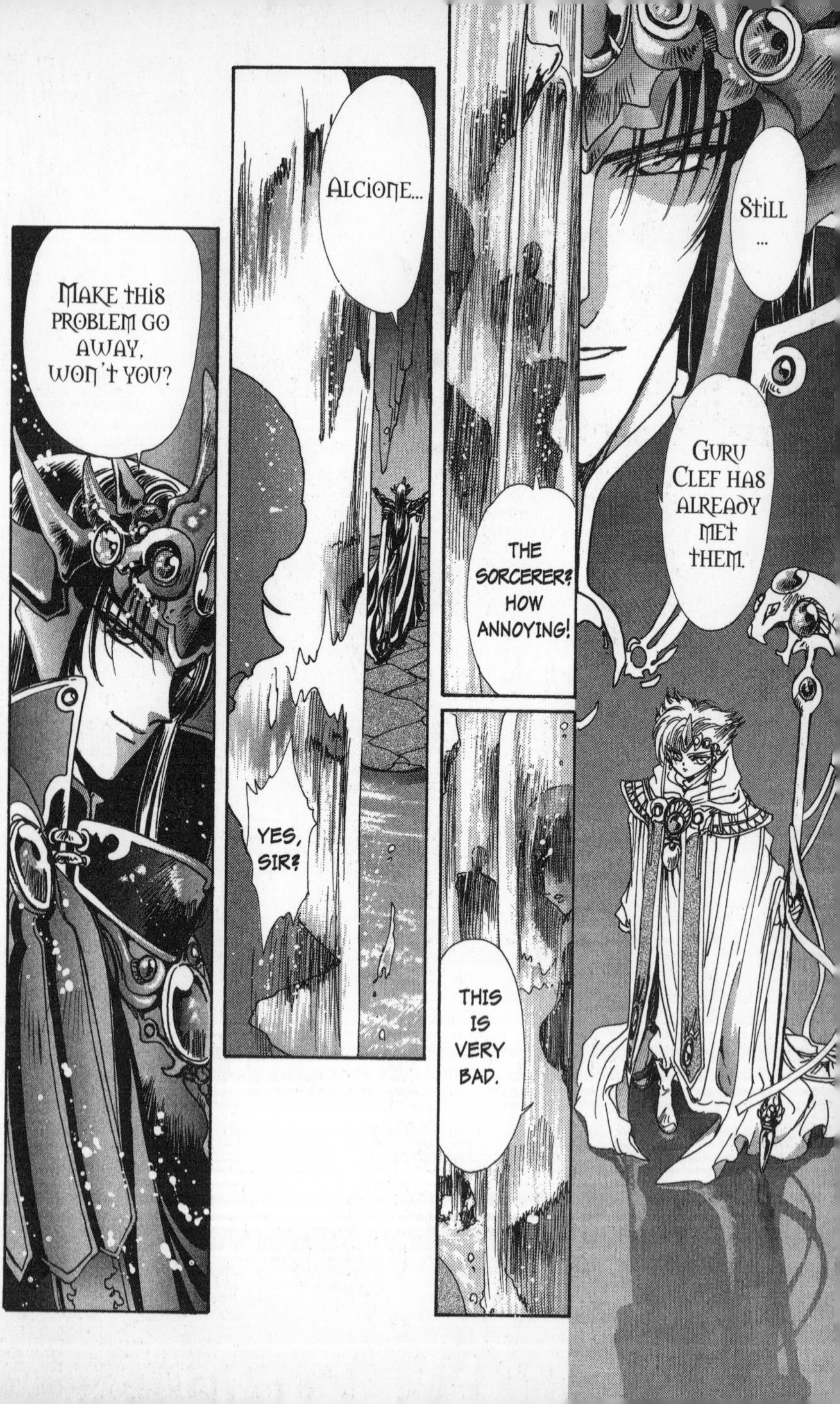
Still ...
Guru Clef has already met them.
THE SORCERER? HOW ANNOYING!
THIS IS VERY BAD.
Alcione...
YES, SIR?
Make this problem go away, won't you?

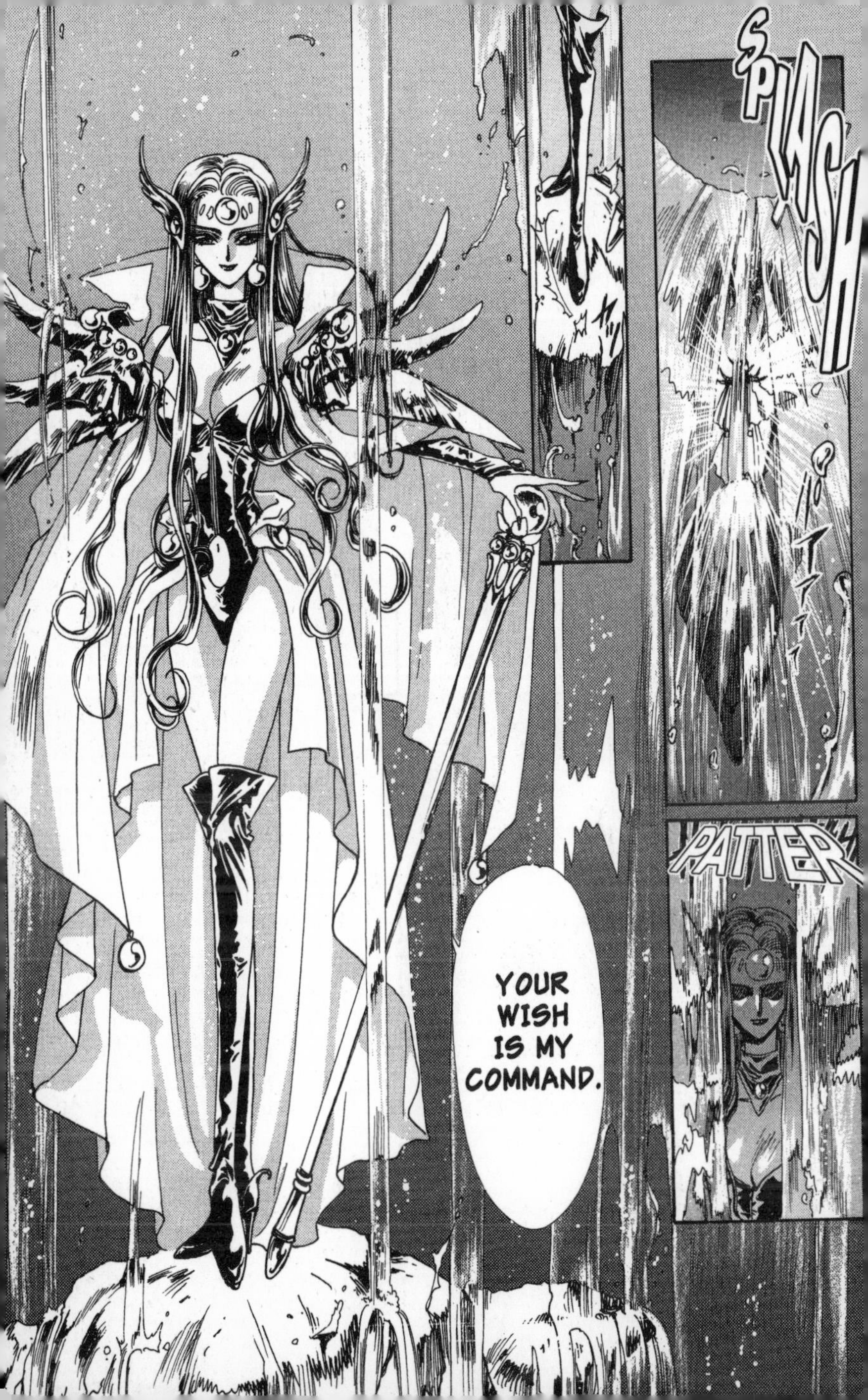
SPLASH
PATTER
YOUR WISH IS MY COMMAND.

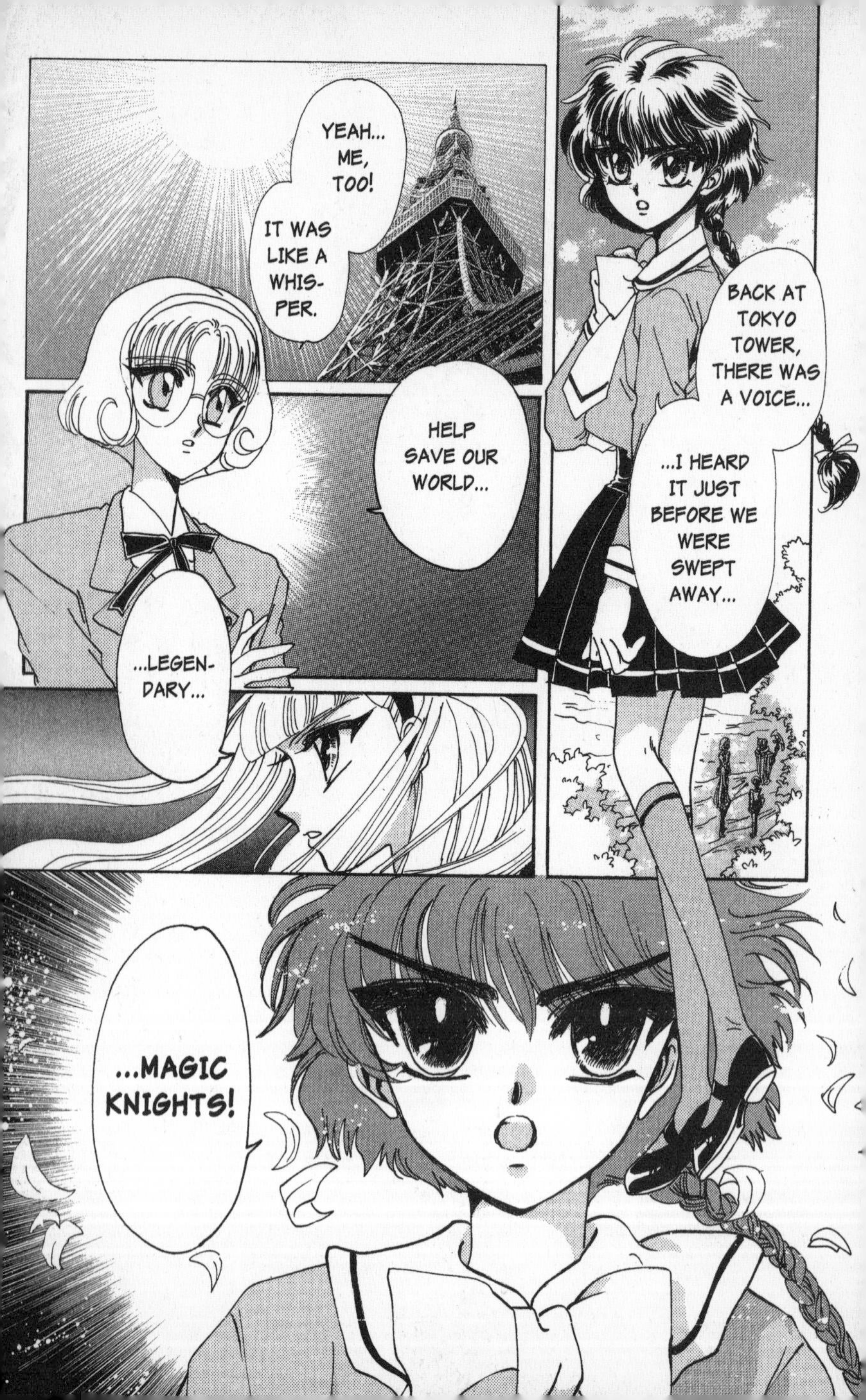
BACK AT TOKYO TOWER, THERE WAS A VOICE...
...I HEARD IT JUST BEFORE WE WERE SWEPT AWAY...
YEAH... ME, TOO!
IT WAS LIKE A WHISPER.
HELP SAVE OUR WORLD...
...LEGENDARY...
...MAGIC KNIGHTS!

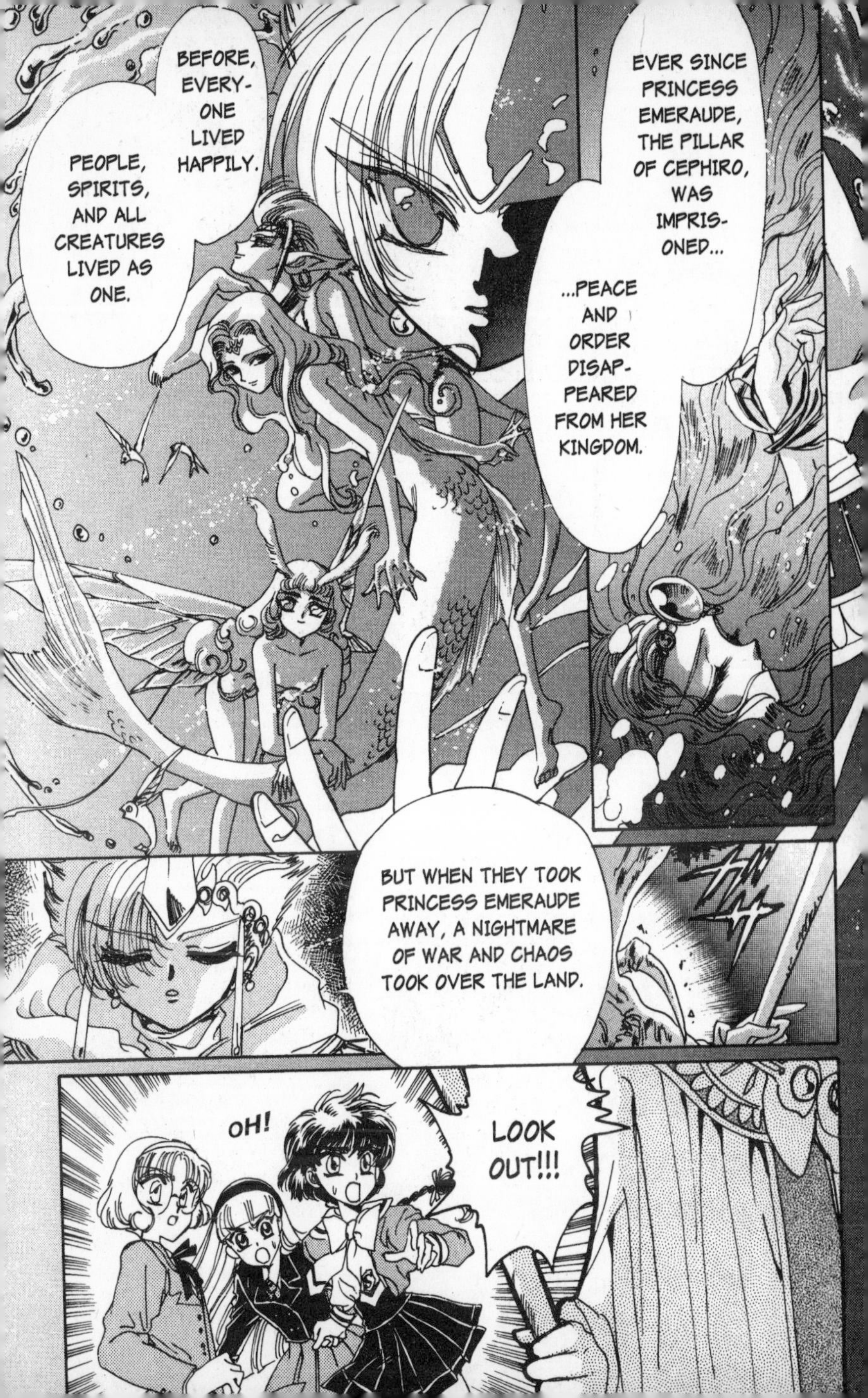
EVER SINCE PRINCESS EMERAUDE, THE PILLAR OF CEPHIRO, WAS IMPRIS-ONED...
...PEACE AND ORDER DISAP-PEARED FROM HER KINGDOM.
BEFORE, EVERY-ONE LIVED HAPPILY.
PEOPLE, SPIRITS, AND ALL CREATURES LIVED AS ONE.
BUT WHEN THEY TOOK PRINCESS EMERAUDE AWAY, A NIGHTMARE OF WAR AND CHAOS TOOK OVER THE LAND.
LOOK OUT!!!
OH!

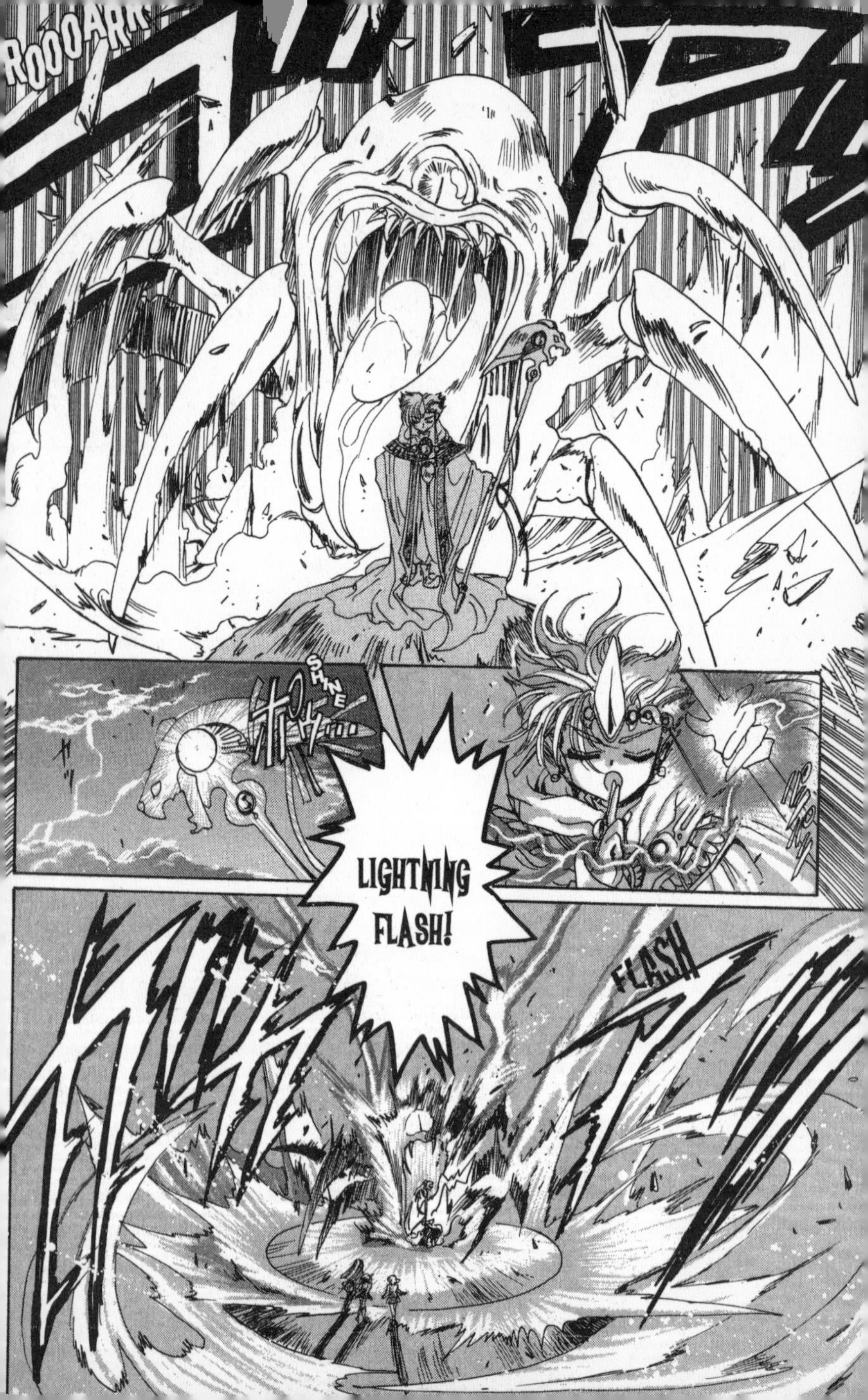
ROOOARR
LIGHTNING FLASH!
SHINE
FLASH

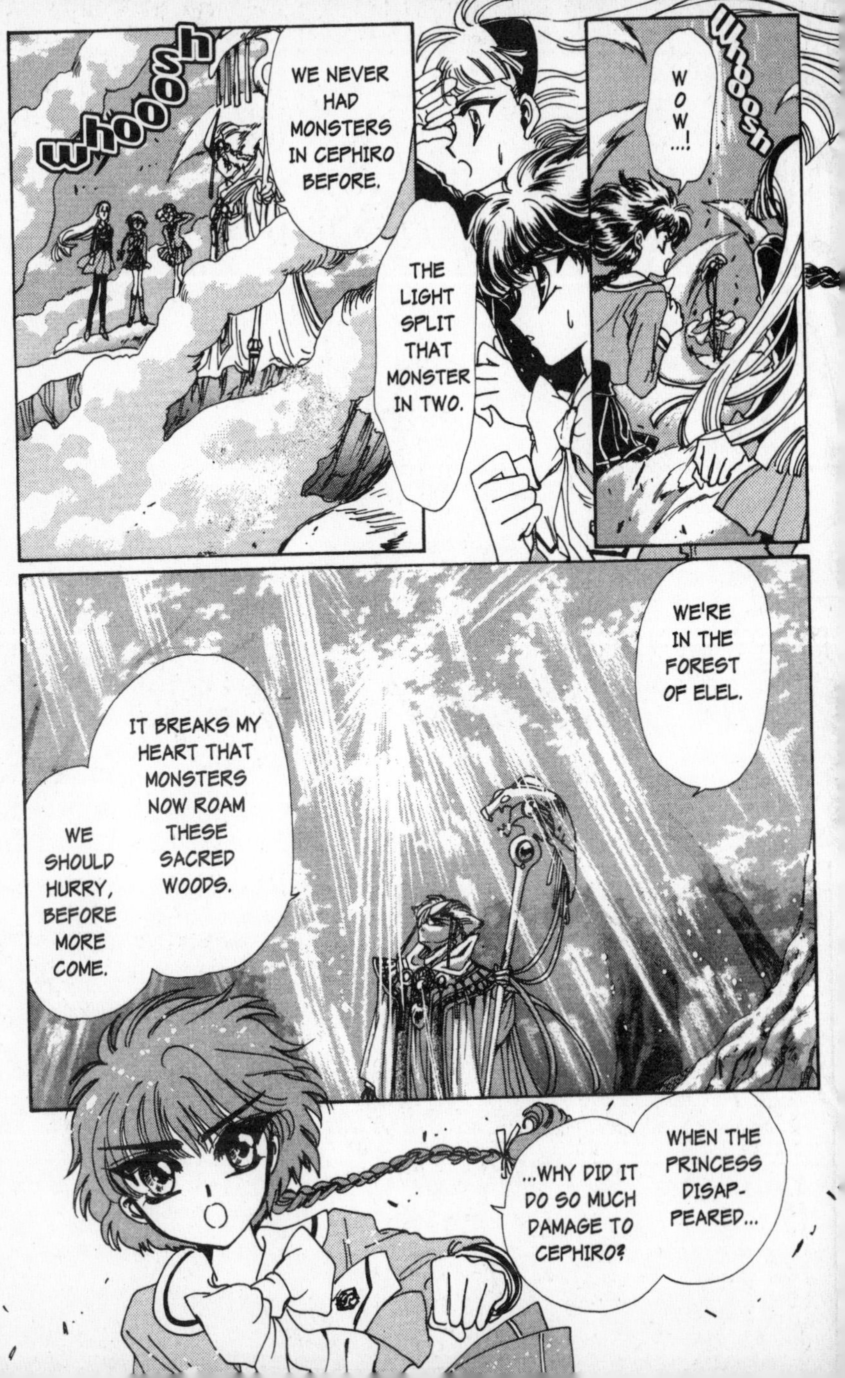
WOW...!
whooosh
whooosh
WE NEVER HAD MONSTERS IN CEPHIRO BEFORE.
THE LIGHT SPLIT THAT MONSTER IN TWO.
WE'RE IN THE FOREST OF ELEL.
IT BREAKS MY HEART THAT MONSTERS NOW ROAM THESE SACRED WOODS.
WE SHOULD HURRY, BEFORE MORE COME.
WHEN THE PRINCESS DISAP-PEARED...
...WHY DID IT DO SO MUCH DAMAGE TO CEPHIRO?

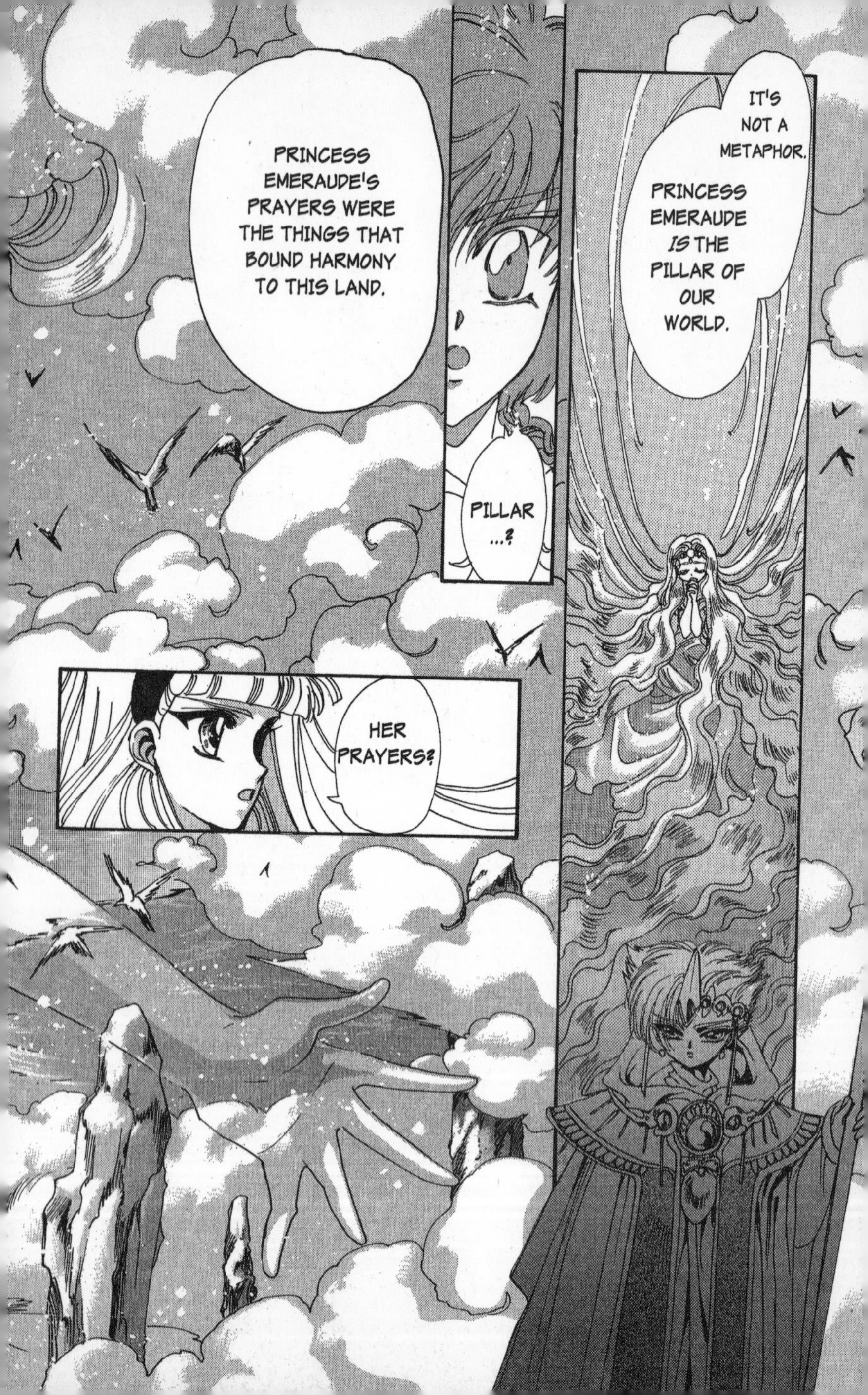
PRINCESS EMERAUDE'S PRAYERS WERE THE THINGS THAT BOUND HARMONY TO THIS LAND.
PILLAR ...?
IT'S NOT A METAPHOR.
PRINCESS EMERAUDE *IS* THE PILLAR OF OUR WORLD.
HER PRAYERS?

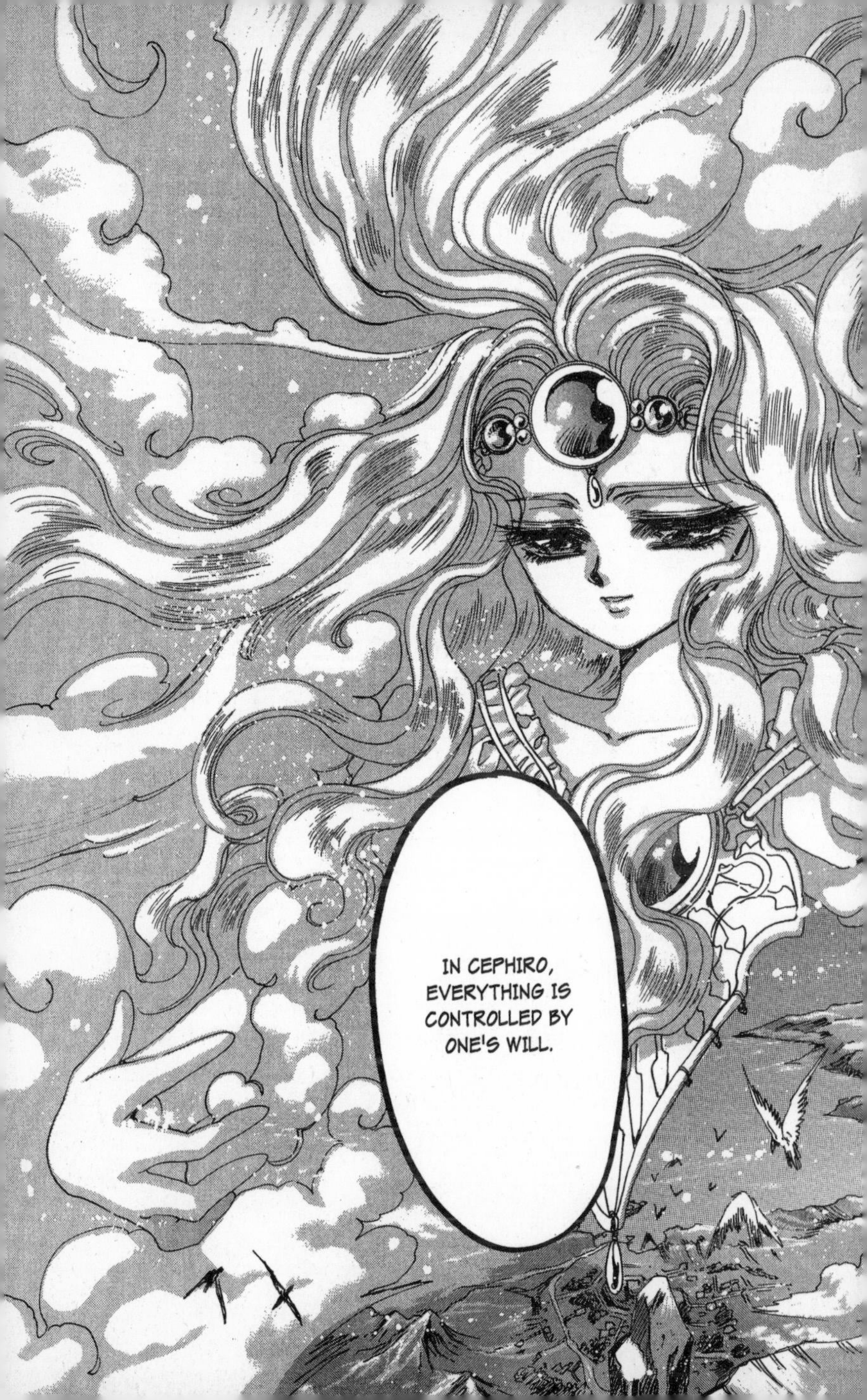
IN CEPHIRO, EVERYTHING IS CONTROLLED BY ONE'S WILL.

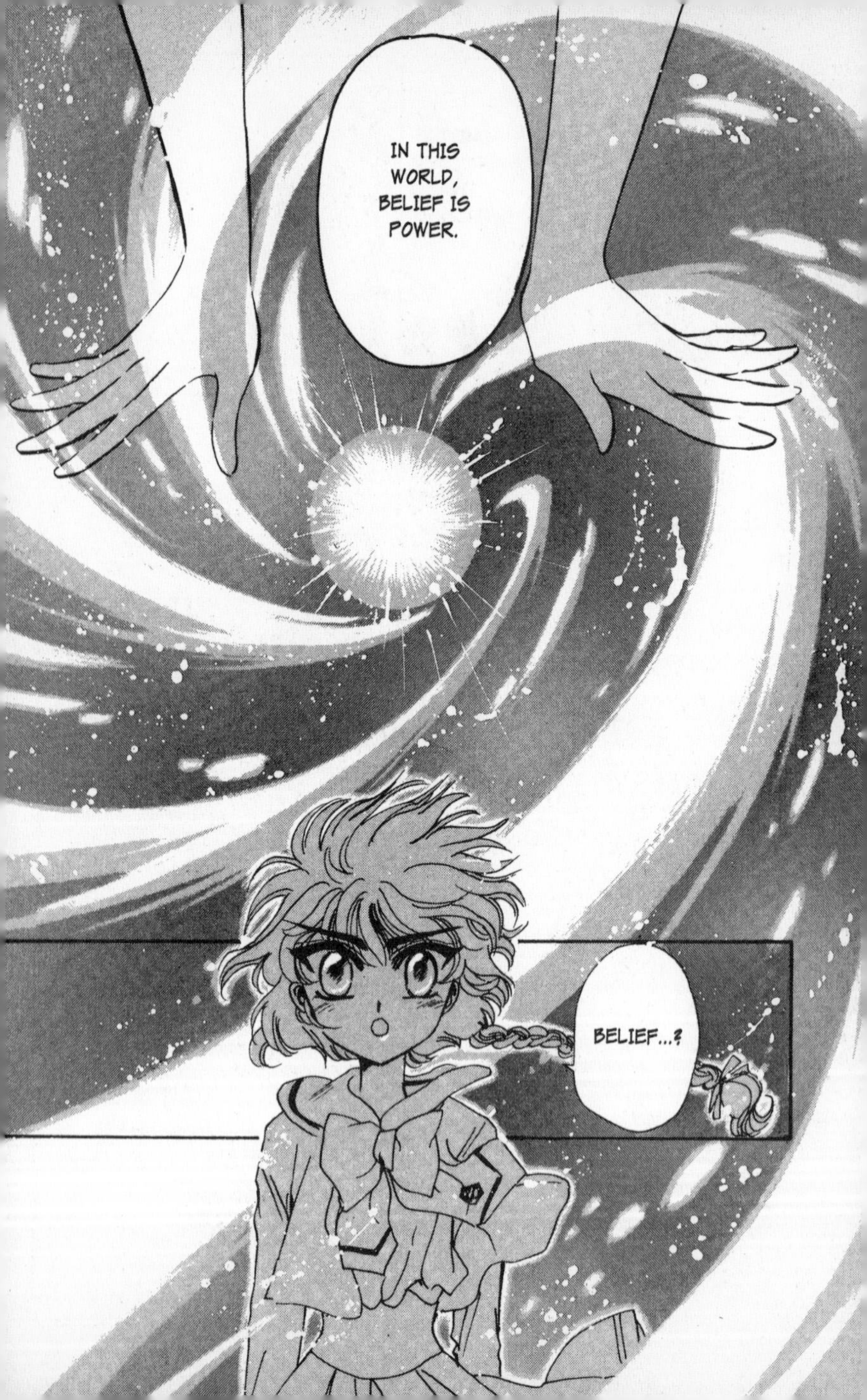
IN THIS WORLD, BELIEF IS POWER.
BELIEF...?

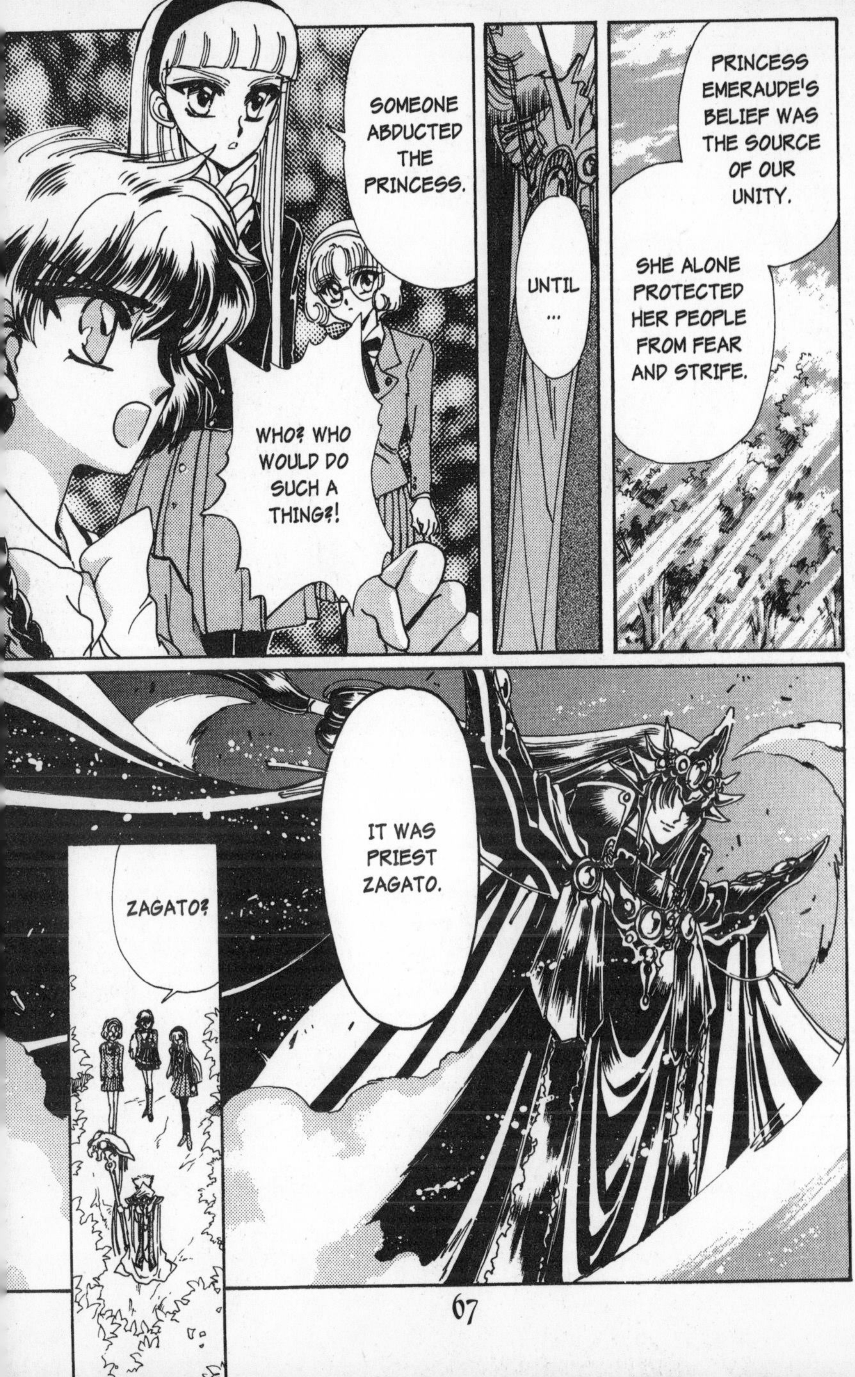
PRINCESS EMERAUDE'S BELIEF WAS THE SOURCE OF OUR UNITY.
SHE ALONE PROTECTED HER PEOPLE FROM FEAR AND STRIFE.
UNTIL ...
SOMEONE ABDUCTED THE PRINCESS.
WHO? WHO WOULD DO SUCH A THING?!
IT WAS PRIEST ZAGATO.
ZAGATO?

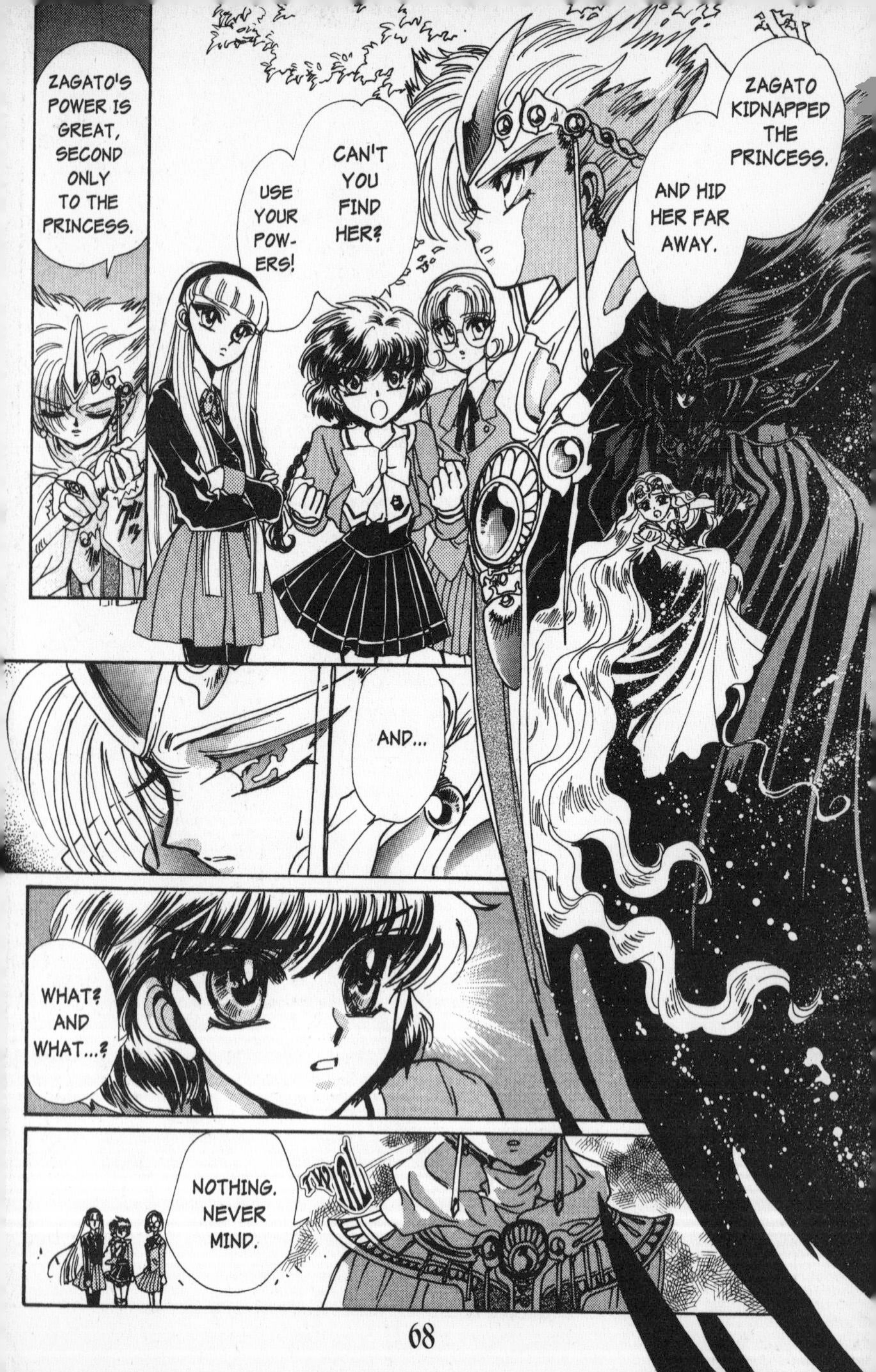
ZAGATO KIDNAPPED THE PRINCESS.
AND HID HER FAR AWAY.
CAN'T YOU FIND HER?
USE YOUR POW-ERS!
ZAGATO'S POWER IS GREAT, SECOND ONLY TO THE PRINCESS.
AND...
WHAT? AND WHAT...?
NOTHING. NEVER MIND.

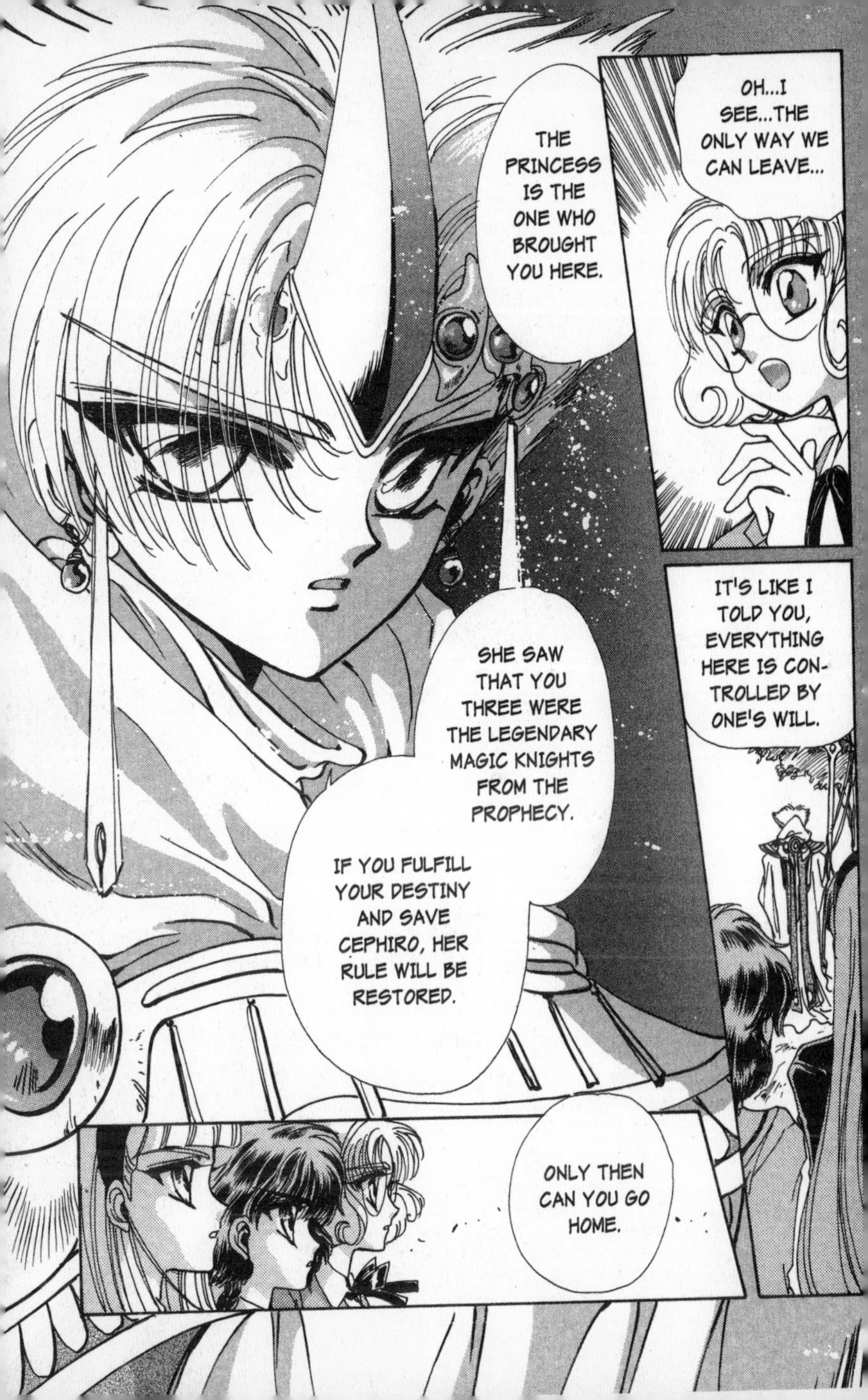
OH...I SEE...THE ONLY WAY WE CAN LEAVE...
IT'S LIKE I TOLD YOU, EVERYTHING HERE IS CONTROLLED BY ONE'S WILL.
THE PRINCESS IS THE ONE WHO BROUGHT YOU HERE.
SHE SAW THAT YOU THREE WERE THE LEGENDARY MAGIC KNIGHTS FROM THE PROPHECY.
IF YOU FULFILL YOUR DESTINY AND SAVE CEPHIRO, HER RULE WILL BE RESTORED.
ONLY THEN CAN YOU GO HOME.

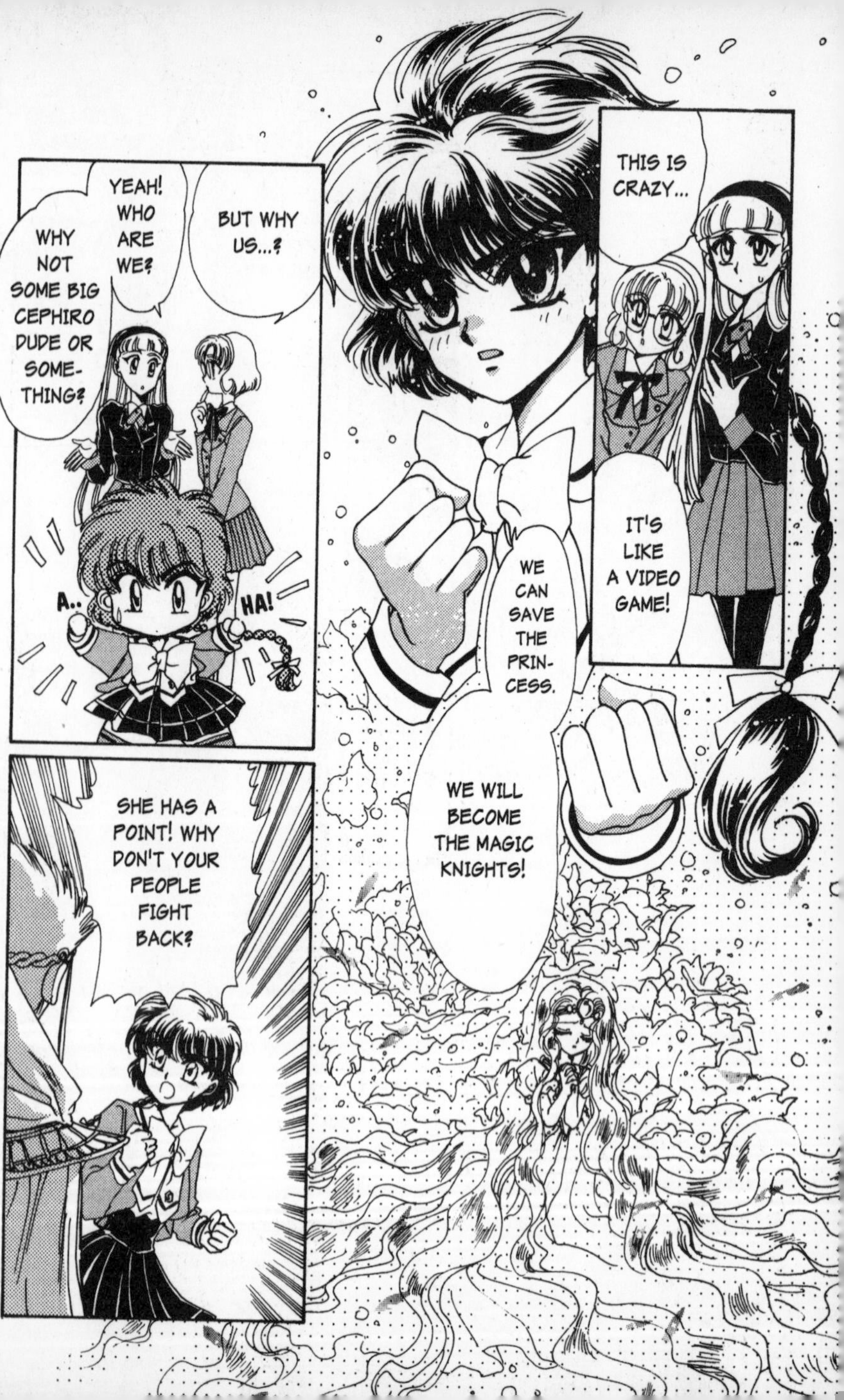
THIS IS CRAZY...
IT'S LIKE A VIDEO GAME!
WE CAN SAVE THE PRINCESS.
WE WILL BECOME THE MAGIC KNIGHTS!
BUT WHY US...?
YEAH! WHO ARE WE?
WHY NOT SOME BIG CEPHIRO DUDE OR SOMETHING?
A.. HA!
SHE HAS A POINT! WHY DON'T YOUR PEOPLE FIGHT BACK?

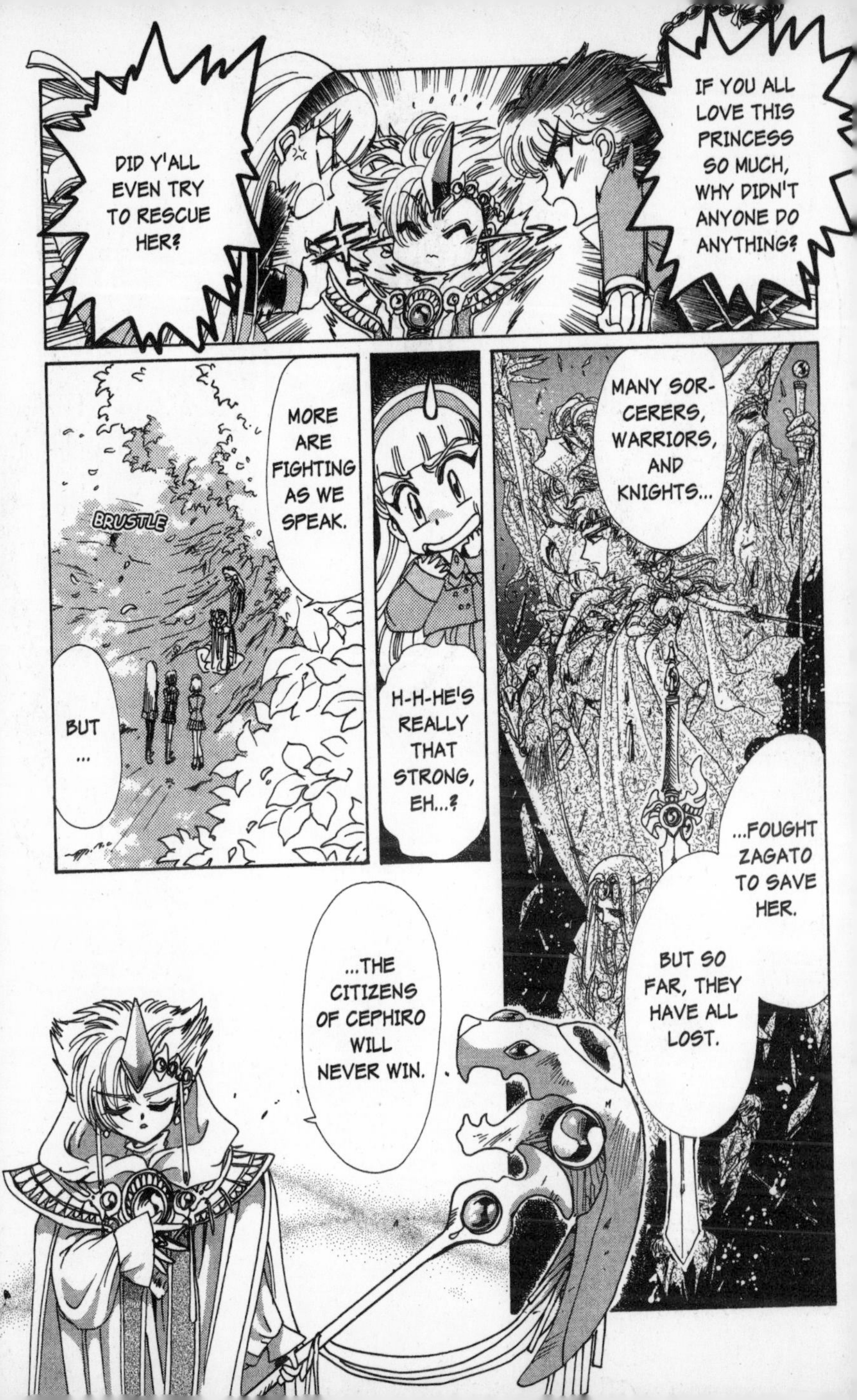
IF YOU ALL LOVE THIS PRINCESS SO MUCH, WHY DIDN'T ANYONE DO ANYTHING?
DID Y'ALL EVEN TRY TO RESCUE HER?
MANY SOR-CERERS, WARRIORS, AND KNIGHTS...
...FOUGHT ZAGATO TO SAVE HER.
BUT SO FAR, THEY HAVE ALL LOST.
H-H-HE'S REALLY THAT STRONG, EH...?
MORE ARE FIGHTING AS WE SPEAK.
BRUSTLE
BUT ...
...THE CITIZENS OF CEPHIRO WILL NEVER WIN.

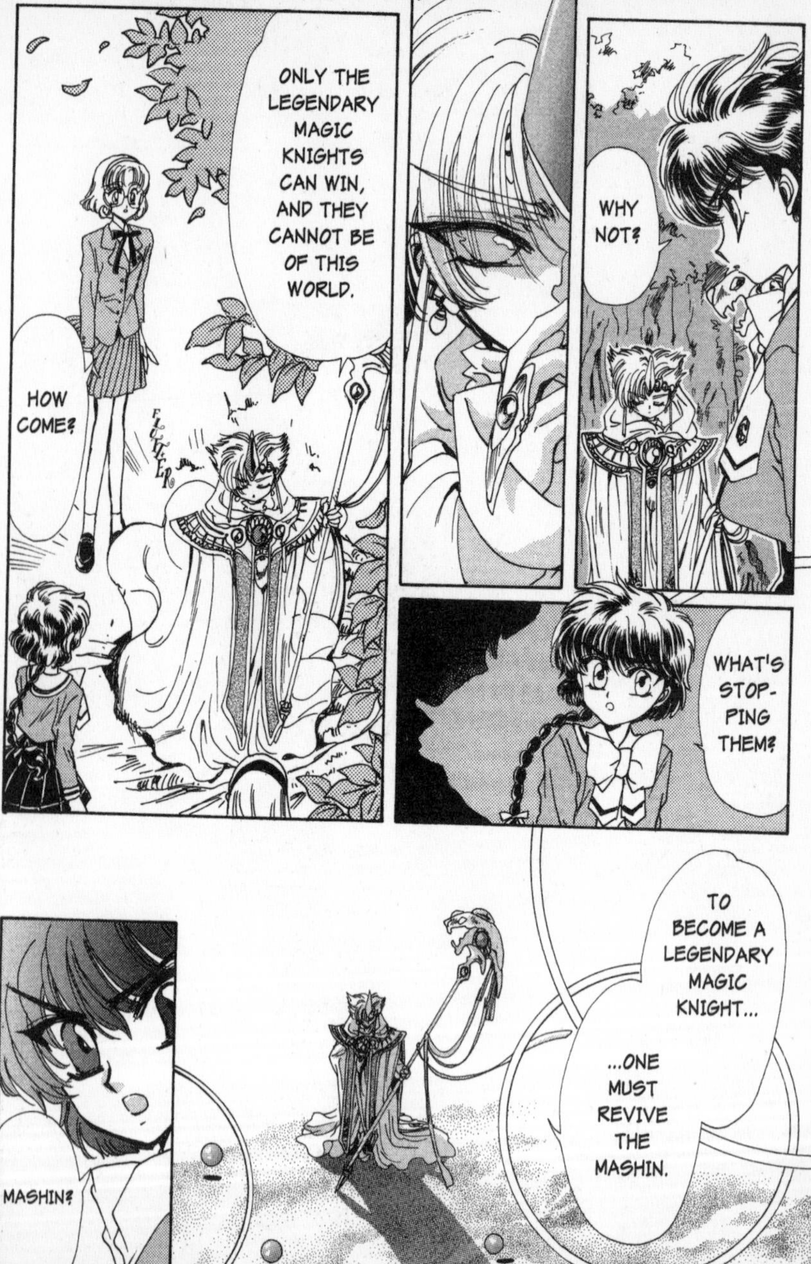
WHY NOT?
WHAT'S STOP-PING THEM?
ONLY THE LEGENDARY MAGIC KNIGHTS CAN WIN, AND THEY CANNOT BE OF THIS WORLD.
FLUTTER
HOW COME?
TO BECOME A LEGENDARY MAGIC KNIGHT...
...ONE MUST REVIVE THE MASHIN.
MASHIN?

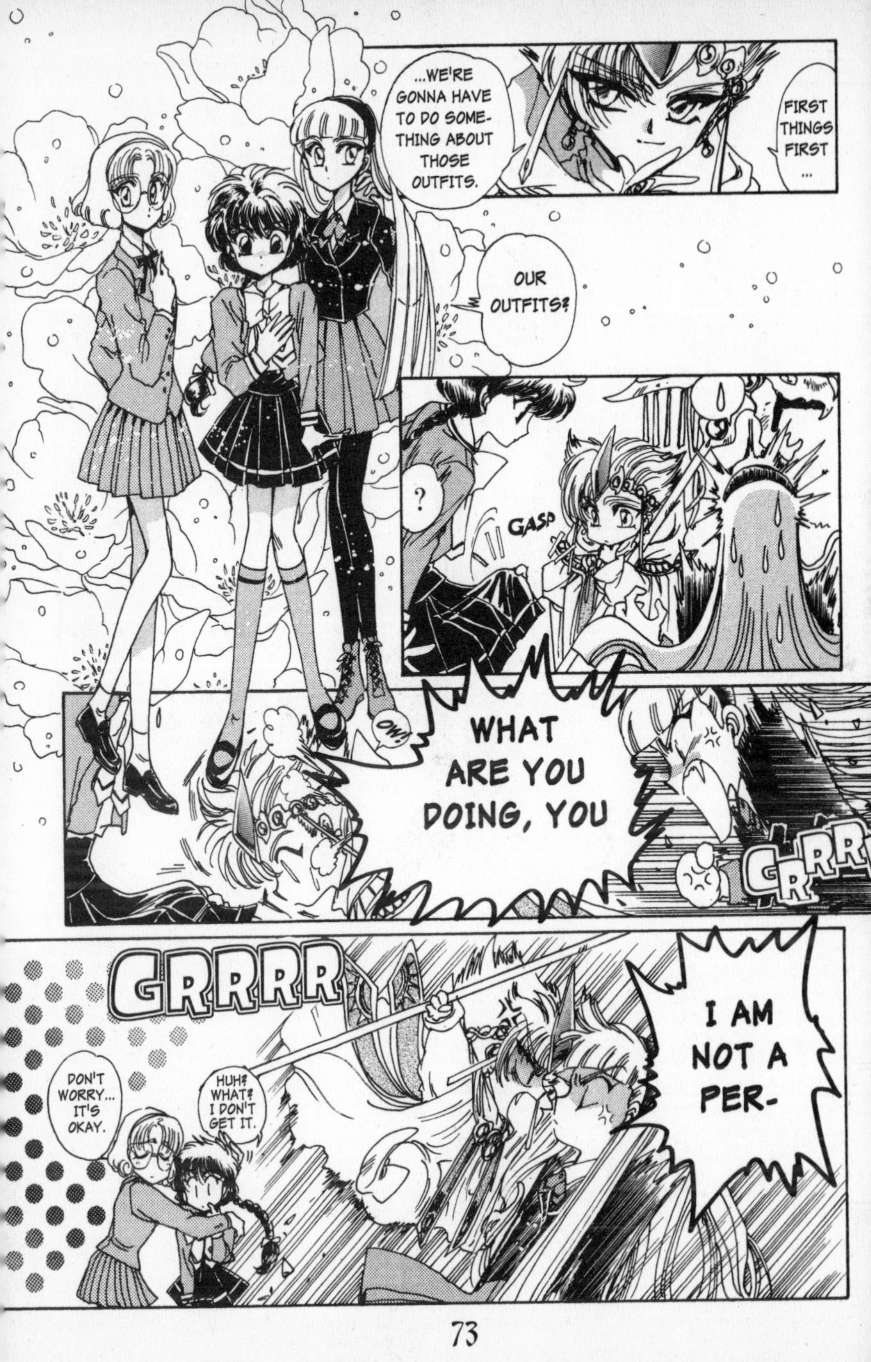
FIRST THINGS FIRST ...
...WE'RE GONNA HAVE TO DO SOME-THING ABOUT THOSE OUTFITS.
OUR OUTFITS?
?
GASP
GRRR
WHAT ARE YOU DOING, YOU
OW!
I AM NOT A PER-
GRRRR
HUH? WHAT? I DON'T GET IT.
DON'T WORRY... IT'S OKAY.

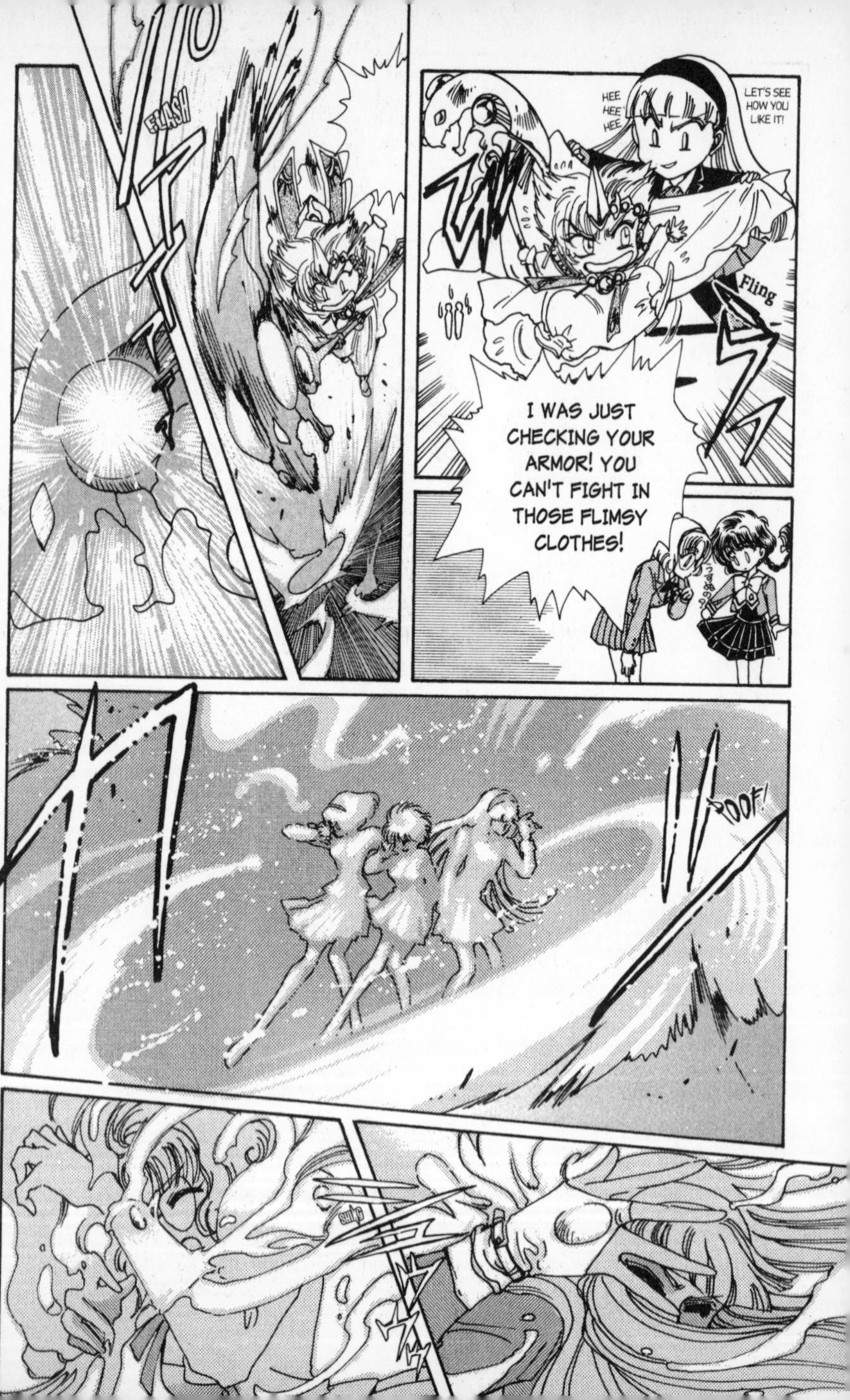
HEE
HEE
HEE
LET'S SEE HOW YOU LIKE IT!
Fling
I WAS JUST CHECKING YOUR ARMOR! YOU CAN'T FIGHT IN THOSE FLIMSY CLOTHES!
FLASH
POOF!

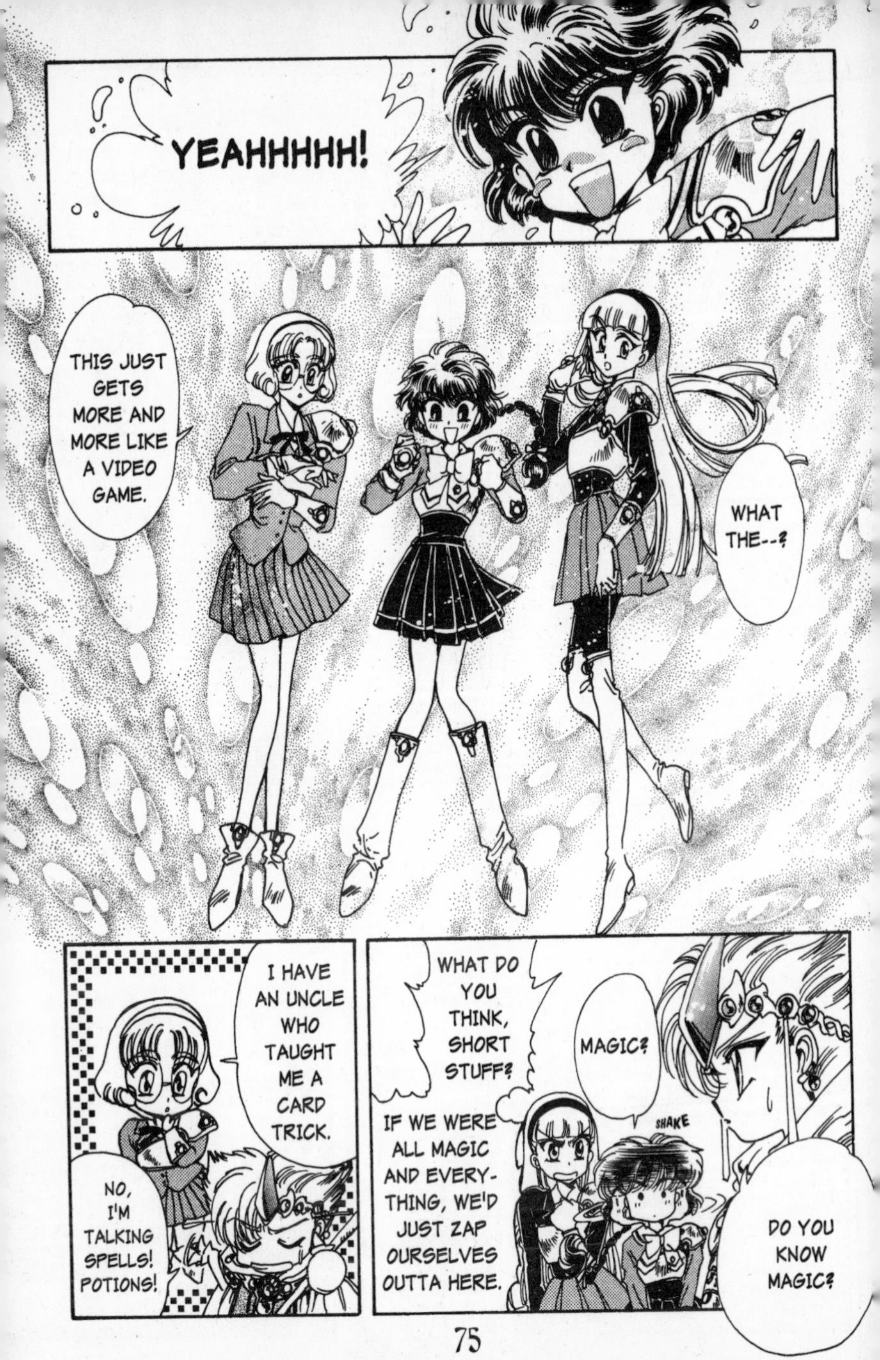
YEAHHHHH!
WHAT THE--?
THIS JUST GETS MORE AND MORE LIKE A VIDEO GAME.
DO YOU KNOW MAGIC?
MAGIC?
WHAT DO YOU THINK, SHORT STUFF?
IF WE WERE ALL MAGIC AND EVERY-THING, WE'D JUST ZAP OURSELVES OUTTA HERE.
SHAKE
I HAVE AN UNCLE WHO TAUGHT ME A CARD TRICK.
NO, I'M TALKING SPELLS! POTIONS!

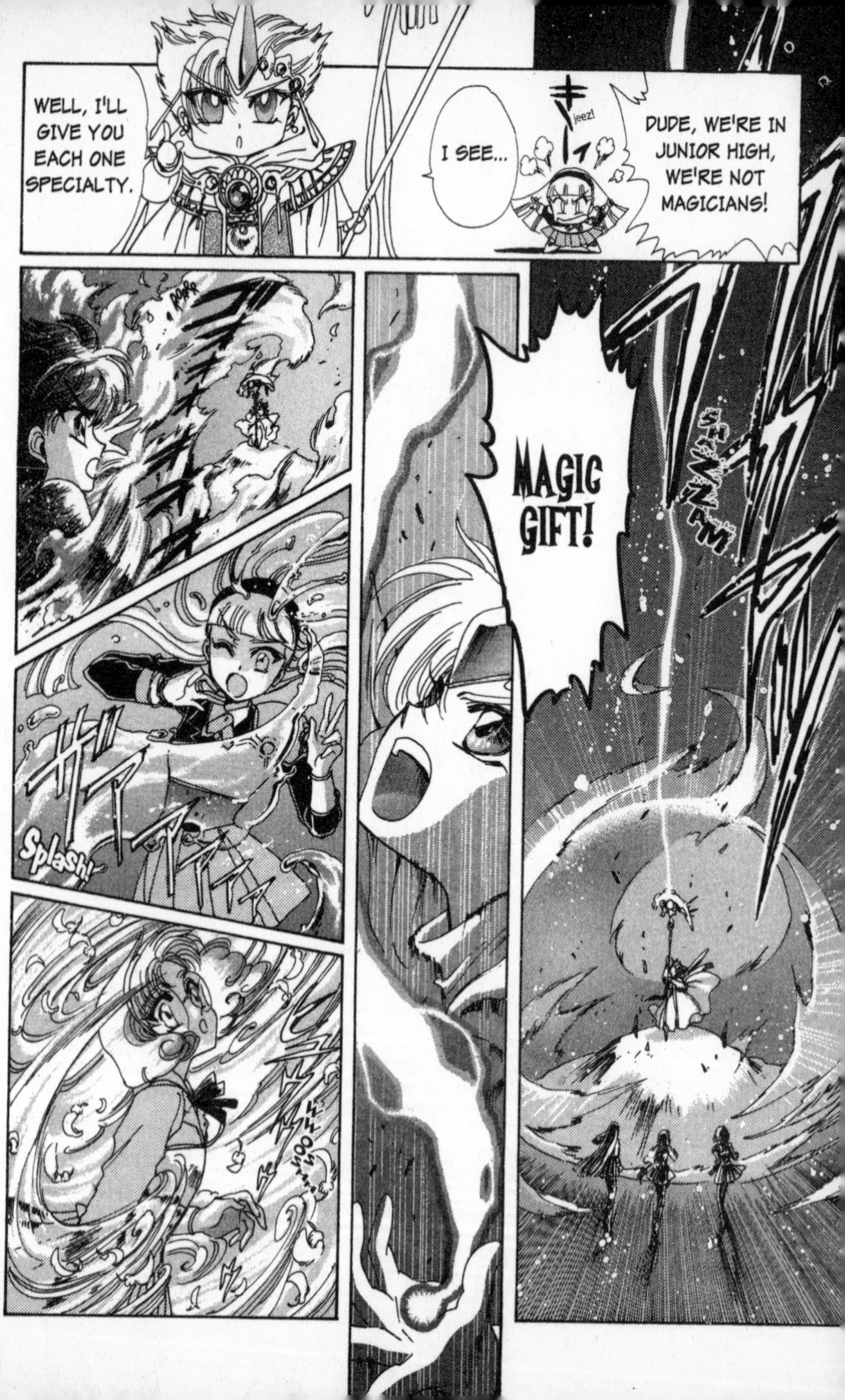

DUDE, WE'RE IN JUNIOR HIGH, WE'RE NOT MAGICIANS!
jeez!
I SEE...
WELL, I'LL GIVE YOU EACH ONE SPECIALTY.
MAGIC GIFT!
SHZZAM
ROARR
Splash!

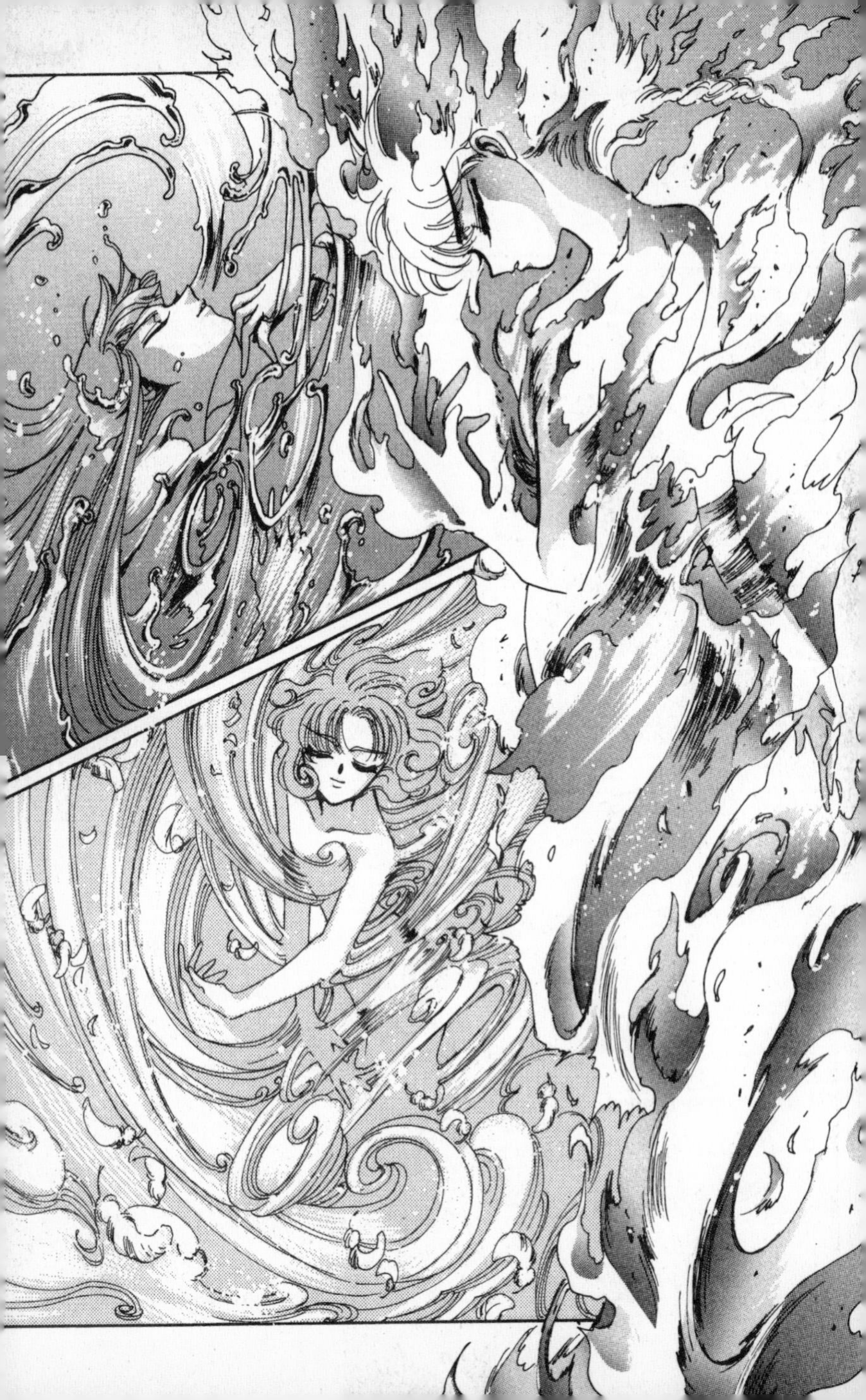

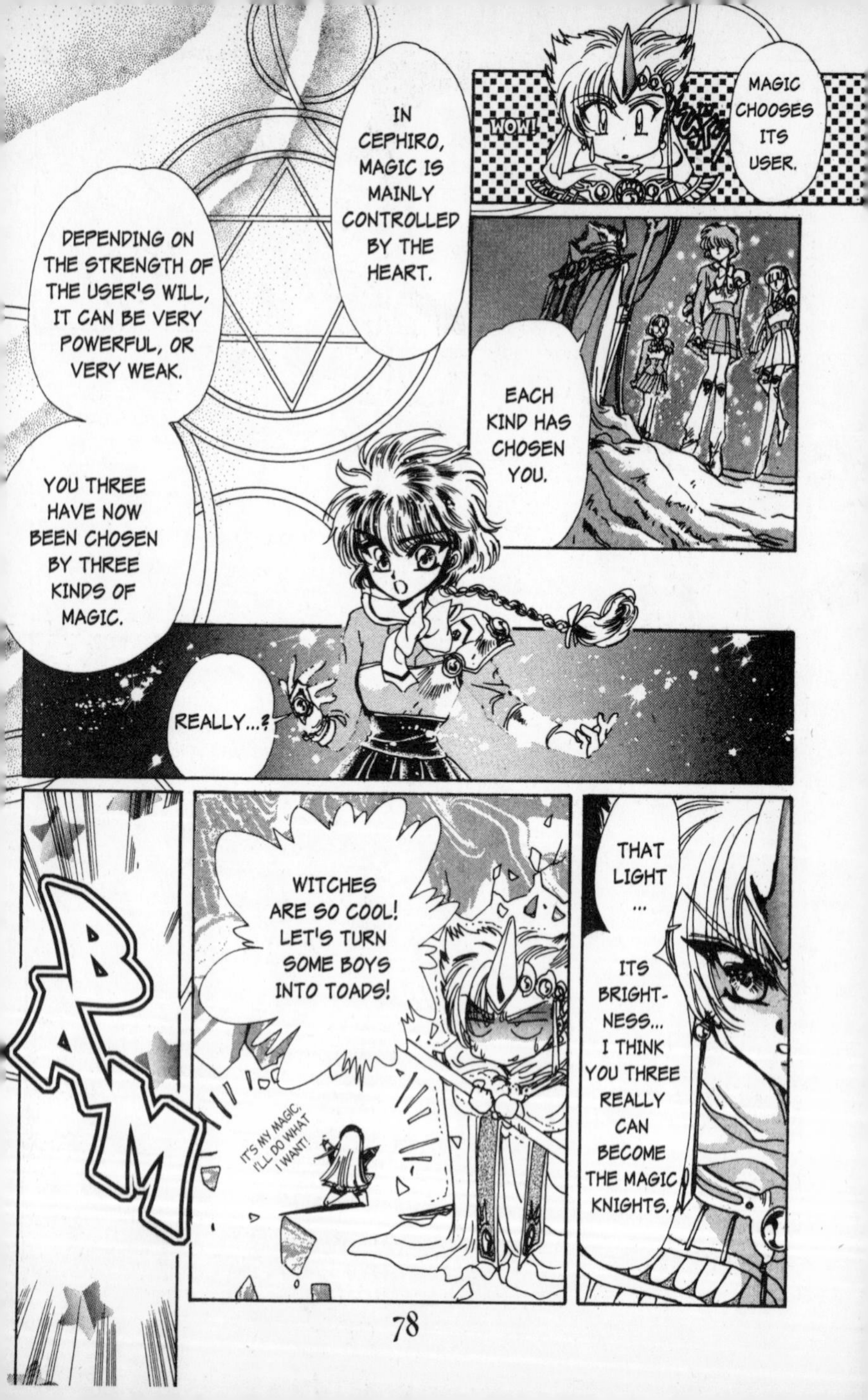

MAGIC CHOOSES ITS USER.
WOW!
IN CEPHIRO, MAGIC IS MAINLY CONTROLLED BY THE HEART.
DEPENDING ON THE STRENGTH OF THE USER'S WILL, IT CAN BE VERY POWERFUL, OR VERY WEAK.
EACH KIND HAS CHOSEN YOU.
YOU THREE HAVE NOW BEEN CHOSEN BY THREE KINDS OF MAGIC.
REALLY...?
THAT LIGHT ...
ITS BRIGHTNESS... I THINK YOU THREE REALLY CAN BECOME THE MAGIC KNIGHTS.
WITCHES ARE SO COOL! LET'S TURN SOME BOYS INTO TOADS!
IT'S MY MAGIC, I'LL DO WHAT I WANT!
BAM

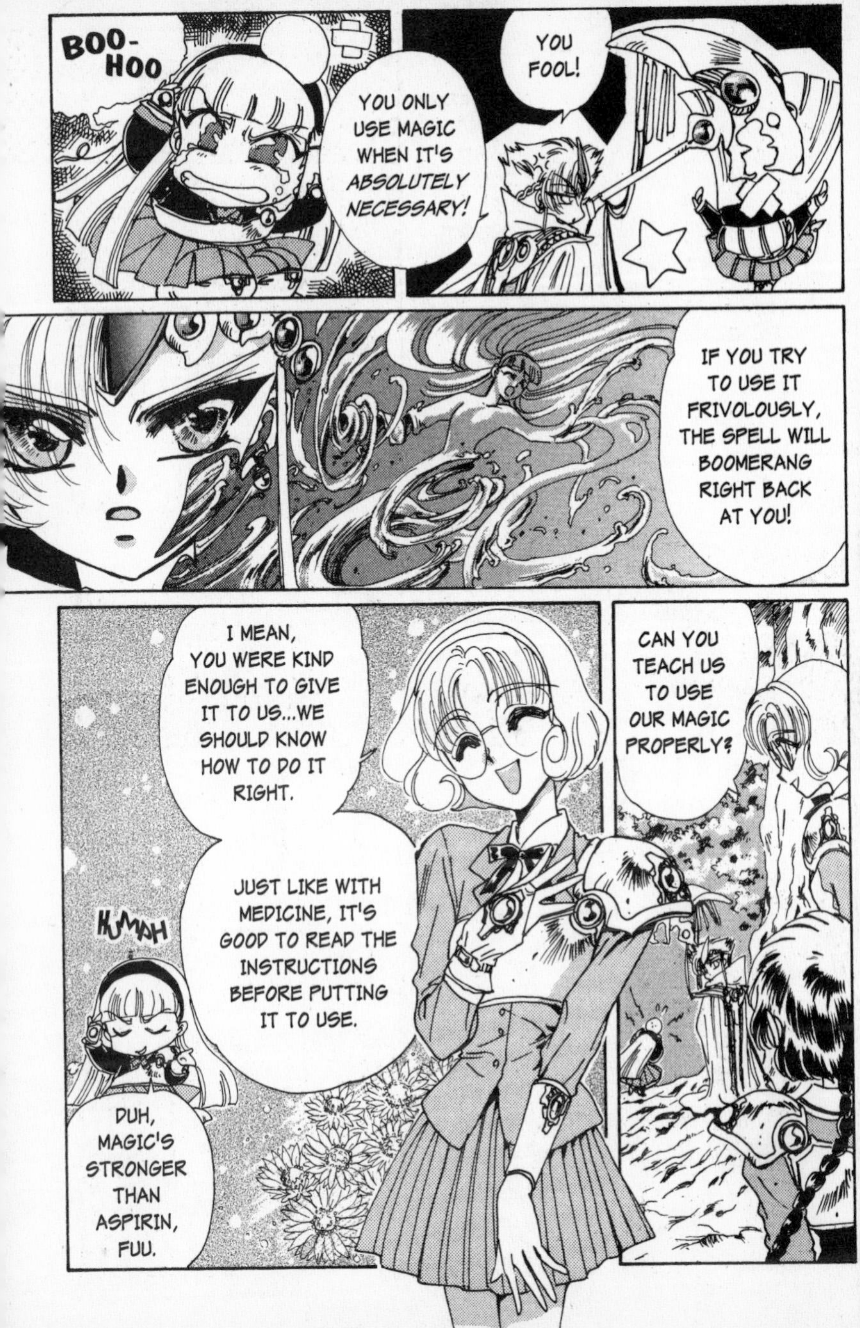
YOU FOOL!
YOU ONLY USE MAGIC WHEN IT'S ABSOLUTELY NECESSARY!
BOO-HOO
IF YOU TRY TO USE IT FRIVOLOUSLY, THE SPELL WILL BOOMERANG RIGHT BACK AT YOU!
CAN YOU TEACH US TO USE OUR MAGIC PROPERLY?
I MEAN, YOU WERE KIND ENOUGH TO GIVE IT TO US...WE SHOULD KNOW HOW TO DO IT RIGHT.
JUST LIKE WITH MEDICINE, IT'S GOOD TO READ THE INSTRUCTIONS BEFORE PUTTING IT TO USE.
HUMPH
DUH, MAGIC'S STRONGER THAN ASPIRIN, FUU.

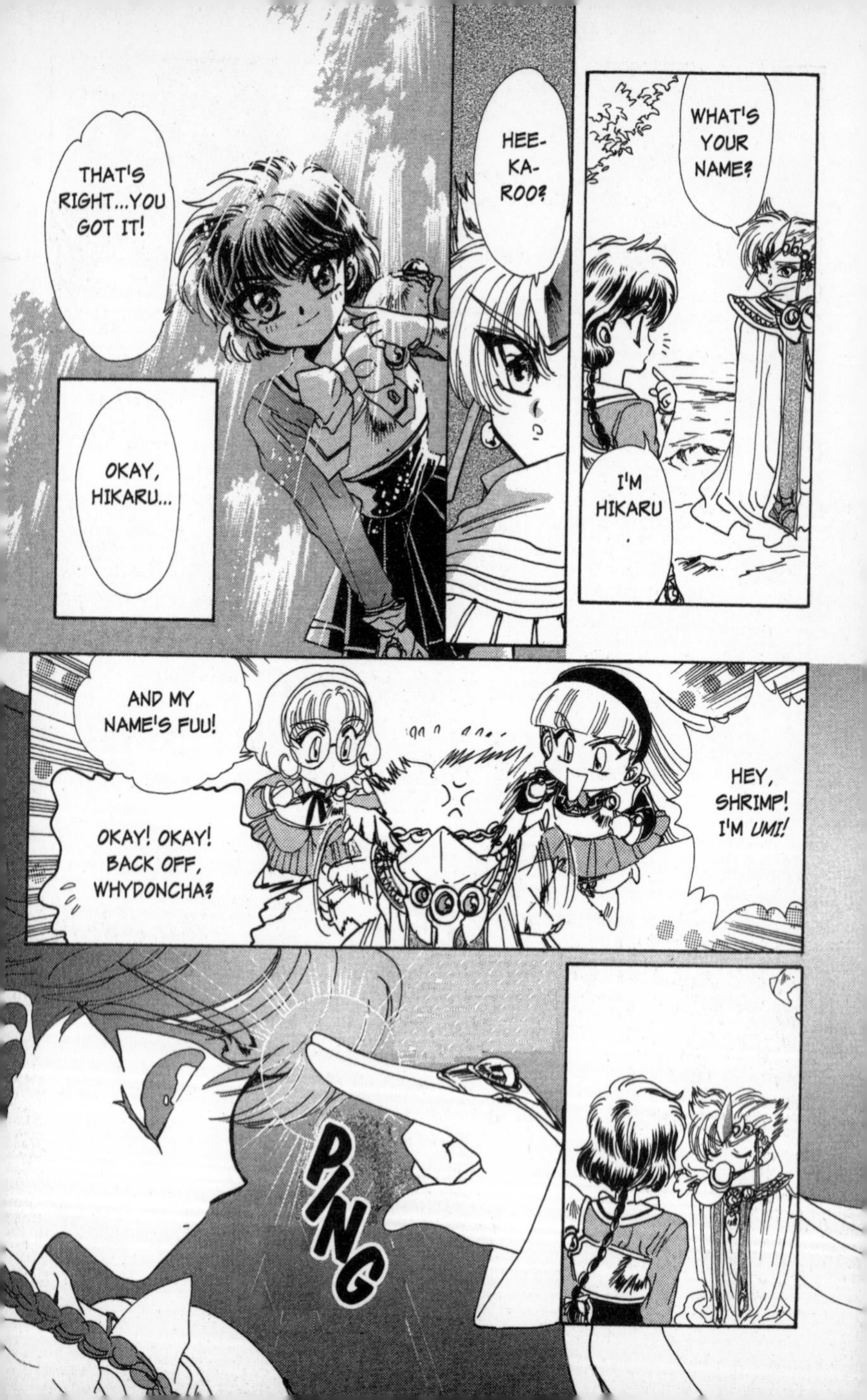
WHAT'S YOUR NAME?
I'M HIKARU.
HEE-KA-ROO?
THAT'S RIGHT...YOU GOT IT!
OKAY, HIKARU...
HEY, SHRIMP! I'M UMI!
AND MY NAME'S FUU!
OKAY! OKAY! BACK OFF, WHYDONCHA?
PING

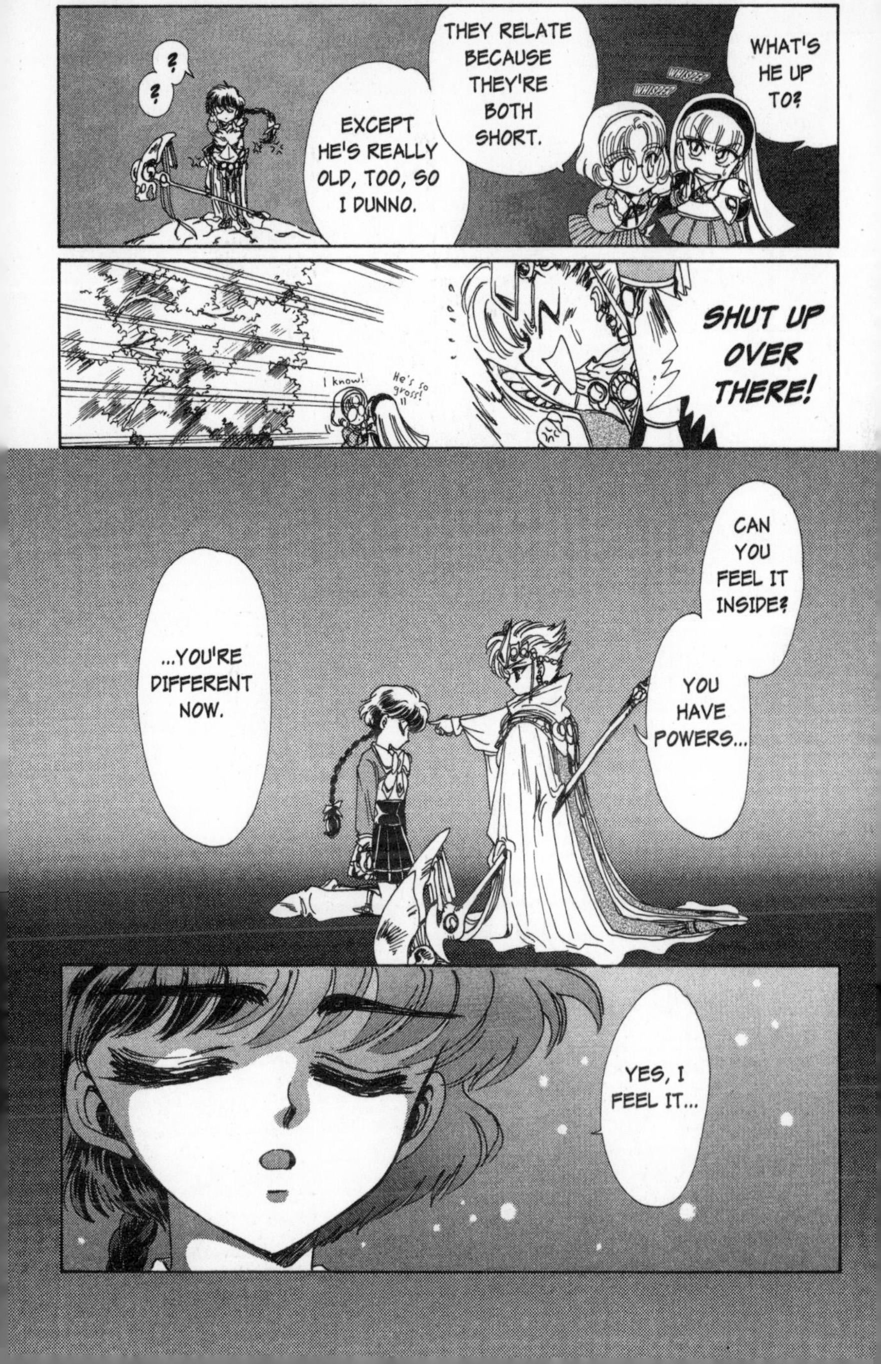
WHAT'S HE UP TO?
WHISPER
WHISPER
THEY RELATE BECAUSE THEY'RE BOTH SHORT.
EXCEPT HE'S REALLY OLD, TOO, SO I DUNNO.
?
?
SHUT UP OVER THERE!
He's so gross!
I know!
CAN YOU FEEL IT INSIDE?
YOU HAVE POWERS...
...YOU'RE DIFFERENT NOW.
YES, I FEEL IT...

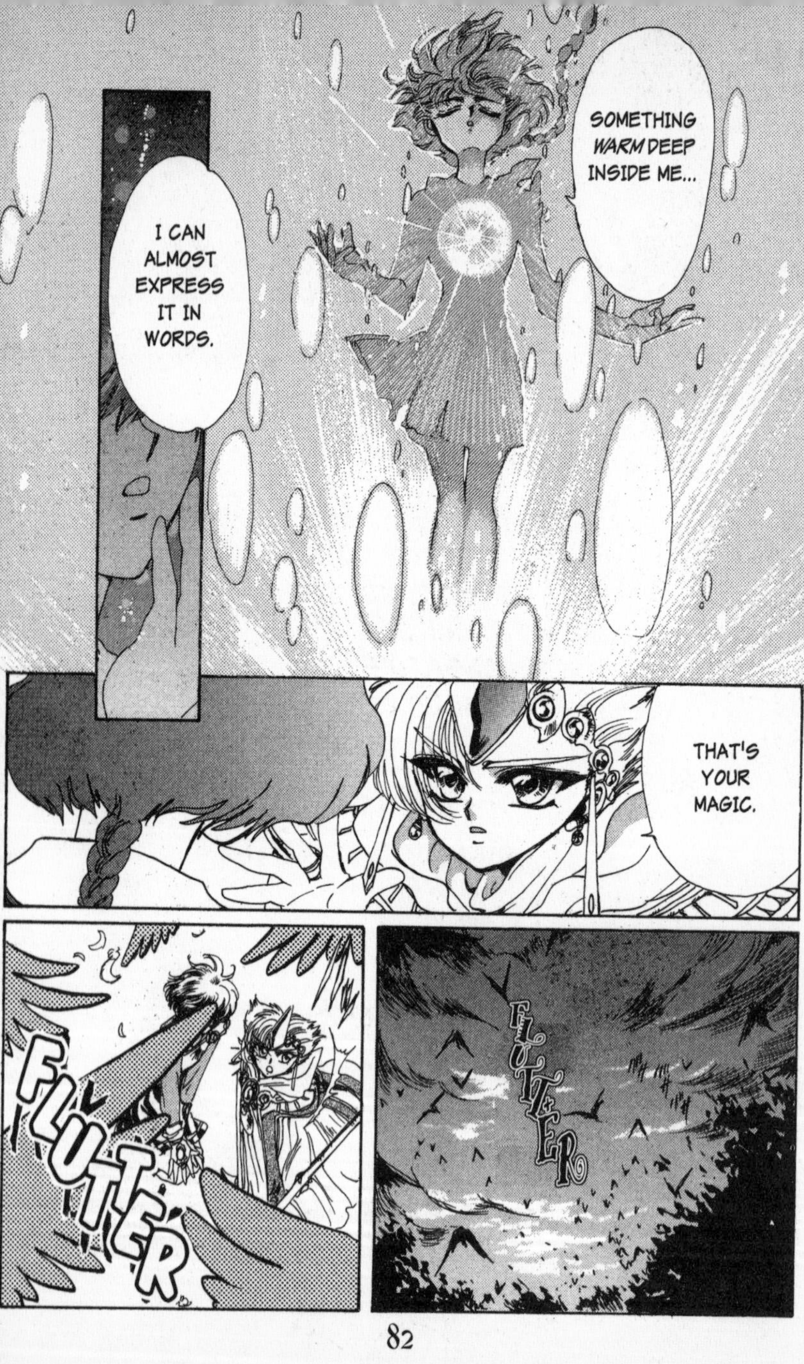
SOMETHING WARM DEEP INSIDE ME...
I CAN ALMOST EXPRESS IT IN WORDS.
THAT'S YOUR MAGIC.
FLUTTER
FLUTTER

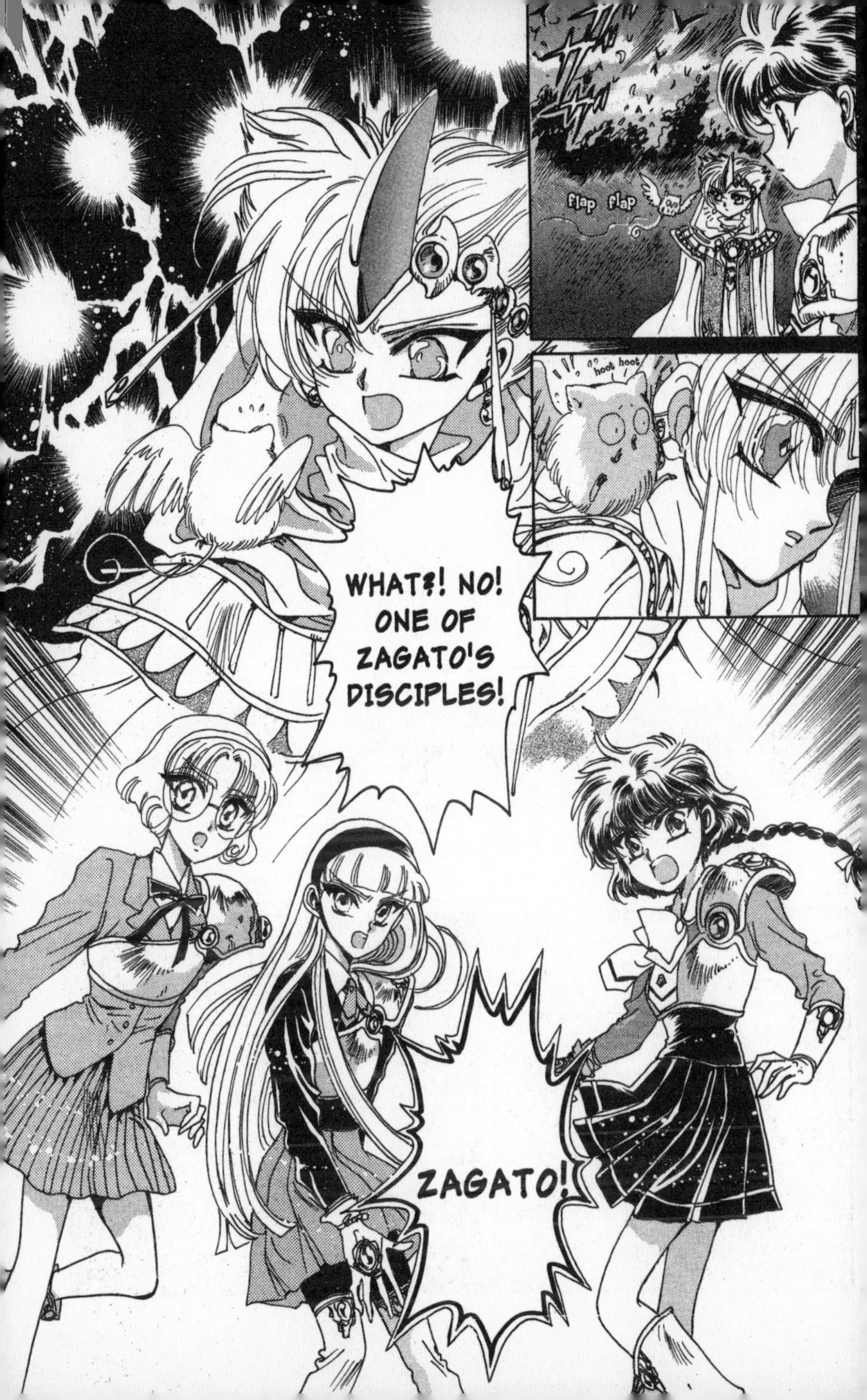
flap flap
hoot hoot
WHAT?! NO! ONE OF ZAGATO'S DISCIPLES!
ZAGATO!

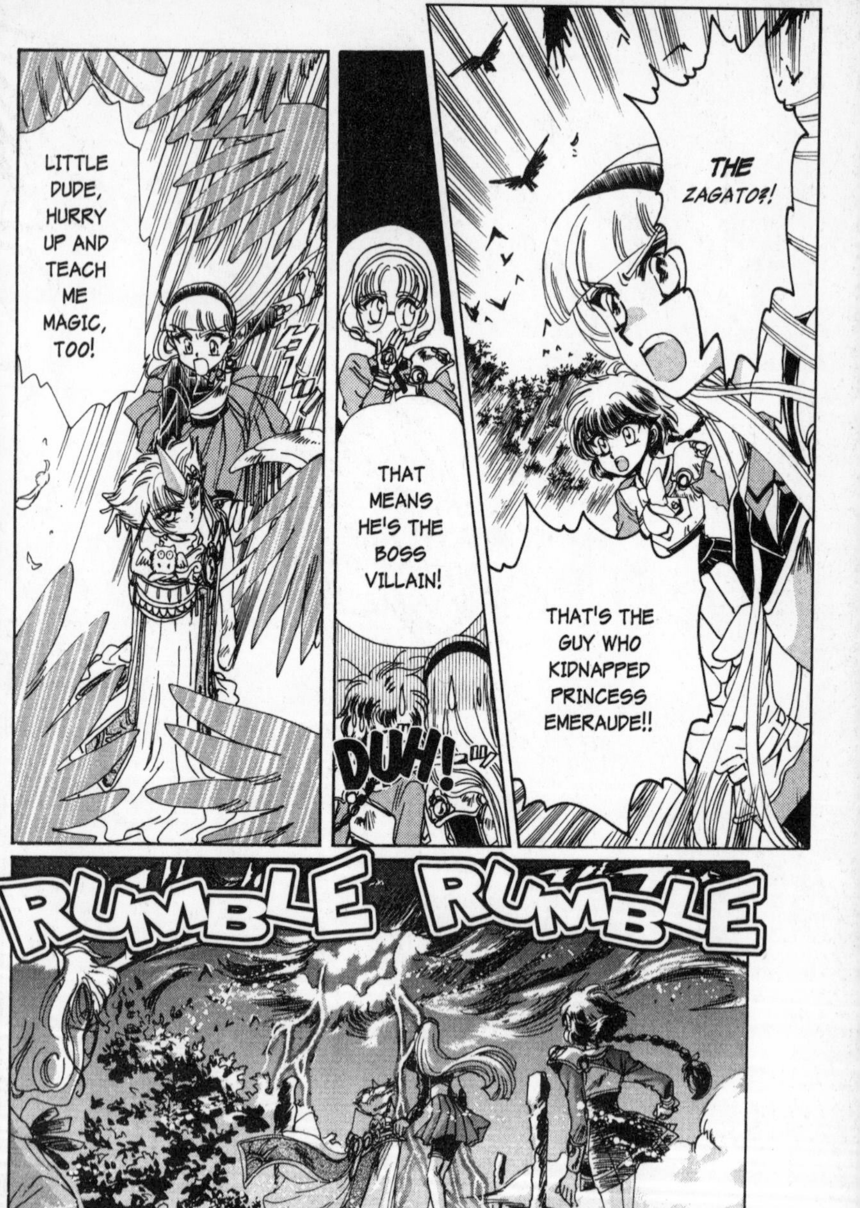
THE ZAGATO?!
THAT'S THE GUY WHO KIDNAPPED PRINCESS EMERAUDE!!
THAT MEANS HE'S THE BOSS VILLAIN!
DUH!
LITTLE DUDE, HURRY UP AND TEACH ME MAGIC, TOO!
RUMBLE RUMBLE

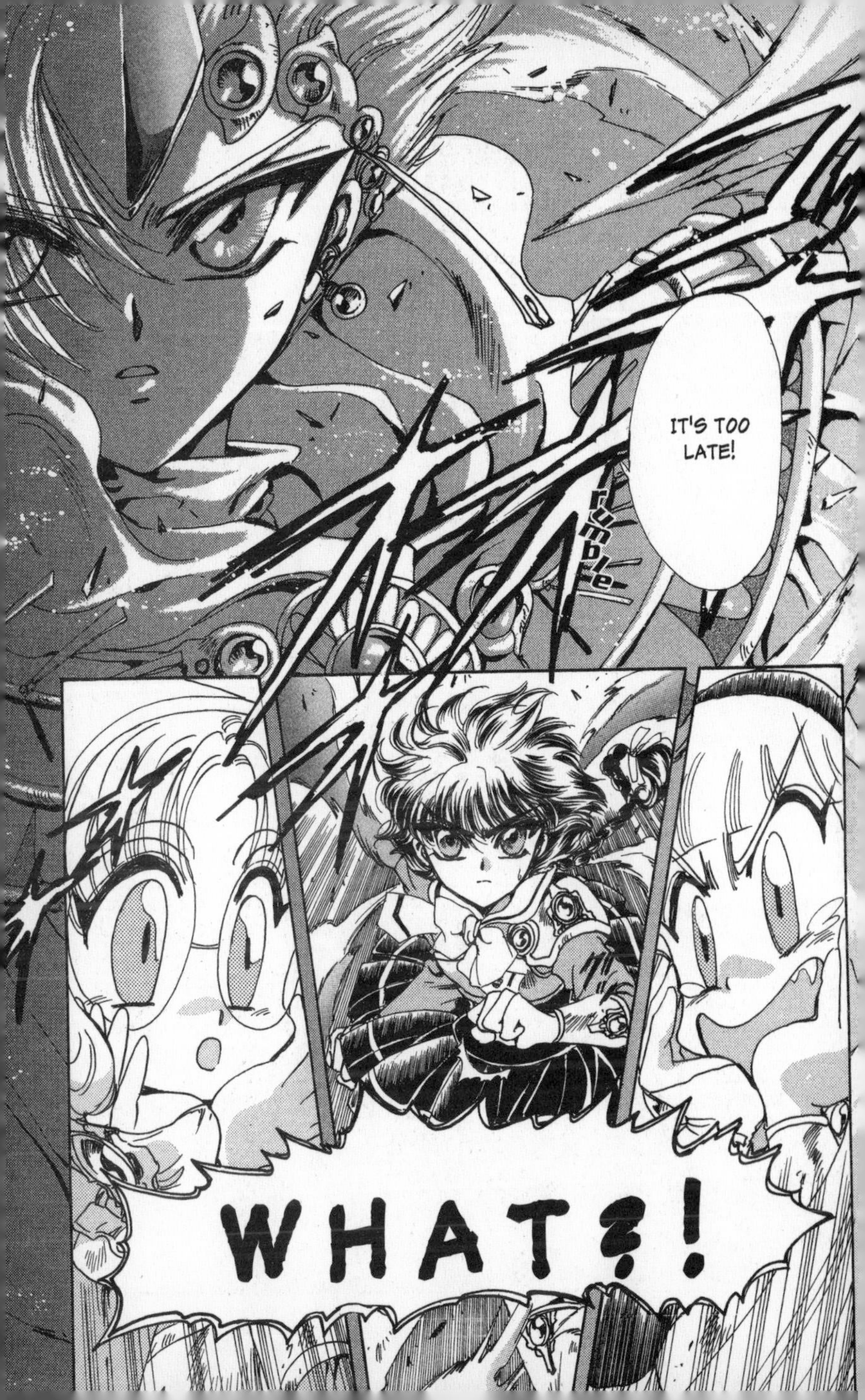
IT'S TOO LATE!
rumble
WHAT?!

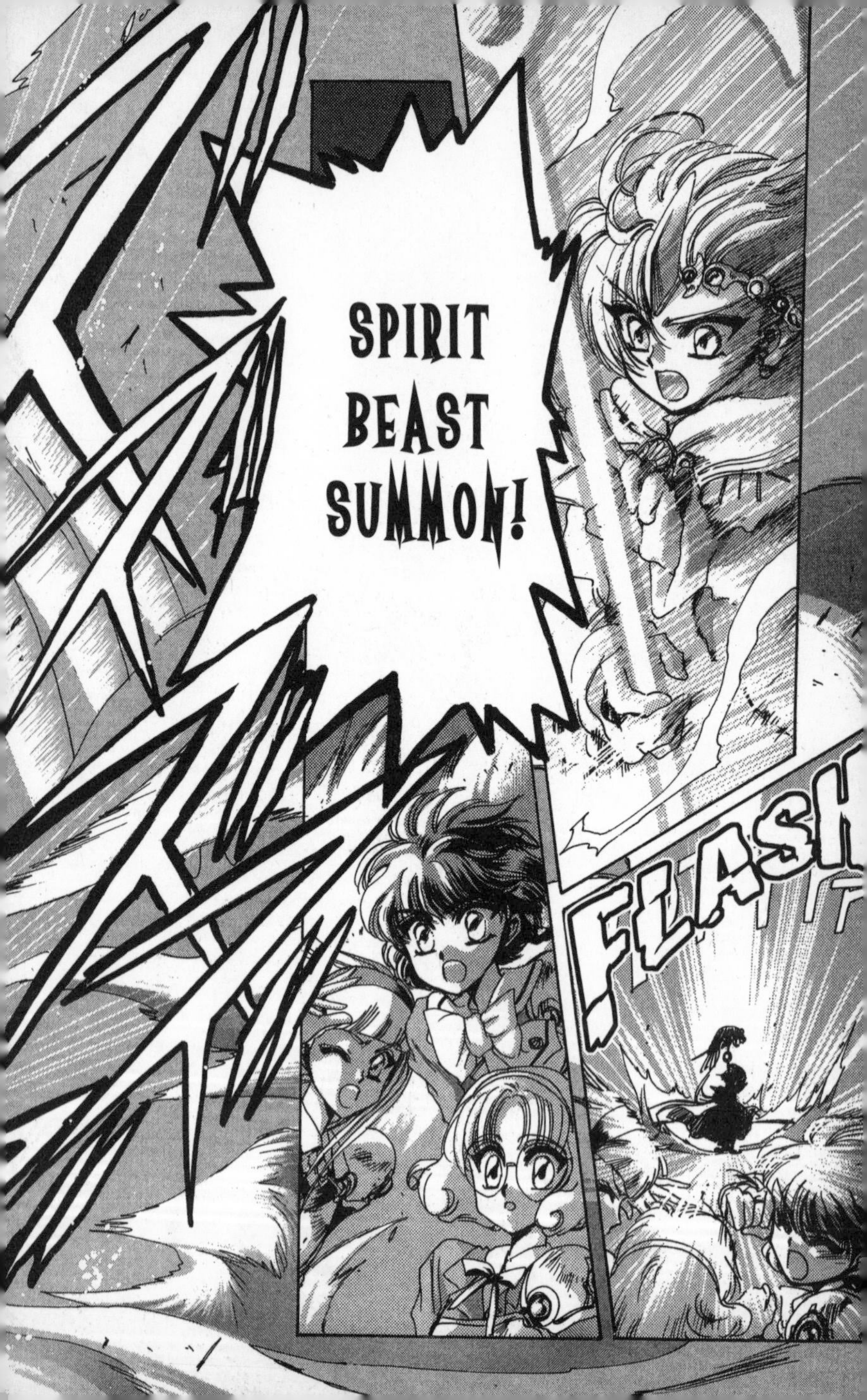
SPIRIT BEAST SUMMON!
FLASH

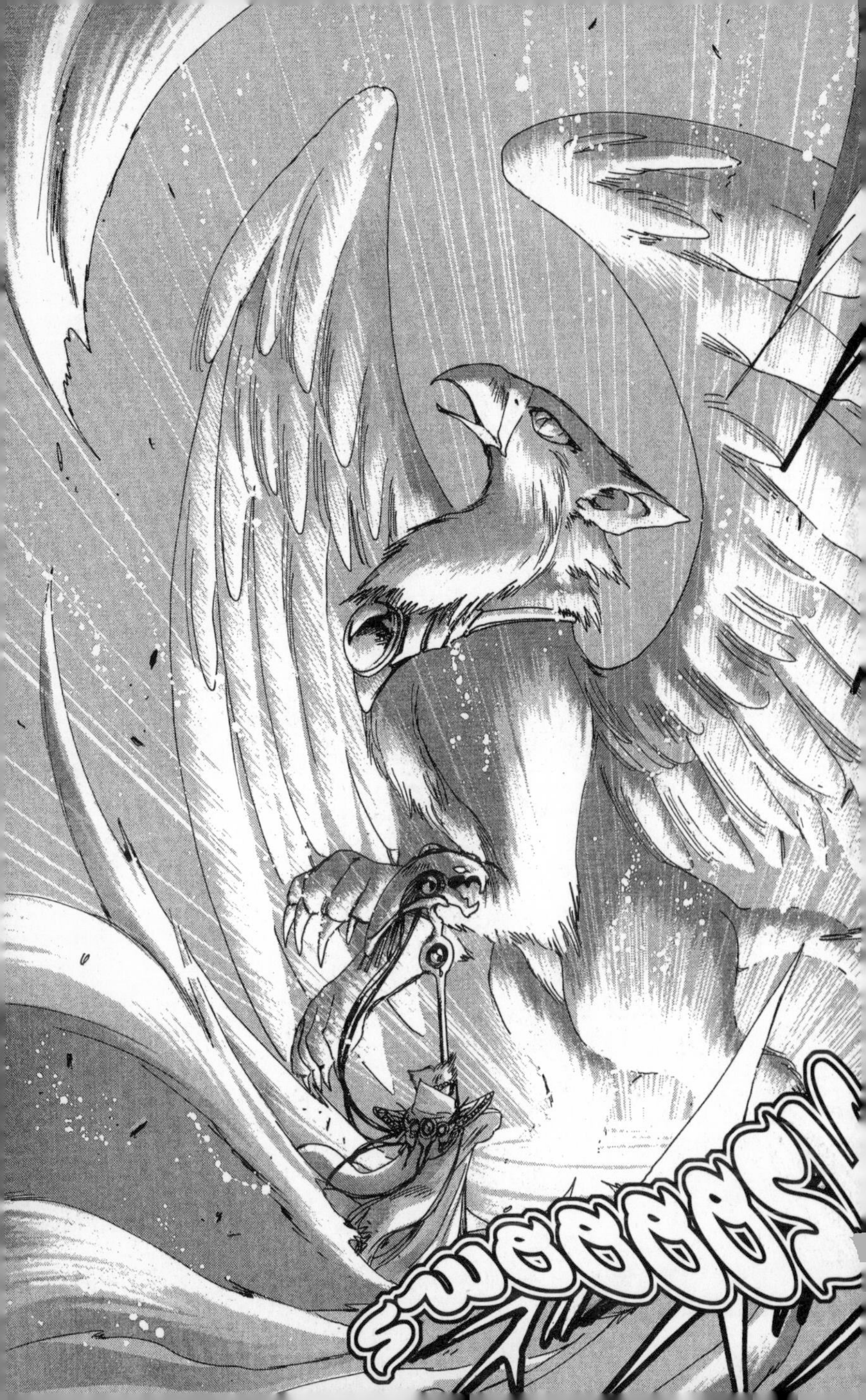
SWOOOOSH

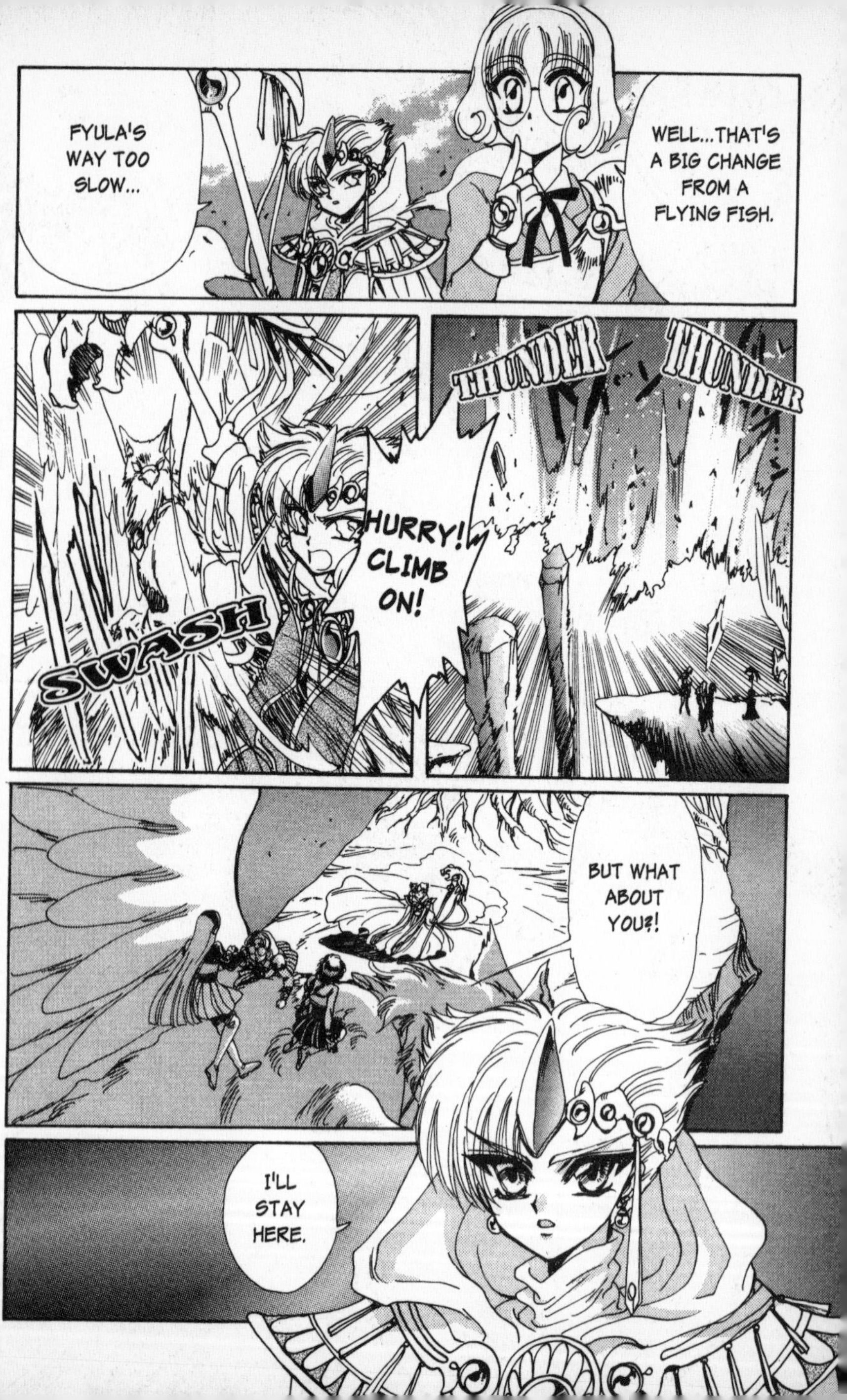
WELL...THAT'S A BIG CHANGE FROM A FLYING FISH.
FYULA'S WAY TOO SLOW...
THUNDER
THUNDER
HURRY! CLIMB ON!
SWASH
BUT WHAT ABOUT YOU?!
I'LL STAY HERE.

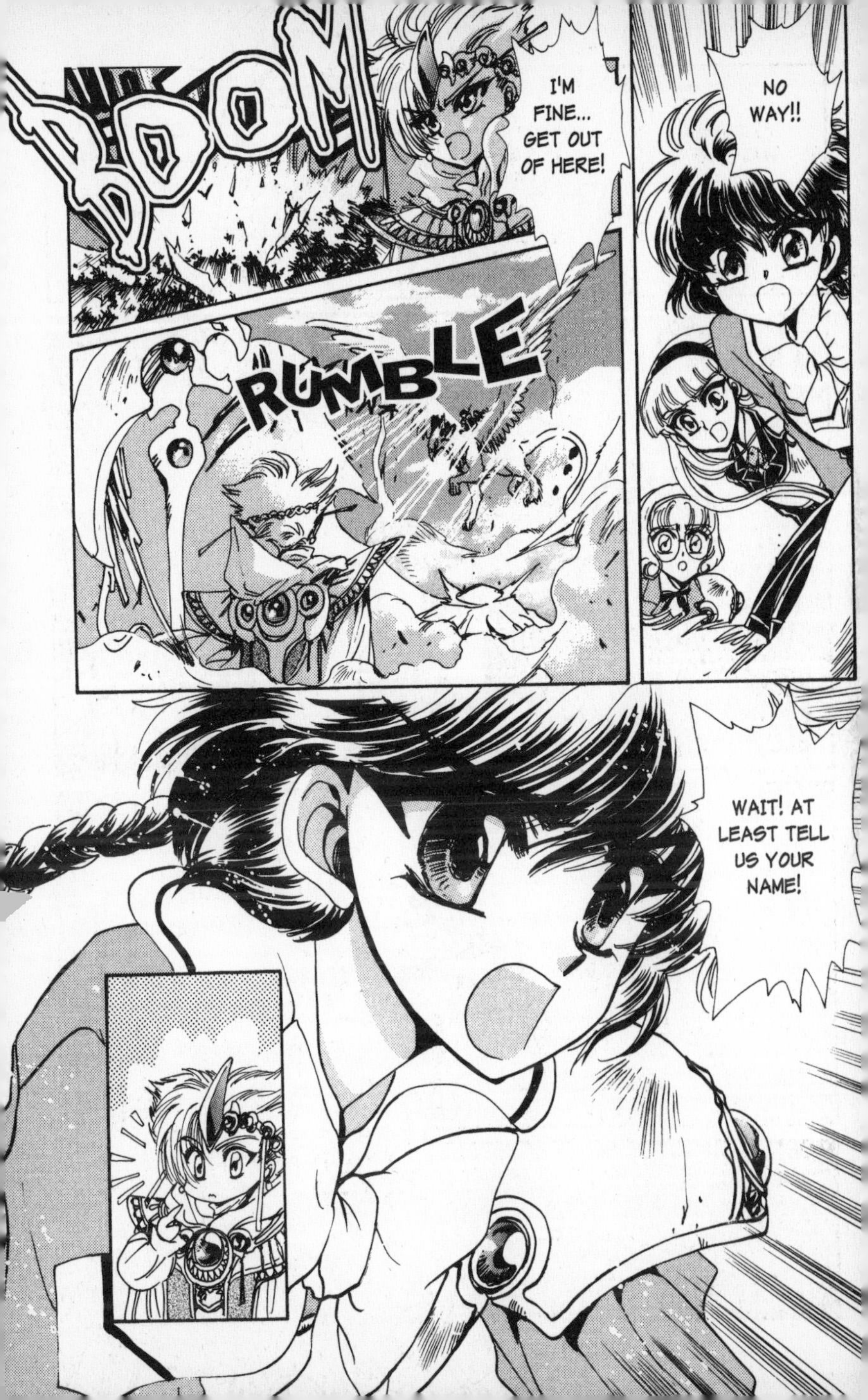
NO WAY!!
I'M FINE... GET OUT OF HERE!
BOOM
RUMBLE
WAIT! AT LEAST TELL US YOUR NAME!

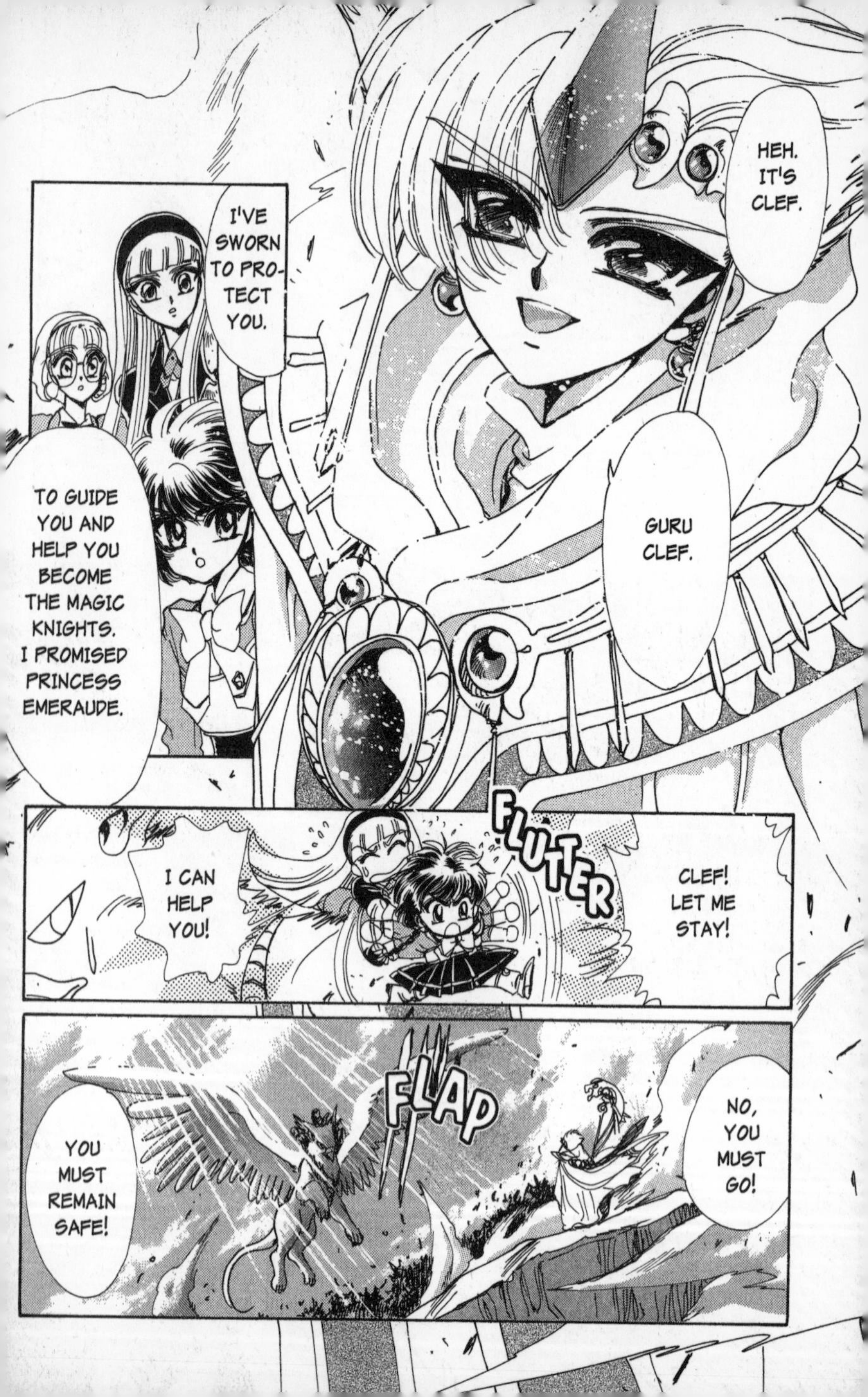
HEH. IT'S CLEF.
GURU CLEF.
I'VE SWORN TO PROTECT YOU.
TO GUIDE YOU AND HELP YOU BECOME THE MAGIC KNIGHTS. I PROMISED PRINCESS EMERAUDE.
CLEF! LET ME STAY!
FLUTTER
I CAN HELP YOU!
NO, YOU MUST GO!
FLAP
YOU MUST REMAIN SAFE!

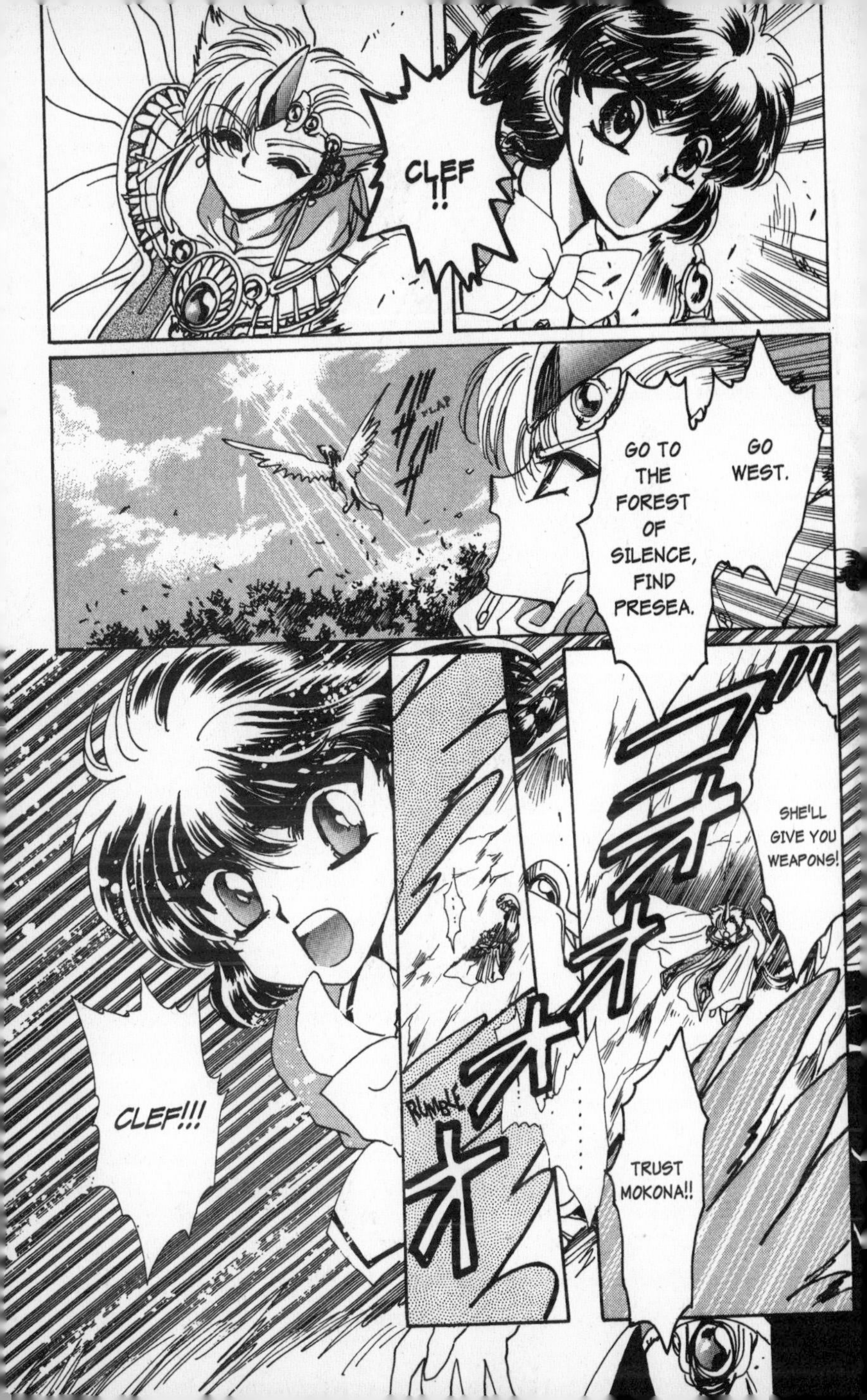
CLEF !!
GO WEST.
GO TO THE FOREST OF SILENCE, FIND PRESEA.
SHE'LL GIVE YOU WEAPONS!
TRUST MOKONA!!
RUMBLE
CLEF!!!

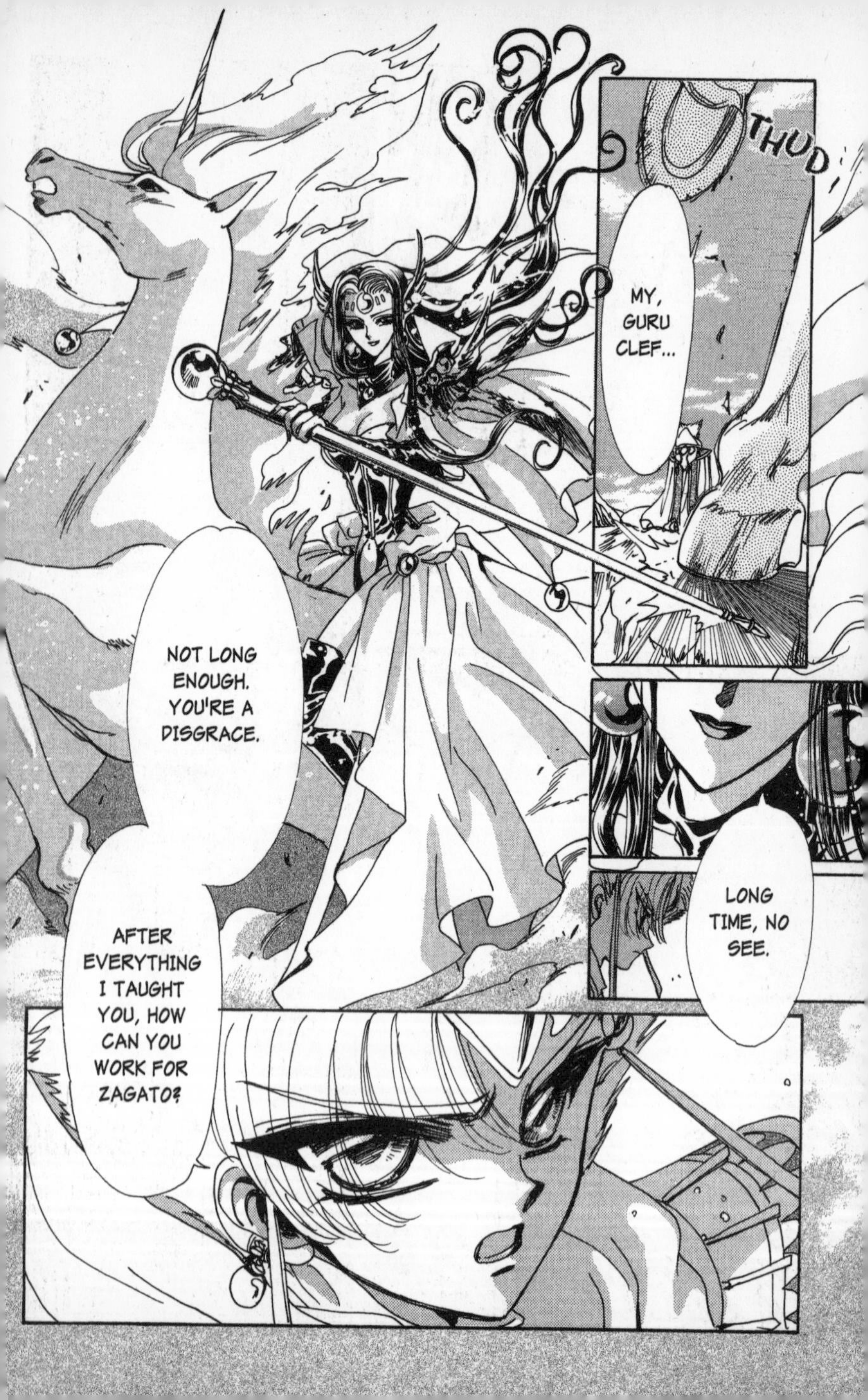
THUD
MY, GURU CLEF...
LONG TIME, NO SEE.
NOT LONG ENOUGH. YOU'RE A DISGRACE.
AFTER EVERYTHING I TAUGHT YOU, HOW CAN YOU WORK FOR ZAGATO?

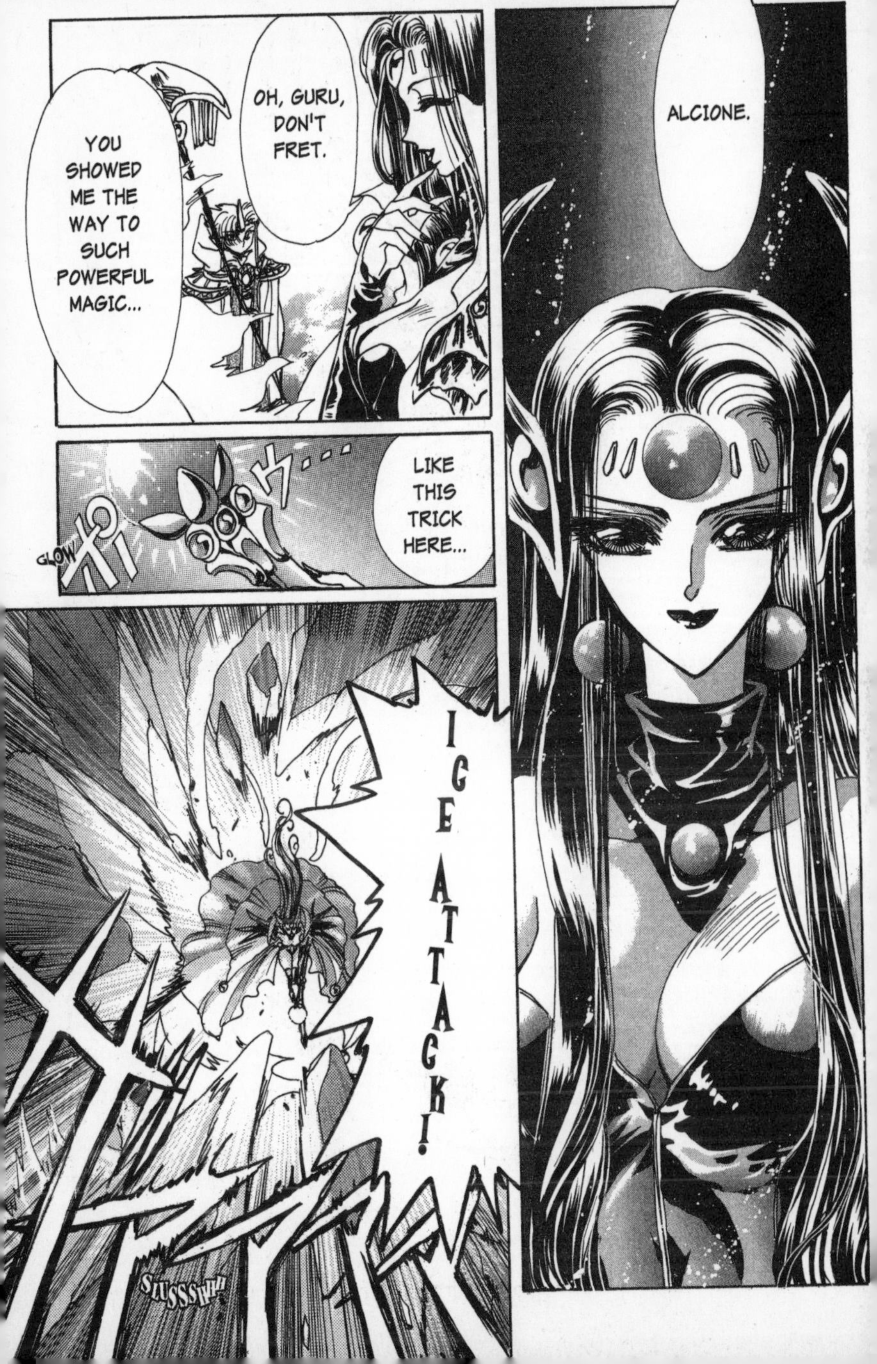
ALCIONE.
OH, GURU, DON'T FRET.
YOU SHOWED ME THE WAY TO SUCH POWERFUL MAGIC...
LIKE THIS TRICK HERE...
GLOW
ICE ATTACK!

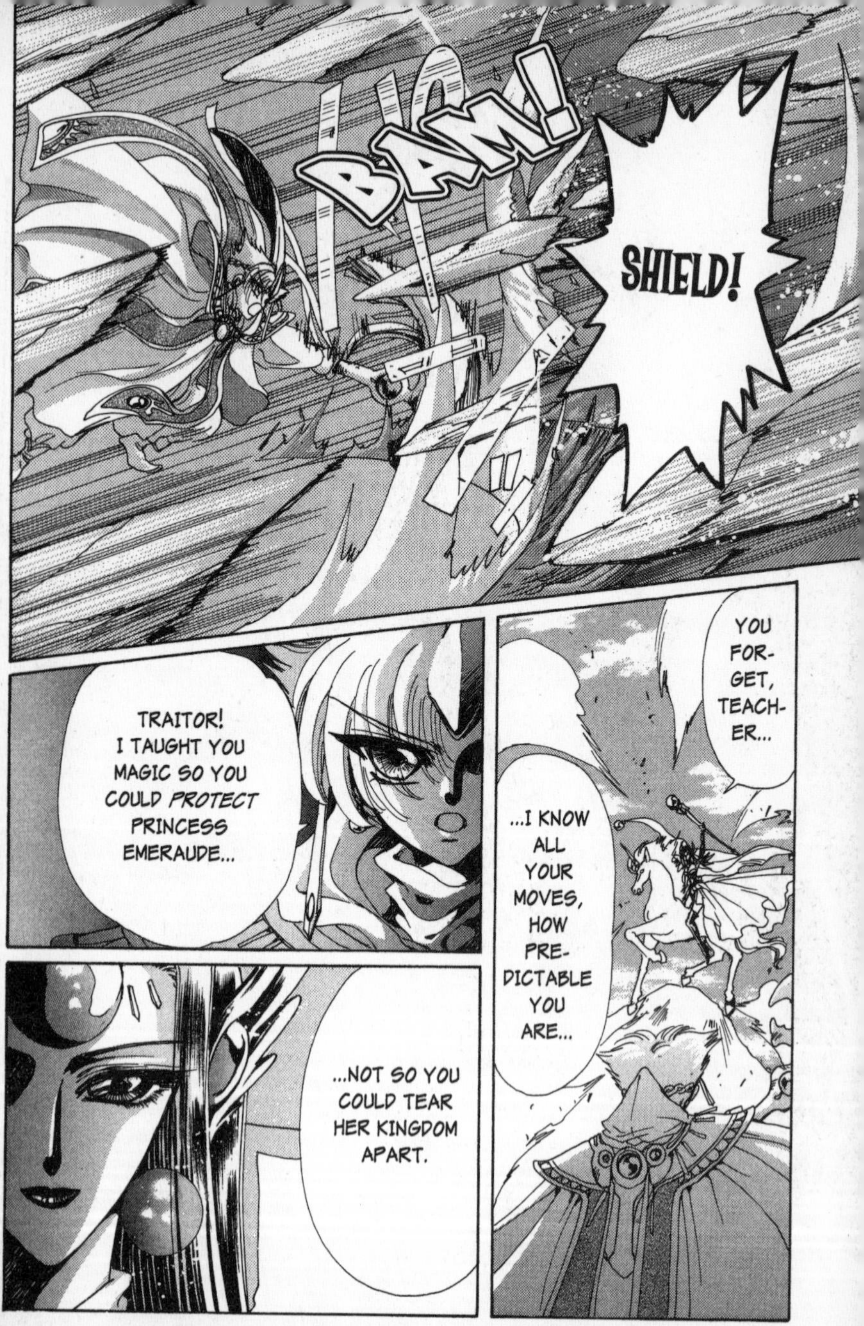
SHIELD!
BAM!
YOU FOR-GET, TEACH-ER...
...I KNOW ALL YOUR MOVES, HOW PRE-DICTABLE YOU ARE...
TRAITOR! I TAUGHT YOU MAGIC SO YOU COULD *PROTECT* PRINCESS EMERAUDE...
...NOT SO YOU COULD TEAR HER KINGDOM APART.

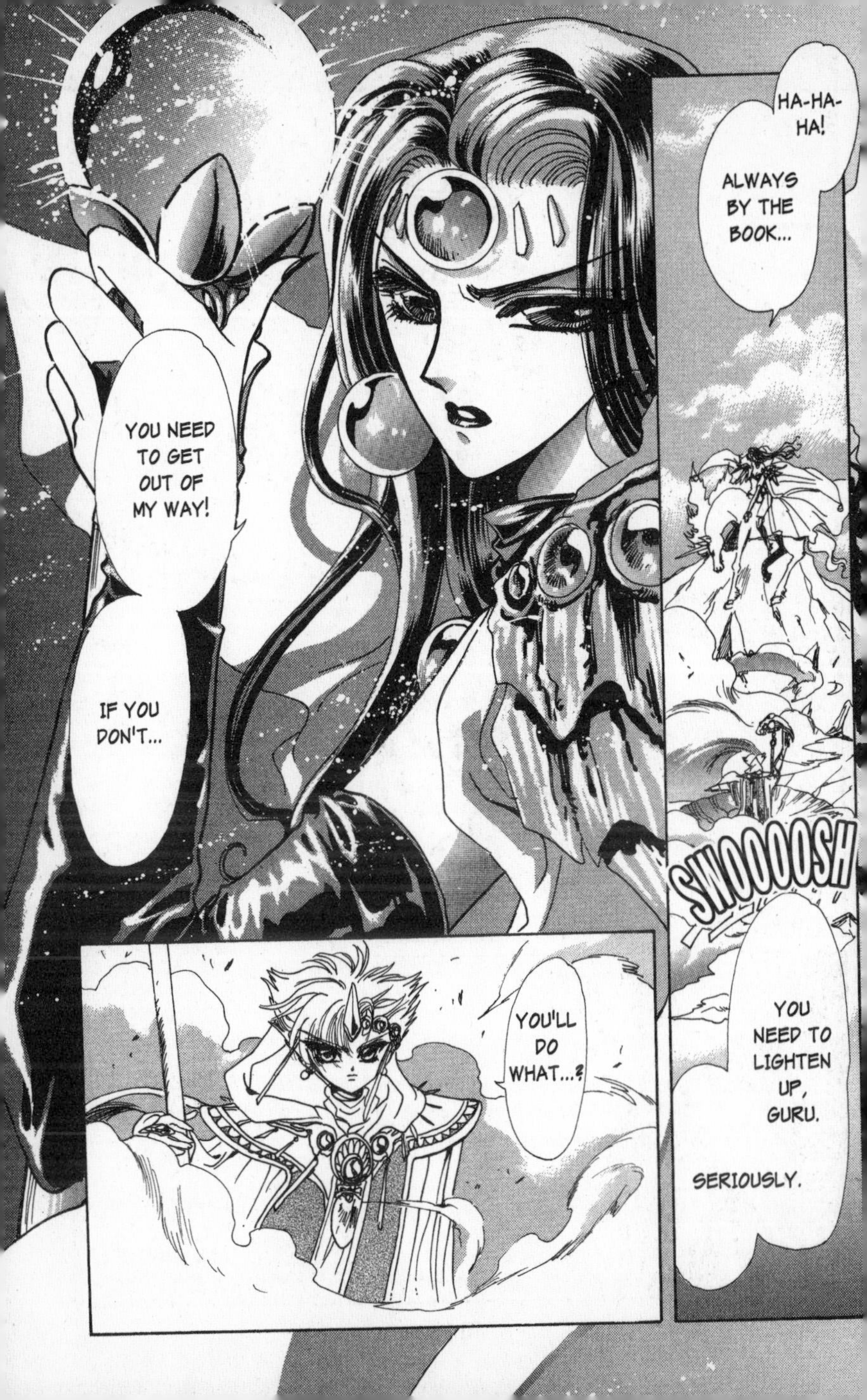
HA-HA-HA!
ALWAYS BY THE BOOK...
SWOOOOSH
YOU NEED TO LIGHTEN UP, GURU.
SERIOUSLY.
YOU NEED TO GET OUT OF MY WAY!
IF YOU DON'T...
YOU'LL DO WHAT...?

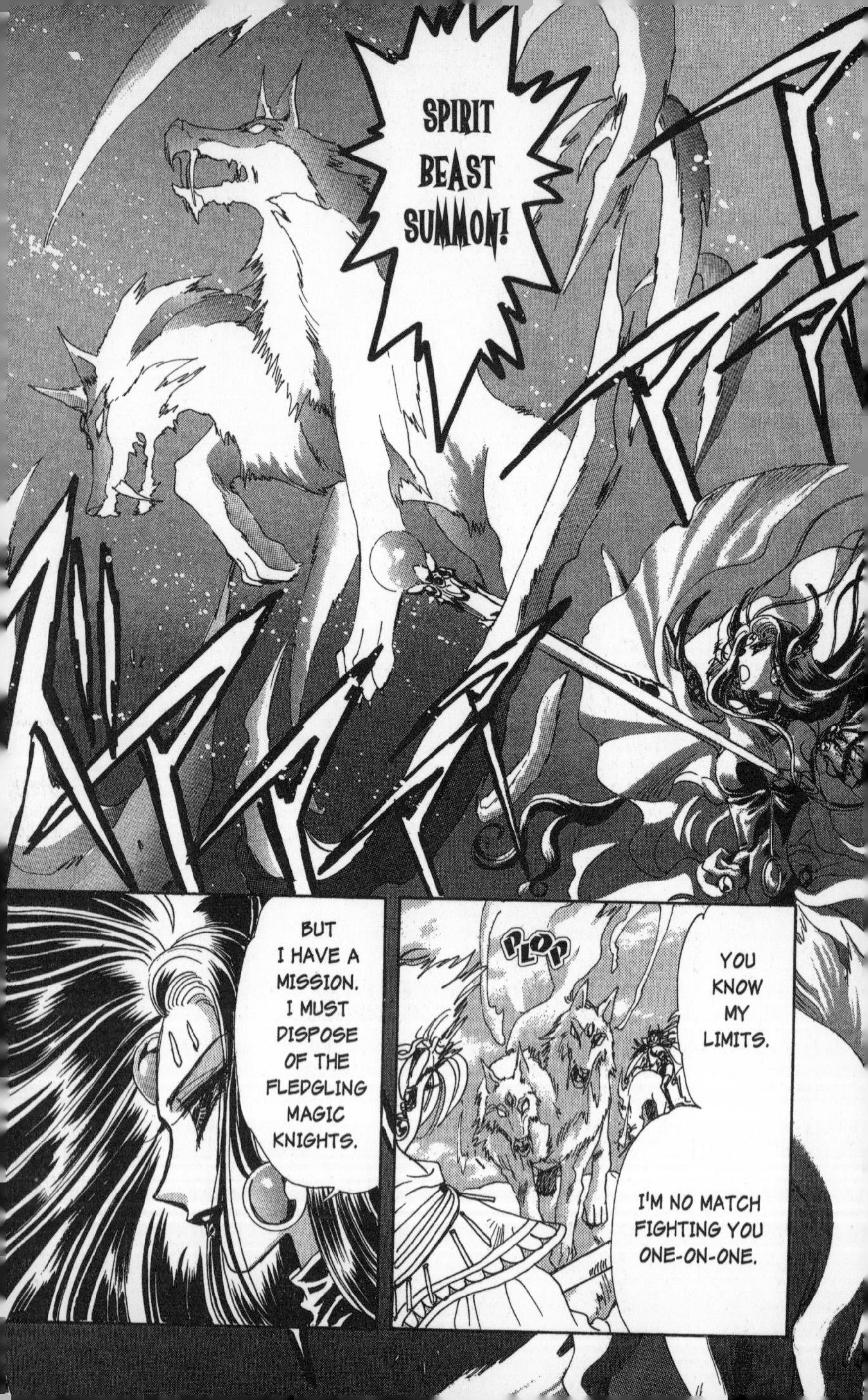
SPIRIT BEAST SUMMON!
PLOP
YOU KNOW MY LIMITS.
I'M NO MATCH FIGHTING YOU ONE-ON-ONE.
BUT I HAVE A MISSION. I MUST DISPOSE OF THE FLEDGLING MAGIC KNIGHTS.

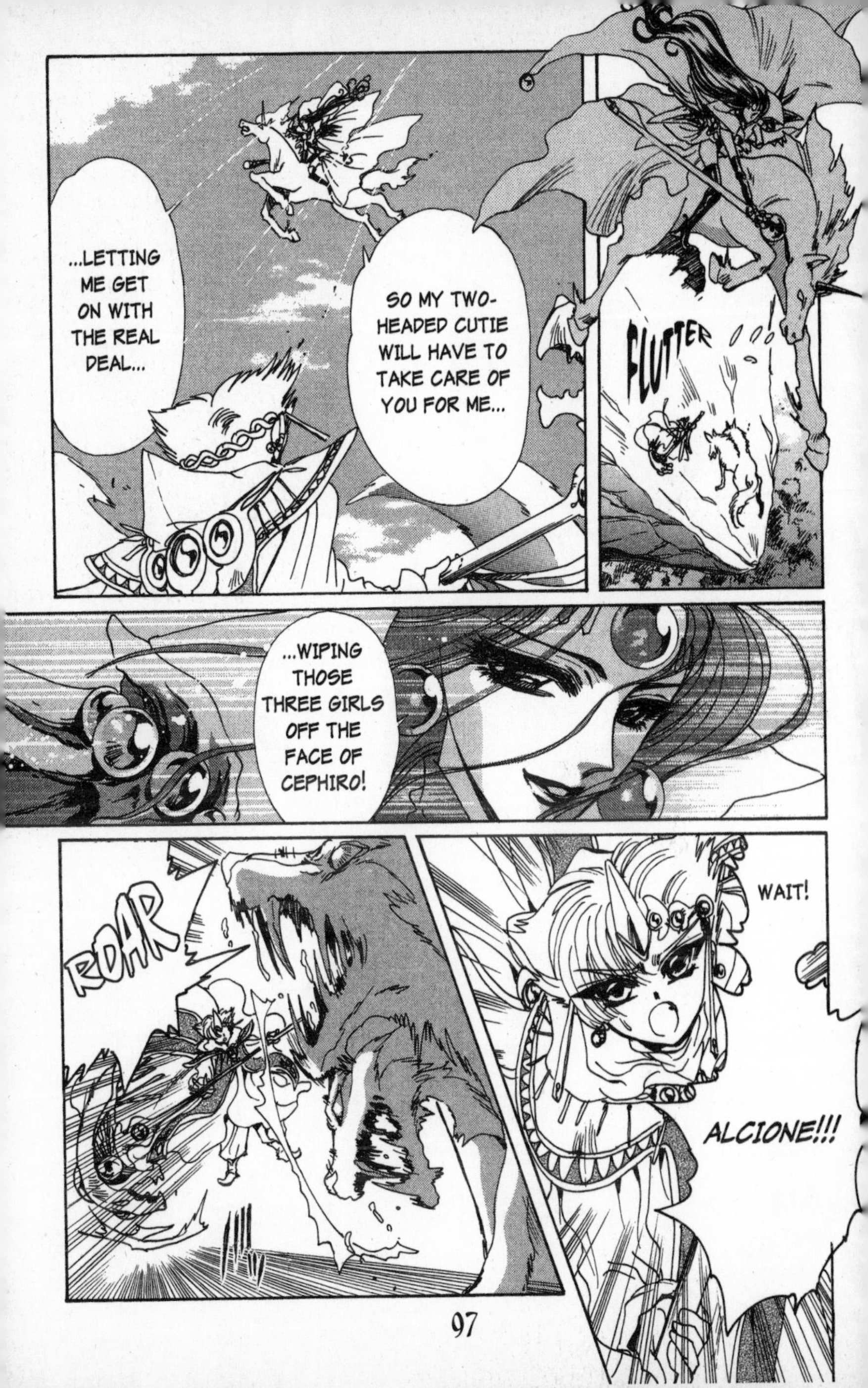
FLUTTER
SO MY TWO-HEADED CUTIE WILL HAVE TO TAKE CARE OF YOU FOR ME...
...LETTING ME GET ON WITH THE REAL DEAL...
...WIPING THOSE THREE GIRLS OFF THE FACE OF CEPHIRO!
WAIT!
ALCIONE!!!
ROAR

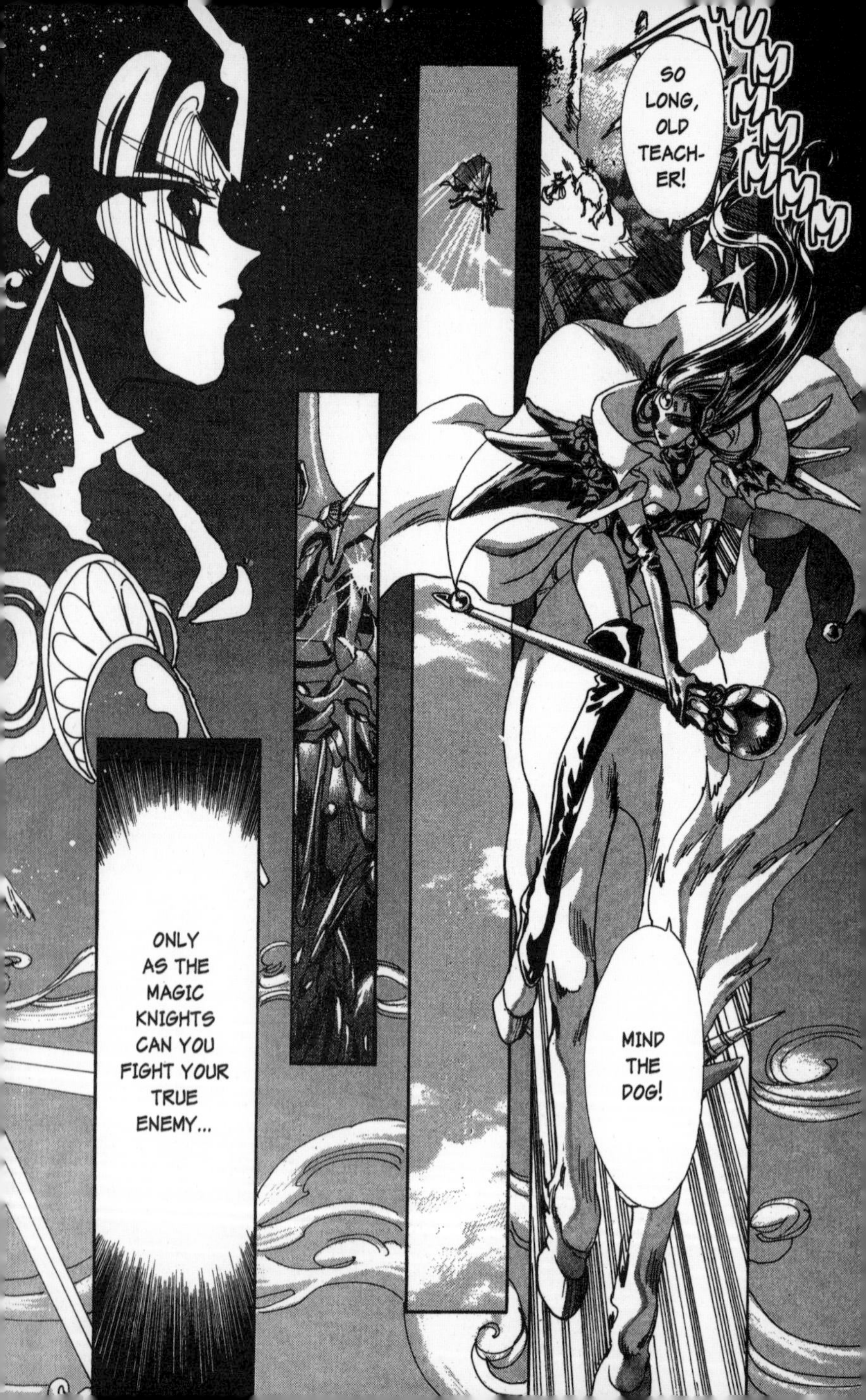
UMMMMMM
SO LONG, OLD TEACHER!
MIND THE DOG!
ONLY AS THE MAGIC KNIGHTS CAN YOU FIGHT YOUR TRUE ENEMY...

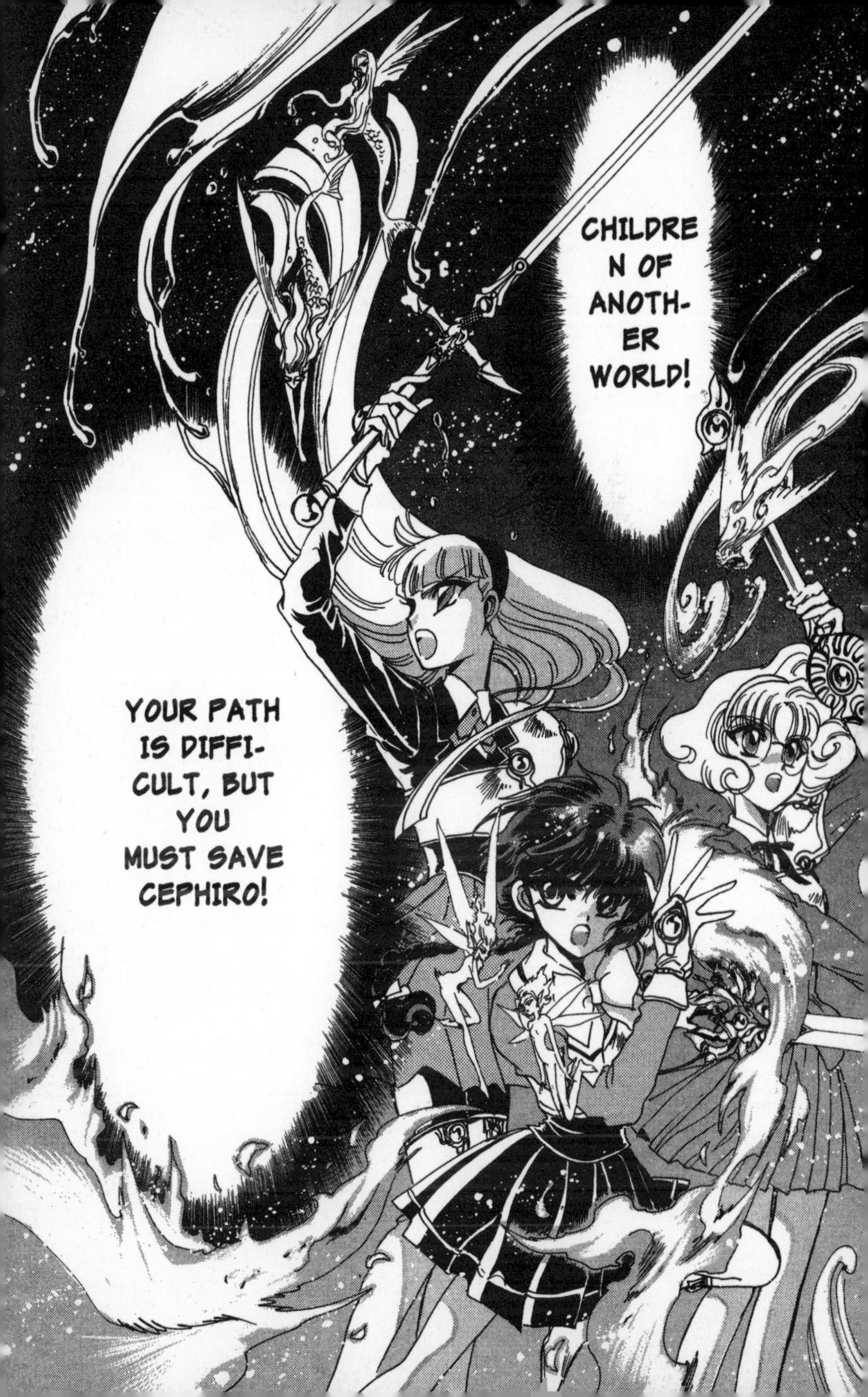
CHILDRE N OF ANOTH- ER WORLD!
YOUR PATH IS DIFFI- CULT, BUT YOU MUST SAVE CEPHIRO!

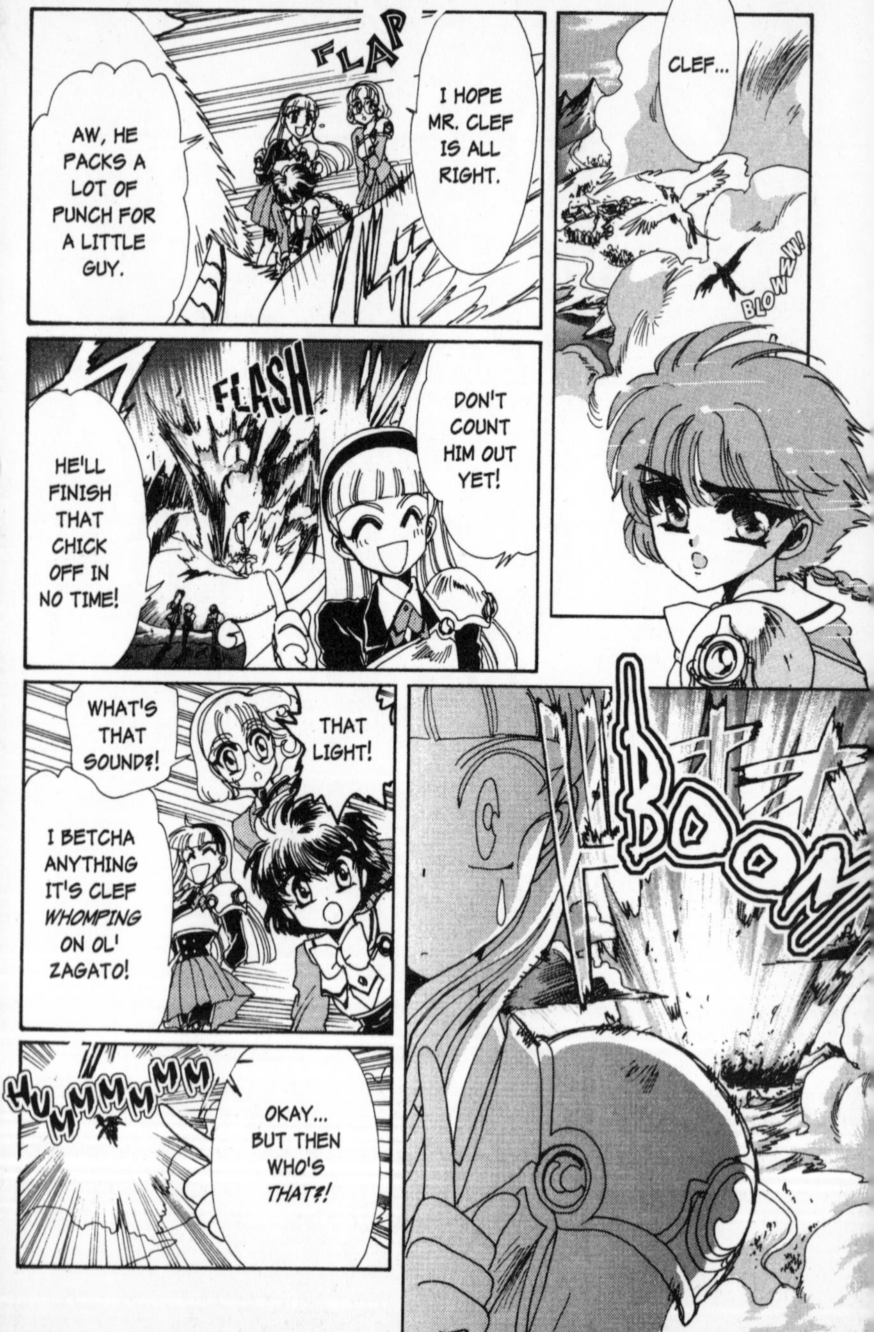
CLEF...
BLOWWW!
FLAP
I HOPE MR. CLEF IS ALL RIGHT.
AW, HE PACKS A LOT OF PUNCH FOR A LITTLE GUY.
FLASH
DON'T COUNT HIM OUT YET!
HE'LL FINISH THAT CHICK OFF IN NO TIME!
BOOM
THAT LIGHT!
WHAT'S THAT SOUND?!
I BETCHA ANYTHING IT'S CLEF *WHOMPING* ON OL' ZAGATO!
OKAY... BUT THEN WHO'S *THAT*?!
HUMMMMMMM

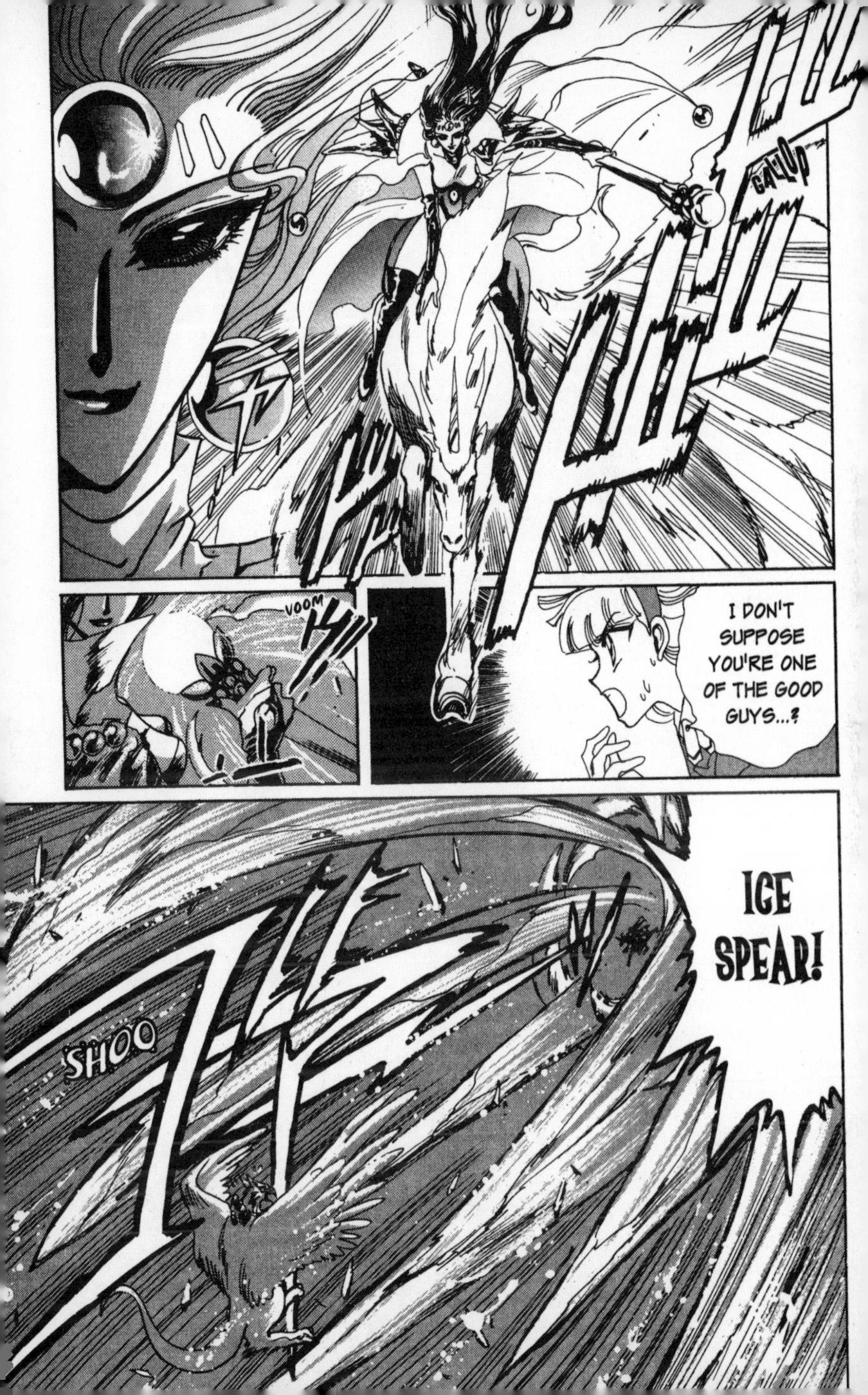
GALLOP
I DON'T SUPPOSE YOU'RE ONE OF THE GOOD GUYS...?
VOOM
ICE SPEAR!
SHOO

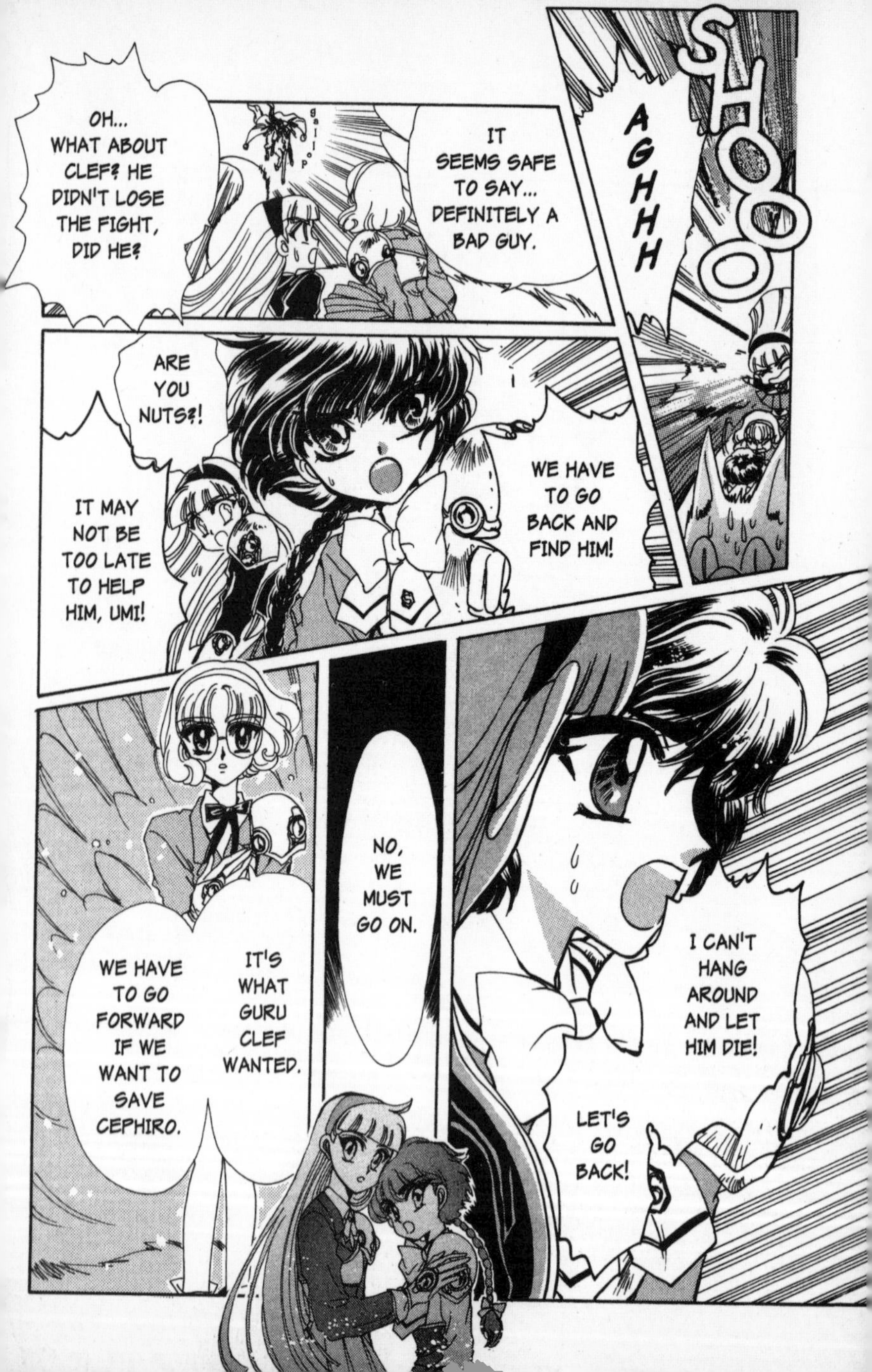
SHOOO
AGHHH
gallop
IT SEEMS SAFE TO SAY... DEFINITELY A BAD GUY.
OH... WHAT ABOUT CLEF? HE DIDN'T LOSE THE FIGHT, DID HE?
ARE YOU NUTS?!
WE HAVE TO GO BACK AND FIND HIM!
IT MAY NOT BE TOO LATE TO HELP HIM, UMI!
I CAN'T HANG AROUND AND LET HIM DIE!
LET'S GO BACK!
NO, WE MUST GO ON.
IT'S WHAT GURU CLEF WANTED.
WE HAVE TO GO FORWARD IF WE WANT TO SAVE CEPHIRO.

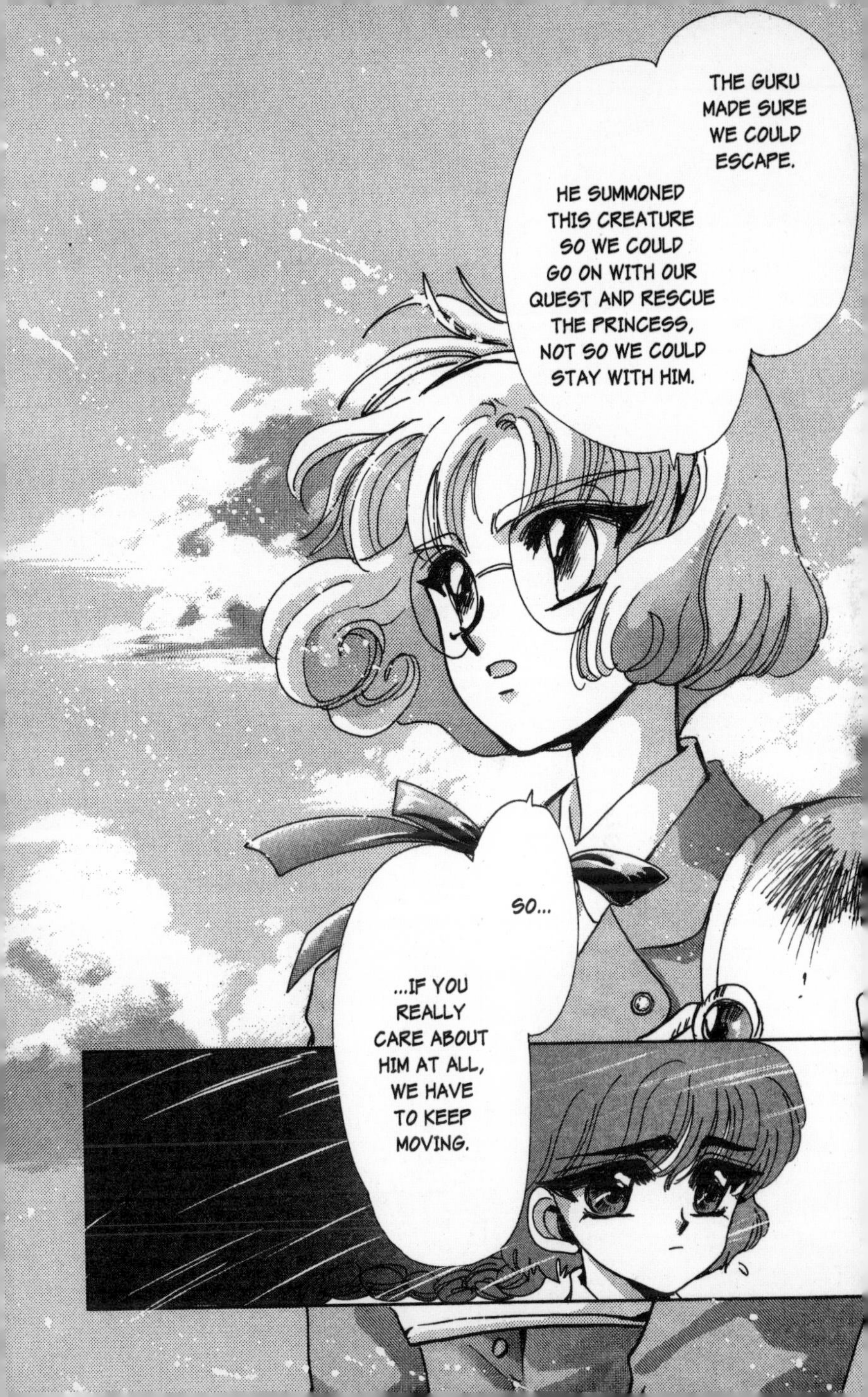
THE GURU MADE SURE WE COULD ESCAPE.
HE SUMMONED THIS CREATURE SO WE COULD GO ON WITH OUR QUEST AND RESCUE THE PRINCESS, NOT SO WE COULD STAY WITH HIM.
SO...
...IF YOU REALLY CARE ABOUT HIM AT ALL, WE HAVE TO KEEP MOVING.

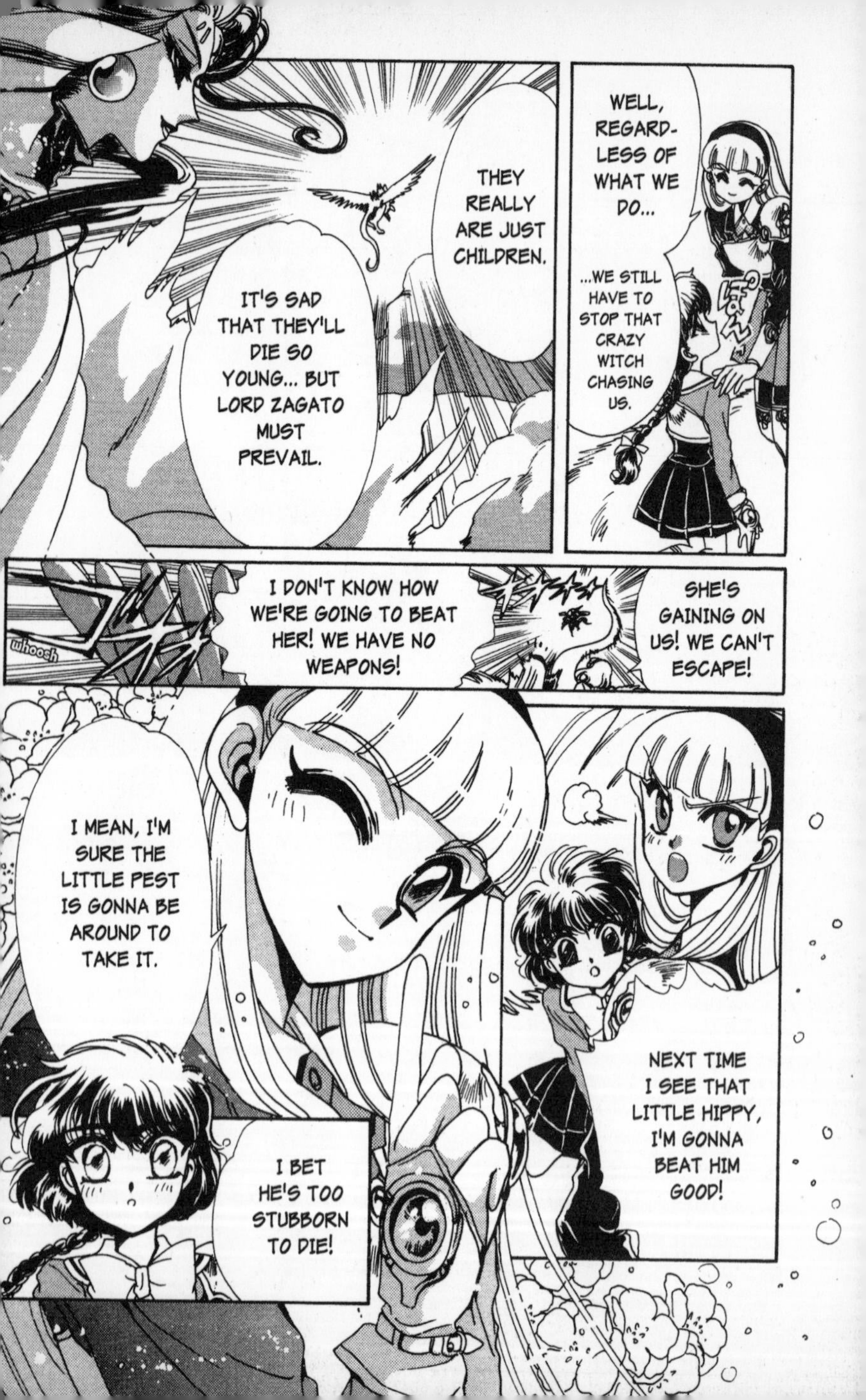
WELL, REGARDLESS OF WHAT WE DO...
...WE STILL HAVE TO STOP THAT CRAZY WITCH CHASING US.
THEY REALLY ARE JUST CHILDREN.
IT'S SAD THAT THEY'LL DIE SO YOUNG... BUT LORD ZAGATO MUST PREVAIL.
SHE'S GAINING ON US! WE CAN'T ESCAPE!
I DON'T KNOW HOW WE'RE GOING TO BEAT HER! WE HAVE NO WEAPONS!
whoosh
NEXT TIME I SEE THAT LITTLE HIPPY, I'M GONNA BEAT HIM GOOD!
I MEAN, I'M SURE THE LITTLE PEST IS GONNA BE AROUND TO TAKE IT.
I BET HE'S TOO STUBBORN TO DIE!

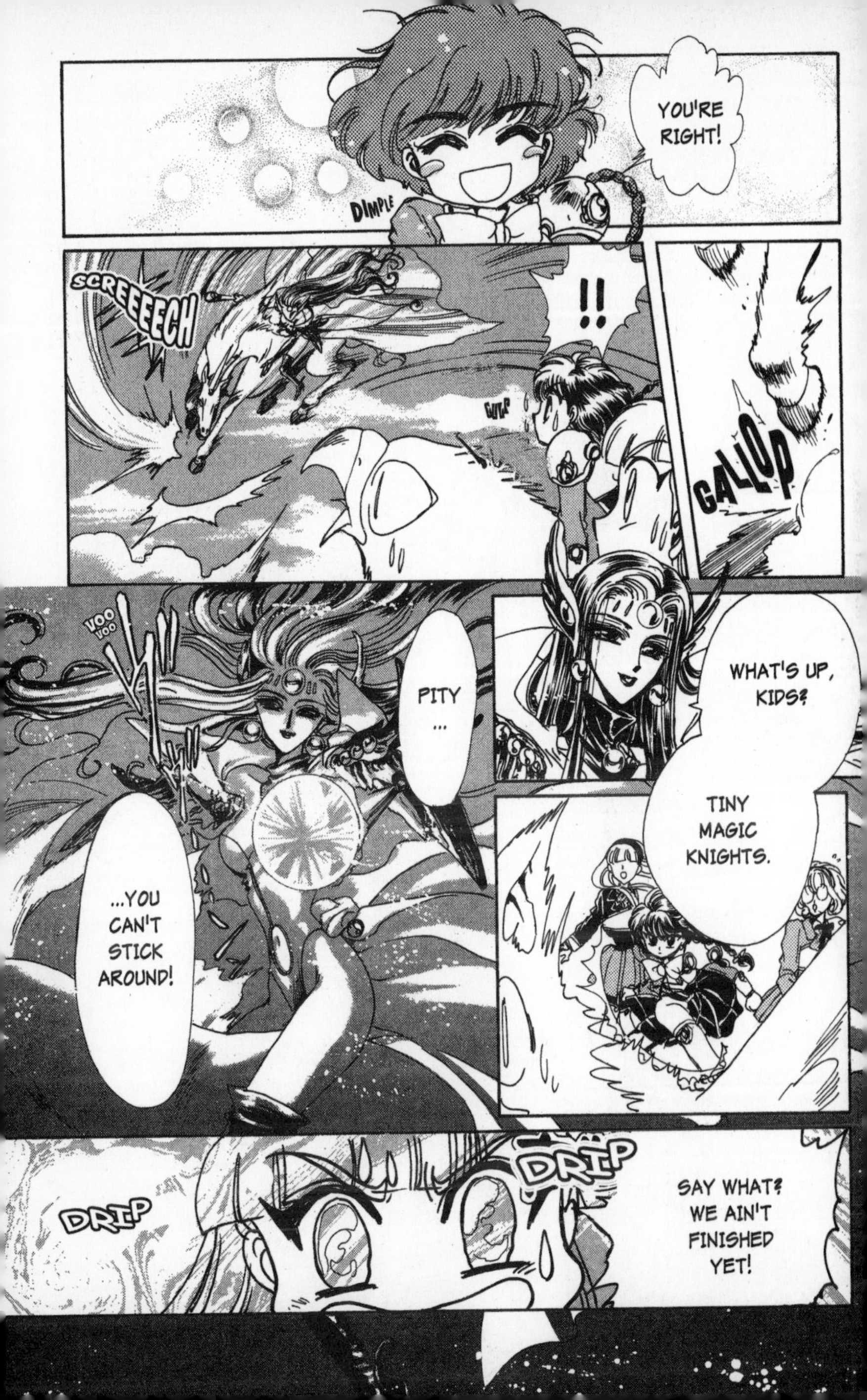
YOU'RE RIGHT!
DIMPLE
GALLOP
!!
SCREEEEECH
GULP
WHAT'S UP, KIDS?
TINY MAGIC KNIGHTS.
PITY ...
VOO VOO
...YOU CAN'T STICK AROUND!
SAY WHAT? WE AIN'T FINISHED YET!
DRIP
DRIP

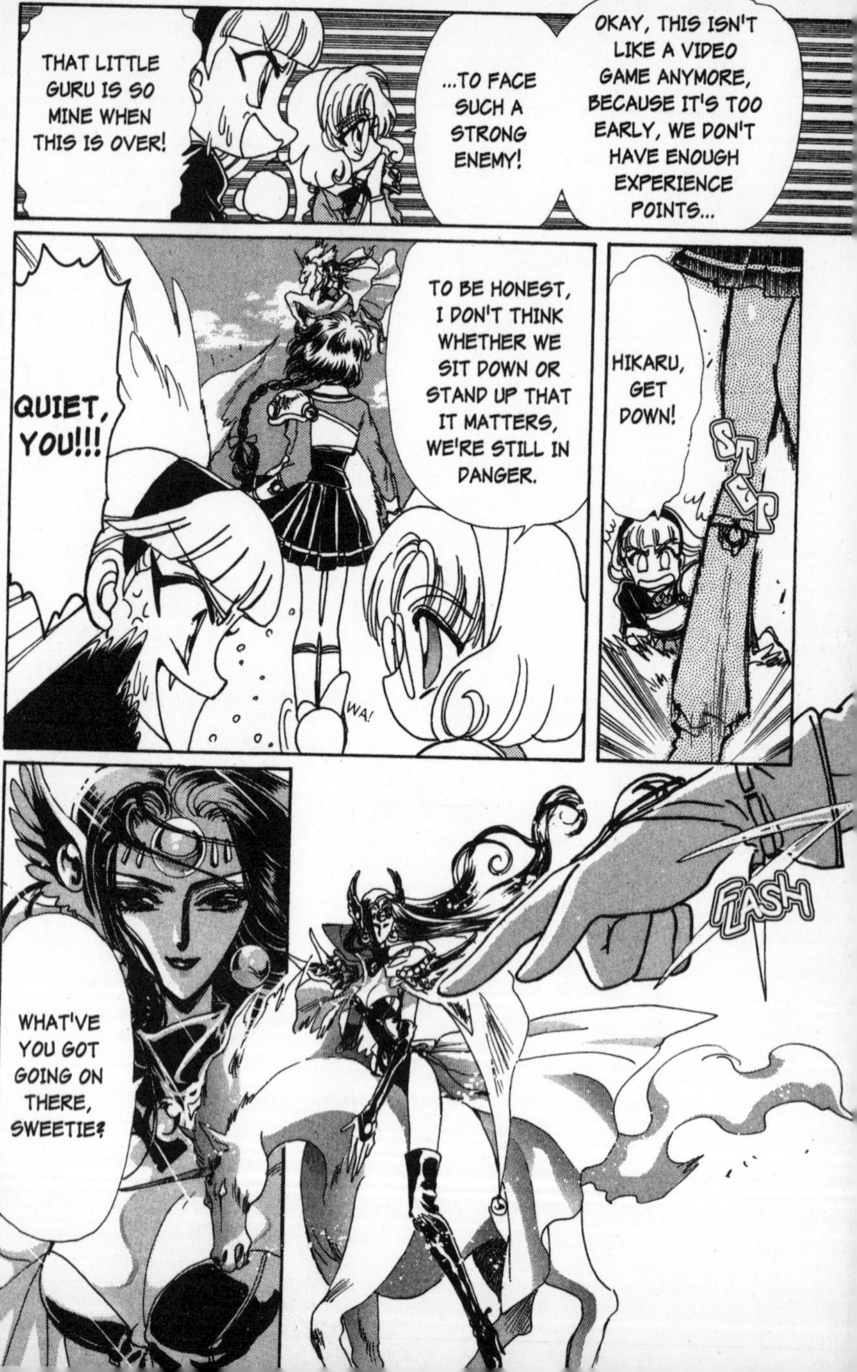
OKAY, THIS ISN'T LIKE A VIDEO GAME ANYMORE, BECAUSE IT'S TOO EARLY, WE DON'T HAVE ENOUGH EXPERIENCE POINTS...
...TO FACE SUCH A STRONG ENEMY!
THAT LITTLE GURU IS SO MINE WHEN THIS IS OVER!
HIKARU, GET DOWN!
STEP
TO BE HONEST, I DON'T THINK WHETHER WE SIT DOWN OR STAND UP THAT IT MATTERS, WE'RE STILL IN DANGER.
QUIET, YOU!!!
WA!
FLASH
WHAT'VE YOU GOT GOING ON THERE, SWEETIE?

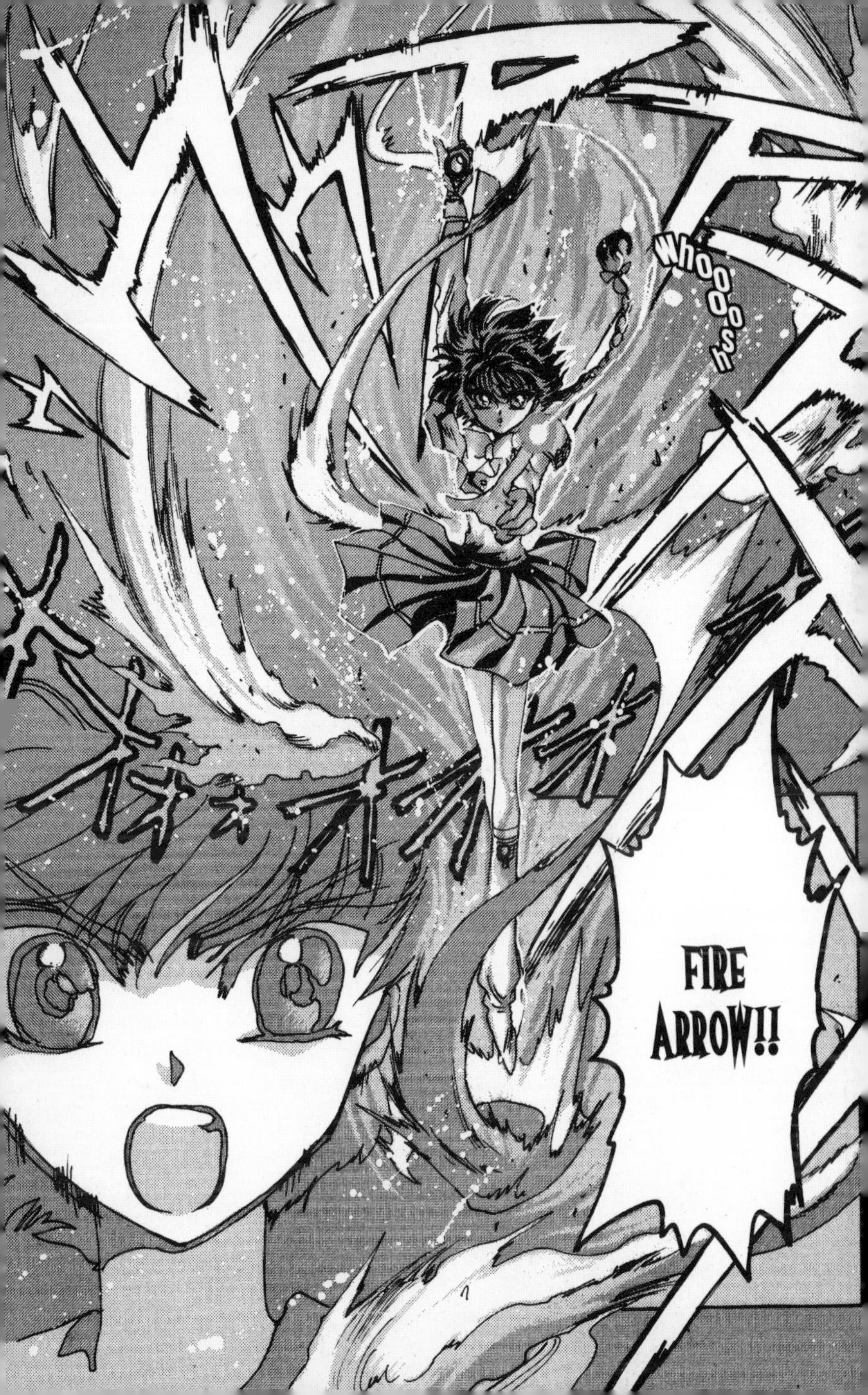
Whooooosh
FIRE ARROW!!

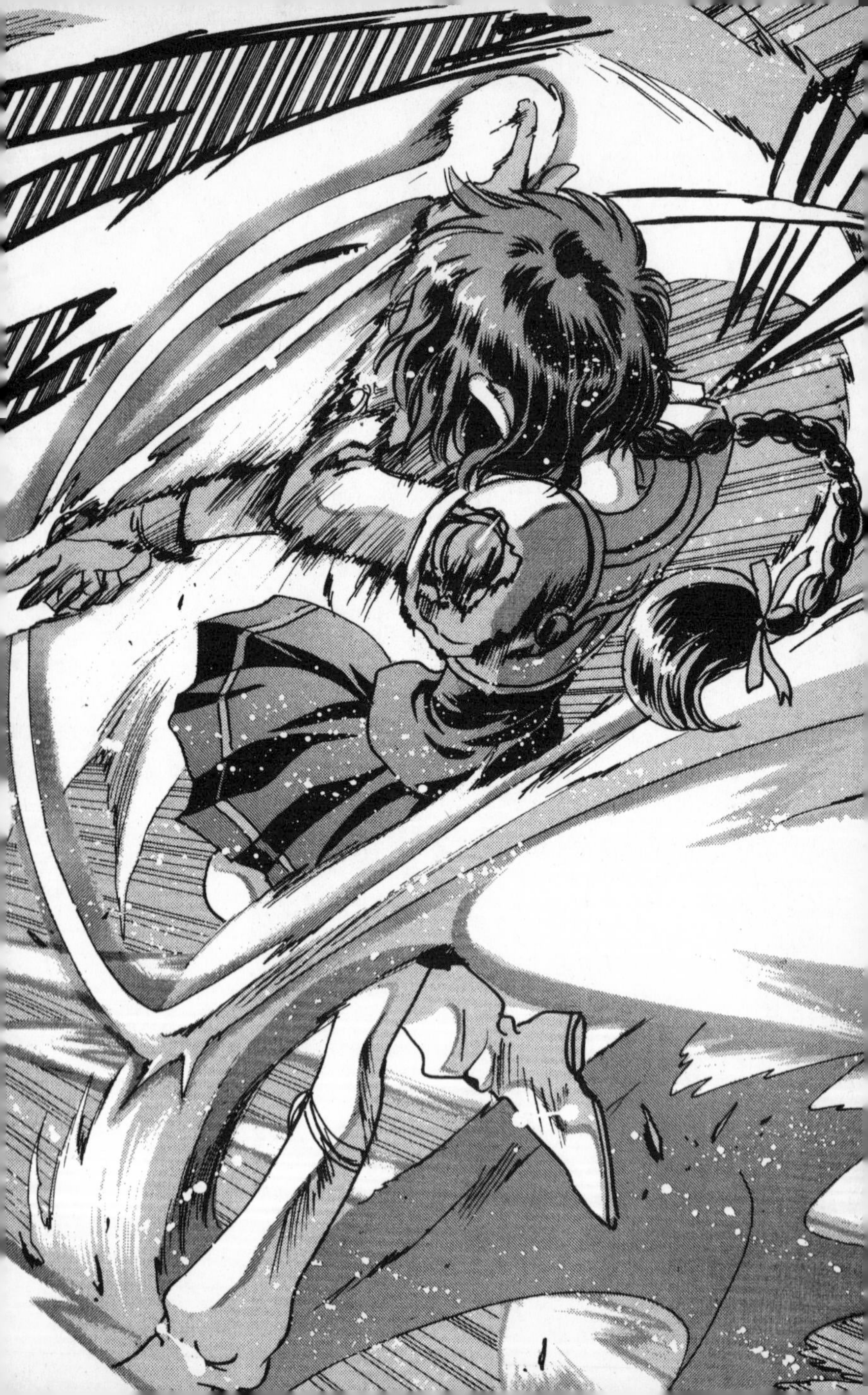

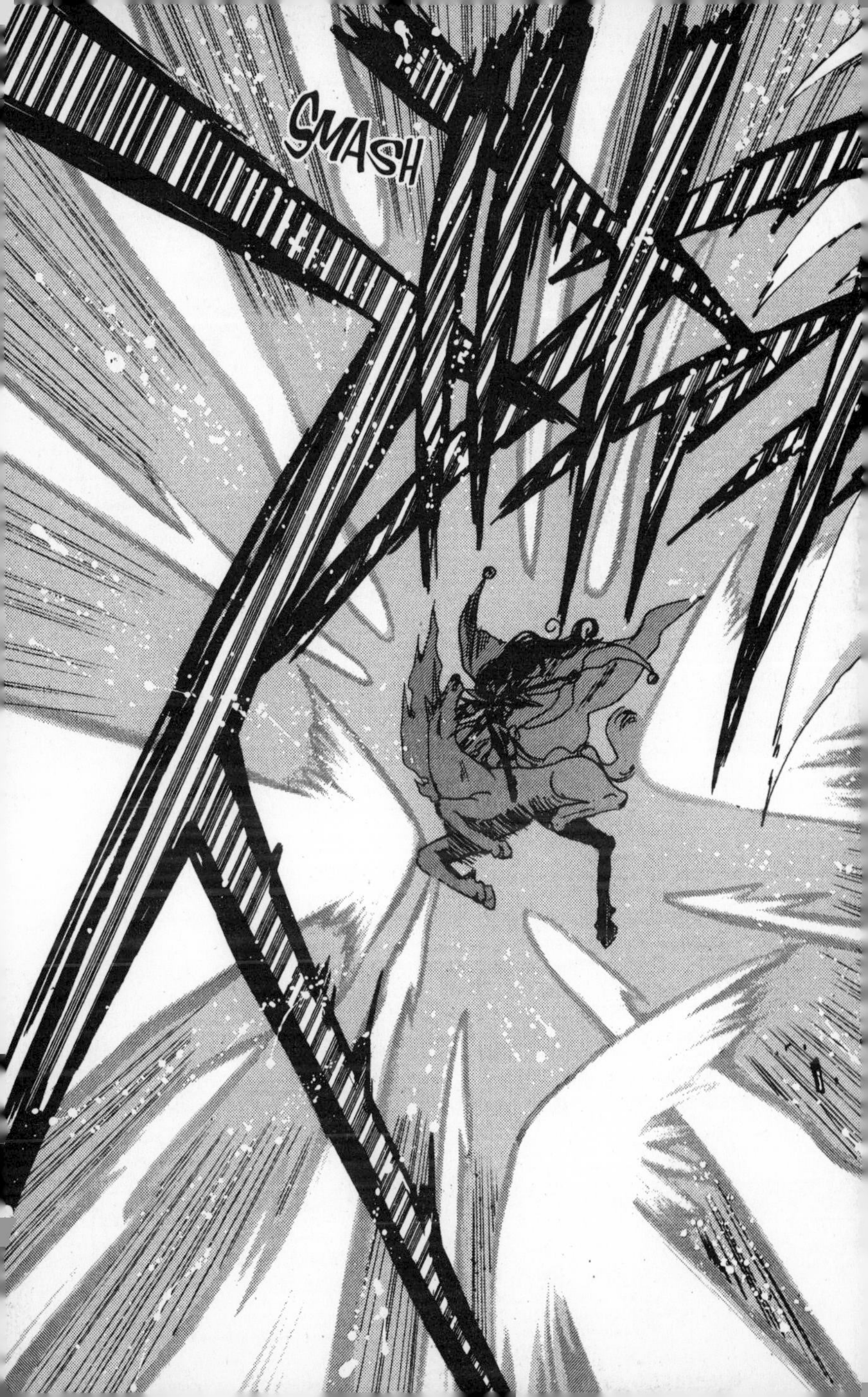
SMASH

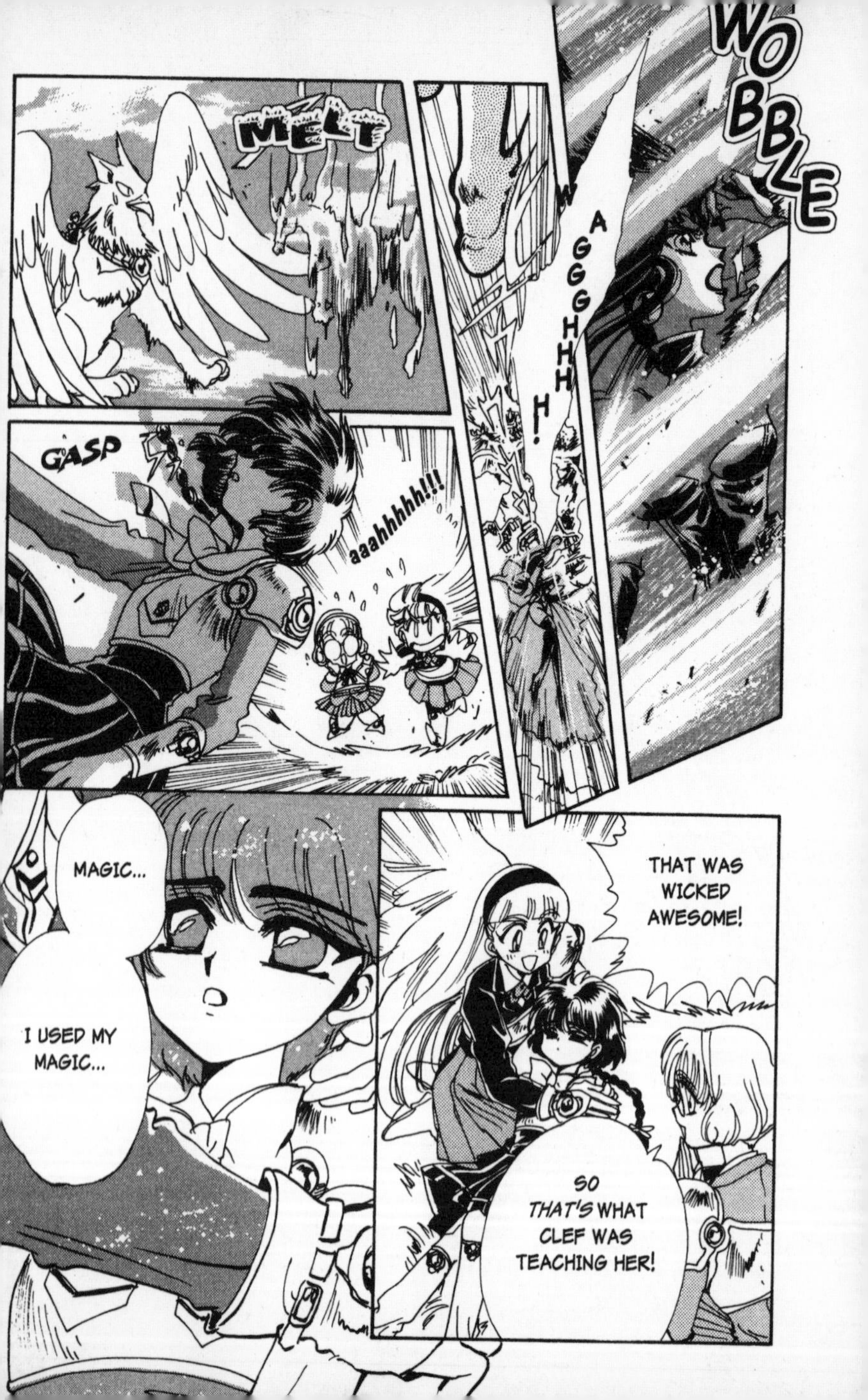
WOBBLE
AGGGHHHH!
MELT
GASP
aaahhhhh!!!
THAT WAS WICKED AWESOME!
SO *THAT'S* WHAT CLEF WAS TEACHING HER!
MAGIC...
I USED MY MAGIC...

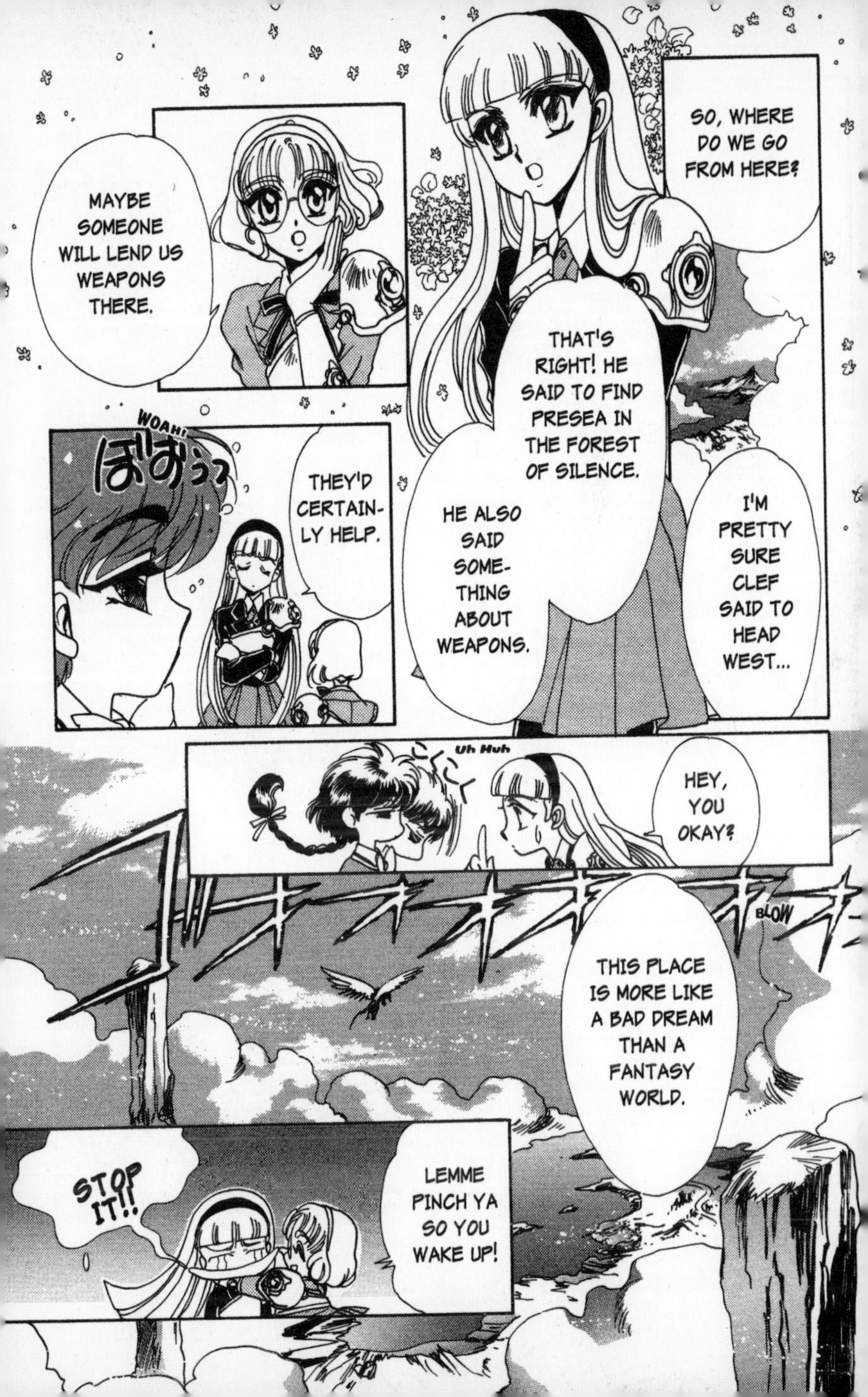
SO, WHERE DO WE GO FROM HERE?
I'M PRETTY SURE CLEF SAID TO HEAD WEST...
THAT'S RIGHT! HE SAID TO FIND PRESEA IN THE FOREST OF SILENCE.
HE ALSO SAID SOMETHING ABOUT WEAPONS.
MAYBE SOMEONE WILL LEND US WEAPONS THERE.
WOAH!
ぼおうっ
THEY'D CERTAINLY HELP.
Uh Huh
HEY, YOU OKAY?
BLOW
THIS PLACE IS MORE LIKE A BAD DREAM THAN A FANTASY WORLD.
LEMME PINCH YA SO YOU WAKE UP!
STOP IT!!

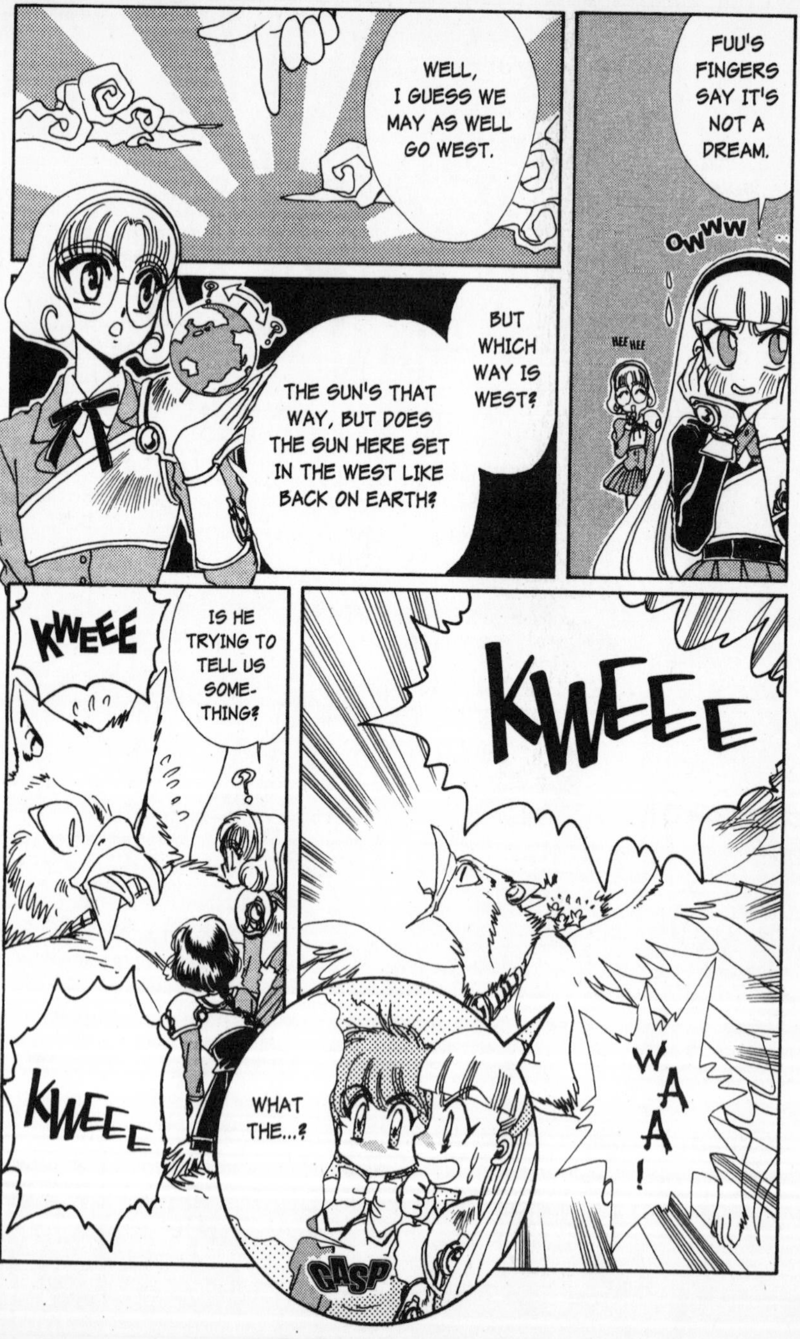
FUU'S FINGERS SAY IT'S NOT A DREAM.
OWWW
HEE HEE
WELL, I GUESS WE MAY AS WELL GO WEST.
BUT WHICH WAY IS WEST?
THE SUN'S THAT WAY, BUT DOES THE SUN HERE SET IN THE WEST LIKE BACK ON EARTH?
KWEEEE
WAA!
WHAT THE...?
GASP
KWEEE
IS HE TRYING TO TELL US SOME-THING?
KWEEEE

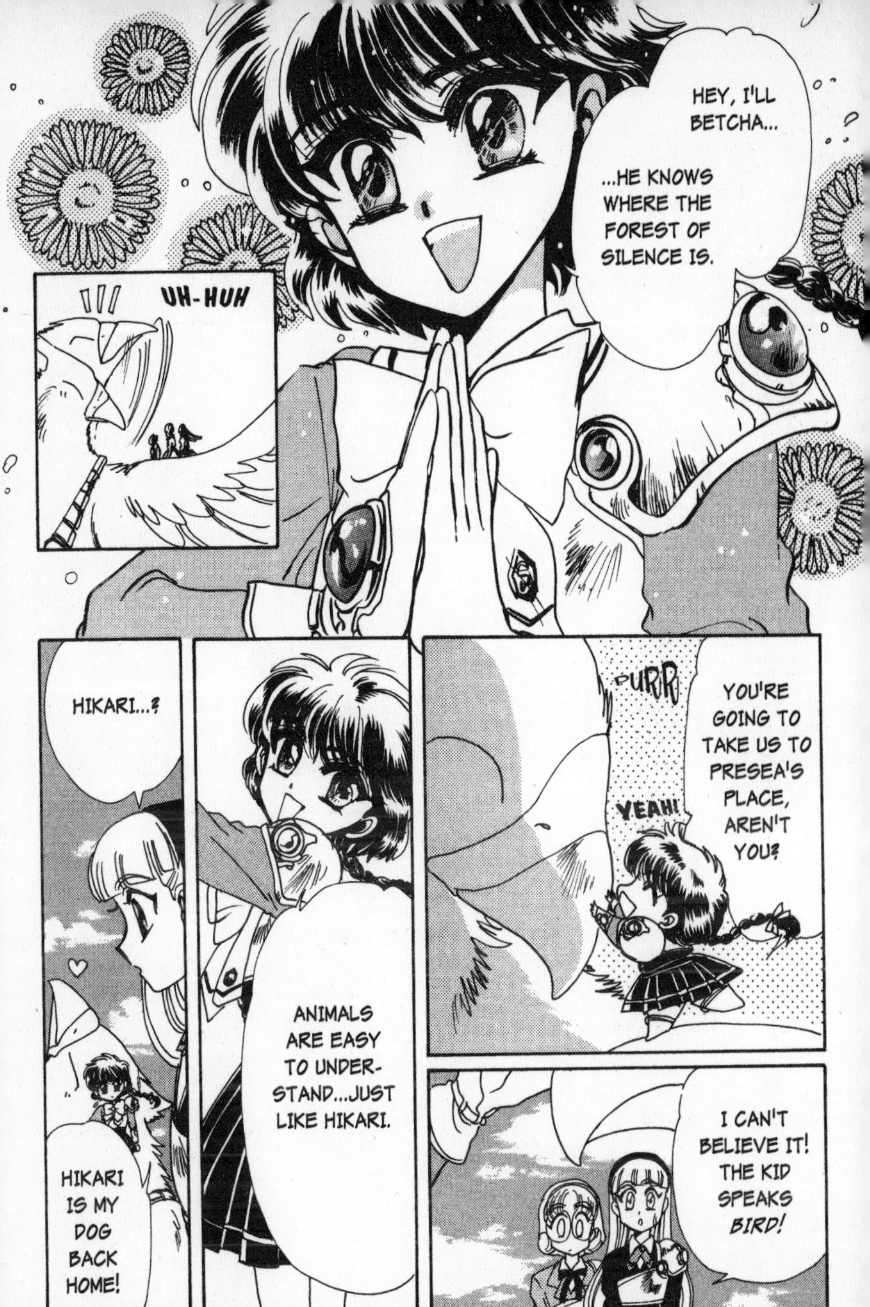
HEY, I'LL BETCHA...
...HE KNOWS WHERE THE FOREST OF SILENCE IS.
UH-HUH
YOU'RE GOING TO TAKE US TO PRESEA'S PLACE, AREN'T YOU?
PURR
YEAH!
I CAN'T BELIEVE IT! THE KID SPEAKS *BIRD*!
ANIMALS ARE EASY TO UNDER-STAND...JUST LIKE HIKARI.
HIKARI...?
HIKARI IS MY DOG BACK HOME!

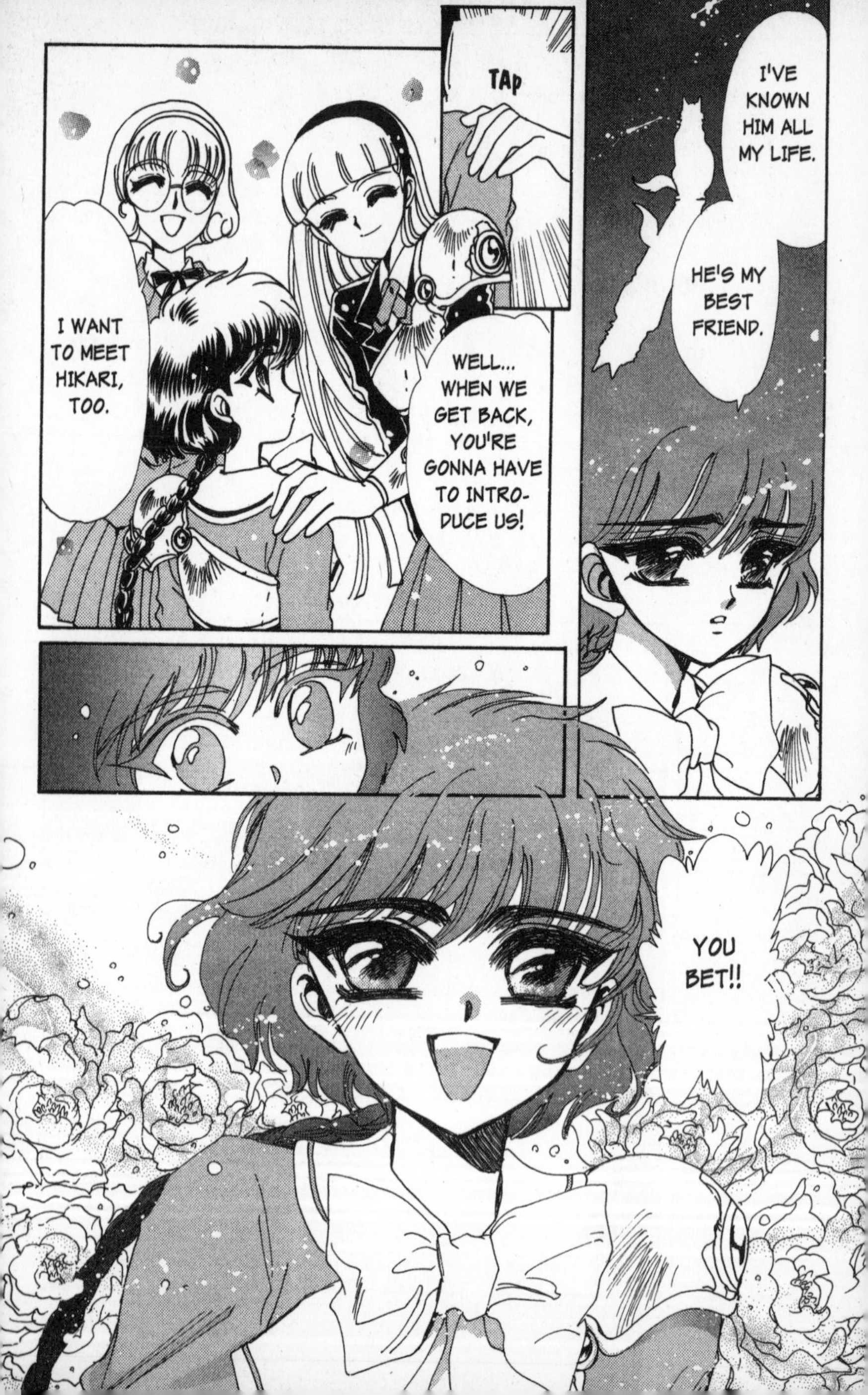
I'VE KNOWN HIM ALL MY LIFE.
HE'S MY BEST FRIEND.
TAP
WELL... WHEN WE GET BACK, YOU'RE GONNA HAVE TO INTRO-DUCE US!
I WANT TO MEET HIKARI, TOO.
YOU BET!!

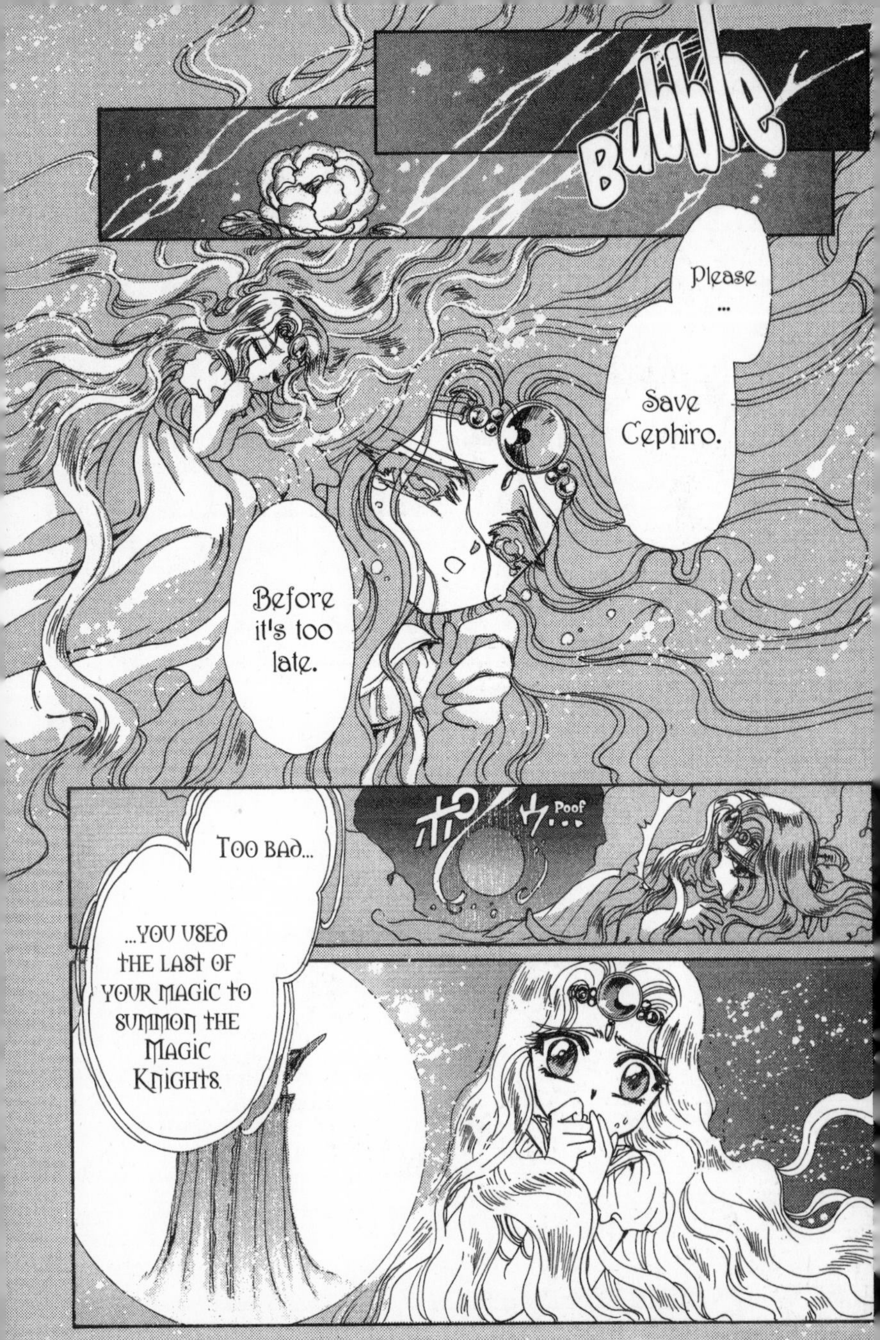
Bubble
Please ...
Save Cephiro.
Before it's too late.
Poof
TOO BAD...
...YOU USED THE LAST OF YOUR MAGIC TO SUMMON THE MAGIC KNIGHTS.

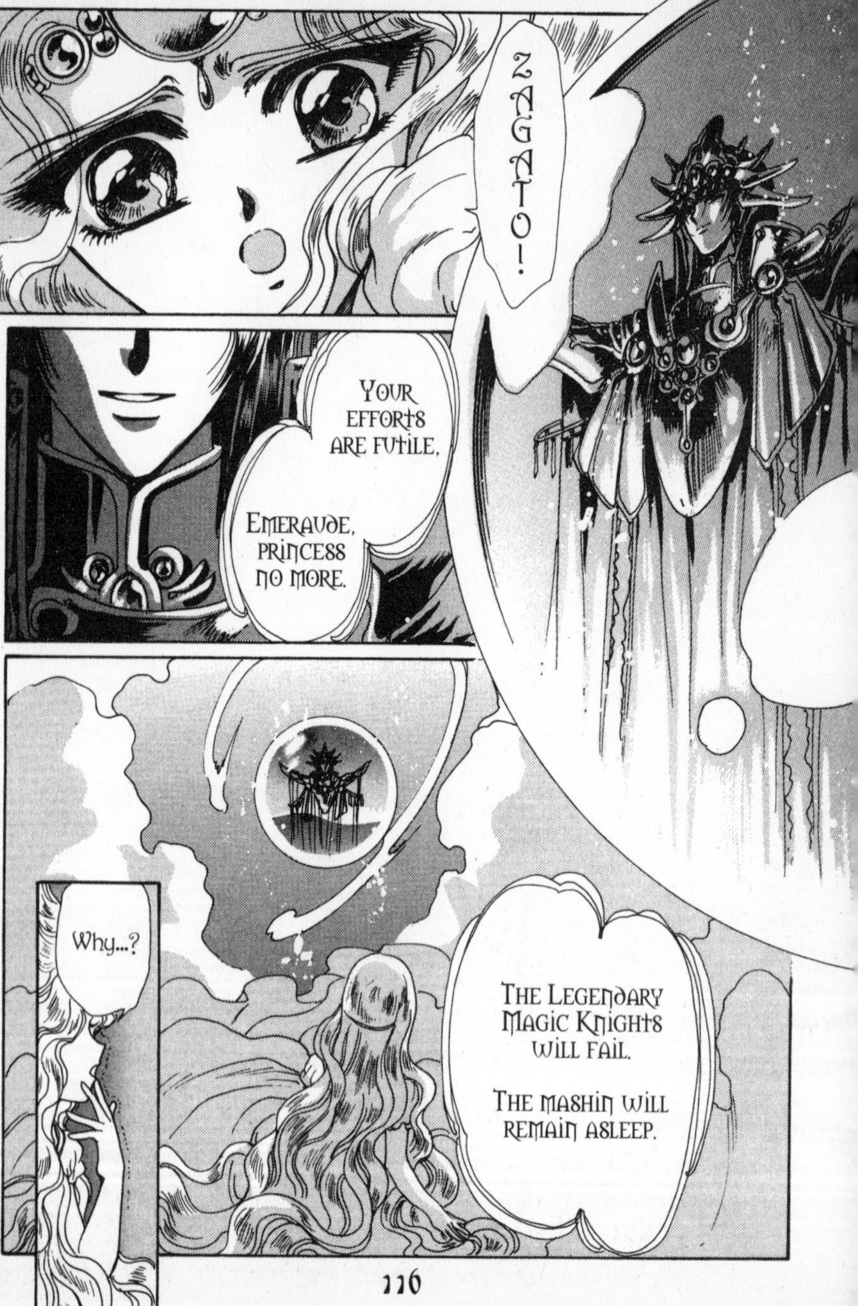
ZAGATO!
YOUR EFFORTS ARE FUTILE,
EMERAUDE, PRINCESS NO MORE.
THE LEGENDARY MAGIC KNIGHTS WILL FAIL.
THE MASHIN WILL REMAIN ASLEEP.
Why...?

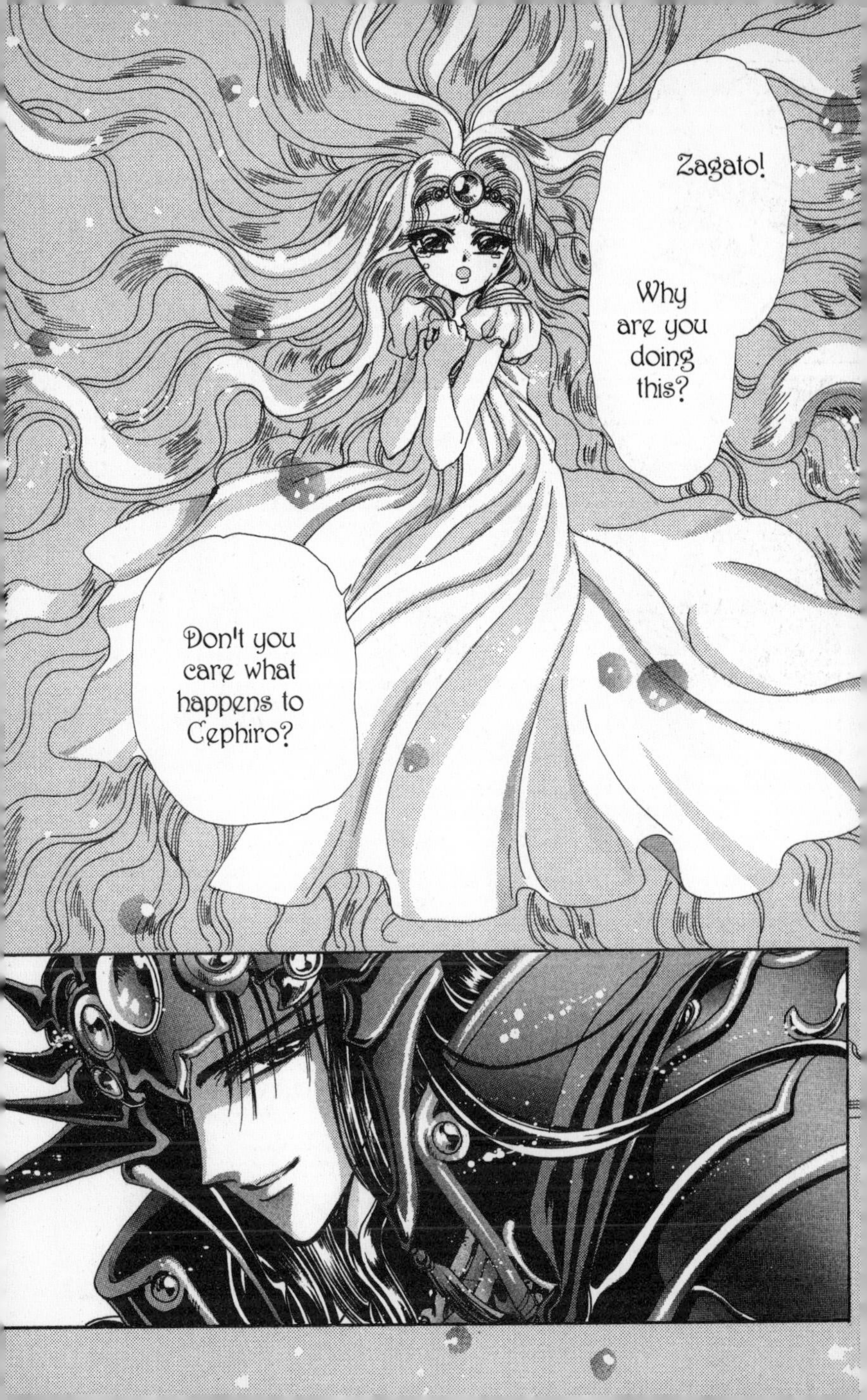
Zagato!
Why are you doing this?
Don't you care what happens to Cephiro?

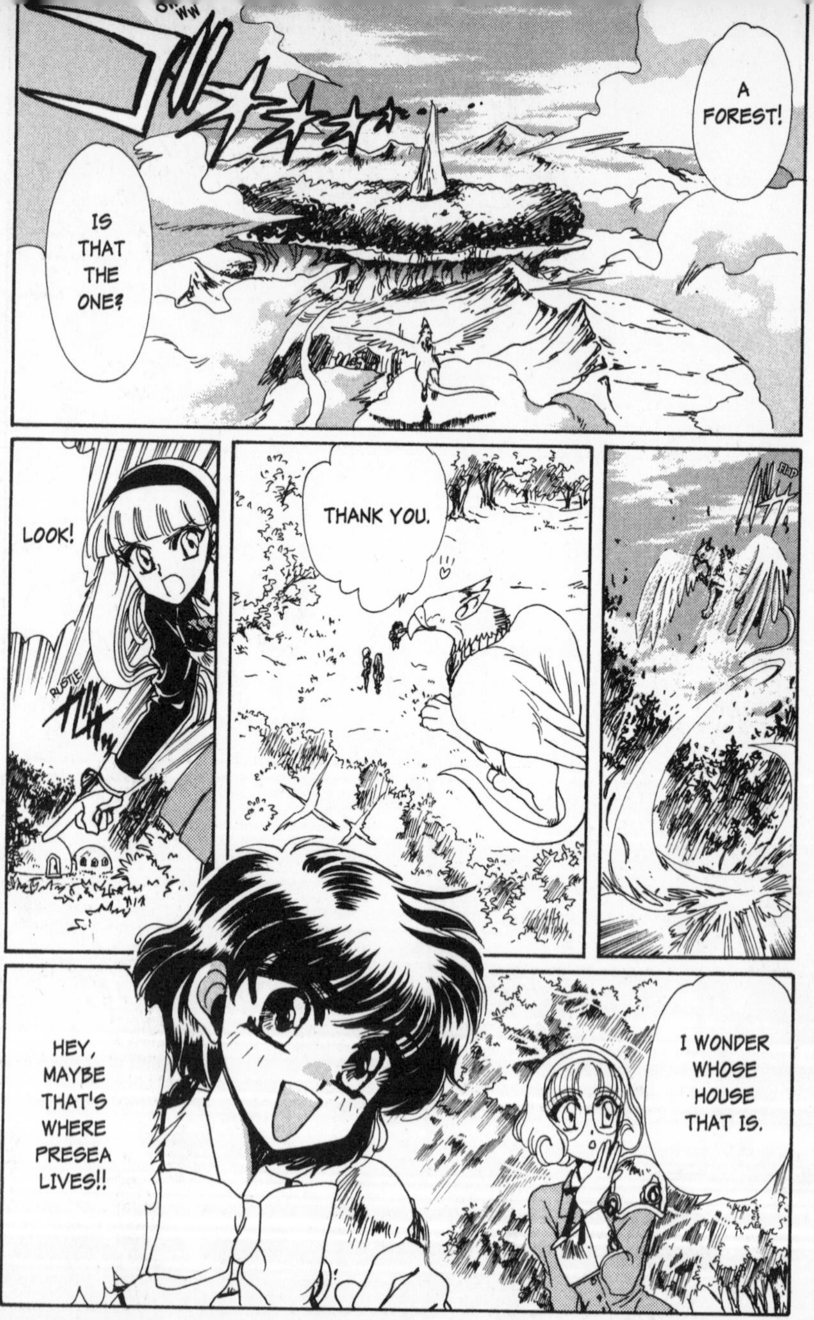
A FOREST!
IS THAT THE ONE?
Flap
THANK YOU.
LOOK!
RUSTLE
I WONDER WHOSE HOUSE THAT IS.
HEY, MAYBE THAT'S WHERE PRESEA LIVES!!

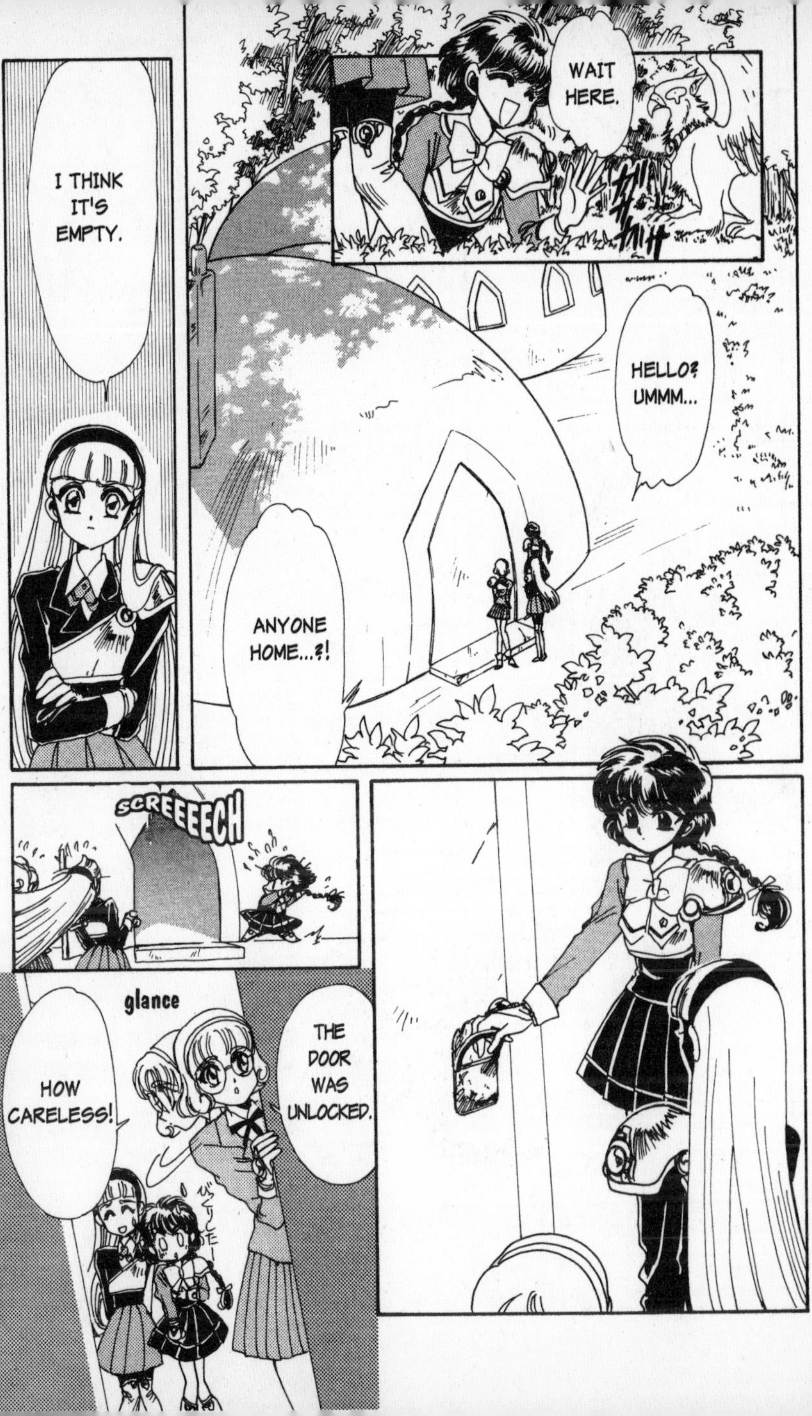
WAIT HERE.
HELLO? UMMM...
ANYONE HOME...?!
I THINK IT'S EMPTY.
SCREEEEECH
THE DOOR WAS UNLOCKED.
glance
HOW CARELESS!

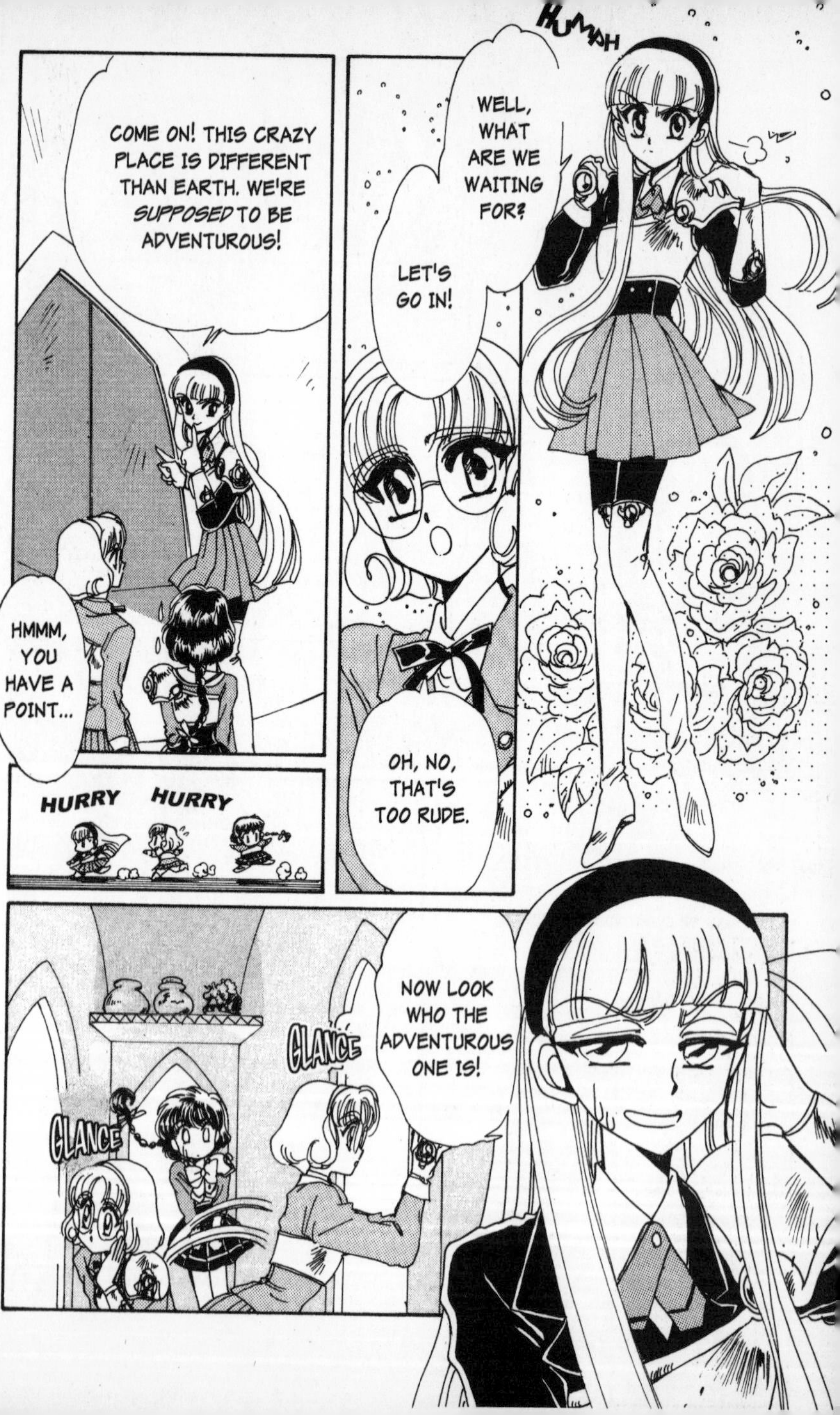
HUMPH
WELL, WHAT ARE WE WAITING FOR?
LET'S GO IN!
OH, NO, THAT'S TOO RUDE.
COME ON! THIS CRAZY PLACE IS DIFFERENT THAN EARTH. WE'RE *SUPPOSED* TO BE ADVENTUROUS!
HMMM, YOU HAVE A POINT...
HURRY HURRY
NOW LOOK WHO THE ADVENTUROUS ONE IS!
GLANCE
GLANCE

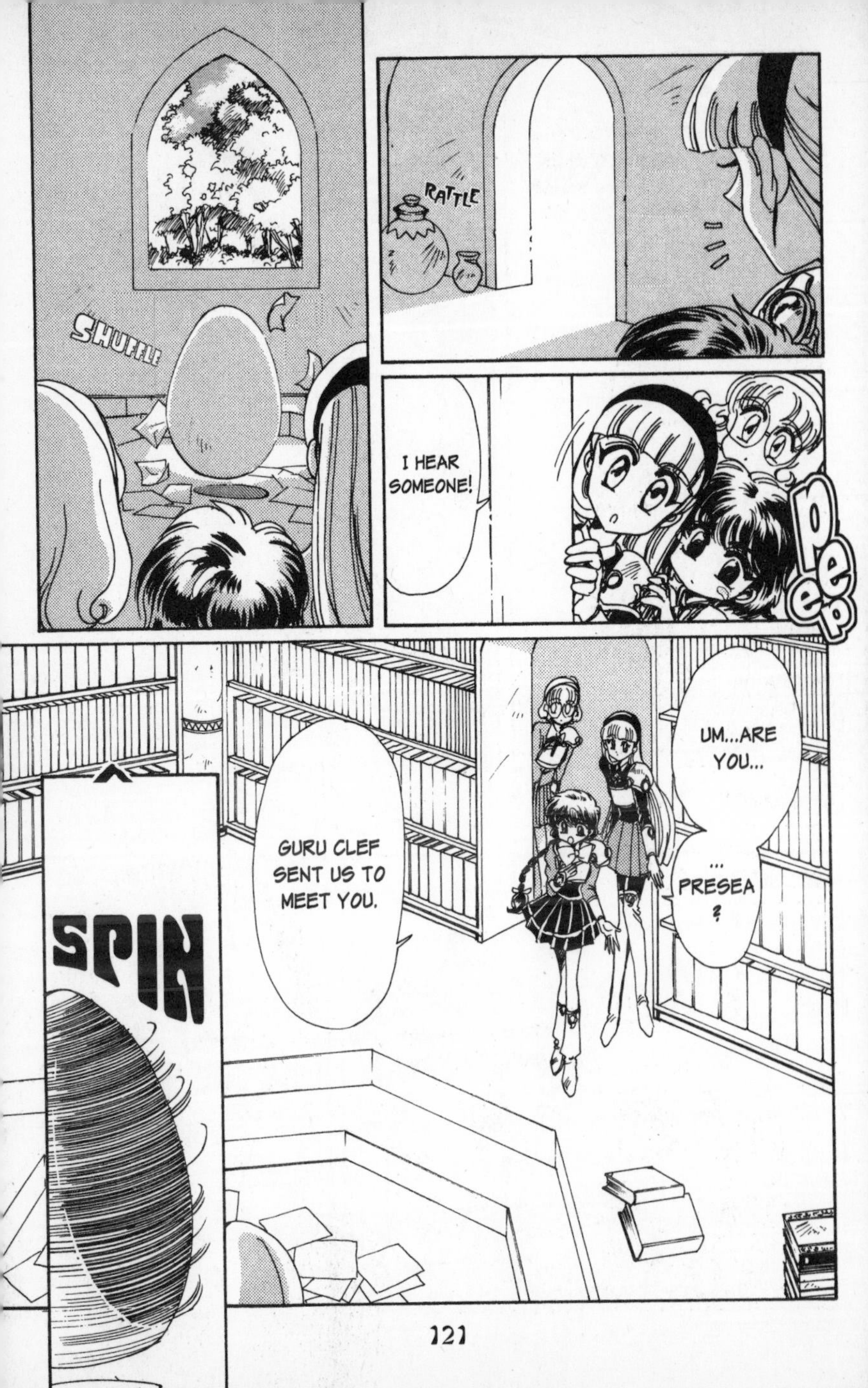
RATTLE
I HEAR SOMEONE!
peep
SHUFFLE
UM...ARE YOU...
... PRESEA?
GURU CLEF SENT US TO MEET YOU.
SPIN

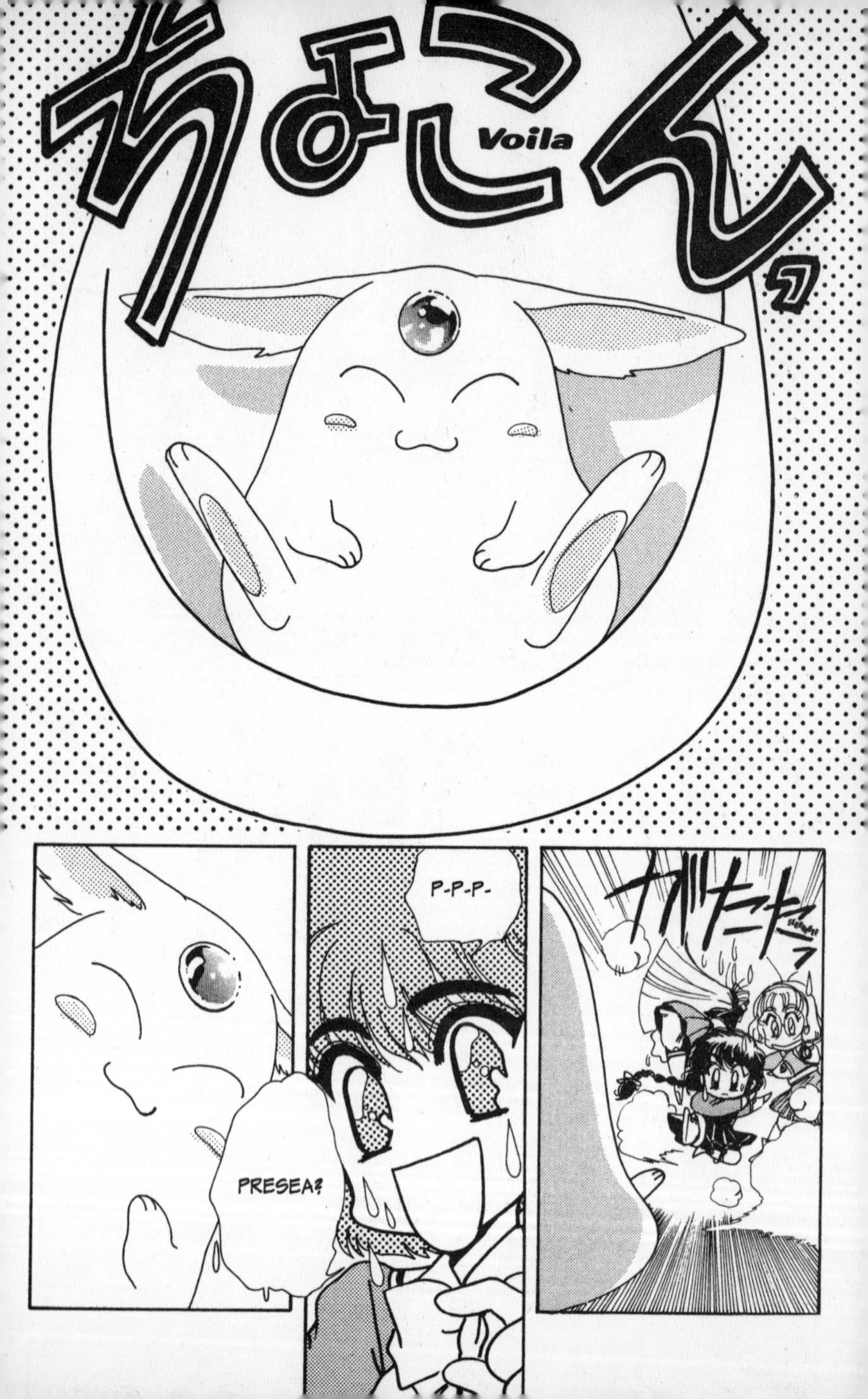

ちょこん
Voila
ガターッ
P-P-P-
PRESEA?

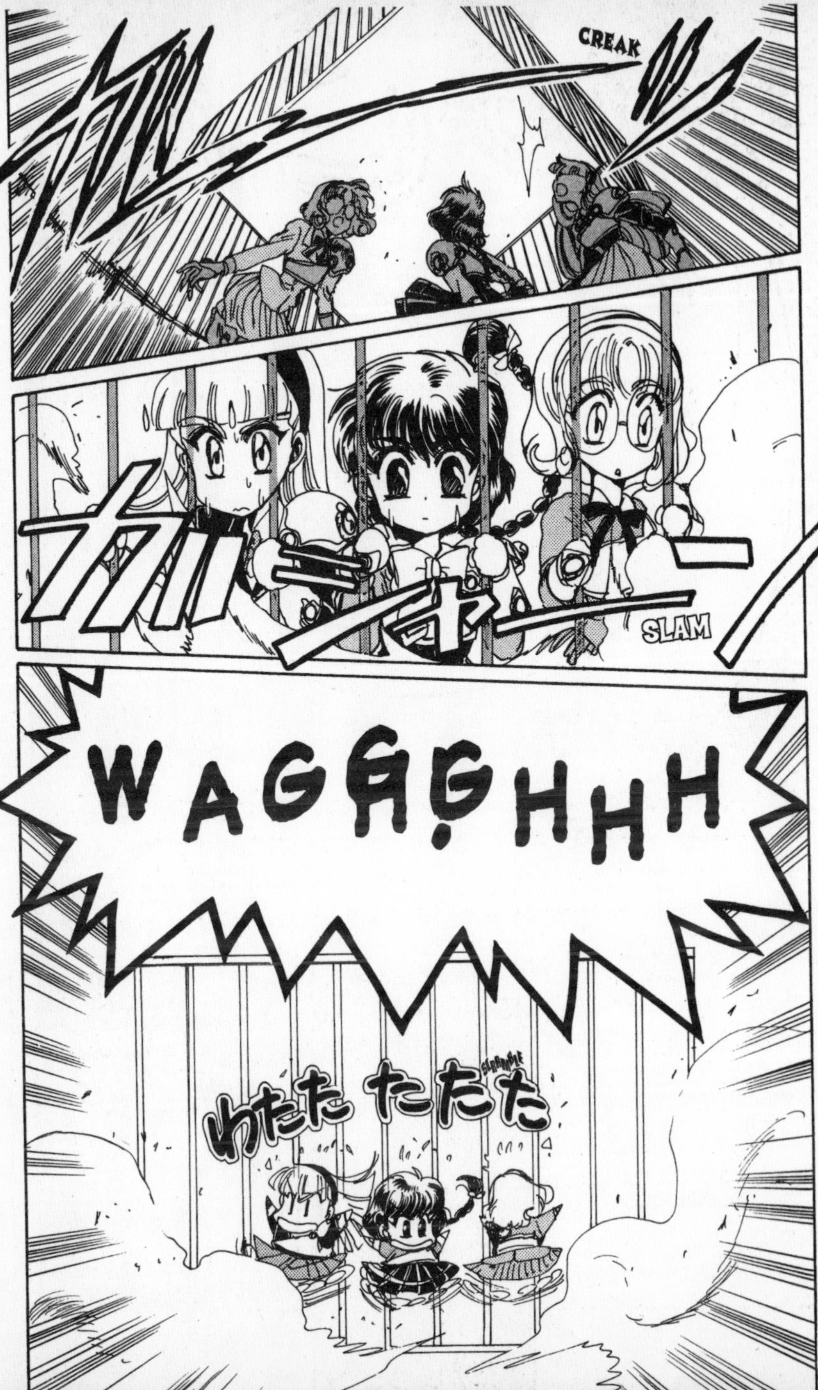
CREAK
SLAM
WAGAGHHH
SCRAMBLE

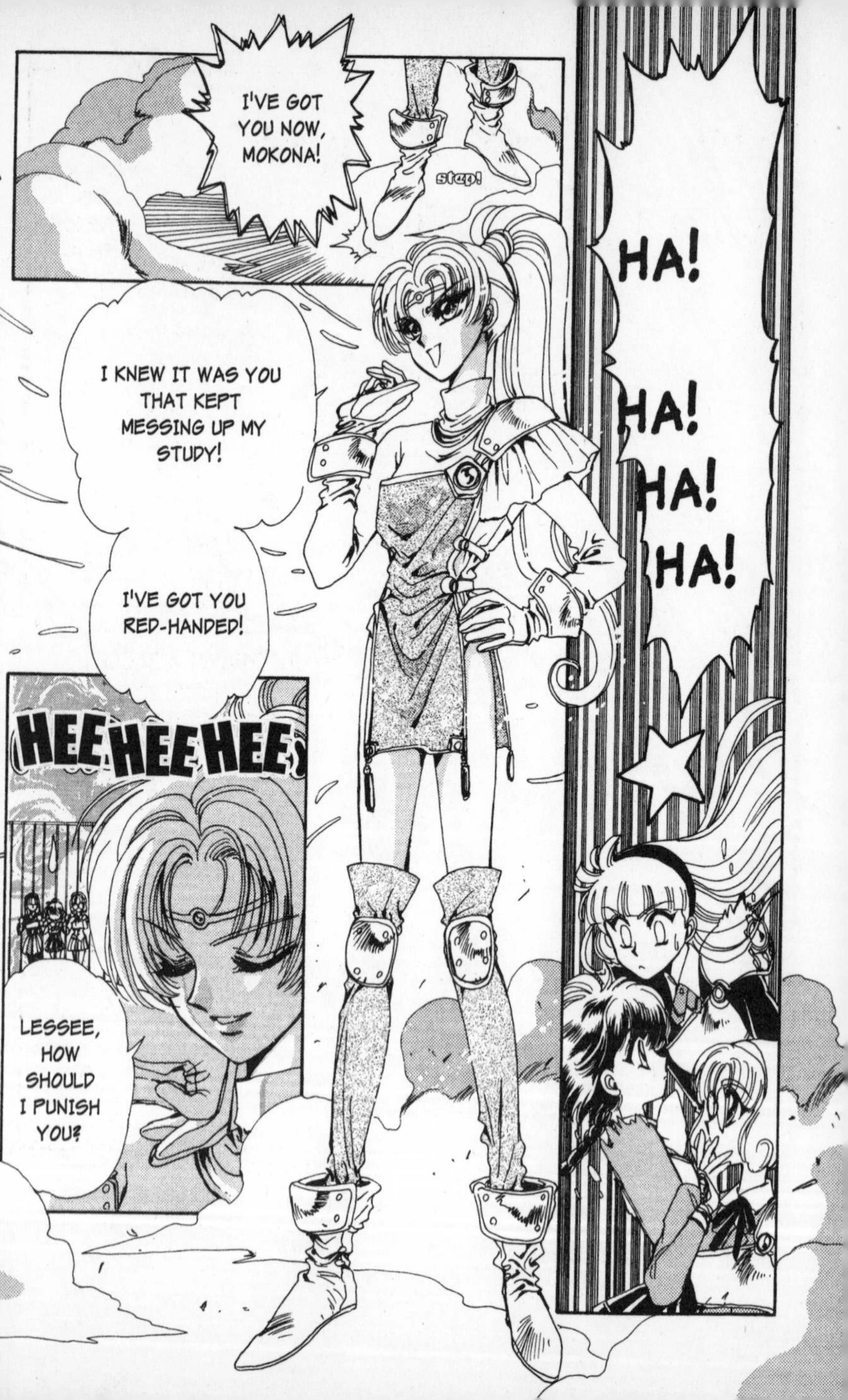
HA! HA! HA! HA!
I'VE GOT YOU NOW, MOKONA!
step!
I KNEW IT WAS YOU THAT KEPT MESSING UP MY STUDY!
I'VE GOT YOU RED-HANDED!
HEE HEE HEE
LESSEE, HOW SHOULD I PUNISH YOU?

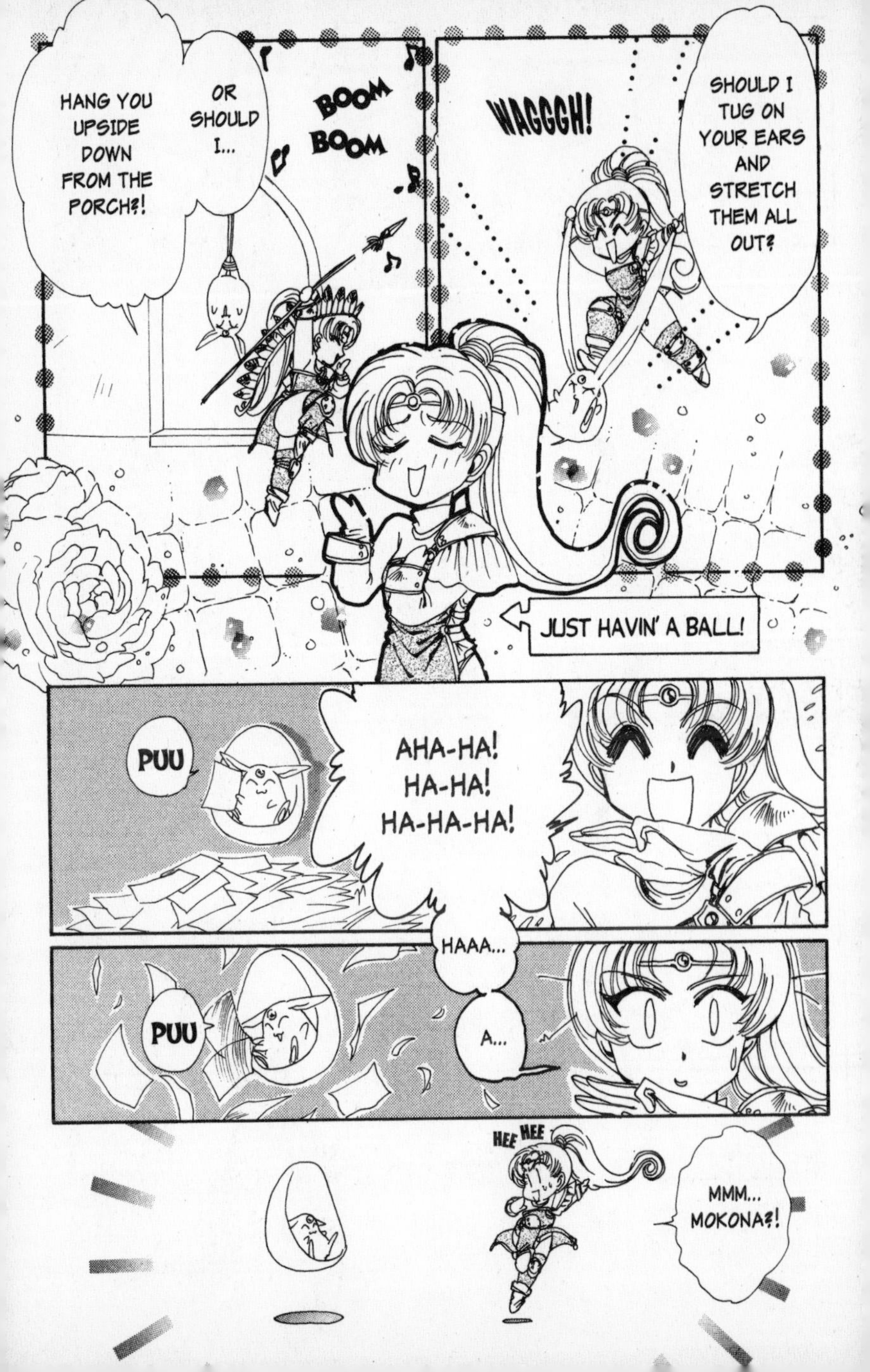
WAGGGH!
SHOULD I TUG ON YOUR EARS AND STRETCH THEM ALL OUT?
BOOM BOOM
OR SHOULD I...
HANG YOU UPSIDE DOWN FROM THE PORCH?!
JUST HAVIN' A BALL!
AHA-HA! HA-HA! HA-HA-HA!
PUU
HAAA...
A...
PUU
HEE HEE
MMM... MOKONA?!

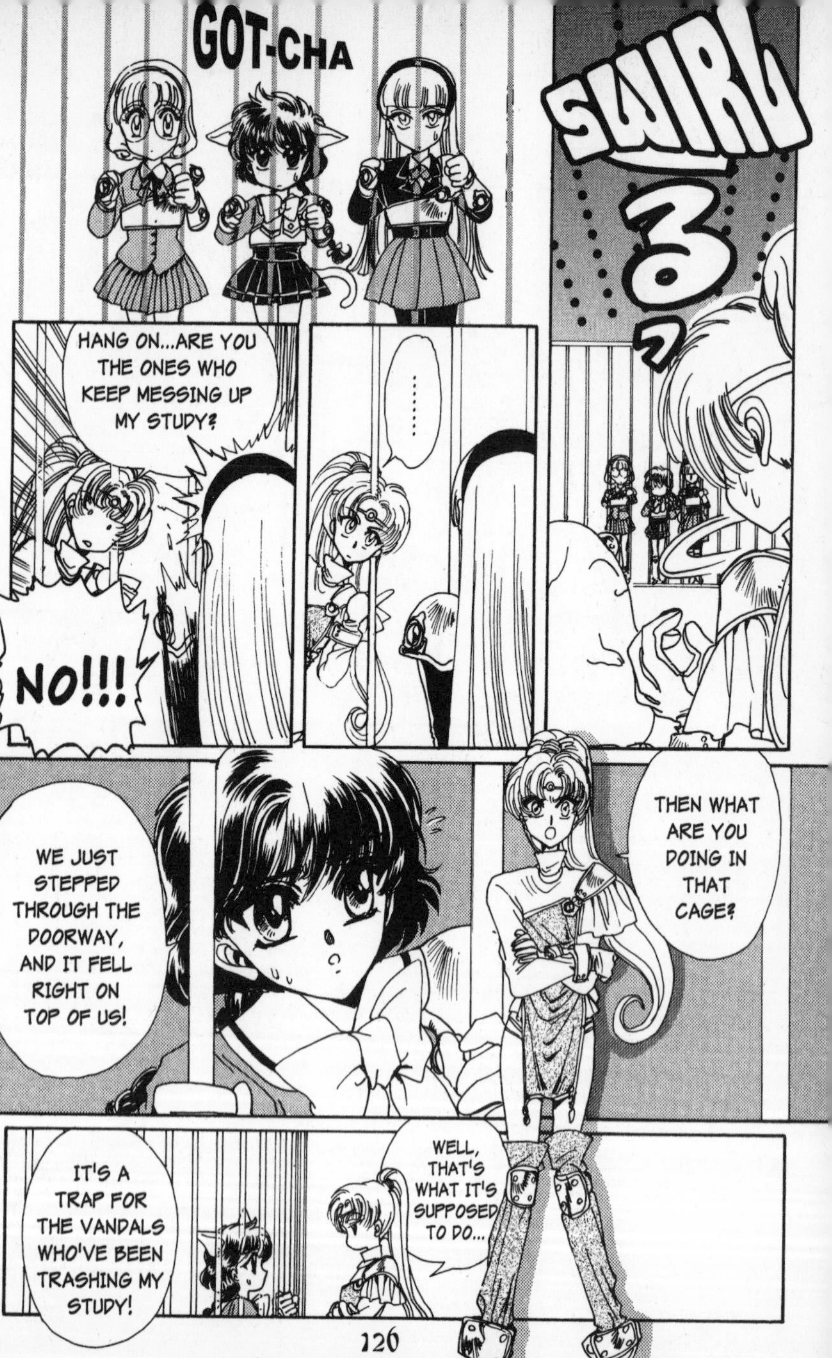
SWIRL
GOT-CHA
......
HANG ON...ARE YOU THE ONES WHO KEEP MESSING UP MY STUDY?
NO!!!
THEN WHAT ARE YOU DOING IN THAT CAGE?
WE JUST STEPPED THROUGH THE DOORWAY, AND IT FELL RIGHT ON TOP OF US!
WELL, THAT'S WHAT IT'S SUPPOSED TO DO...
IT'S A TRAP FOR THE VANDALS WHO'VE BEEN TRASHING MY STUDY!

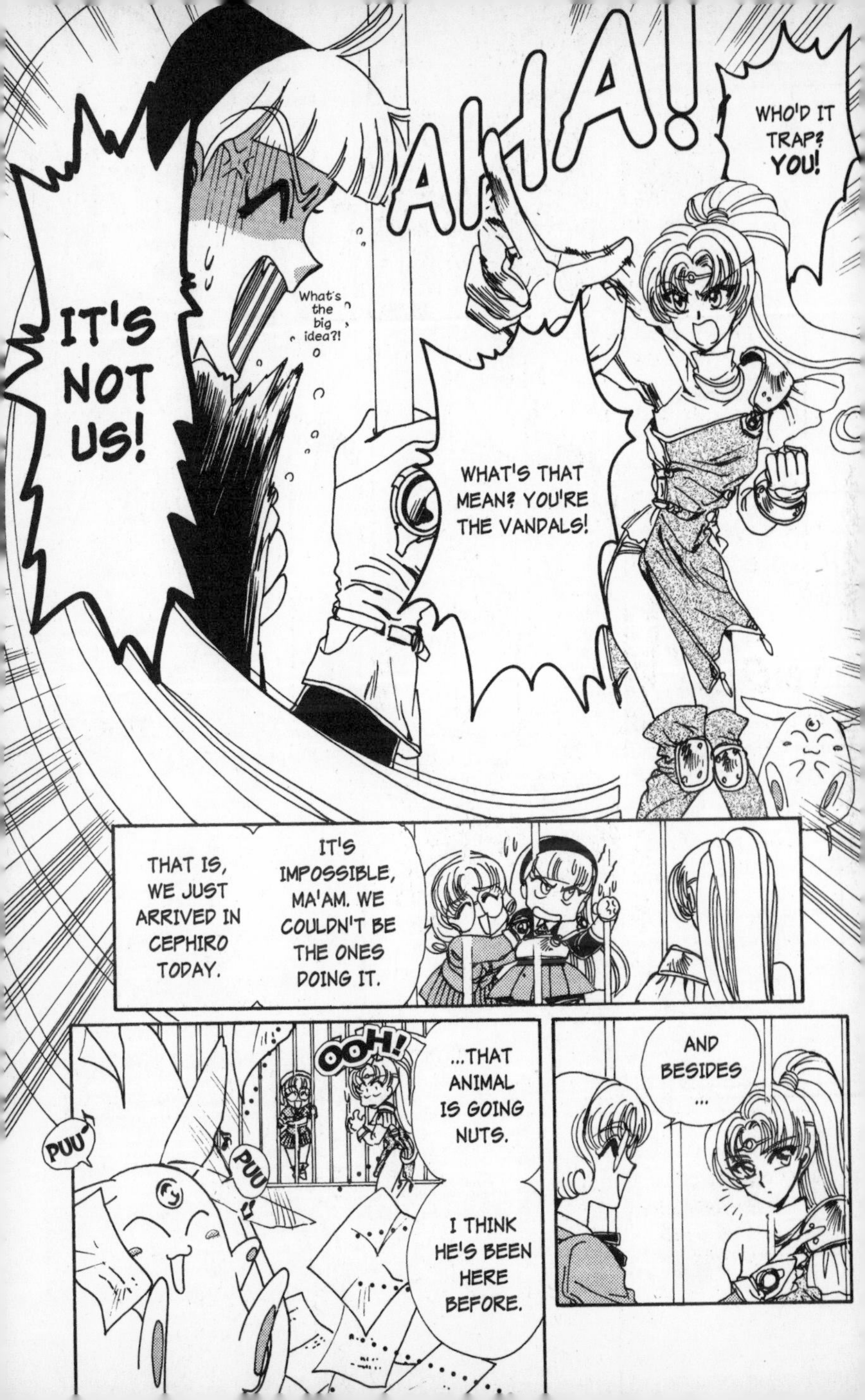
AHA!
WHO'D IT TRAP? YOU!
WHAT'S THAT MEAN? YOU'RE THE VANDALS!
What's the big idea?!
IT'S NOT US!
IT'S IMPOSSIBLE, MA'AM. WE COULDN'T BE THE ONES DOING IT.
THAT IS, WE JUST ARRIVED IN CEPHIRO TODAY.
AND BESIDES ...
...THAT ANIMAL IS GOING NUTS.
I THINK HE'S BEEN HERE BEFORE.
OOH!
PUU
PUU-

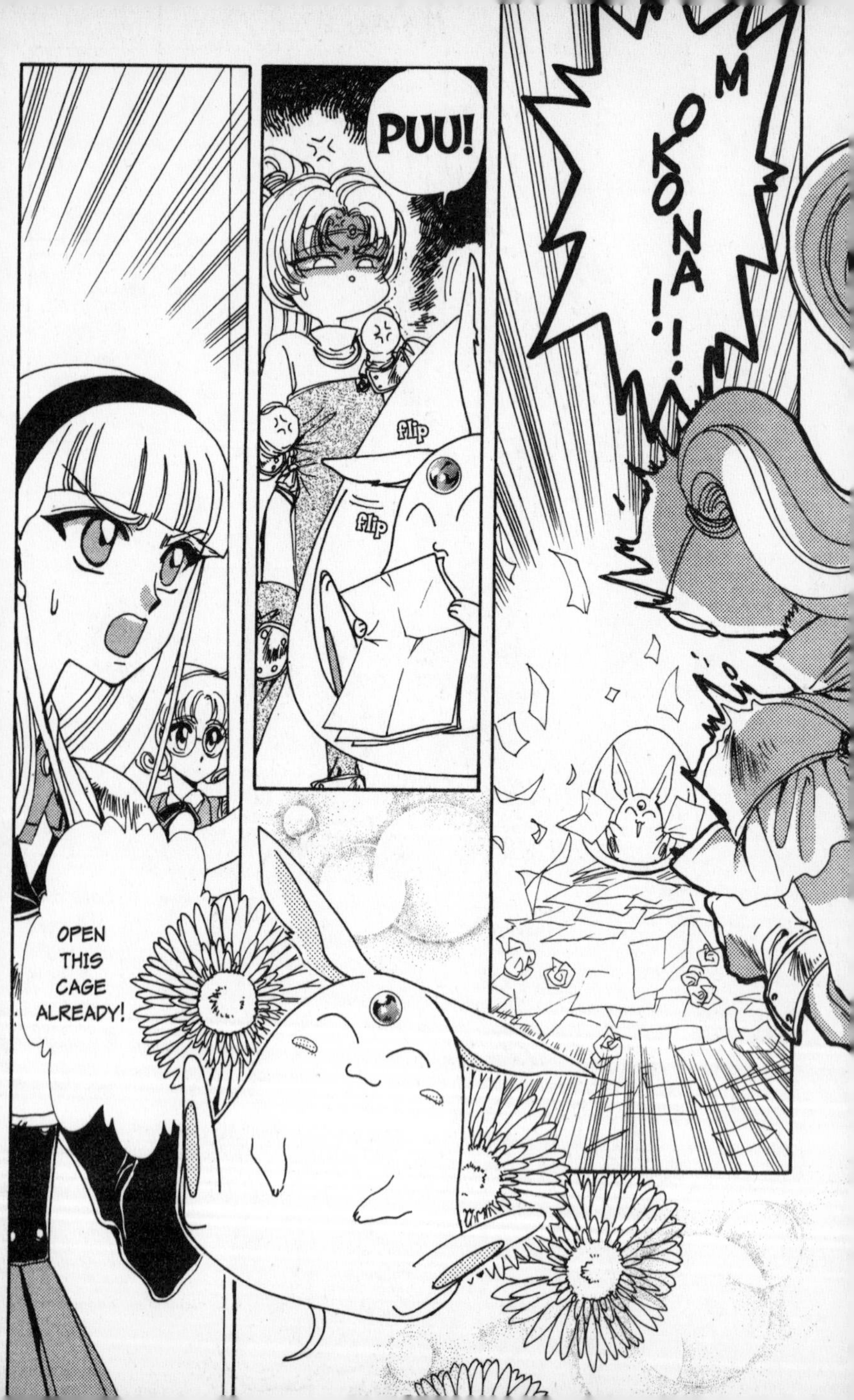
MOKONA!!
PUU!
flip
flip
OPEN THIS CAGE ALREADY!

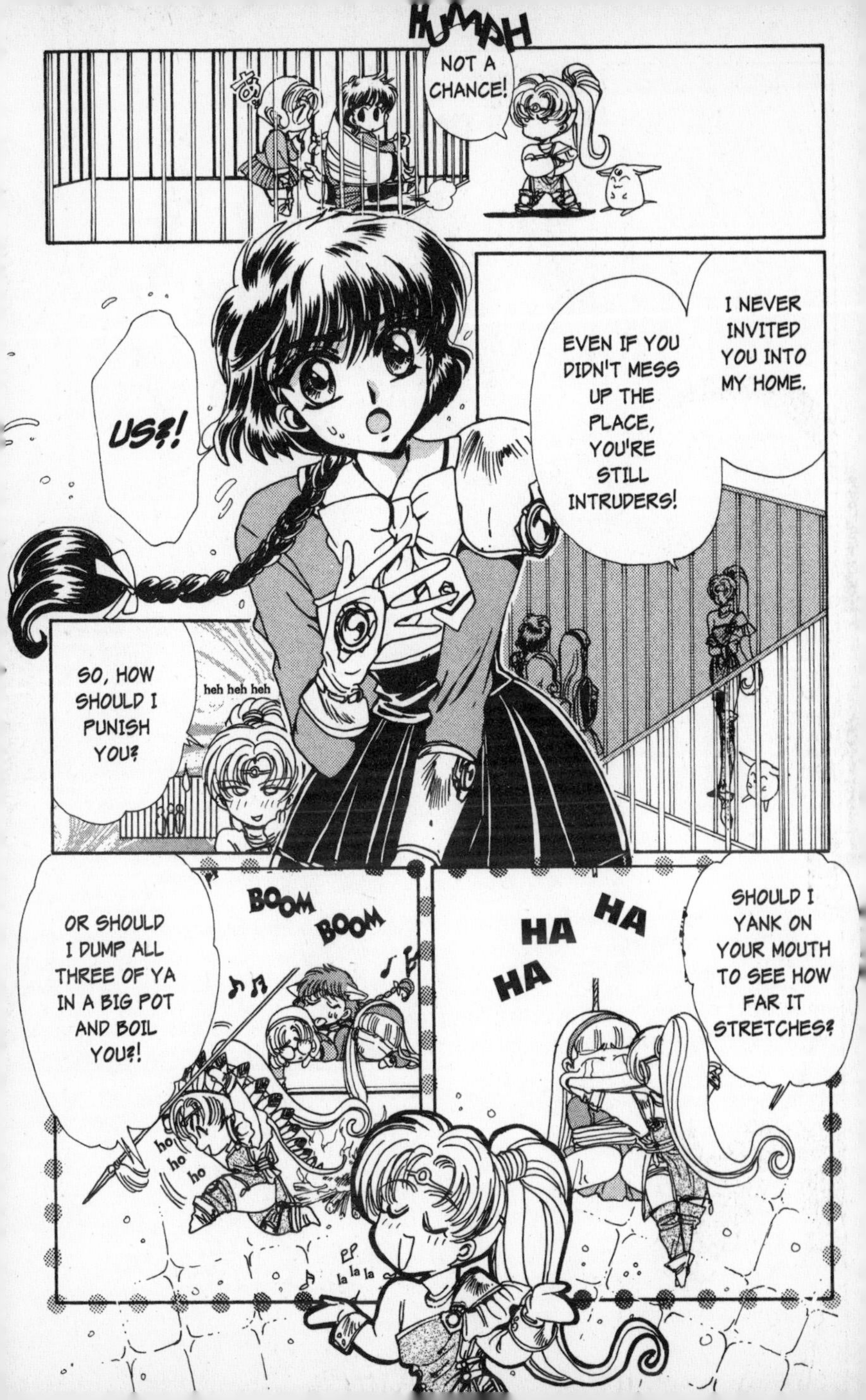
HUMPH
NOT A CHANCE!
I NEVER INVITED YOU INTO MY HOME.
EVEN IF YOU DIDN'T MESS UP THE PLACE, YOU'RE STILL INTRUDERS!
US?!
SO, HOW SHOULD I PUNISH YOU?
heh heh heh
SHOULD I YANK ON YOUR MOUTH TO SEE HOW FAR IT STRETCHES?
HA HA HA
OR SHOULD I DUMP ALL THREE OF YA IN A BIG POT AND BOIL YOU?!
BOOM BOOM
ho ho ho
la la la

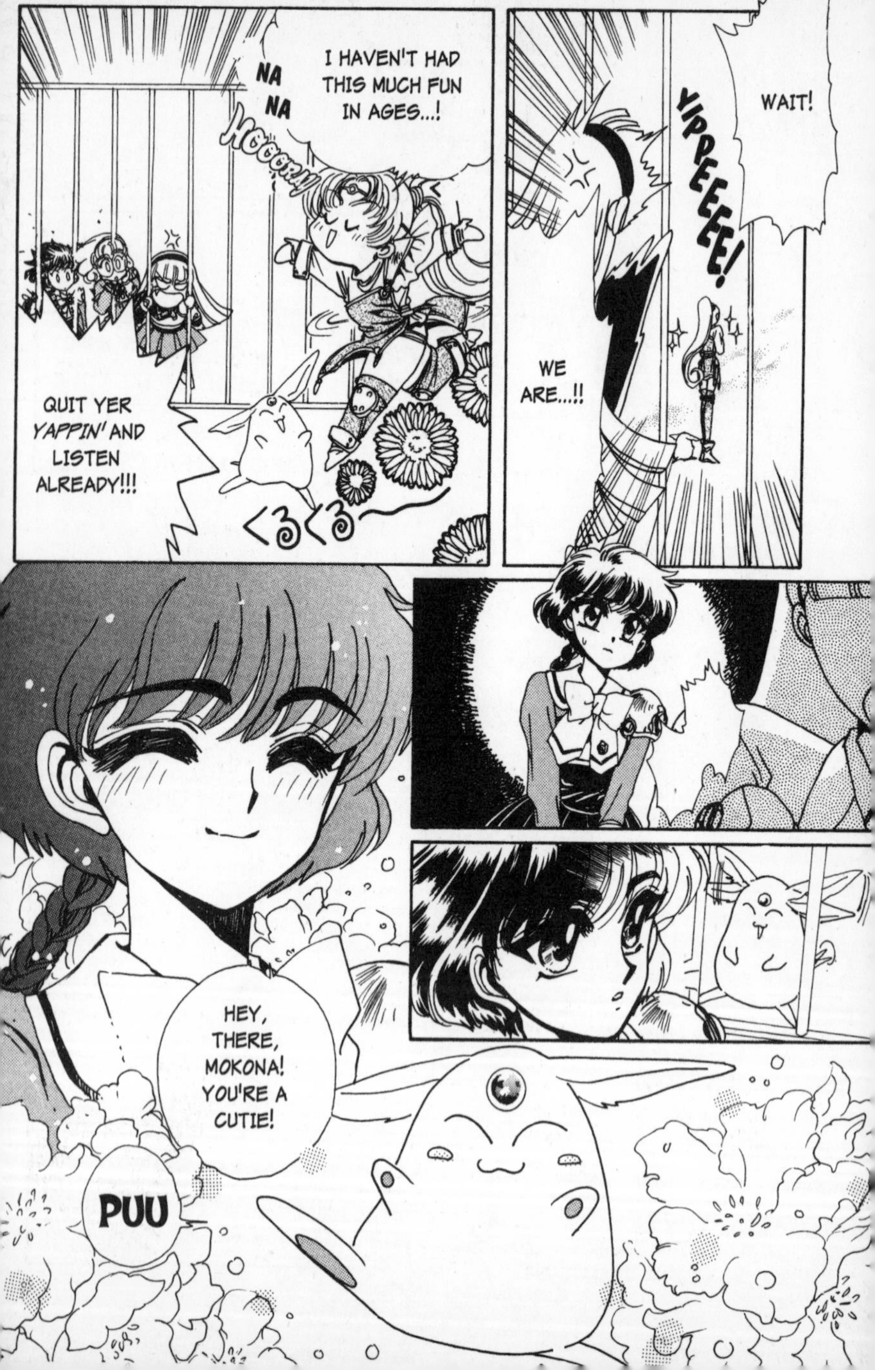
WAIT!
YIPPEEEE!
WE ARE...!!
I HAVEN'T HAD THIS MUCH FUN IN AGES...!
NA NA
QUIT YER *YAPPIN'* AND LISTEN ALREADY!!!
くるくる
HEY, THERE, MOKONA! YOU'RE A CUTIE!
PUU

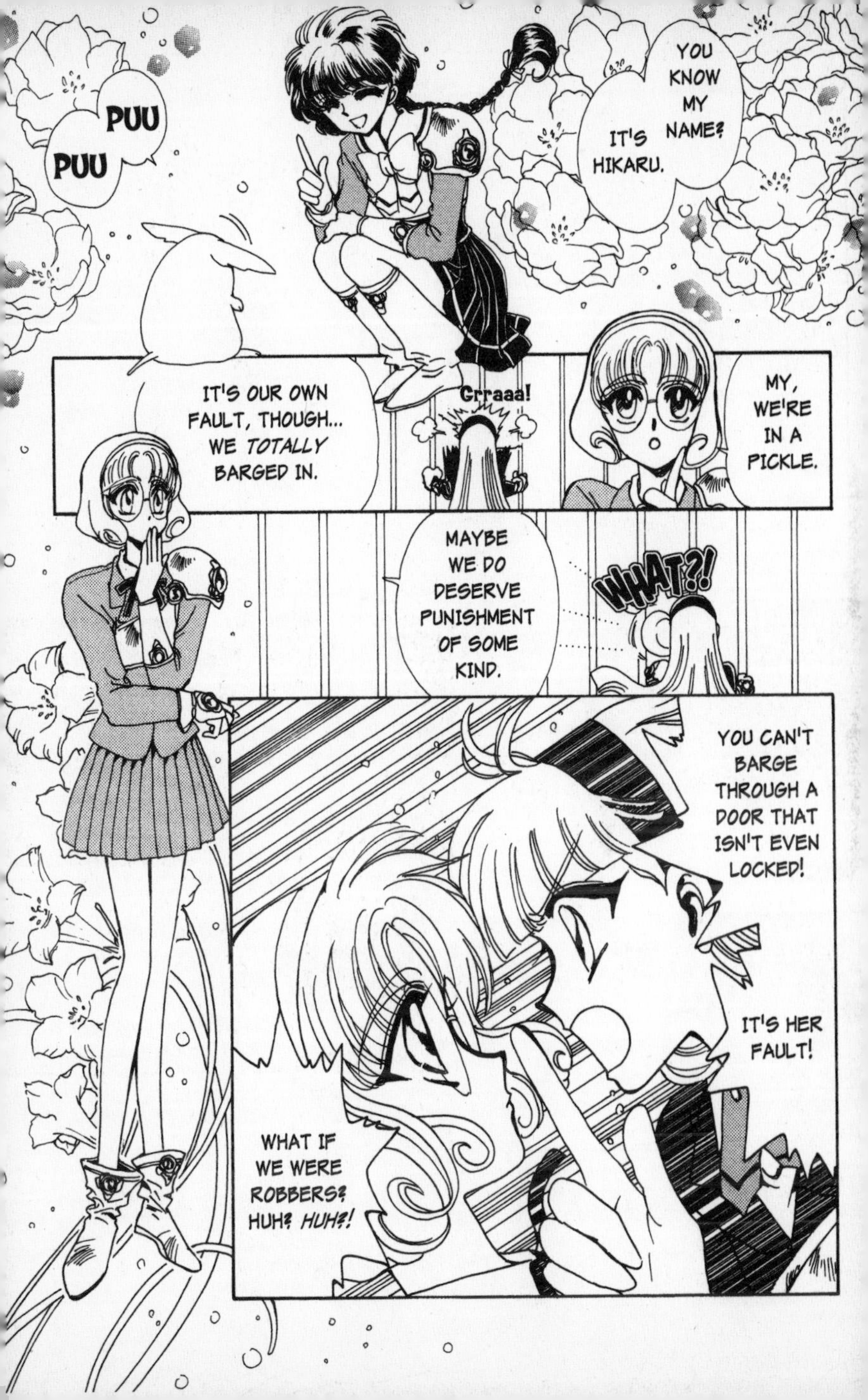
YOU KNOW MY NAME?
IT'S HIKARU.
PUU
PUU
MY, WE'RE IN A PICKLE.
Grraaa!
IT'S OUR OWN FAULT, THOUGH... WE *TOTALLY* BARGED IN.
WHAT?!
MAYBE WE DO DESERVE PUNISHMENT OF SOME KIND.
YOU CAN'T BARGE THROUGH A DOOR THAT ISN'T EVEN LOCKED!
IT'S HER FAULT!
WHAT IF WE WERE ROBBERS? HUH? *HUH?!*

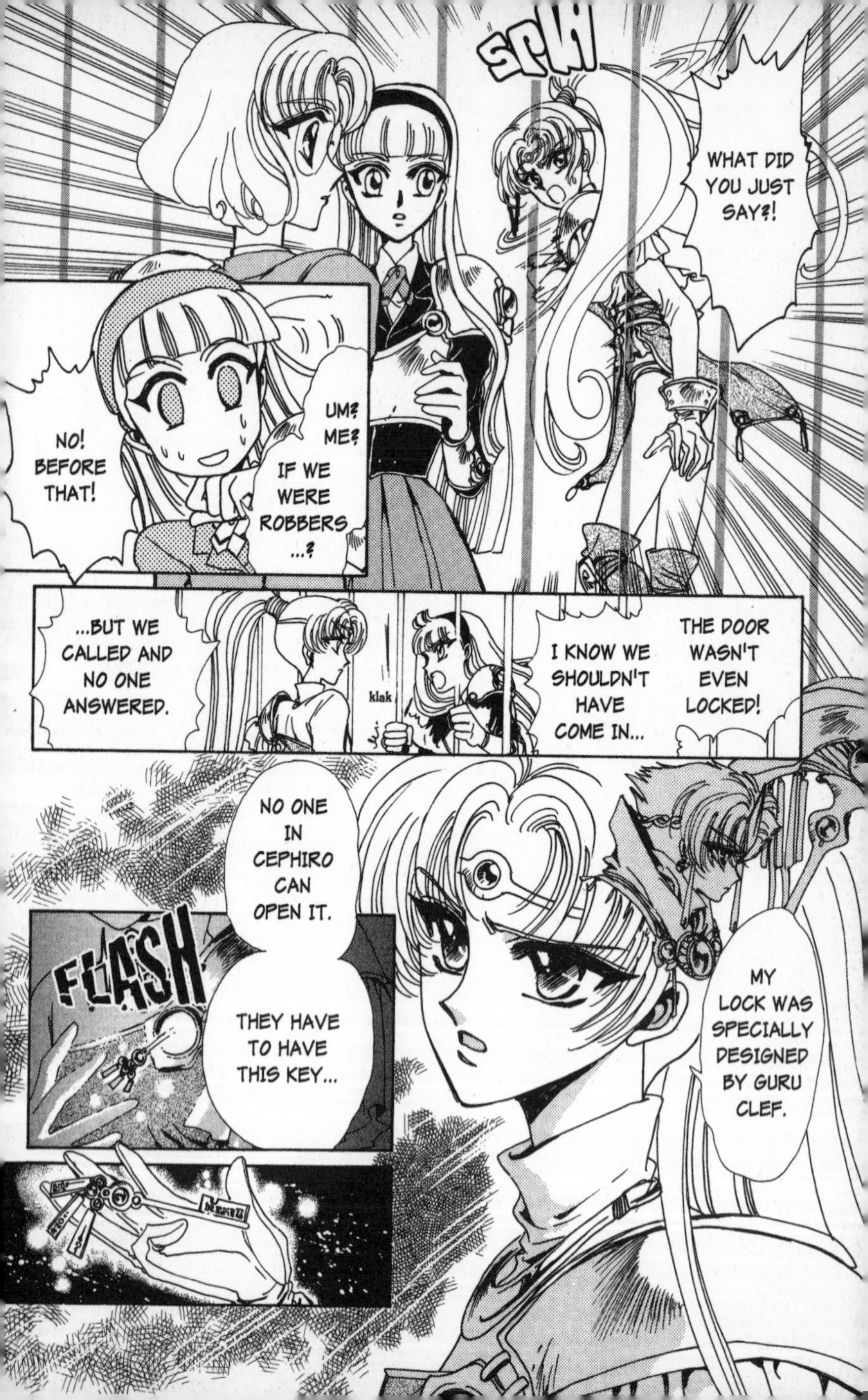
WHAT DID YOU JUST SAY?!
UM? ME?
IF WE WERE ROBBERS ...?
NO! BEFORE THAT!
THE DOOR WASN'T EVEN LOCKED!
I KNOW WE SHOULDN'T HAVE COME IN...
klak
...BUT WE CALLED AND NO ONE ANSWERED.
MY LOCK WAS SPECIALLY DESIGNED BY GURU CLEF.
NO ONE IN CEPHIRO CAN OPEN IT.
THEY HAVE TO HAVE THIS KEY...
FLASH

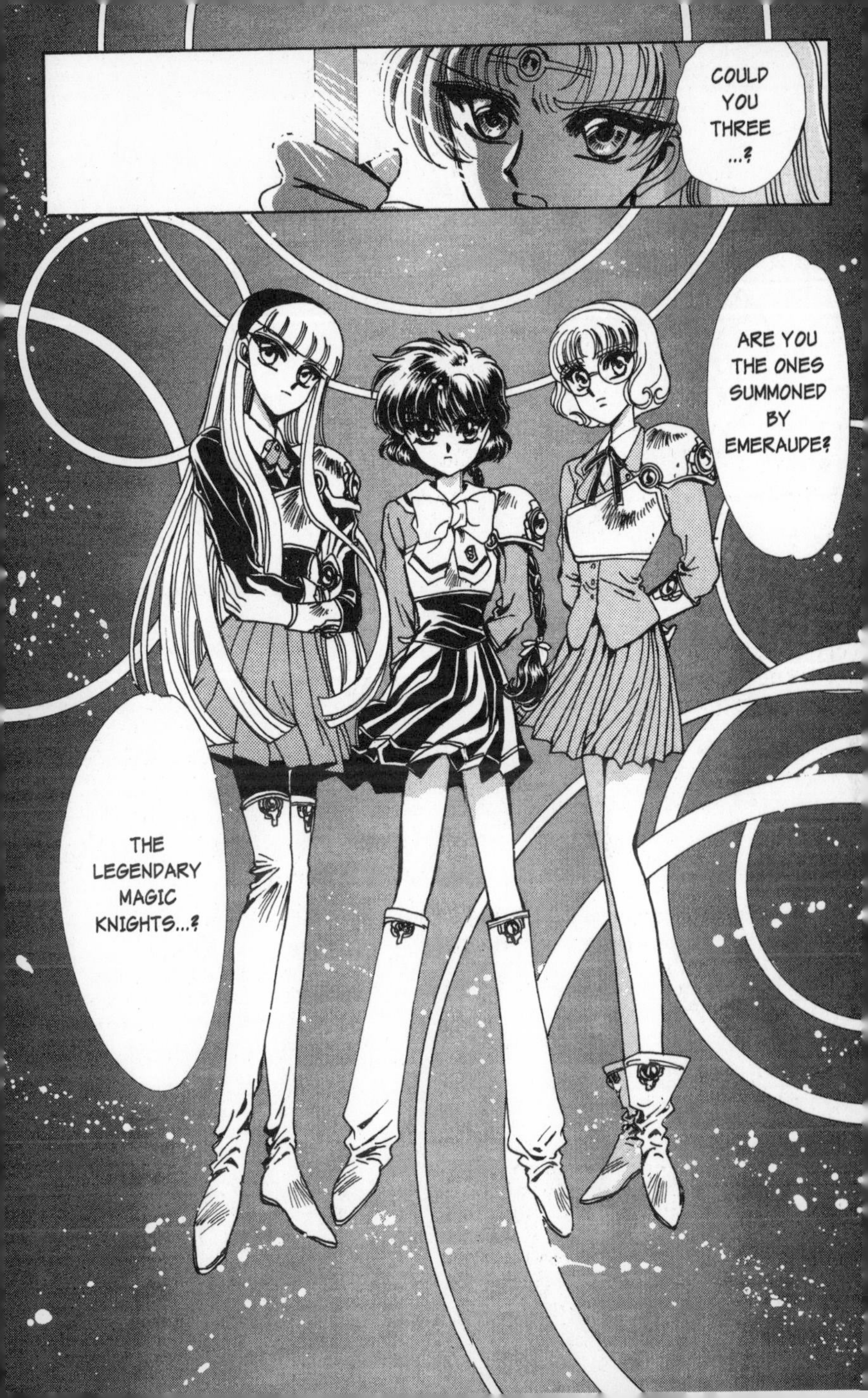
COULD YOU THREE ...?
ARE YOU THE ONES SUMMONED BY EMERAUDE?
THE LEGENDARY MAGIC KNIGHTS...?

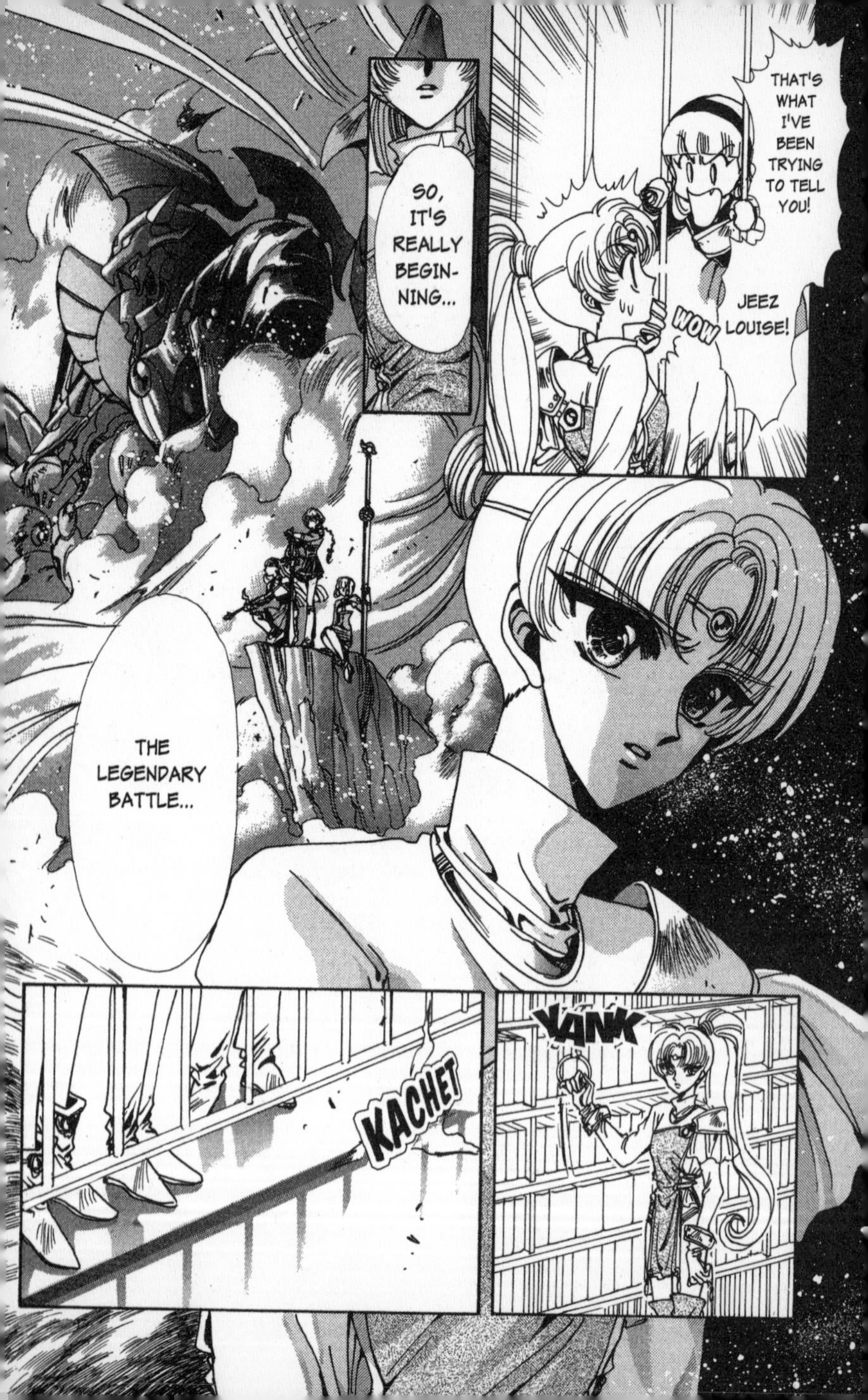
THAT'S WHAT I'VE BEEN TRYING TO TELL YOU!
JEEZ LOUISE!
WOW
SO, IT'S REALLY BEGIN-NING...
THE LEGENDARY BATTLE...
YANK
KACHET

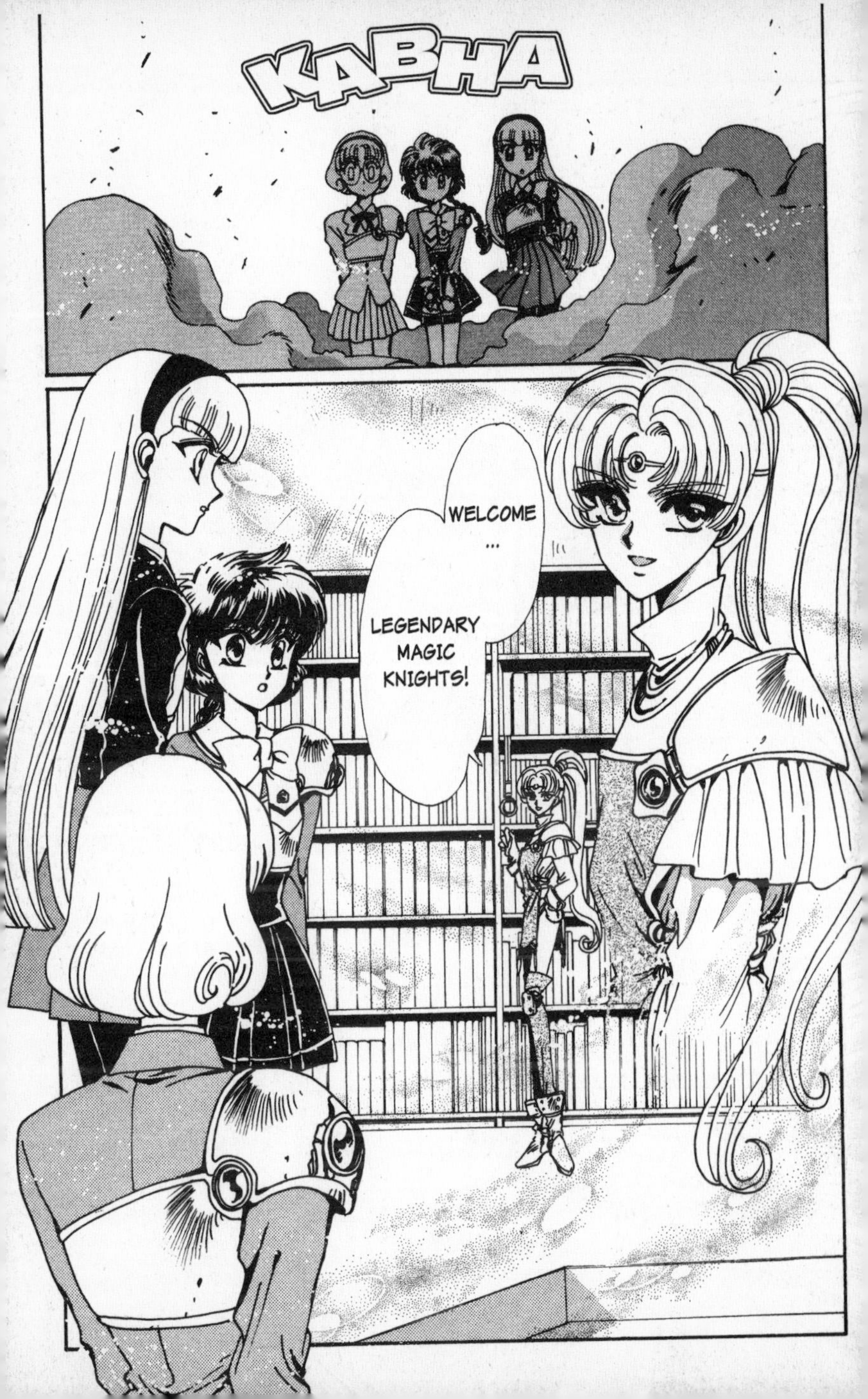
KABHA
WELCOME ...
LEGENDARY MAGIC KNIGHTS!

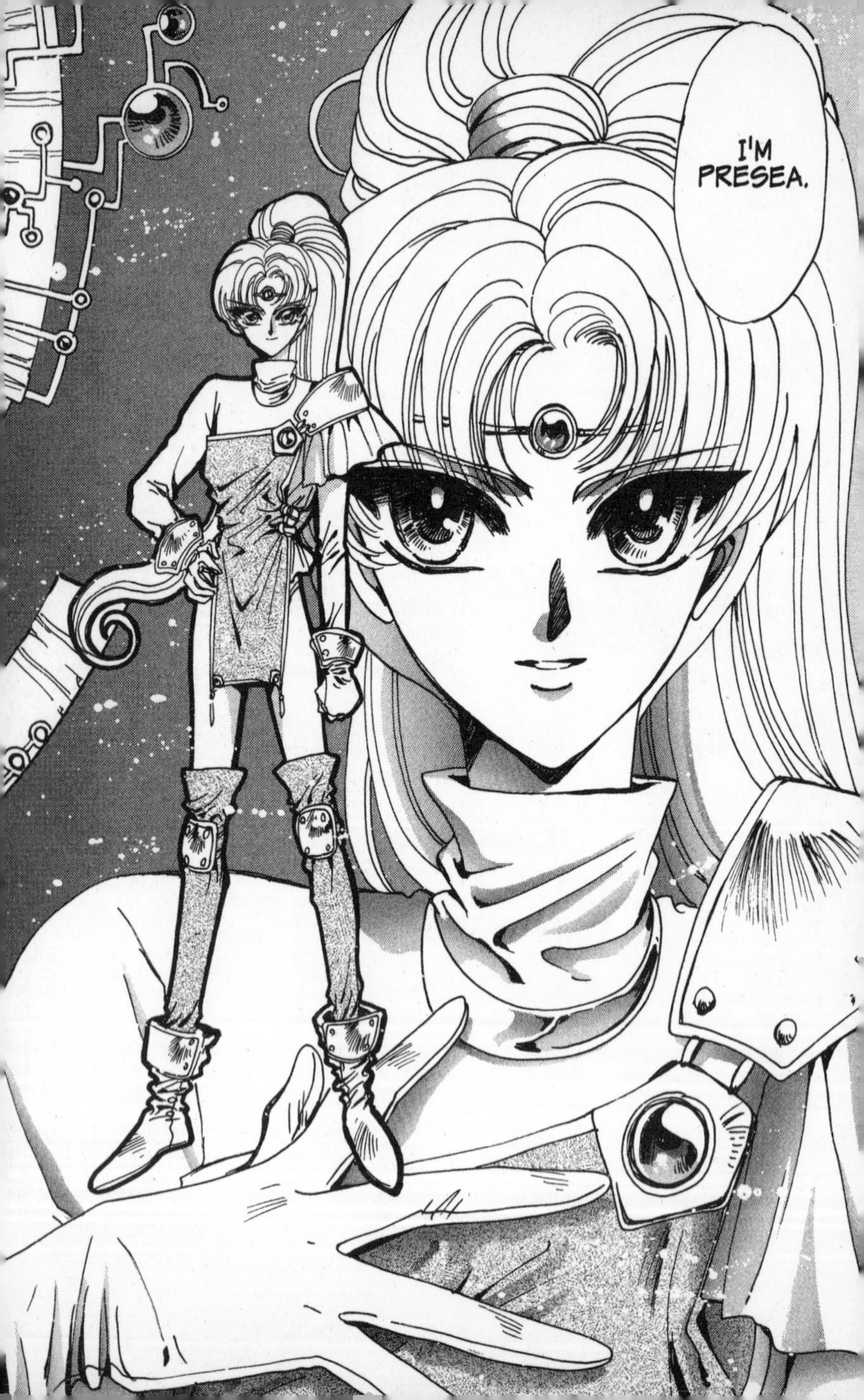
I'M PRESEA.

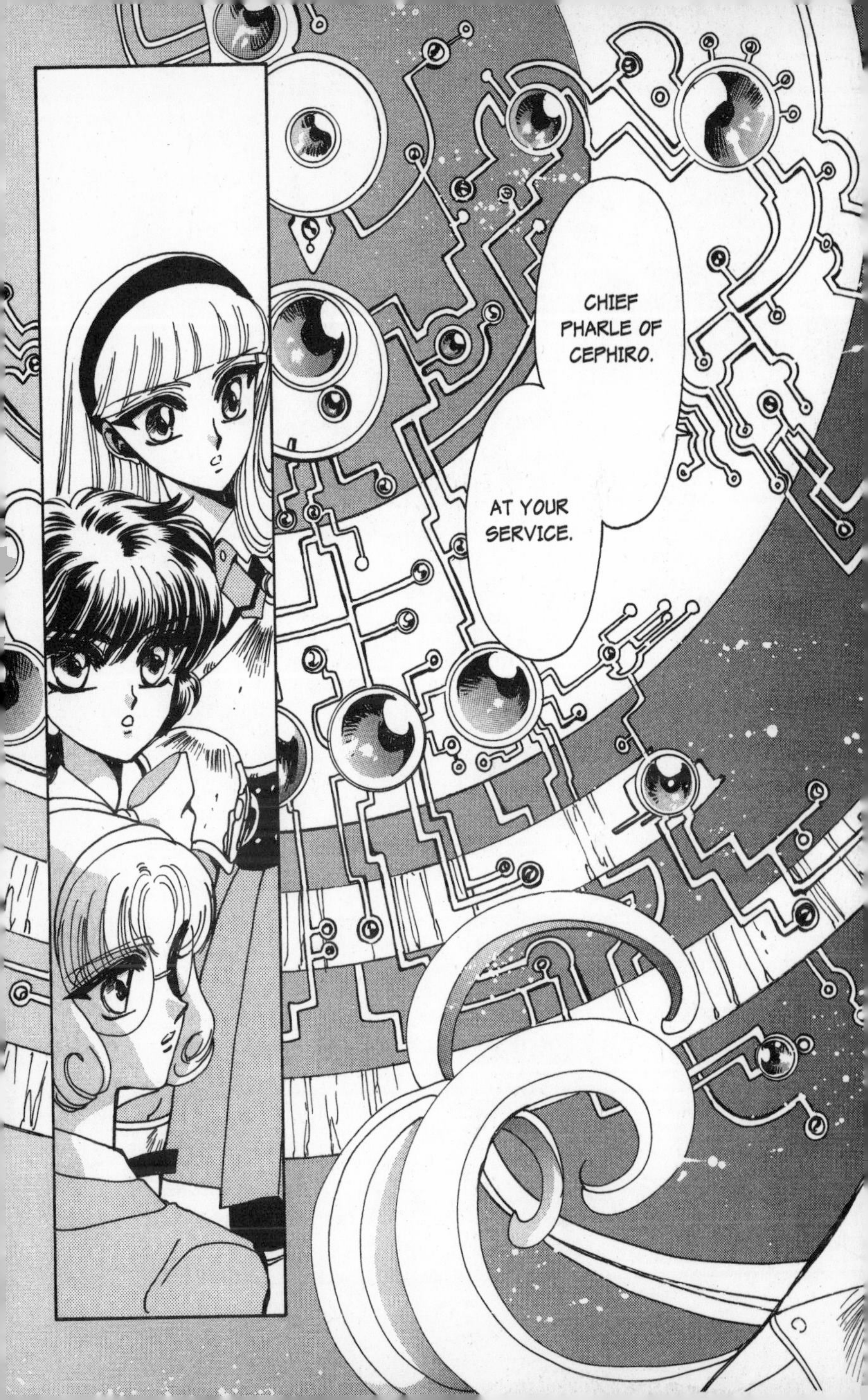
CHIEF PHARLE OF CEPHIRO.
AT YOUR SERVICE.

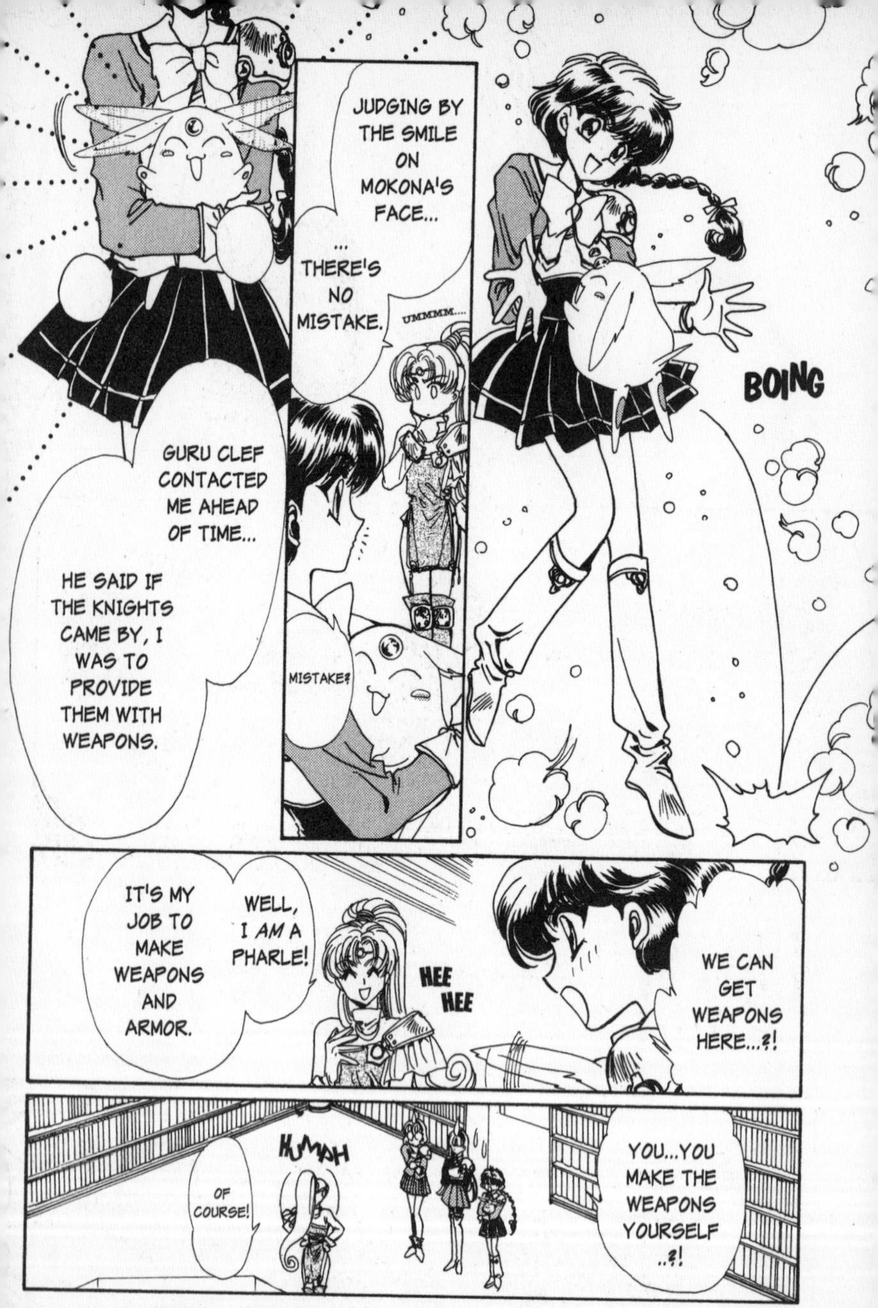
BOING
JUDGING BY THE SMILE ON MOKONA'S FACE...
... THERE'S NO MISTAKE.
UMMMM....
MISTAKE?
GURU CLEF CONTACTED ME AHEAD OF TIME...
HE SAID IF THE KNIGHTS CAME BY, I WAS TO PROVIDE THEM WITH WEAPONS.
WE CAN GET WEAPONS HERE...?!
HEE HEE
WELL, I *AM* A PHARLE!
IT'S MY JOB TO MAKE WEAPONS AND ARMOR.
YOU...YOU MAKE THE WEAPONS YOURSELF ..?!
HUMPH
OF COURSE!

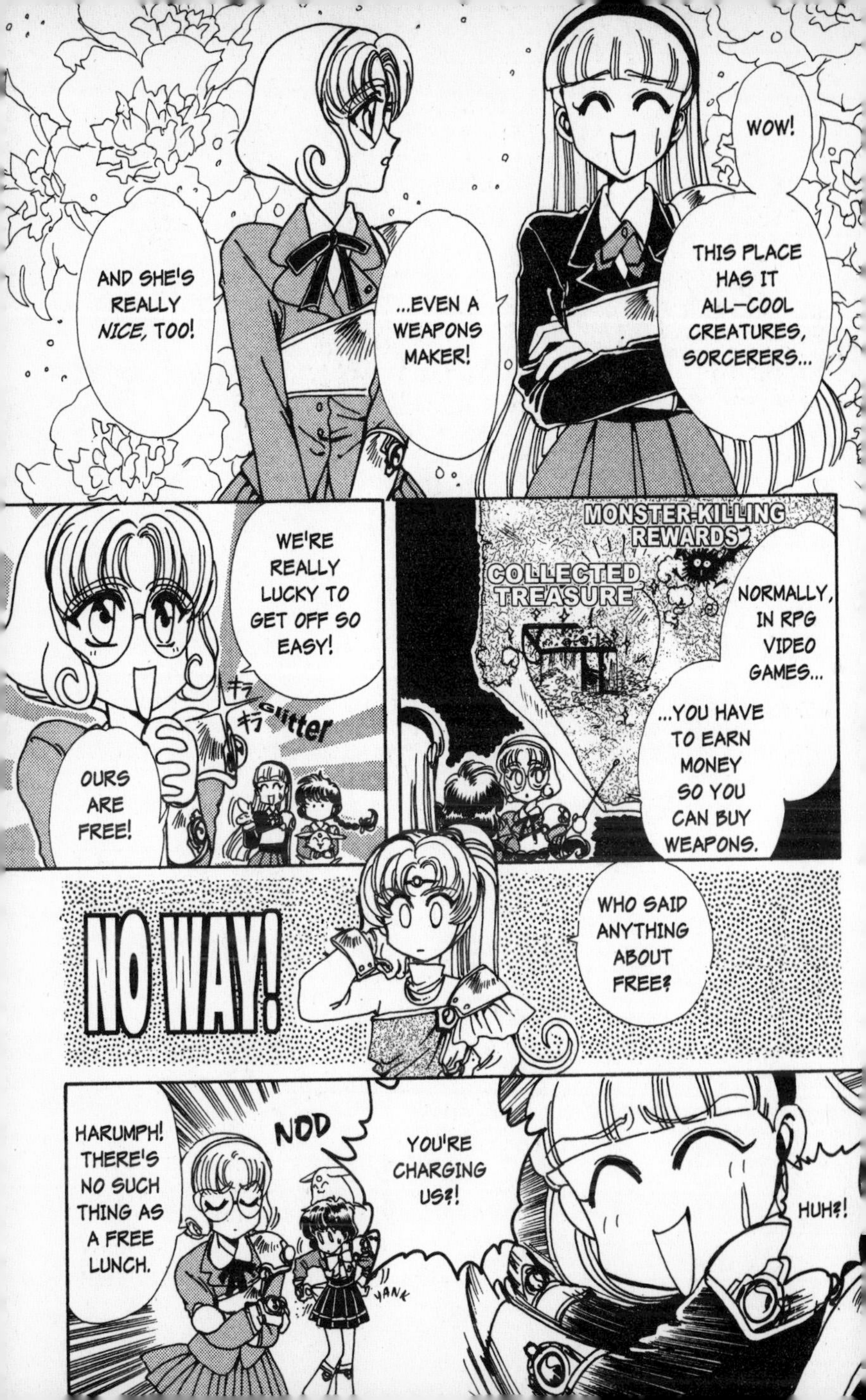

WOW!
THIS PLACE HAS IT ALL—COOL CREATURES, SORCERERS...
...EVEN A WEAPONS MAKER!
AND SHE'S REALLY *NICE*, TOO!
MONSTER-KILLING REWARDS
COLLECTED TREASURE
NORMALLY, IN RPG VIDEO GAMES...
...YOU HAVE TO EARN MONEY SO YOU CAN BUY WEAPONS.
WE'RE REALLY LUCKY TO GET OFF SO EASY!
キラ キラ
Glitter
OURS ARE FREE!
WHO SAID ANYTHING ABOUT FREE?
NO WAY!
HUH?!
YOU'RE CHARGING US?!
NOD
YANK
HARUMPH! THERE'S NO SUCH THING AS A FREE LUNCH.

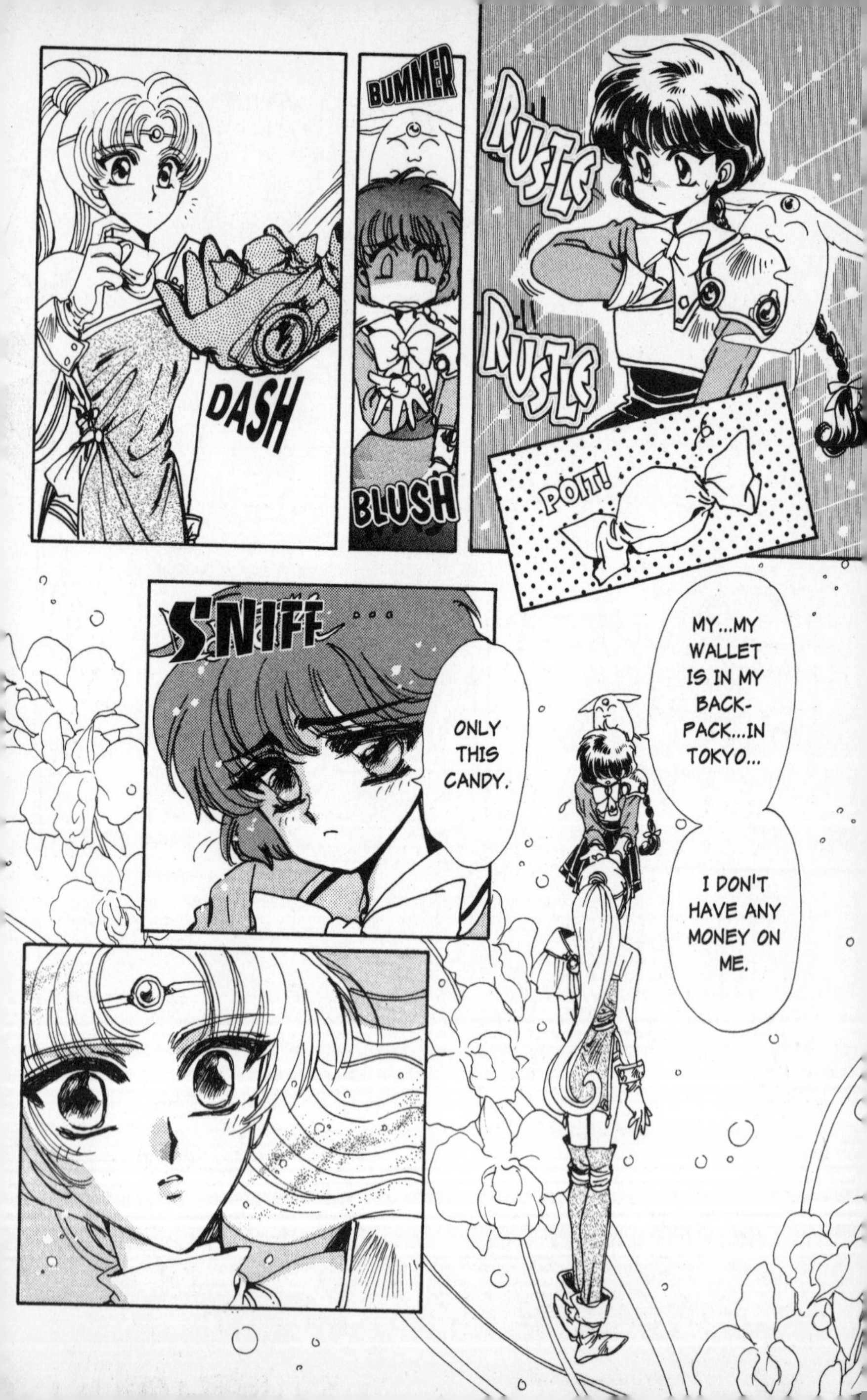
RUSTLE
RUSTLE
POIT!
BUMMER
BLUSH
DASH
MY...MY WALLET IS IN MY BACK-PACK...IN TOKYO...
I DON'T HAVE ANY MONEY ON ME.
S'NIFF...
ONLY THIS CANDY.

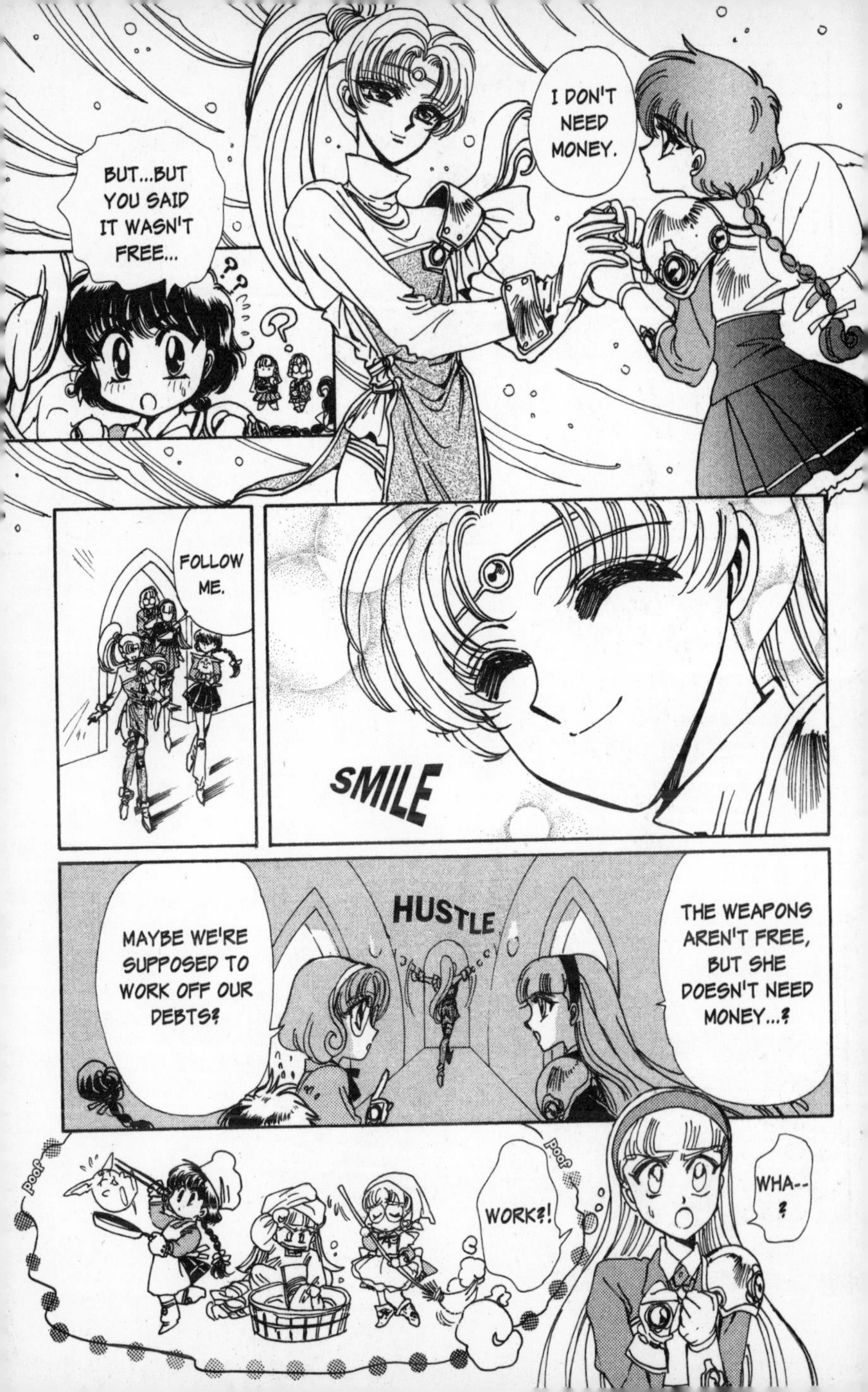
I DON'T NEED MONEY.
BUT...BUT YOU SAID IT WASN'T FREE...
SMILE
FOLLOW ME.
THE WEAPONS AREN'T FREE, BUT SHE DOESN'T NEED MONEY...?
HUSTLE
MAYBE WE'RE SUPPOSED TO WORK OFF OUR DEBTS?
WHA-- ?
WORK?!
poof
poof

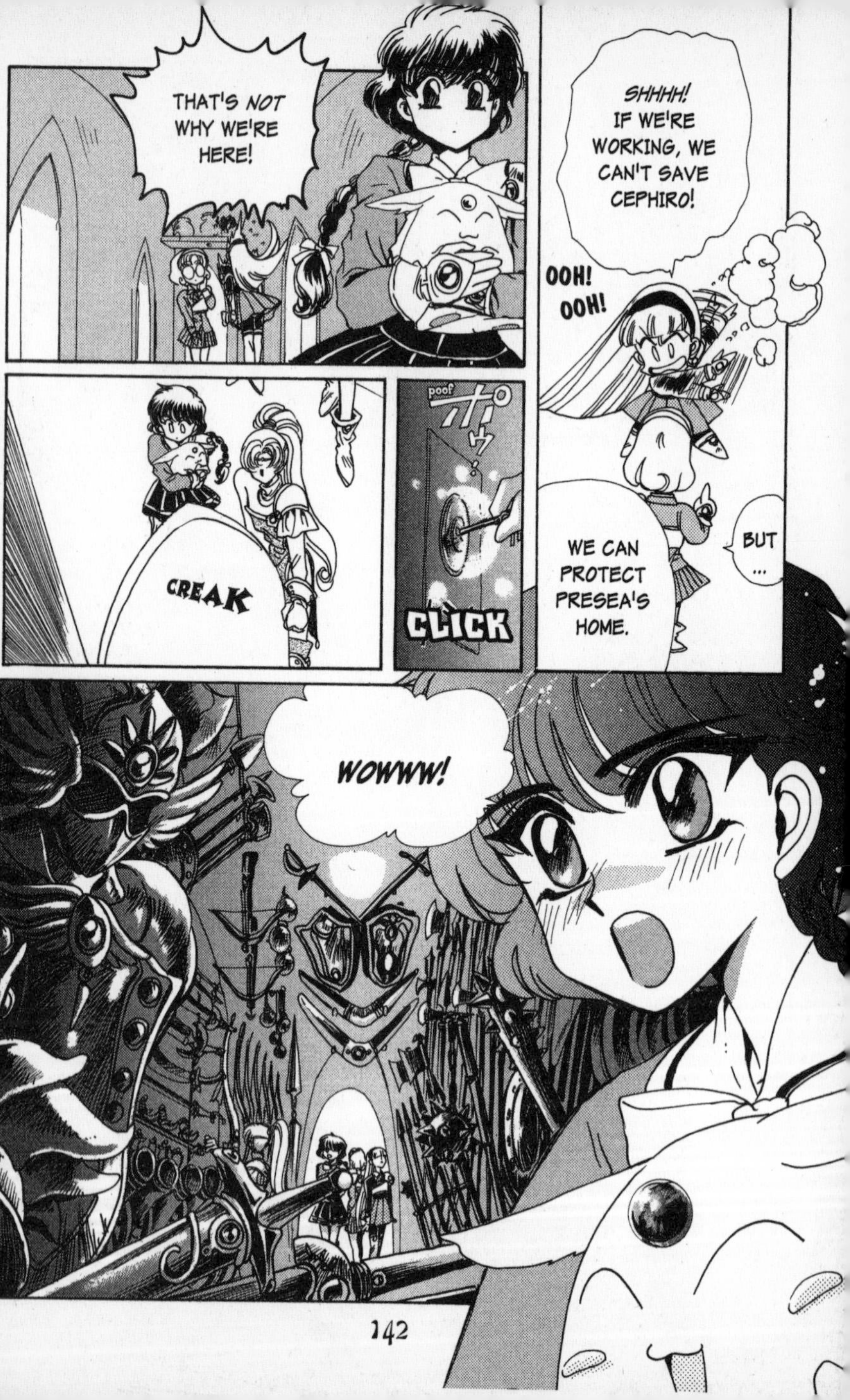
SHHHH! IF WE'RE WORKING, WE CAN'T SAVE CEPHIRO!
OOH! OOH!
WE CAN PROTECT PRESEA'S HOME.
BUT ...
THAT'S NOT WHY WE'RE HERE!
poof
CLICK
CREAK
WOWWW!

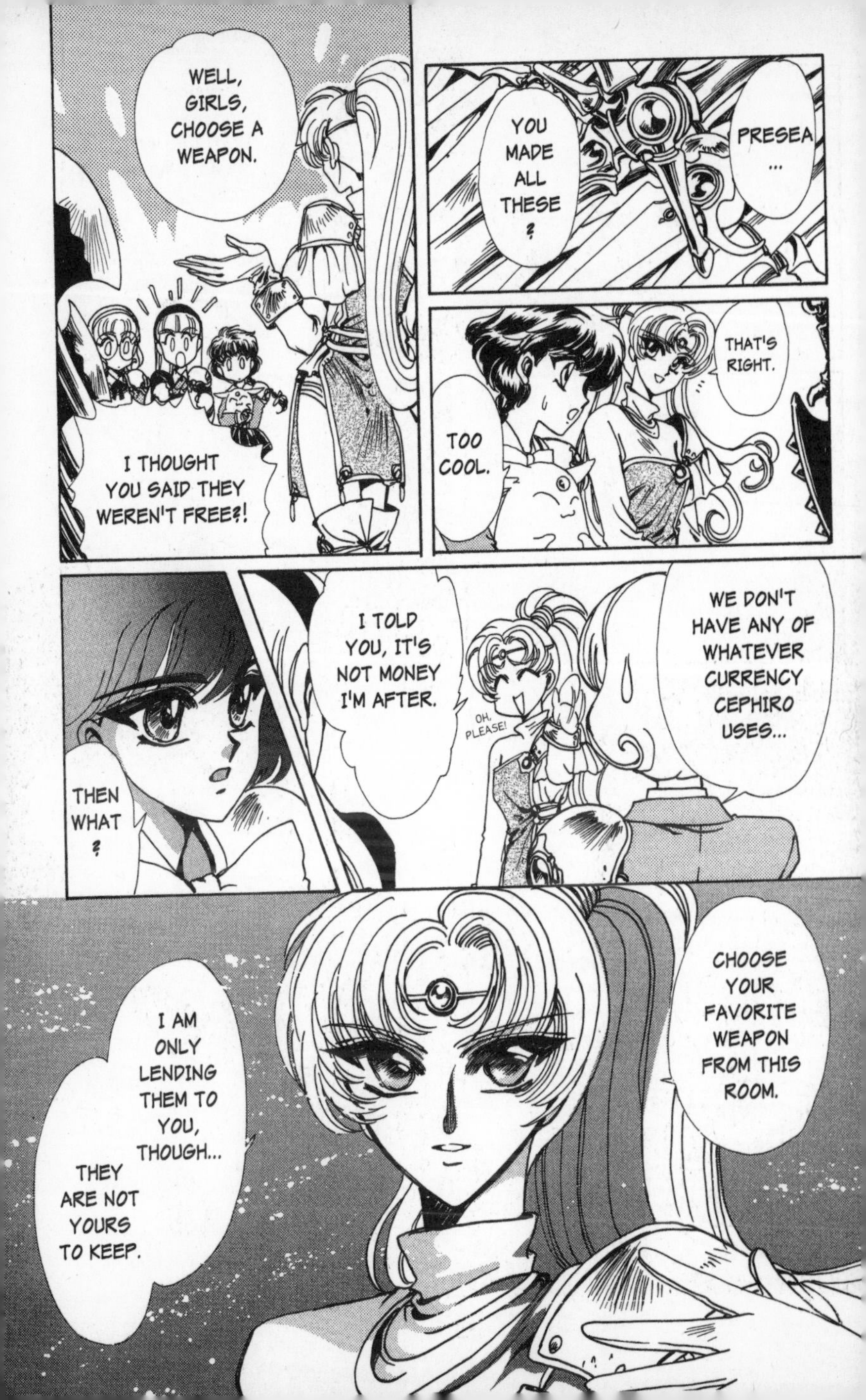
PRESEA ...
YOU MADE ALL THESE?
THAT'S RIGHT.
TOO COOL.
WELL, GIRLS, CHOOSE A WEAPON.
I THOUGHT YOU SAID THEY WEREN'T FREE?!
WE DON'T HAVE ANY OF WHATEVER CURRENCY CEPHIRO USES...
OH, PLEASE!
I TOLD YOU, IT'S NOT MONEY I'M AFTER.
THEN WHAT?
CHOOSE YOUR FAVORITE WEAPON FROM THIS ROOM.
I AM ONLY LENDING THEM TO YOU, THOUGH...
THEY ARE NOT YOURS TO KEEP.

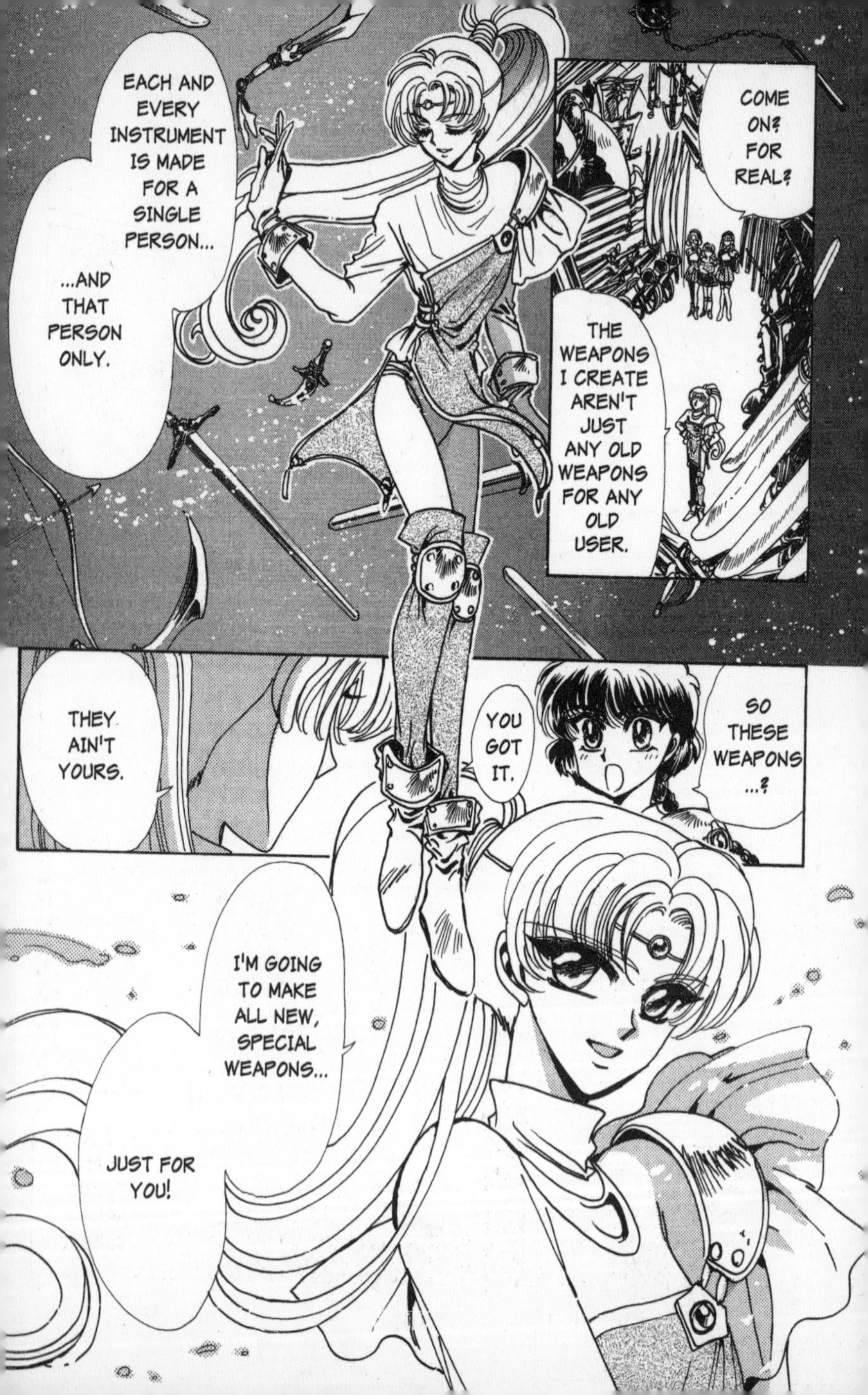
COME ON? FOR REAL?
THE WEAPONS I CREATE AREN'T JUST ANY OLD WEAPONS FOR ANY OLD USER.
EACH AND EVERY INSTRUMENT IS MADE FOR A SINGLE PERSON...
...AND THAT PERSON ONLY.
SO THESE WEAPONS ...?
YOU GOT IT.
THEY AIN'T YOURS.
I'M GOING TO MAKE ALL NEW, SPECIAL WEAPONS...
JUST FOR YOU!

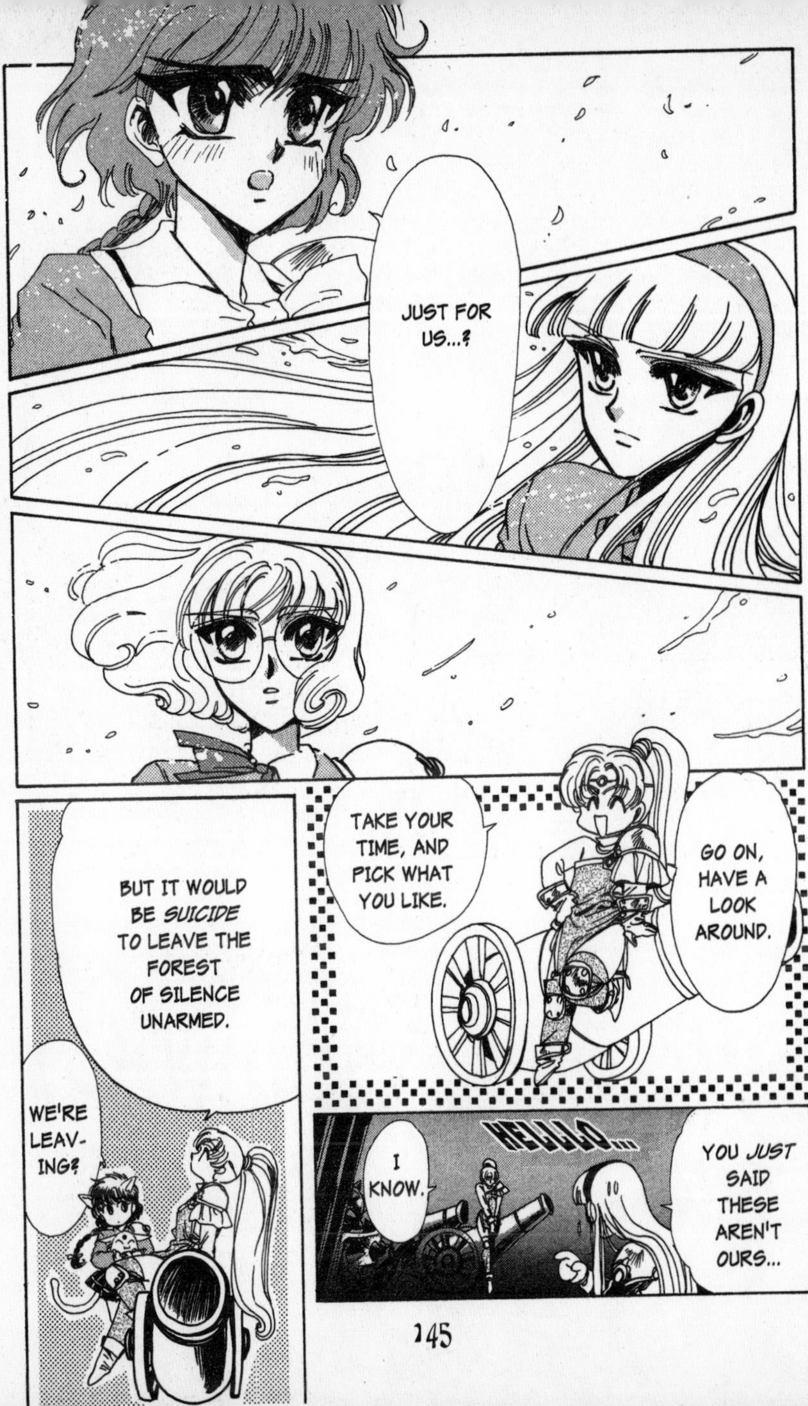
JUST FOR US...?
GO ON, HAVE A LOOK AROUND.
TAKE YOUR TIME, AND PICK WHAT YOU LIKE.
YOU *JUST* SAID THESE AREN'T OURS...
HELLO...
I KNOW.
BUT IT WOULD BE *SUICIDE* TO LEAVE THE FOREST OF SILENCE UNARMED.
WE'RE LEAV-ING?

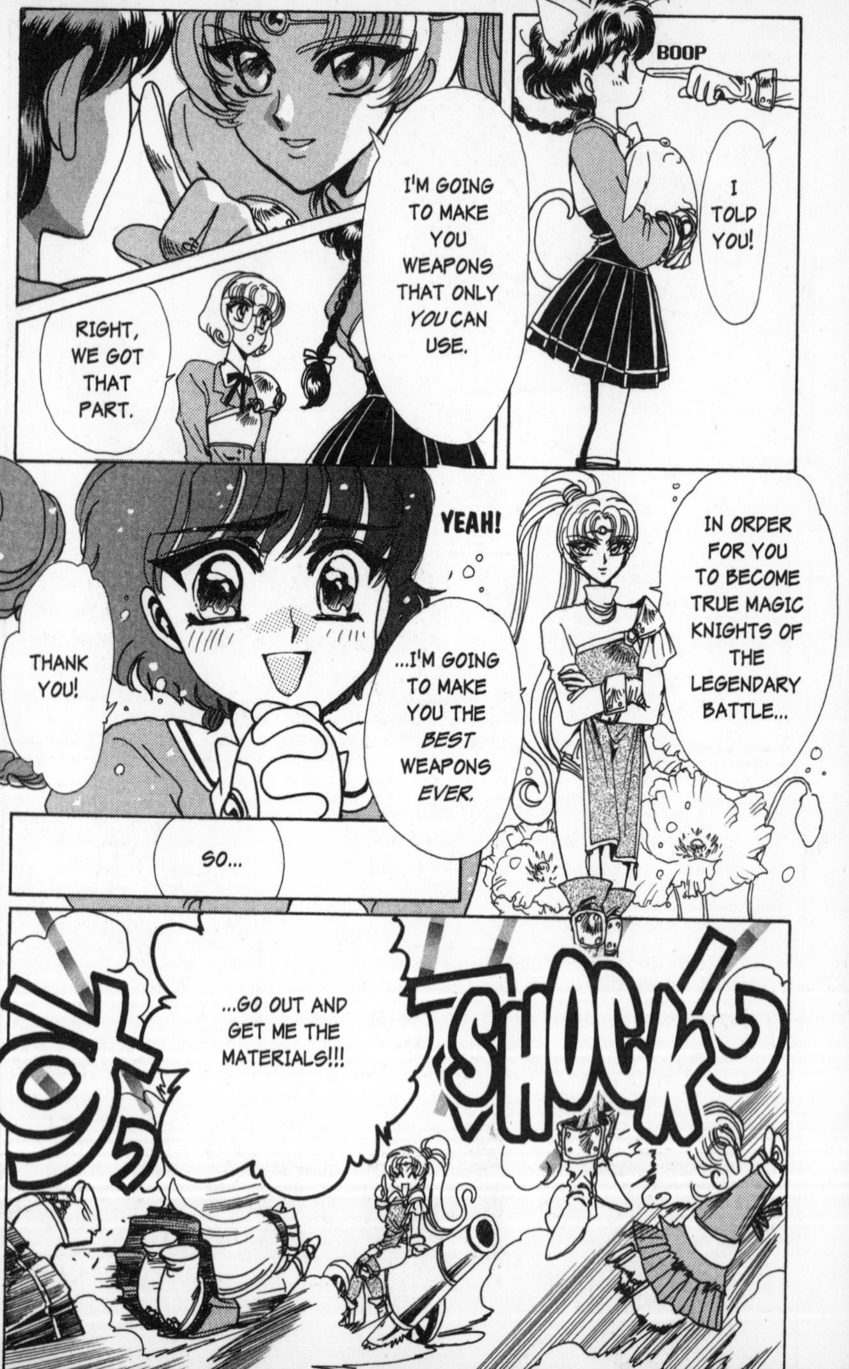
BOOP
I TOLD YOU!
I'M GOING TO MAKE YOU WEAPONS THAT ONLY *YOU* CAN USE.
RIGHT, WE GOT THAT PART.
IN ORDER FOR YOU TO BECOME TRUE MAGIC KNIGHTS OF THE LEGENDARY BATTLE...
...I'M GOING TO MAKE YOU THE *BEST* WEAPONS *EVER.*
YEAH!
THANK YOU!
SO...
SHOCK
...GO OUT AND GET ME THE MATERIALS!!!

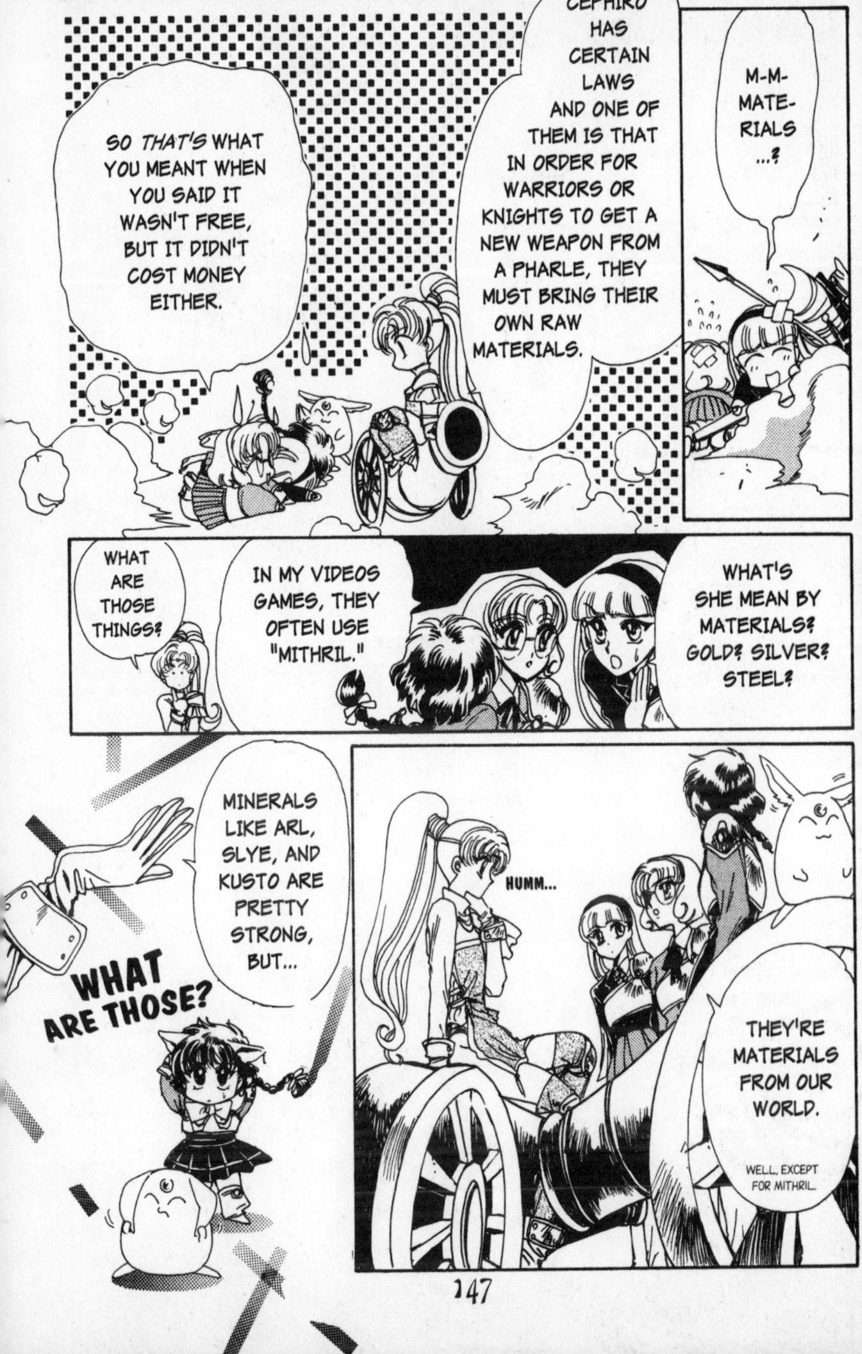
M-M-MATE-RIALS ...?
CEPHIRO HAS CERTAIN LAWS AND ONE OF THEM IS THAT IN ORDER FOR WARRIORS OR KNIGHTS TO GET A NEW WEAPON FROM A PHARLE, THEY MUST BRING THEIR OWN RAW MATERIALS.
SO THAT'S WHAT YOU MEANT WHEN YOU SAID IT WASN'T FREE, BUT IT DIDN'T COST MONEY EITHER.
WHAT'S SHE MEAN BY MATERIALS? GOLD? SILVER? STEEL?
IN MY VIDEOS GAMES, THEY OFTEN USE "MITHRIL."
WHAT ARE THOSE THINGS?
THEY'RE MATERIALS FROM OUR WORLD.
WELL, EXCEPT FOR MITHRIL.
HUMM...
MINERALS LIKE ARL, SLYE, AND KUSTO ARE PRETTY STRONG, BUT...
WHAT ARE THOSE?

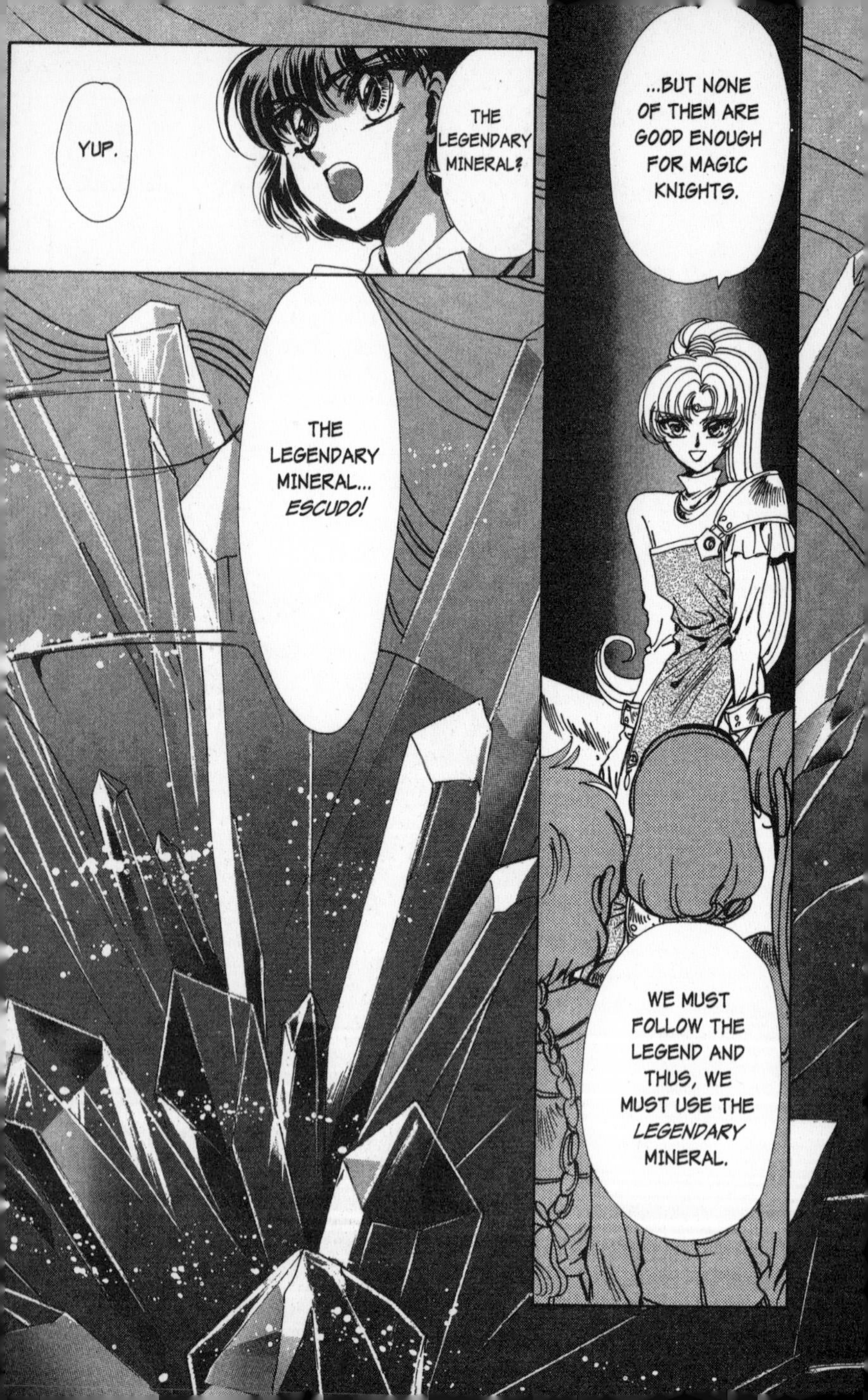
...BUT NONE OF THEM ARE GOOD ENOUGH FOR MAGIC KNIGHTS.
WE MUST FOLLOW THE LEGEND AND THUS, WE MUST USE THE *LEGENDARY* MINERAL.
THE LEGENDARY MINERAL?
YUP.
THE LEGENDARY MINERAL... *ESCUDO!*

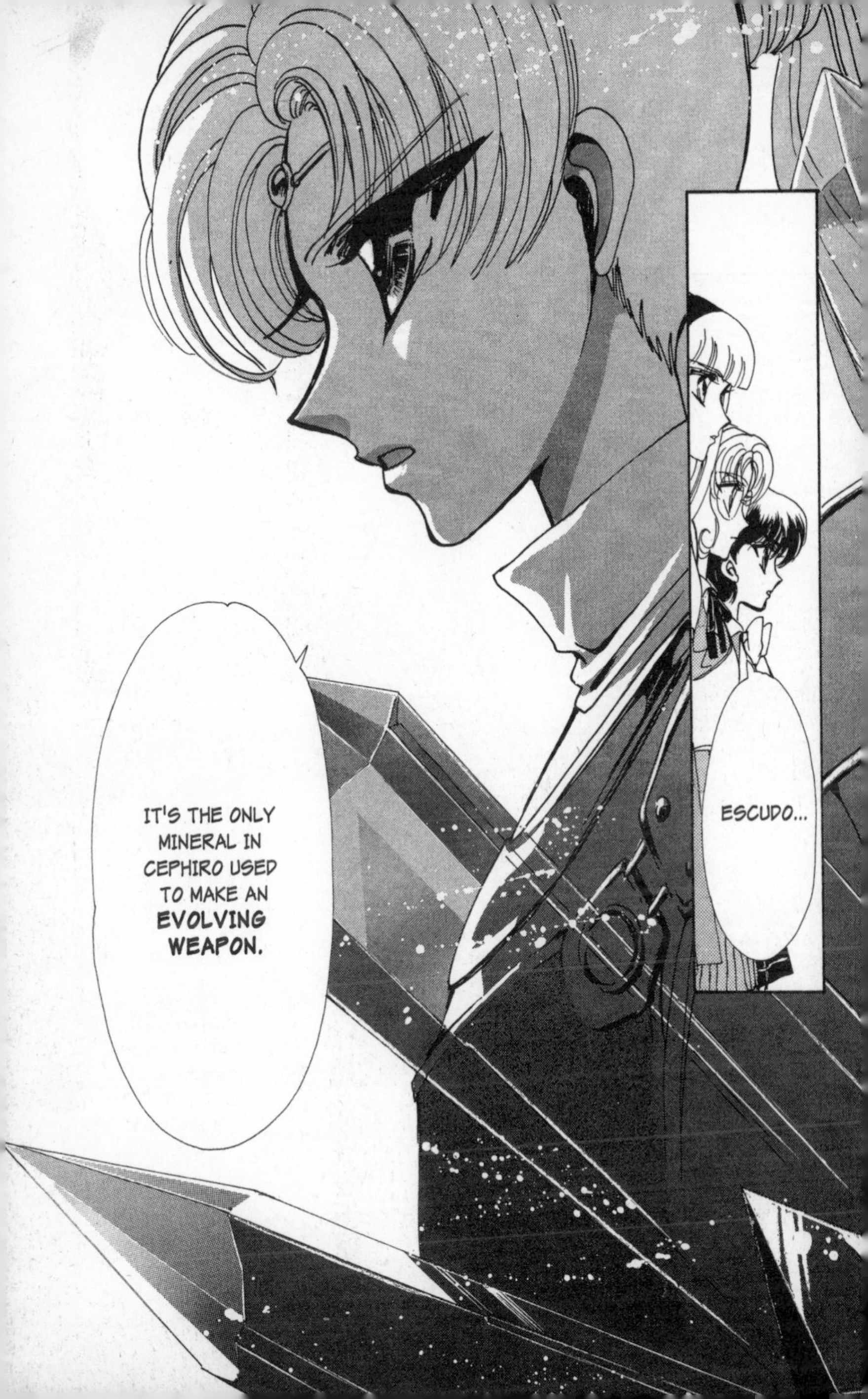
ESCUDO...
IT'S THE ONLY MINERAL IN CEPHIRO USED TO MAKE AN EVOLVING WEAPON.

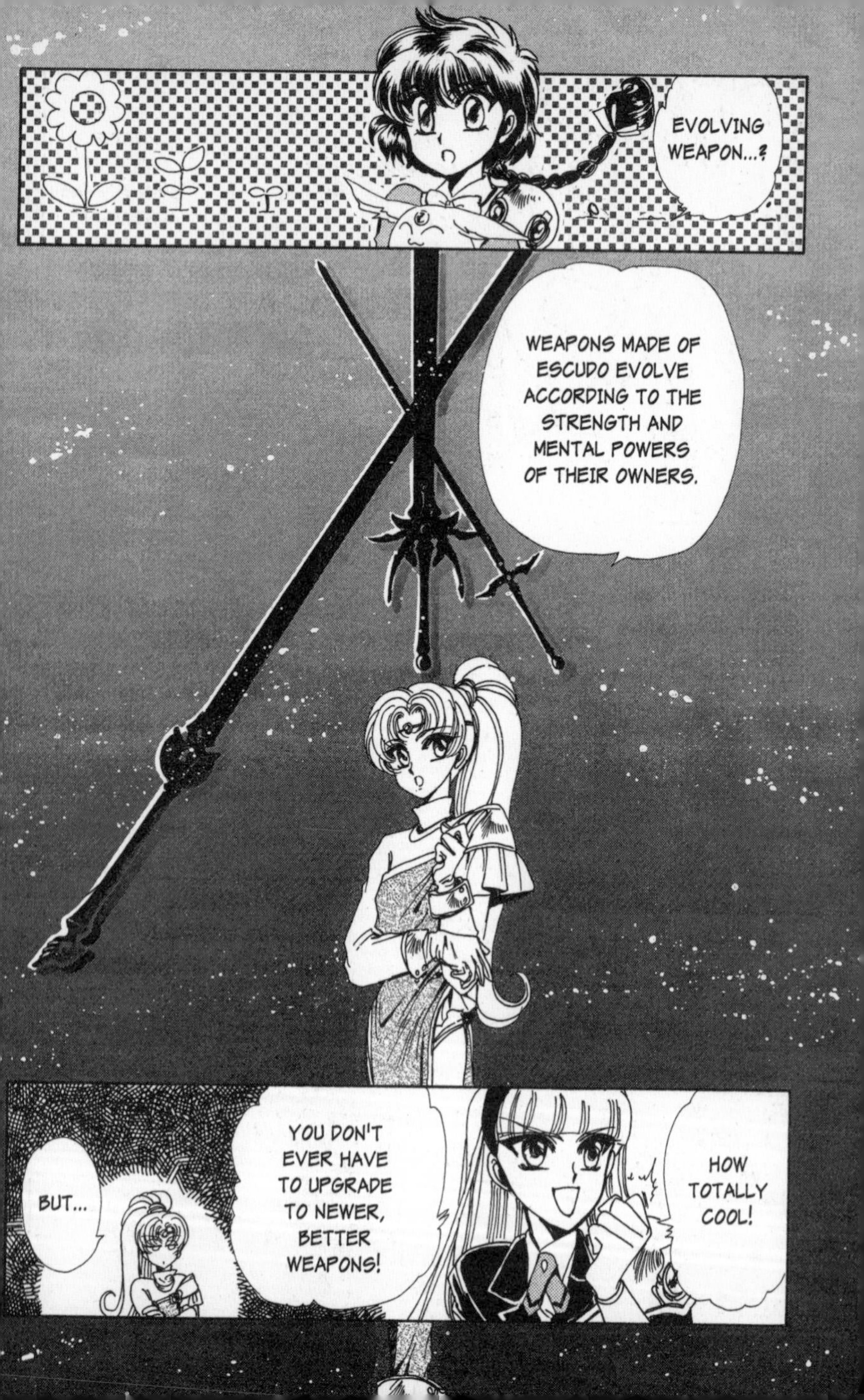
EVOLVING WEAPON...?
WEAPONS MADE OF ESCUDO EVOLVE ACCORDING TO THE STRENGTH AND MENTAL POWERS OF THEIR OWNERS.
HOW TOTALLY COOL!
YOU DON'T EVER HAVE TO UPGRADE TO NEWER, BETTER WEAPONS!
BUT...

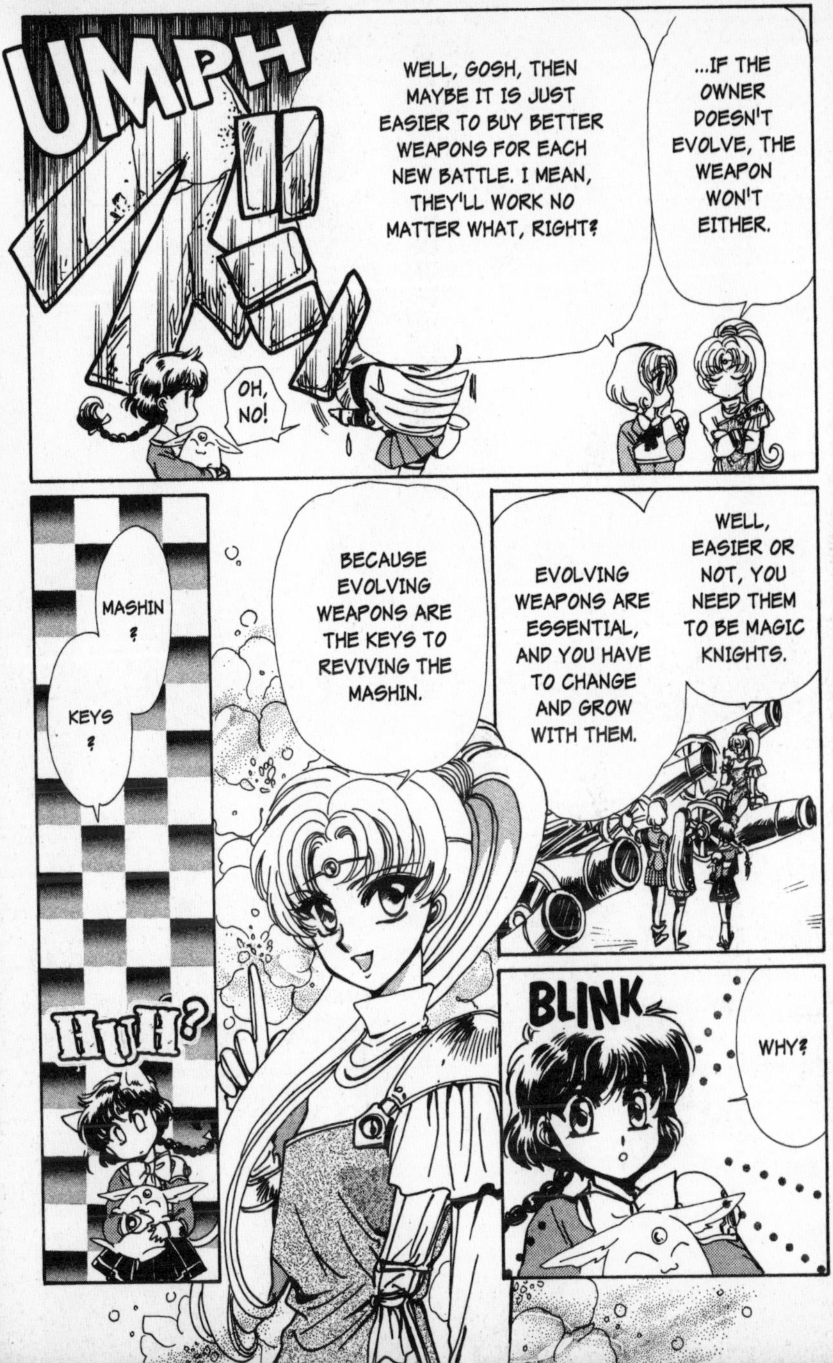
...IF THE OWNER DOESN'T EVOLVE, THE WEAPON WON'T EITHER.
WELL, GOSH, THEN MAYBE IT IS JUST EASIER TO BUY BETTER WEAPONS FOR EACH NEW BATTLE. I MEAN, THEY'LL WORK NO MATTER WHAT, RIGHT?
UMPH
OH, NO!
WELL, EASIER OR NOT, YOU NEED THEM TO BE MAGIC KNIGHTS.
EVOLVING WEAPONS ARE ESSENTIAL, AND YOU HAVE TO CHANGE AND GROW WITH THEM.
BLINK
WHY?
BECAUSE EVOLVING WEAPONS ARE THE KEYS TO REVIVING THE MASHIN.
MASHIN?
KEYS?
HUH?

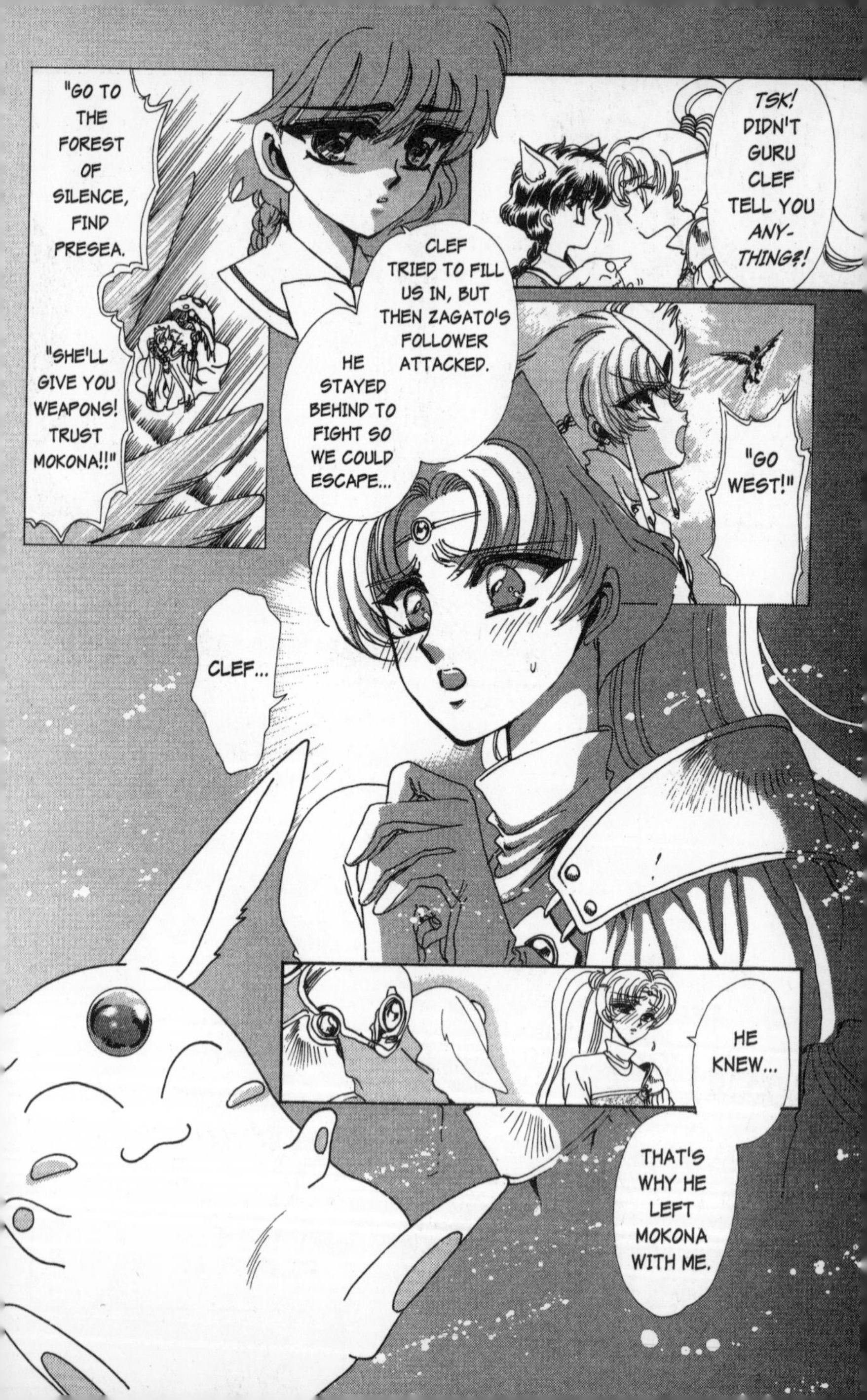
TSK! DIDN'T GURU CLEF TELL YOU ANY-THING?!
CLEF TRIED TO FILL US IN, BUT THEN ZAGATO'S FOLLOWER ATTACKED.
HE STAYED BEHIND TO FIGHT SO WE COULD ESCAPE...
"GO WEST!"
"GO TO THE FOREST OF SILENCE, FIND PRESEA.
"SHE'LL GIVE YOU WEAPONS! TRUST MOKONA!!"
CLEF...
HE KNEW...
THAT'S WHY HE LEFT MOKONA WITH ME.

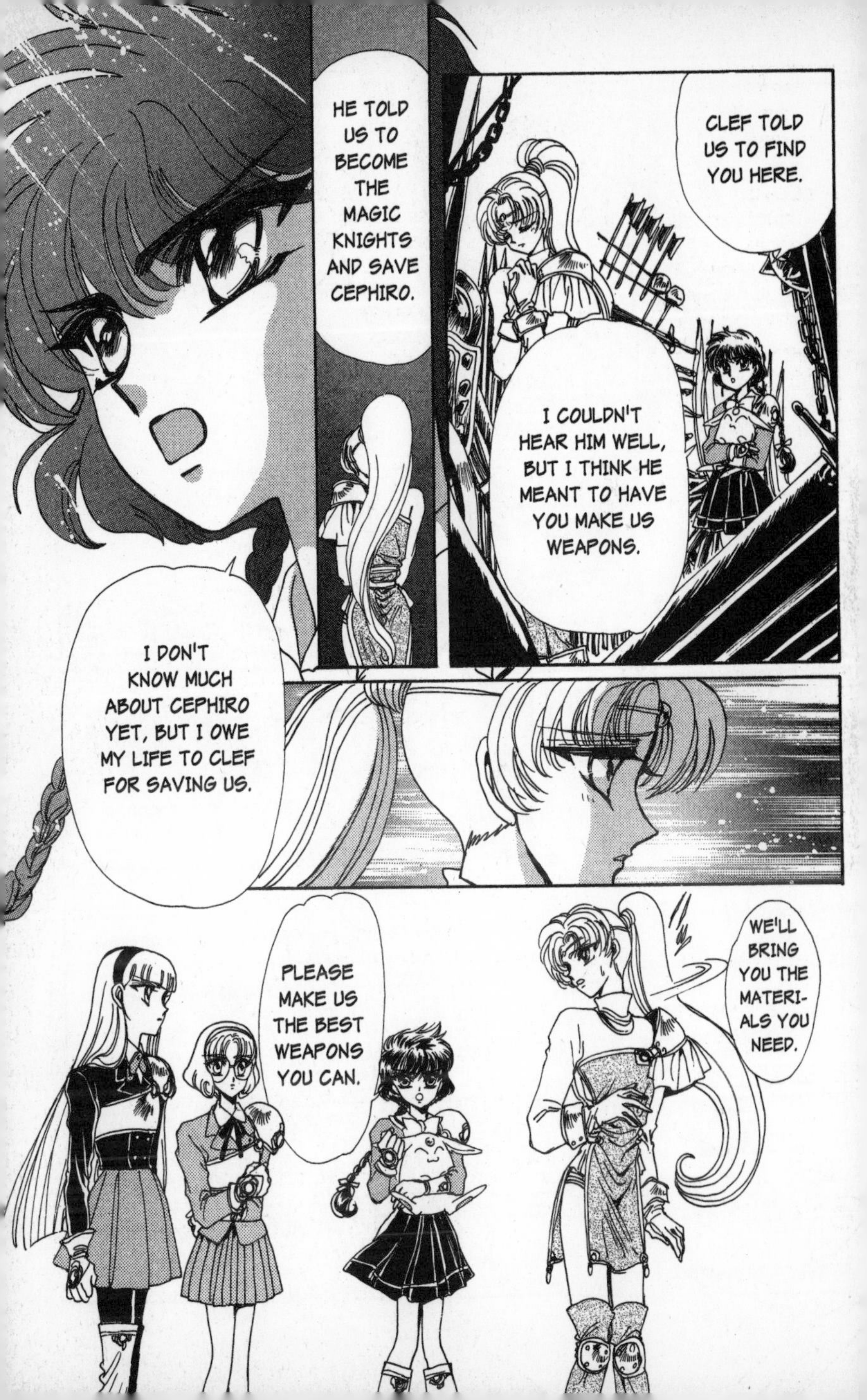
CLEF TOLD US TO FIND YOU HERE.
I COULDN'T HEAR HIM WELL, BUT I THINK HE MEANT TO HAVE YOU MAKE US WEAPONS.
HE TOLD US TO BECOME THE MAGIC KNIGHTS AND SAVE CEPHIRO.
I DON'T KNOW MUCH ABOUT CEPHIRO YET, BUT I OWE MY LIFE TO CLEF FOR SAVING US.
WE'LL BRING YOU THE MATERI-ALS YOU NEED.
PLEASE MAKE US THE BEST WEAPONS YOU CAN.

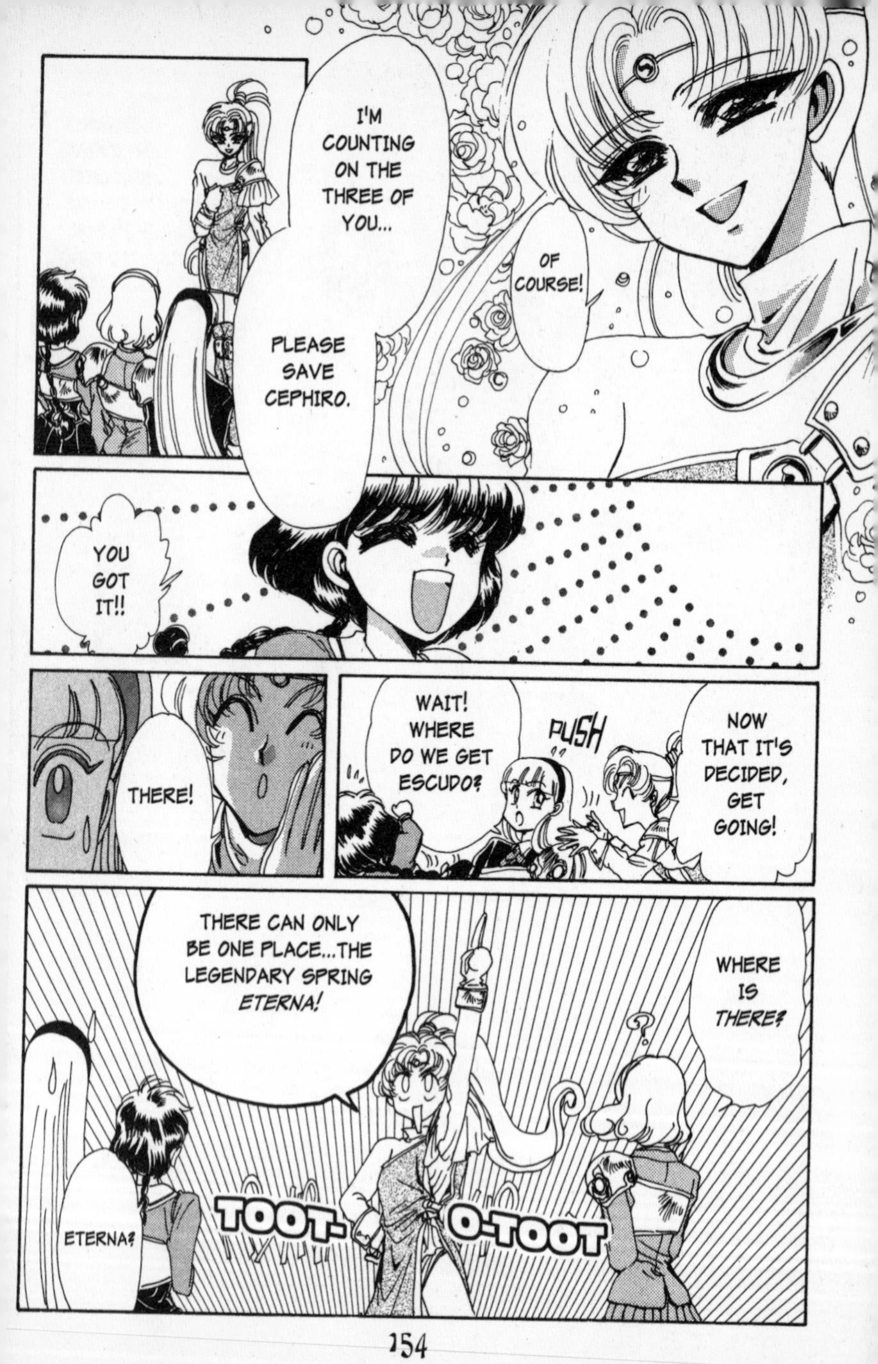
I'M COUNTING ON THE THREE OF YOU...
PLEASE SAVE CEPHIRO.
OF COURSE!
YOU GOT IT!!
NOW THAT IT'S DECIDED, GET GOING!
PUSH
WAIT! WHERE DO WE GET ESCUDO?
THERE!
WHERE IS *THERE*?
THERE CAN ONLY BE ONE PLACE...THE LEGENDARY SPRING *ETERNA!*
ETERNA?
TOOT-O-TOOT

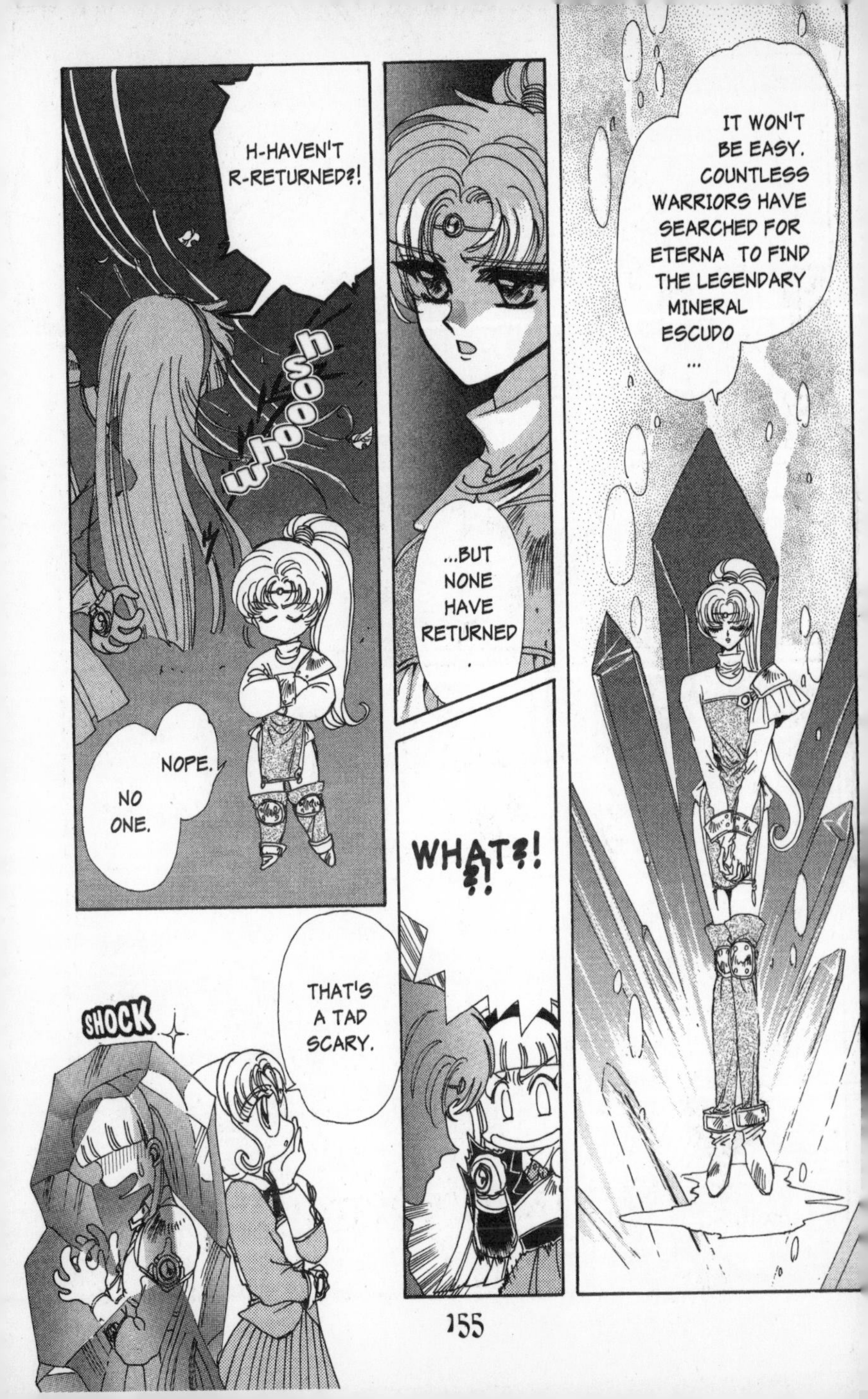
IT WON'T BE EASY. COUNTLESS WARRIORS HAVE SEARCHED FOR ETERNA TO FIND THE LEGENDARY MINERAL ESCUDO ...
...BUT NONE HAVE RETURNED .
H-HAVEN'T R-RETURNED?!
whoooosh
NOPE.
NO ONE.
WHAT?!?!
SHOCK
THAT'S A TAD SCARY.

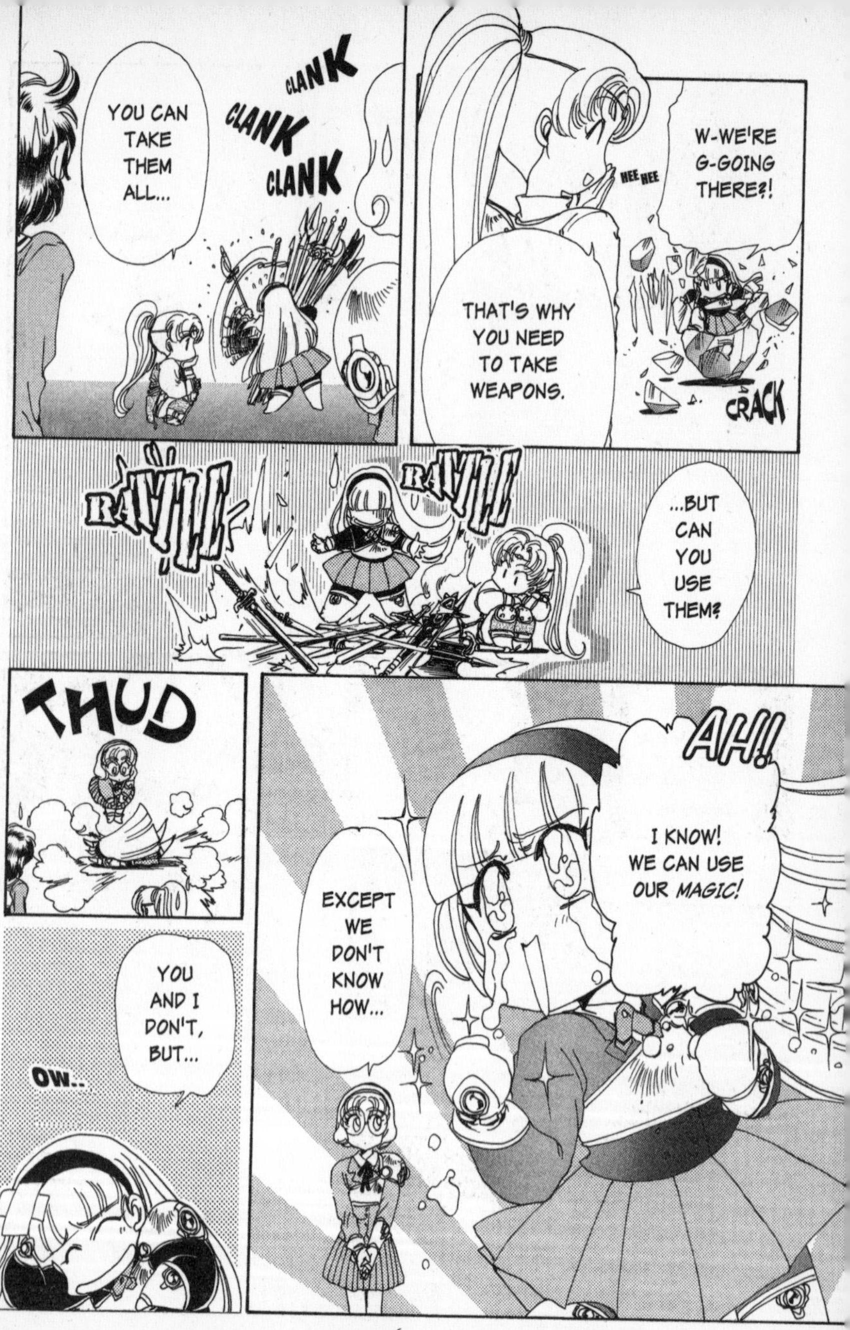
W-WE'RE G-GOING THERE?!
HEE HEE
THAT'S WHY YOU NEED TO TAKE WEAPONS.
CRACK
CLANK
CLANK
CLANK
YOU CAN TAKE THEM ALL...
...BUT CAN YOU USE THEM?
RATTLE
RATTLE
AH!!
I KNOW! WE CAN USE OUR *MAGIC!*
EXCEPT WE DON'T KNOW HOW...
THUD
YOU AND I DON'T, BUT...
OW..

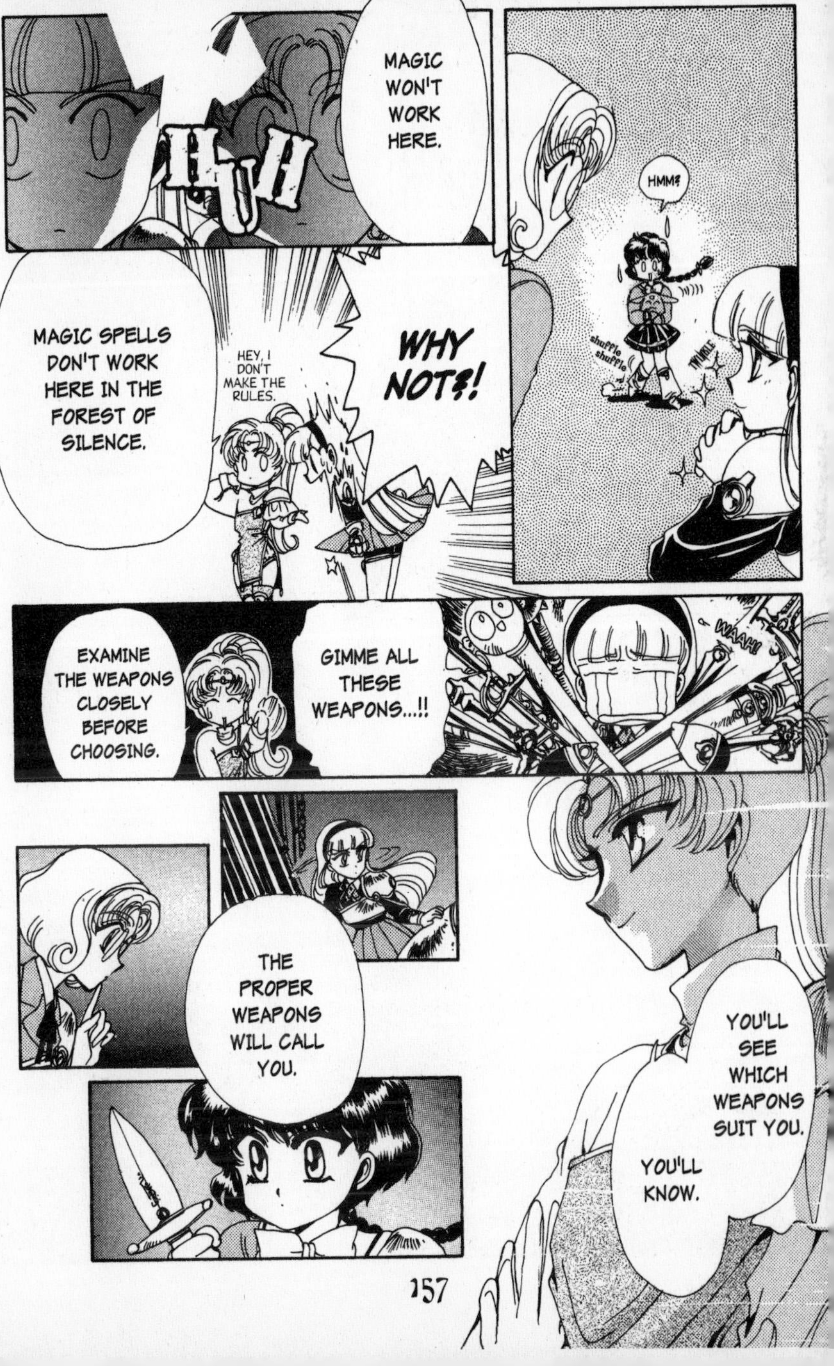
HMM?
shuffle shuffle
TWINKLE
MAGIC WON'T WORK HERE.
HUH
WHY NOT?!
HEY, I DON'T MAKE THE RULES.
MAGIC SPELLS DON'T WORK HERE IN THE FOREST OF SILENCE.
WAAH!
GIMME ALL THESE WEAPONS...!!
EXAMINE THE WEAPONS CLOSELY BEFORE CHOOSING.
YOU'LL SEE WHICH WEAPONS SUIT YOU.
YOU'LL KNOW.
THE PROPER WEAPONS WILL CALL YOU.

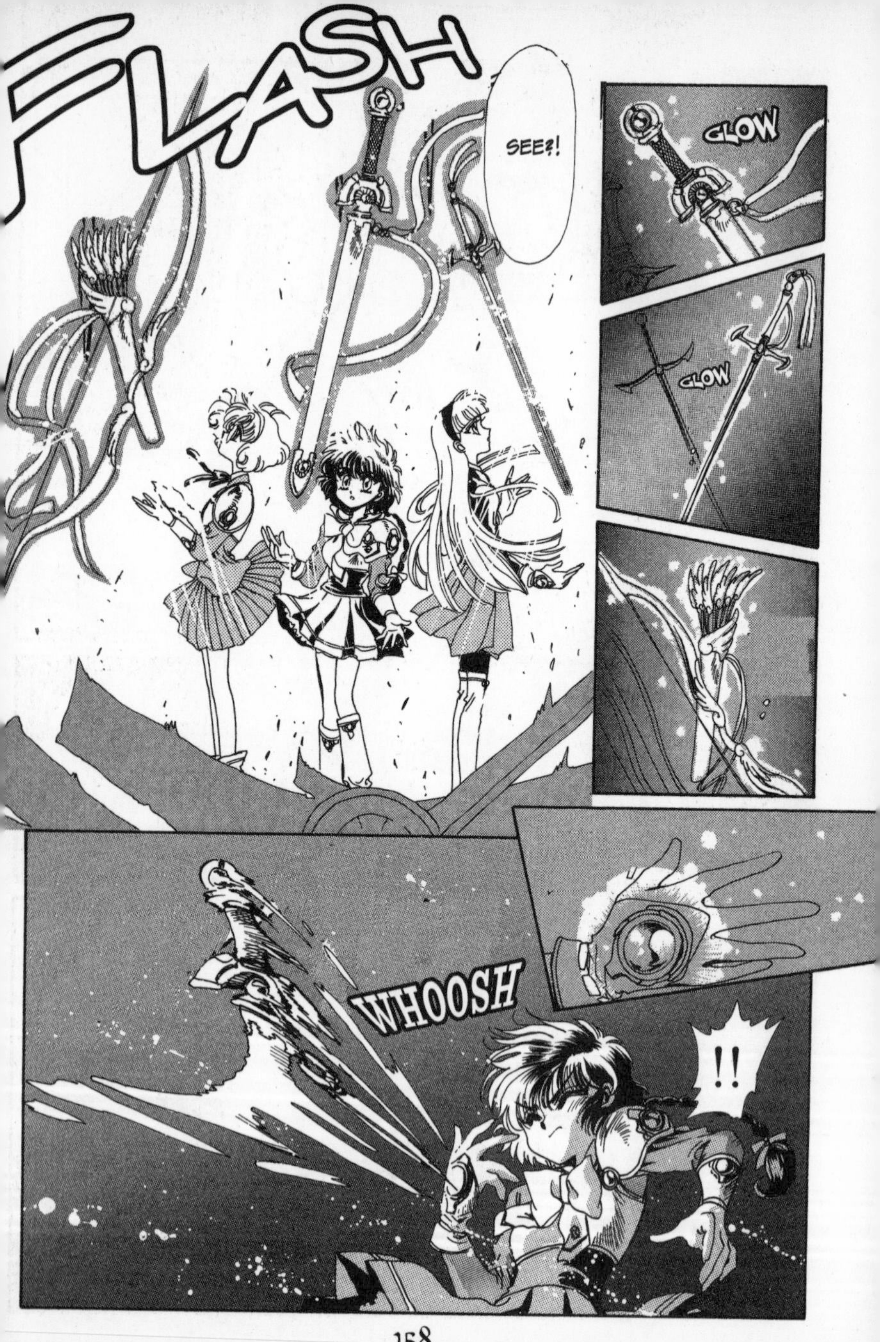
GLOW
GLOW
FLASH
SEE?!
WHOOSH
!!

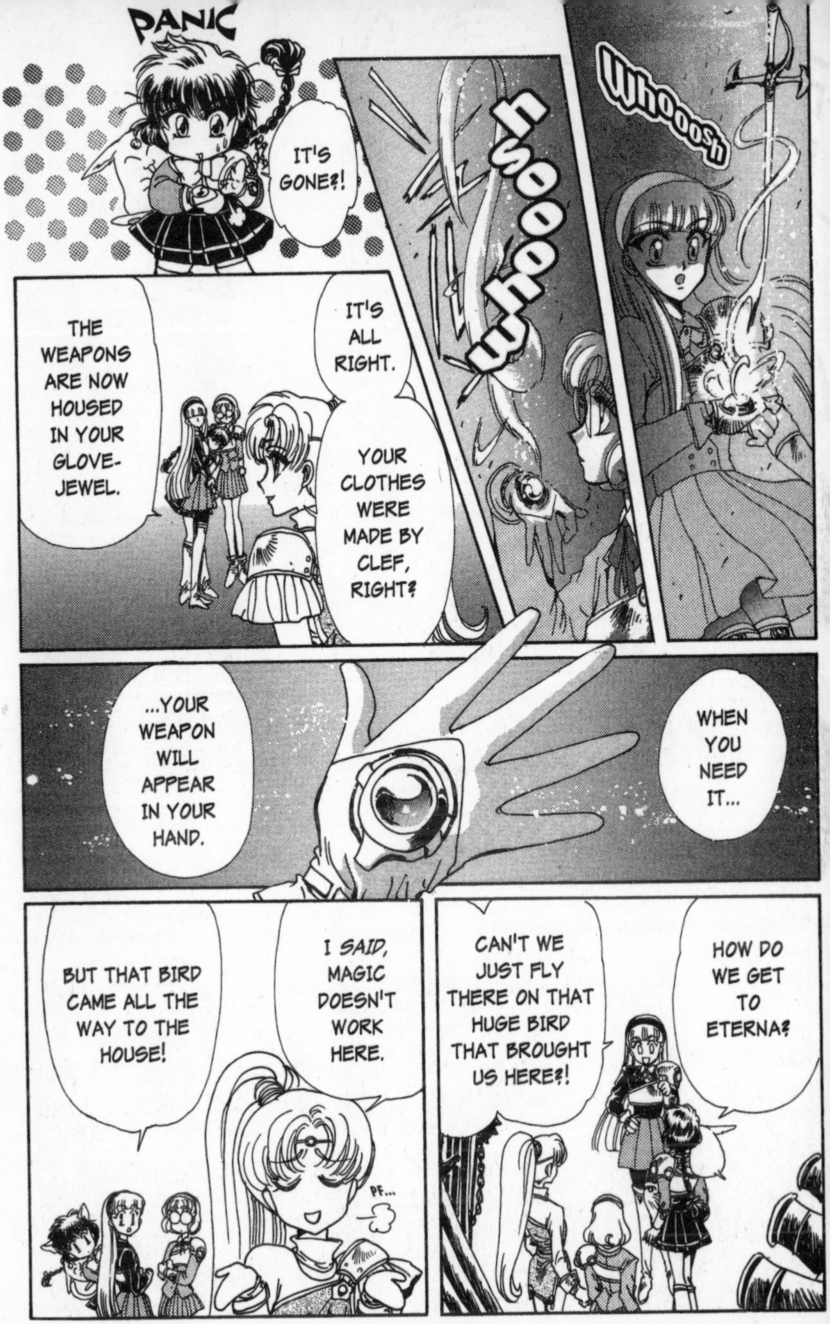
Whoooosh
whoooosh
PANIC
IT'S GONE?!
IT'S ALL RIGHT.
YOUR CLOTHES WERE MADE BY CLEF, RIGHT?
THE WEAPONS ARE NOW HOUSED IN YOUR GLOVE-JEWEL.
WHEN YOU NEED IT...
...YOUR WEAPON WILL APPEAR IN YOUR HAND.
HOW DO WE GET TO ETERNA?
CAN'T WE JUST FLY THERE ON THAT HUGE BIRD THAT BROUGHT US HERE?!
I *SAID*, MAGIC DOESN'T WORK HERE.
BUT THAT BIRD CAME ALL THE WAY TO THE HOUSE!
PF...

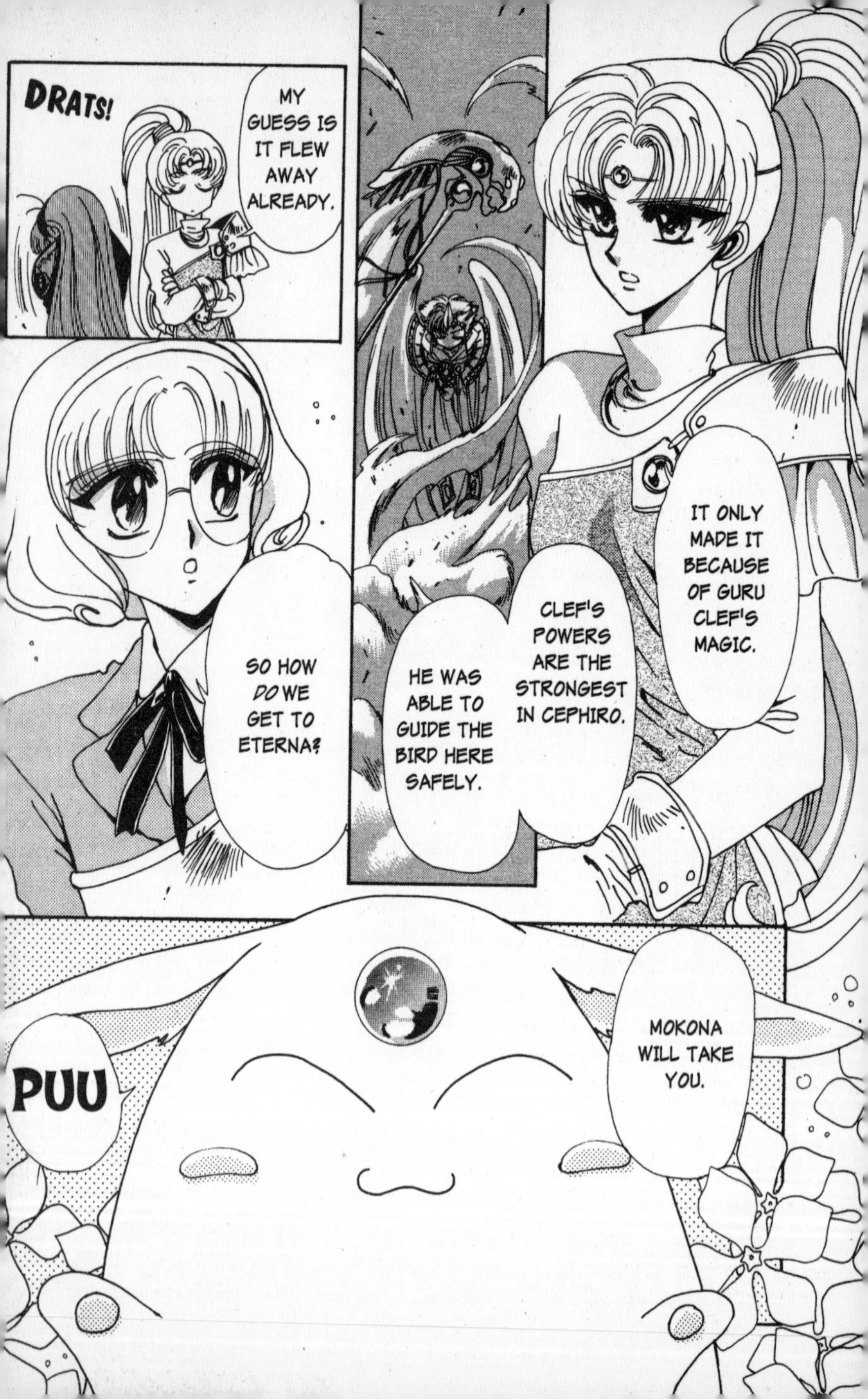
IT ONLY MADE IT BECAUSE OF GURU CLEF'S MAGIC.
CLEF'S POWERS ARE THE STRONGEST IN CEPHIRO.
HE WAS ABLE TO GUIDE THE BIRD HERE SAFELY.
MY GUESS IS IT FLEW AWAY ALREADY.
DRATS!
SO HOW *DO* WE GET TO ETERNA?
MOKONA WILL TAKE YOU.
PUU

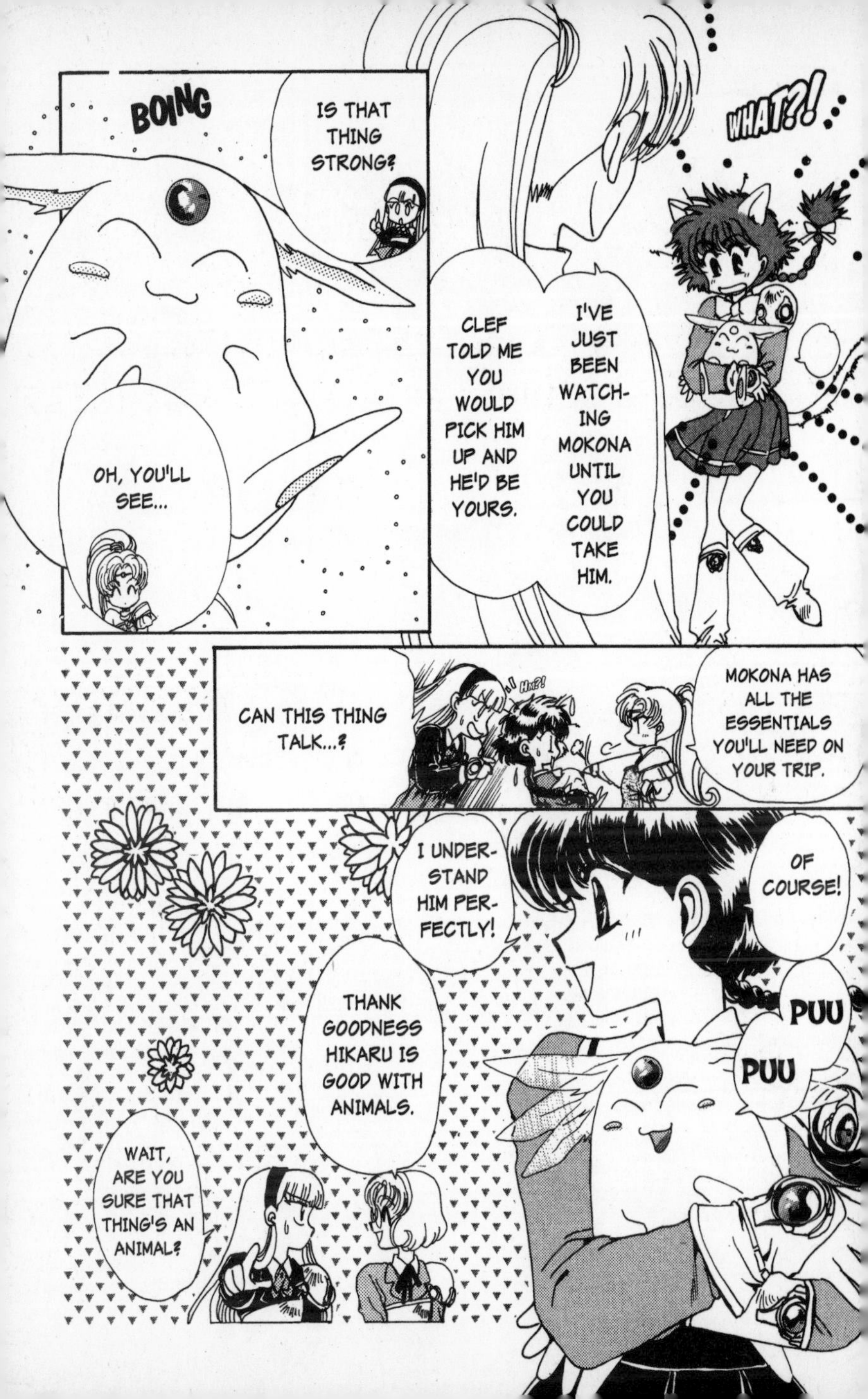
WHAT?!
I'VE JUST BEEN WATCHING MOKONA UNTIL YOU COULD TAKE HIM.
CLEF TOLD ME YOU WOULD PICK HIM UP AND HE'D BE YOURS.
IS THAT THING STRONG?
BOING
OH, YOU'LL SEE...
MOKONA HAS ALL THE ESSENTIALS YOU'LL NEED ON YOUR TRIP.
HM?!
CAN THIS THING TALK...?
OF COURSE!
I UNDERSTAND HIM PERFECTLY!
PUU
PUU
THANK GOODNESS HIKARU IS GOOD WITH ANIMALS.
WAIT, ARE YOU SURE THAT THING'S AN ANIMAL?

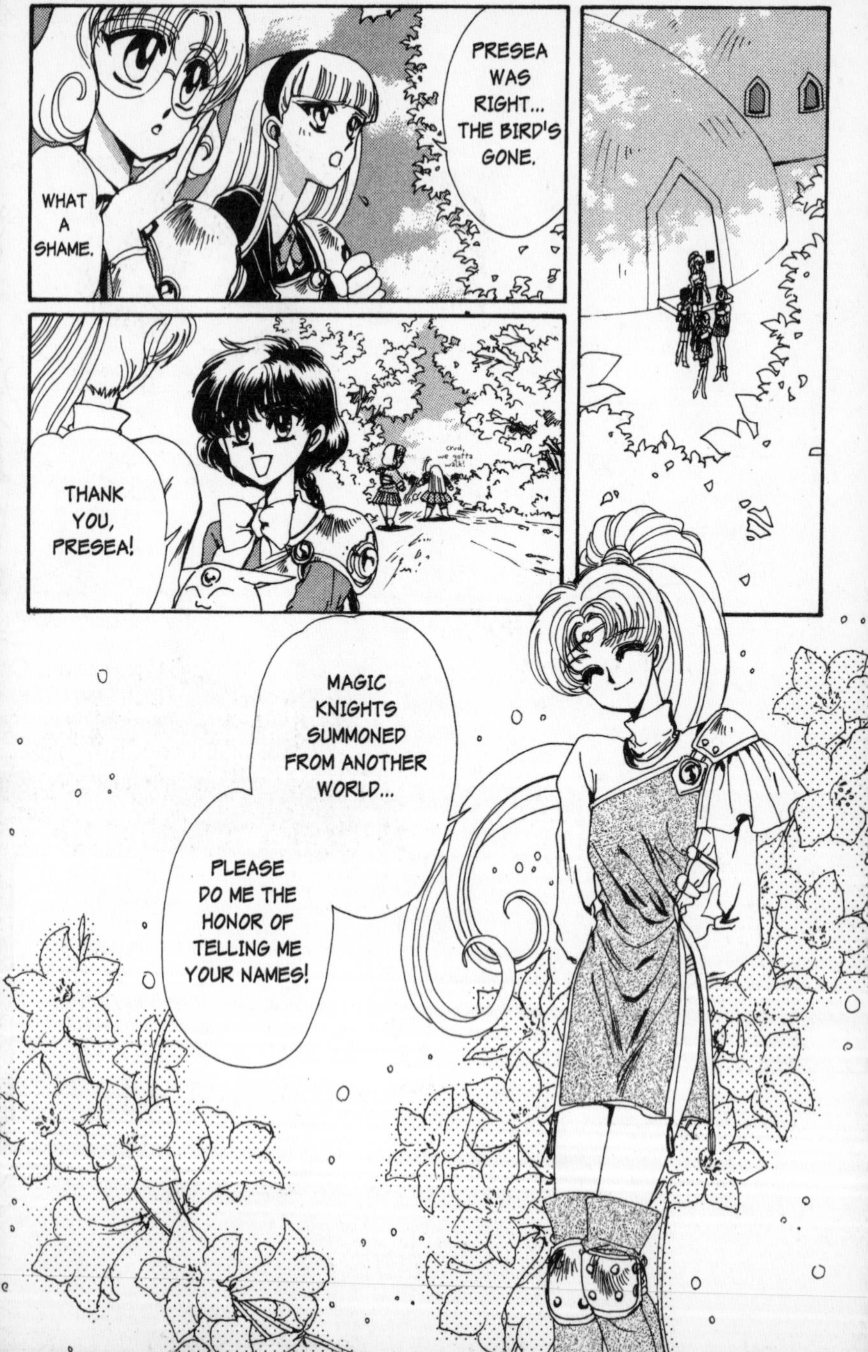
PRESEA WAS RIGHT... THE BIRD'S GONE.
WHAT A SHAME.
crud, we gotta walk!
THANK YOU, PRESEA!
MAGIC KNIGHTS SUMMONED FROM ANOTHER WORLD...
PLEASE DO ME THE HONOR OF TELLING ME YOUR NAMES!

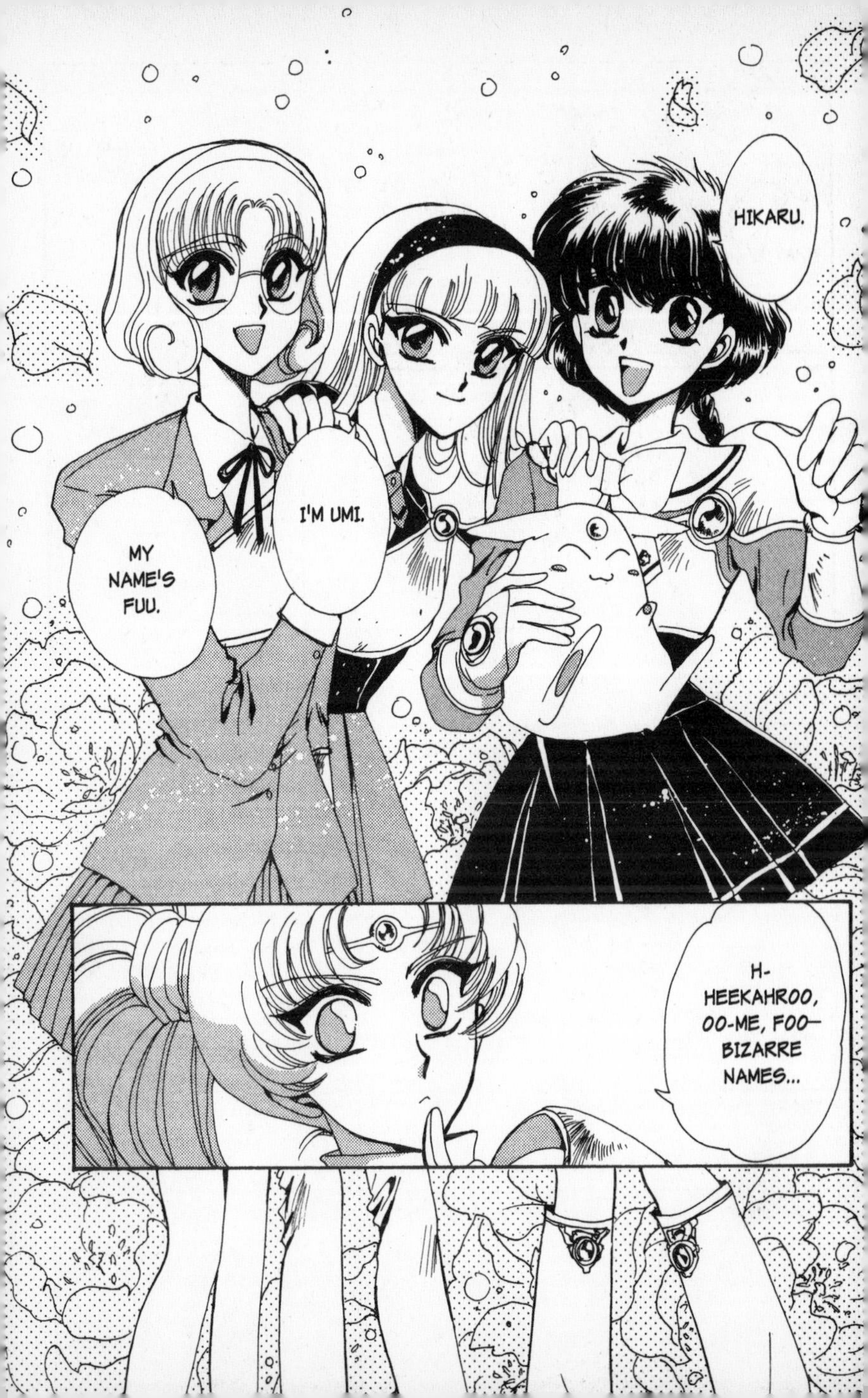
HIKARU.
I'M UMI.
MY NAME'S FUU.
H-HEEKAHROO, OO-ME, FOO—BIZARRE NAMES...

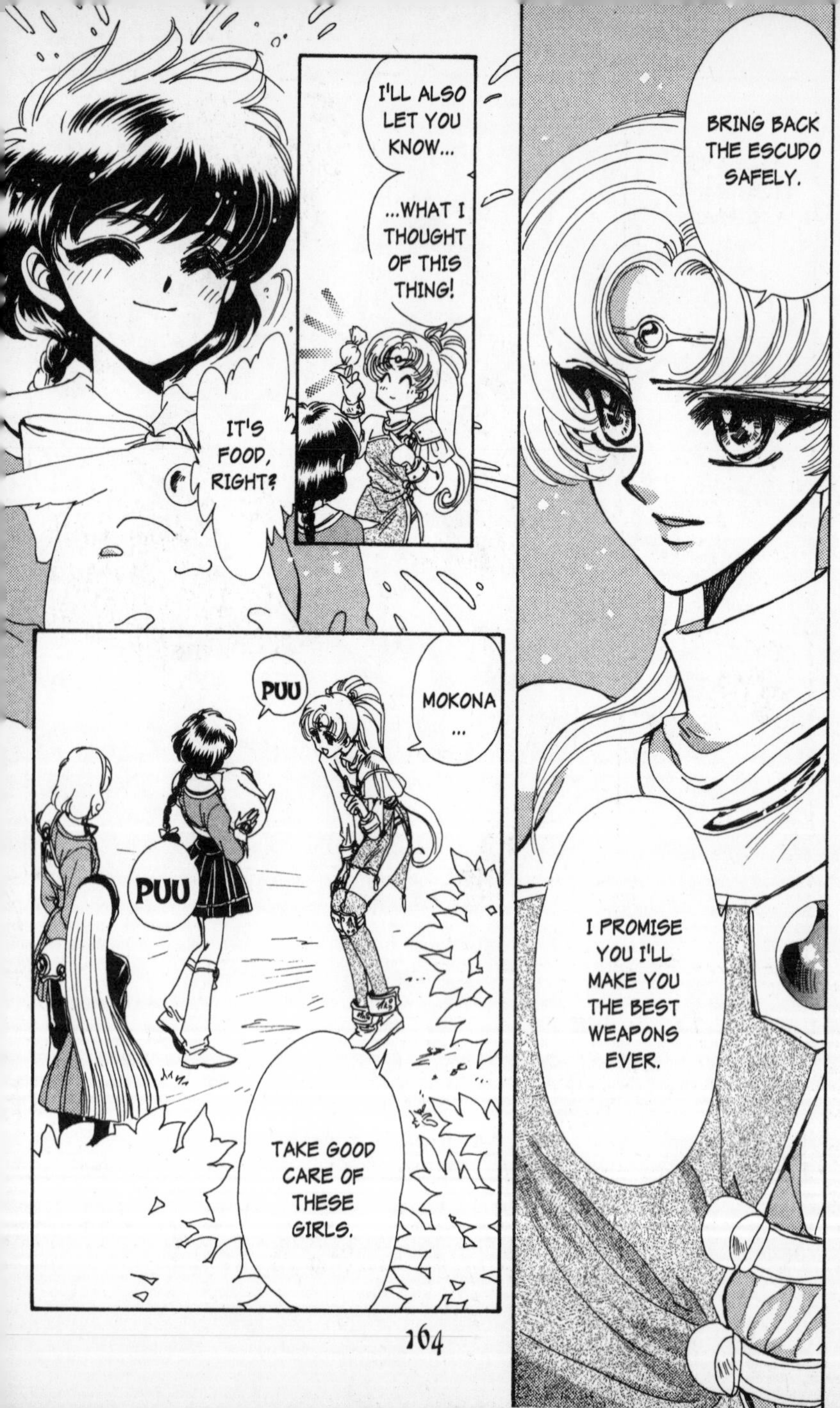
BRING BACK THE ESCUDO SAFELY.
I PROMISE YOU I'LL MAKE YOU THE BEST WEAPONS EVER.
I'LL ALSO LET YOU KNOW...
...WHAT I THOUGHT OF THIS THING!
IT'S FOOD, RIGHT?
MOKONA ...
PUU
PUU
TAKE GOOD CARE OF THESE GIRLS.

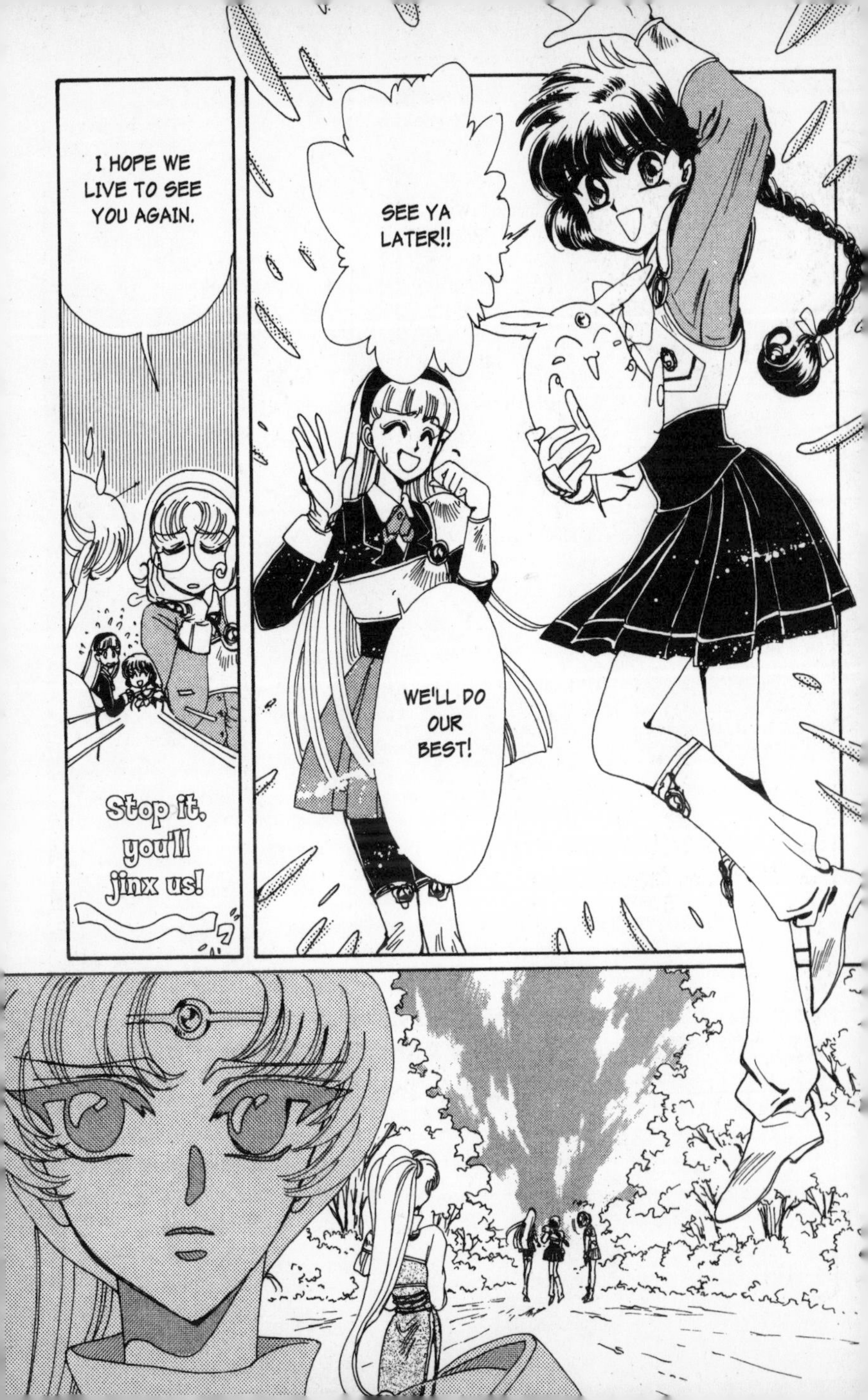
SEE YA LATER!!
WE'LL DO OUR BEST!
I HOPE WE LIVE TO SEE YOU AGAIN.
Stop it, you'll jinx us!

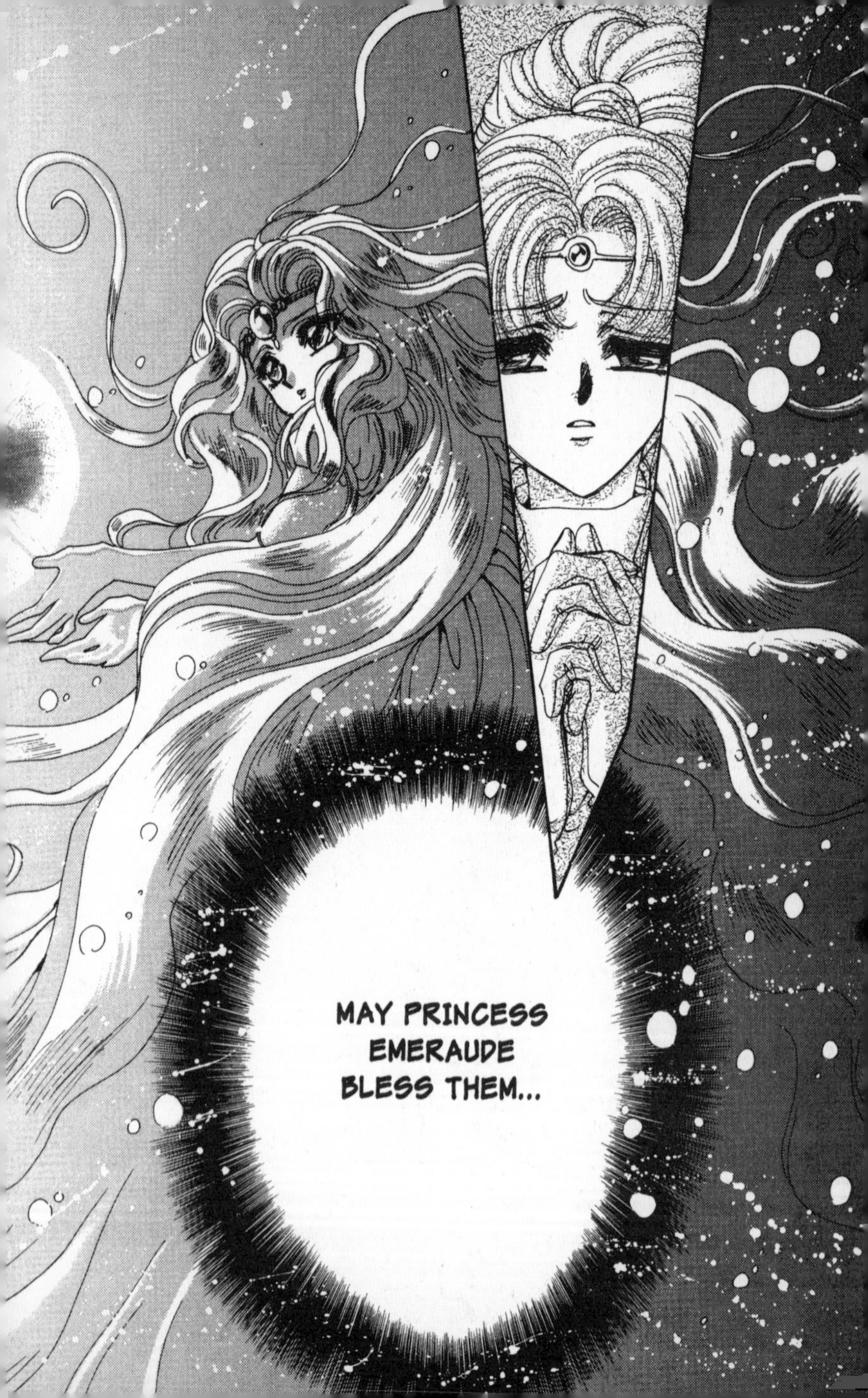
MAY PRINCESS EMERAUDE BLESS THEM...

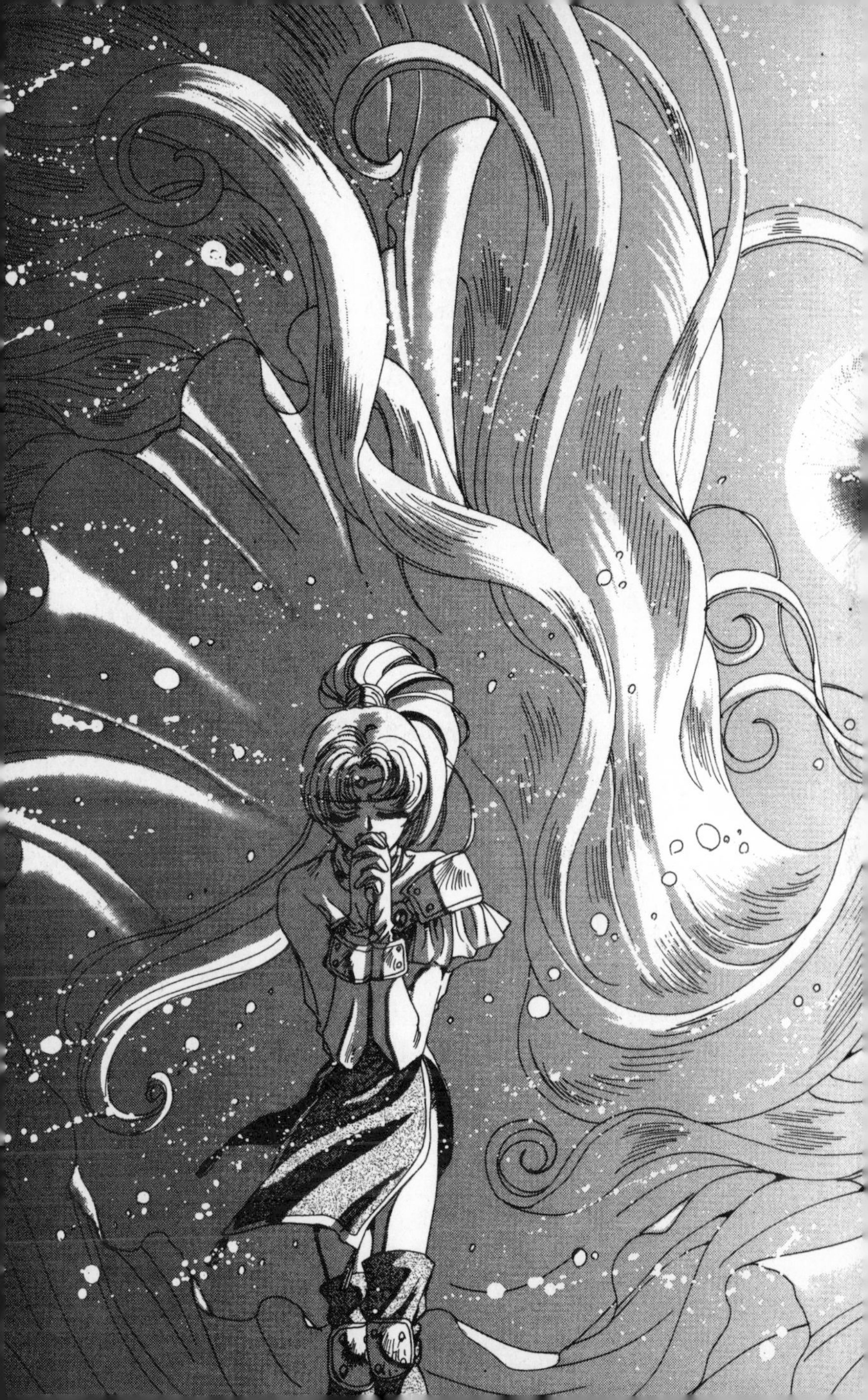

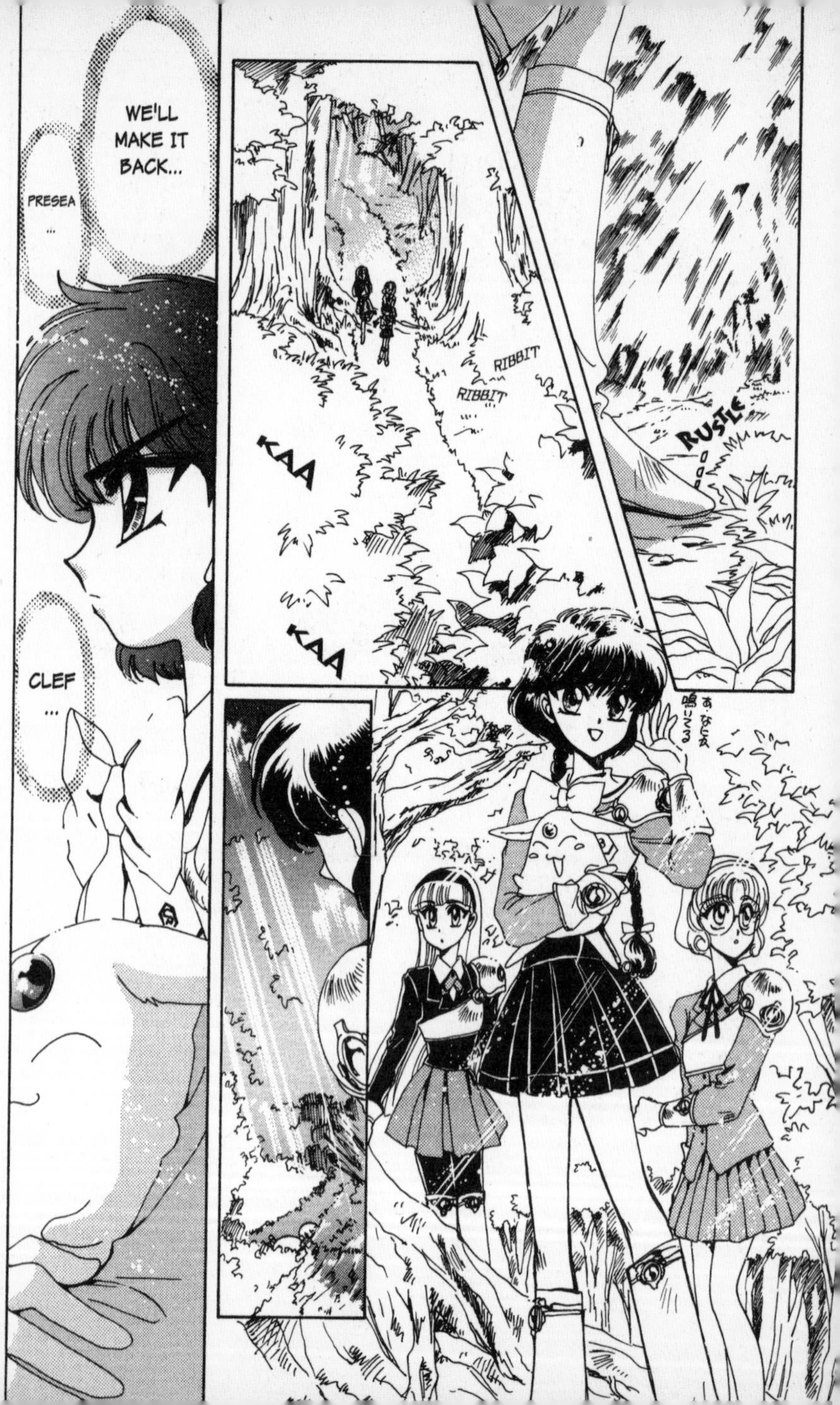
RUSTLE
RIBBIT
RIBBIT
KAA
KAA
あ・なにか鳴いてる
WE'LL MAKE IT BACK...
PRESEA ...
CLEF ...

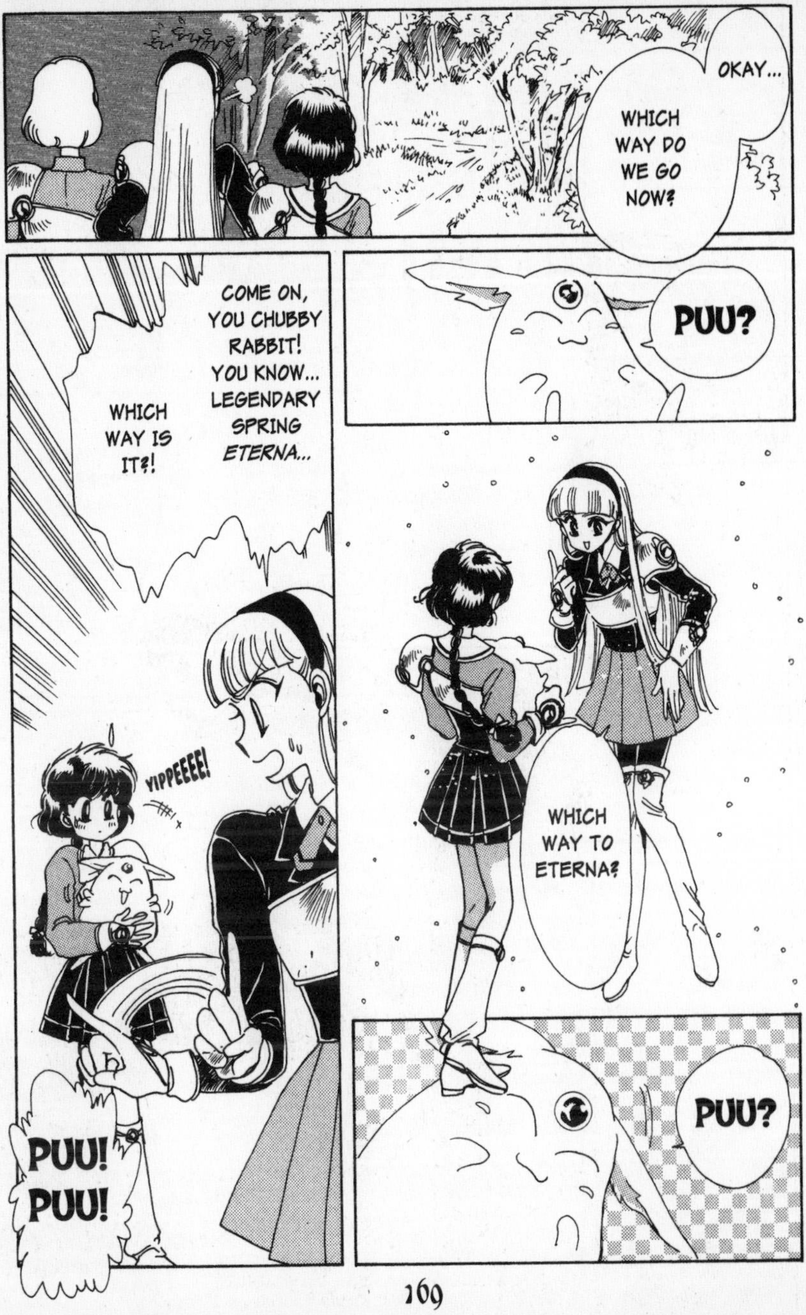
OKAY...
WHICH WAY DO WE GO NOW?
PUU?
WHICH WAY TO ETERNA?
PUU?
COME ON, YOU CHUBBY RABBIT! YOU KNOW... LEGENDARY SPRING *ETERNA*...
WHICH WAY IS IT?!
YIPPEEEE!
PUU! PUU!

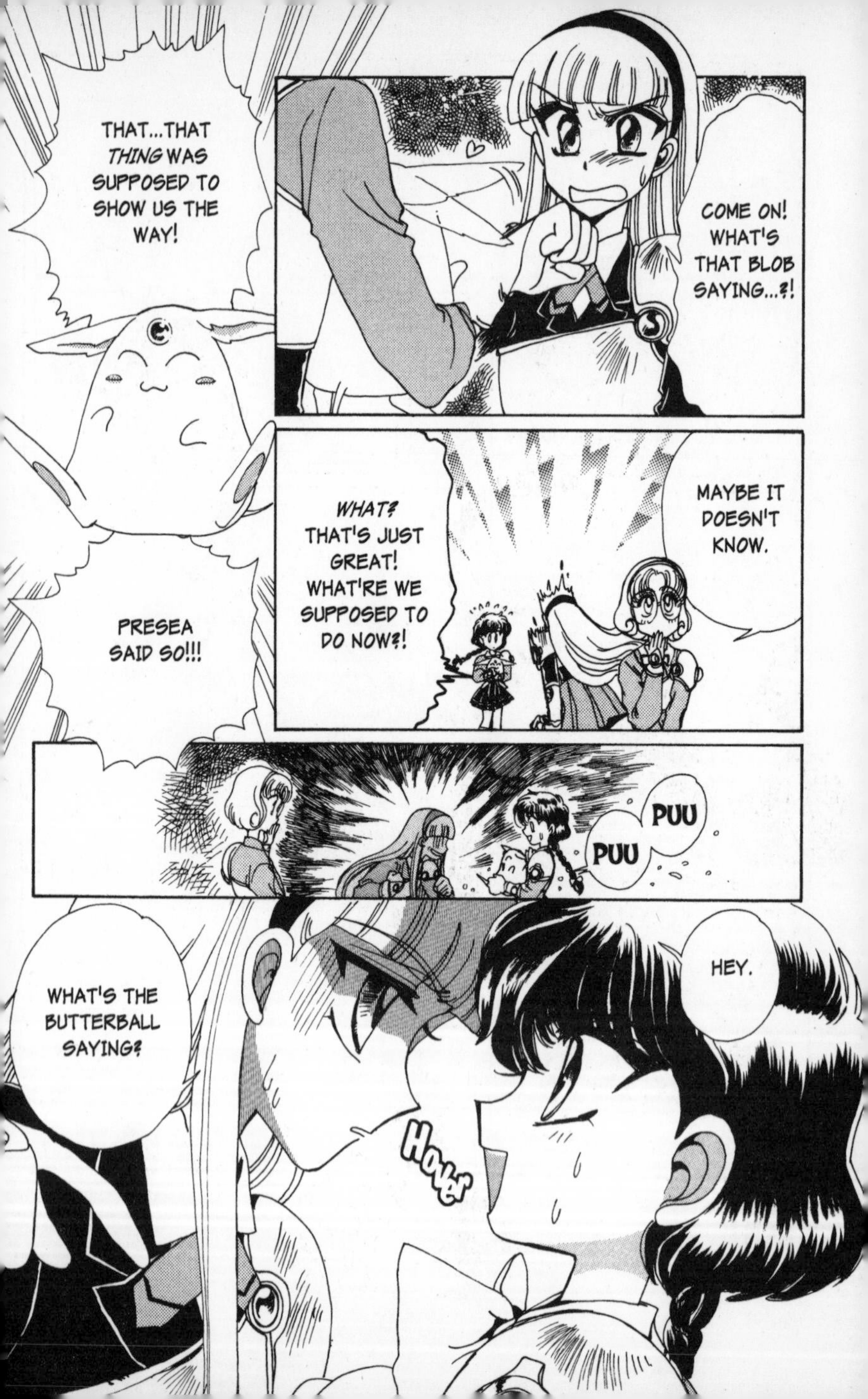
COME ON! WHAT'S THAT BLOB SAYING...?!
THAT...THAT *THING* WAS SUPPOSED TO SHOW US THE WAY!
PRESEA SAID SO!!!
MAYBE IT DOESN'T KNOW.
WHAT? THAT'S JUST GREAT! WHAT'RE WE SUPPOSED TO DO NOW?!
PUU
PUU
HEY.
Hover
WHAT'S THE BUTTERBALL SAYING?

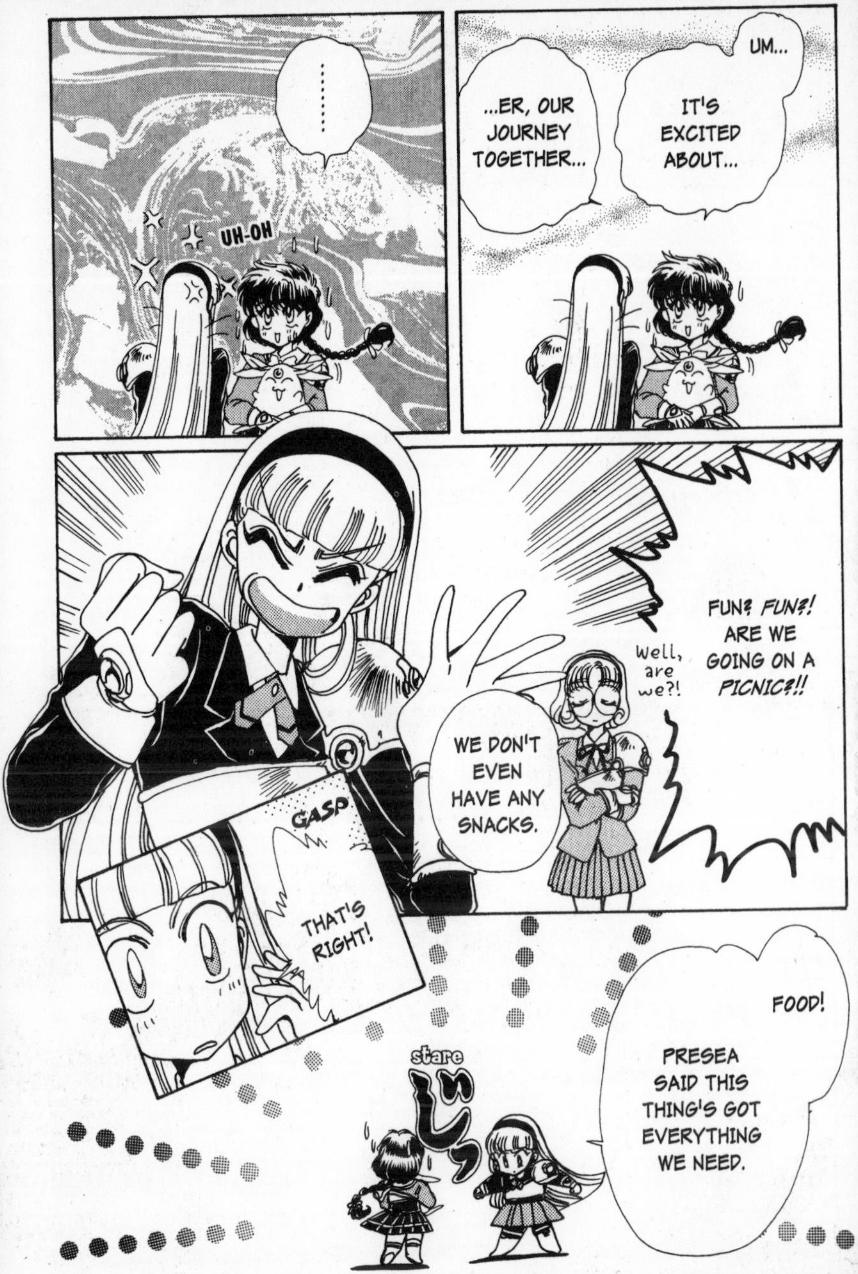
UM...
IT'S EXCITED ABOUT...
...ER, OUR JOURNEY TOGETHER...
......
UH-OH
FUN? FUN?! ARE WE GOING ON A PICNIC?!!
Well, are we?!
WE DON'T EVEN HAVE ANY SNACKS.
GASP
THAT'S RIGHT!
FOOD!
PRESEA SAID THIS THING'S GOT EVERYTHING WE NEED.
stare

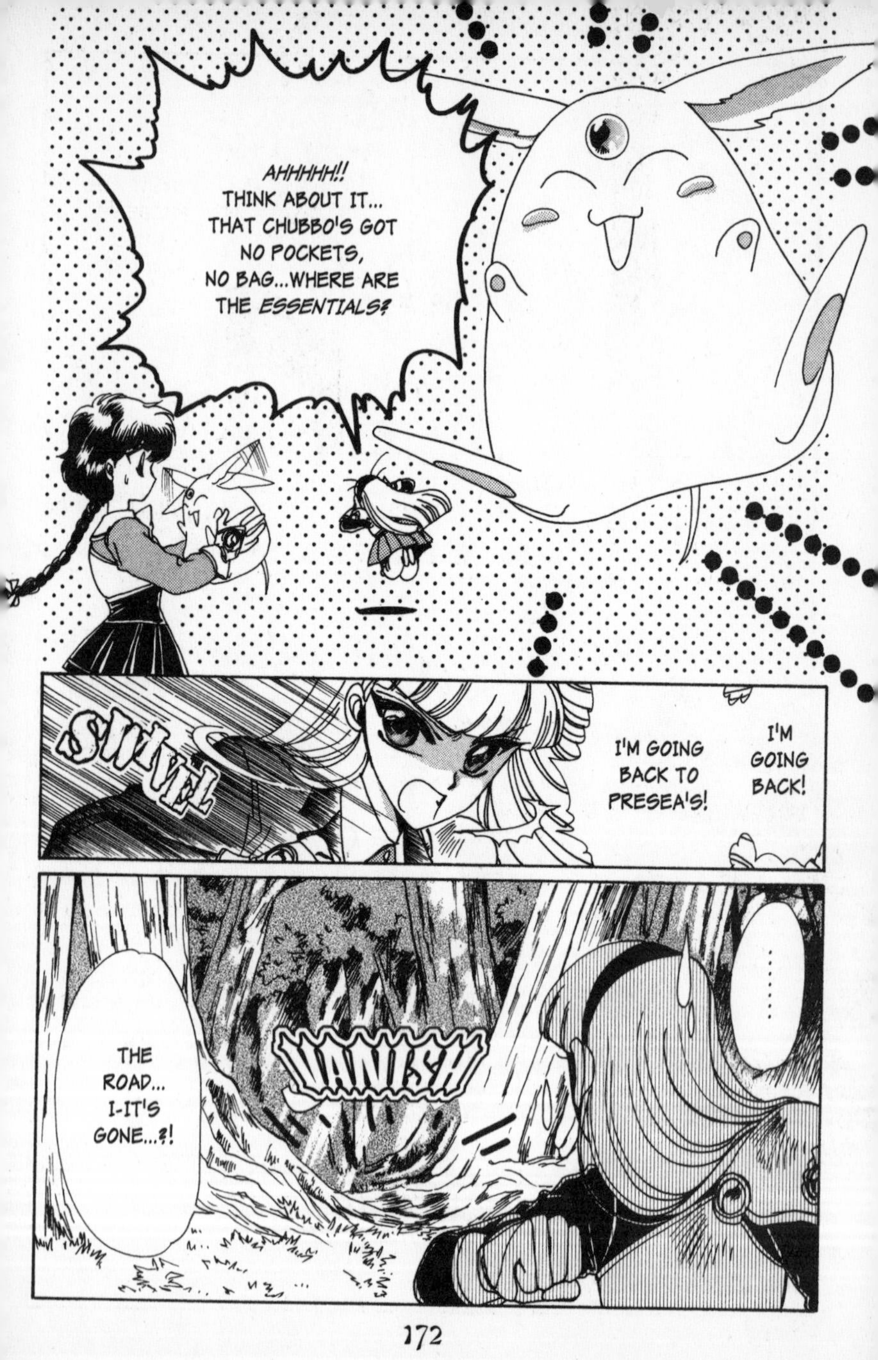
AHHHHH!! THINK ABOUT IT... THAT CHUBBO'S GOT NO POCKETS, NO BAG...WHERE ARE THE ESSENTIALS?
I'M GOING BACK!
I'M GOING BACK TO PRESEA'S!
SWIVEL
......
VANISH
THE ROAD... I-IT'S GONE...?!

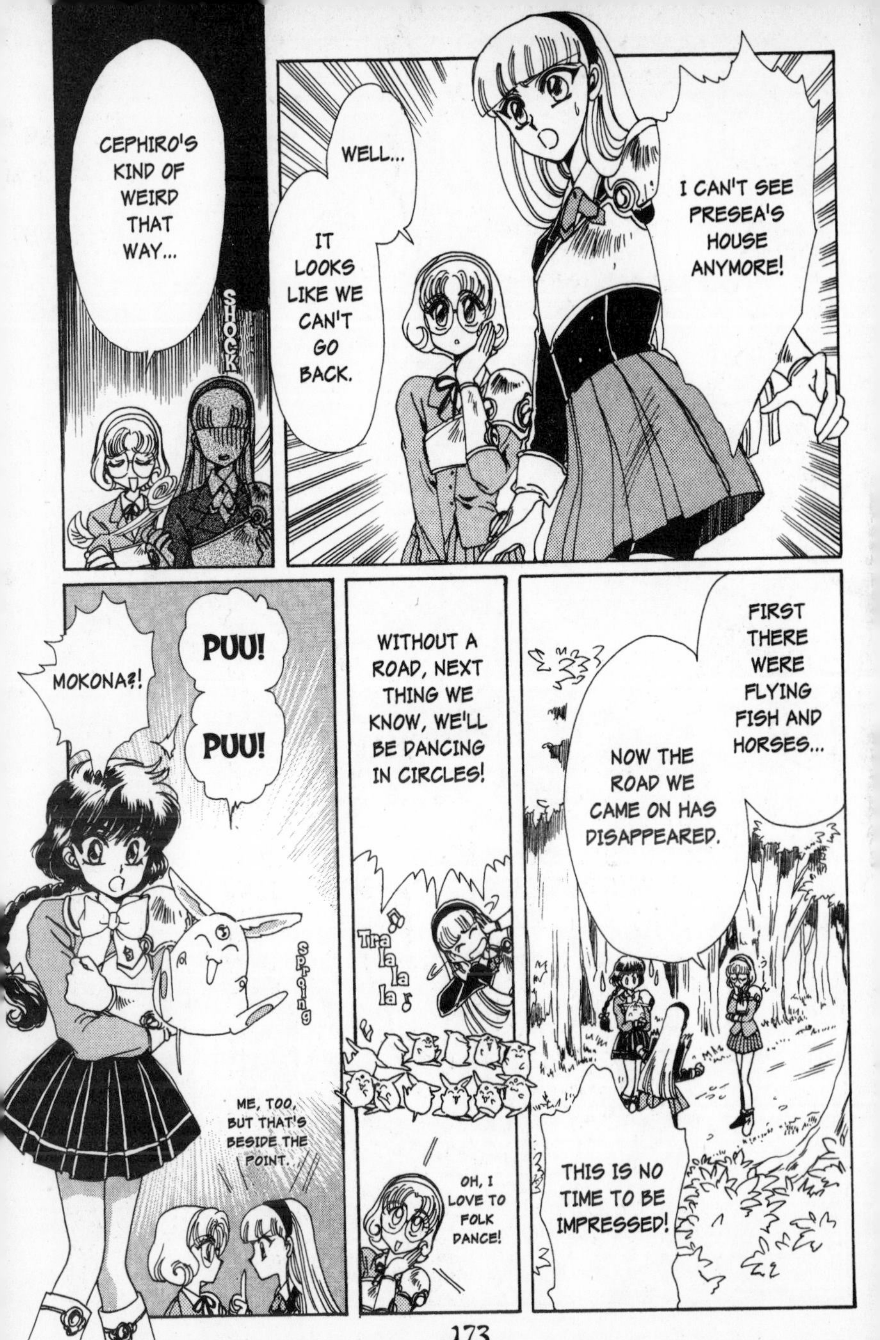
I CAN'T SEE PRESEA'S HOUSE ANYMORE!
WELL...
IT LOOKS LIKE WE CAN'T GO BACK.
CEPHIRO'S KIND OF WEIRD THAT WAY...
SHOCK
FIRST THERE WERE FLYING FISH AND HORSES...
NOW THE ROAD WE CAME ON HAS DISAPPEARED.
THIS IS NO TIME TO BE IMPRESSED!
WITHOUT A ROAD, NEXT THING WE KNOW, WE'LL BE DANCING IN CIRCLES!
Tra la la la
OH, I LOVE TO FOLK DANCE!
MOKONA?!
PUU!
PUU!
spring
ME, TOO, BUT THAT'S BESIDE THE POINT.

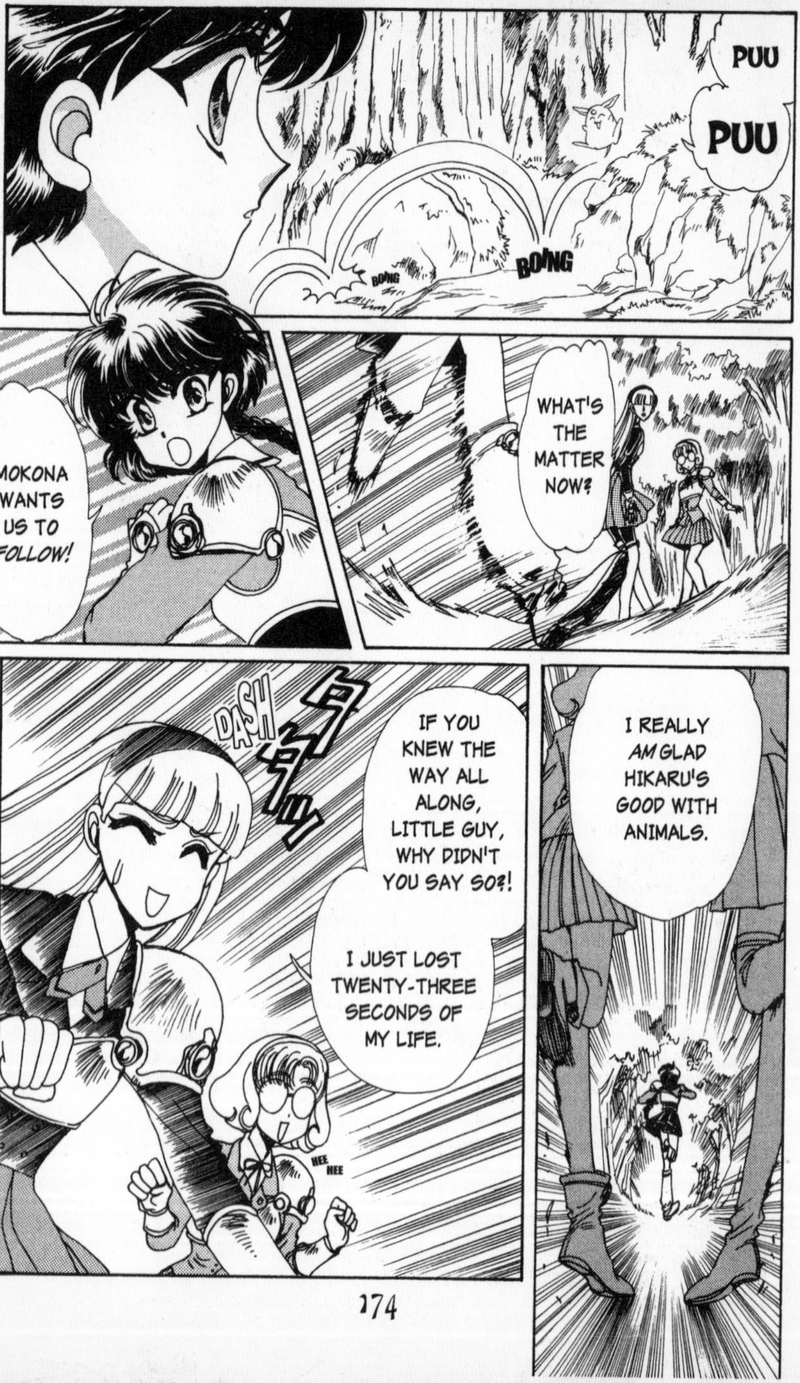
PUU
PUU
BOING
BOING
WHAT'S THE MATTER NOW?
MOKONA WANTS US TO *FOLLOW!*
I REALLY *AM* GLAD HIKARU'S GOOD WITH ANIMALS.
DASH
IF YOU KNEW THE WAY ALL ALONG, LITTLE GUY, WHY DIDN'T YOU SAY SO?!
I JUST LOST TWENTY-THREE SECONDS OF MY LIFE.
HEE HEE

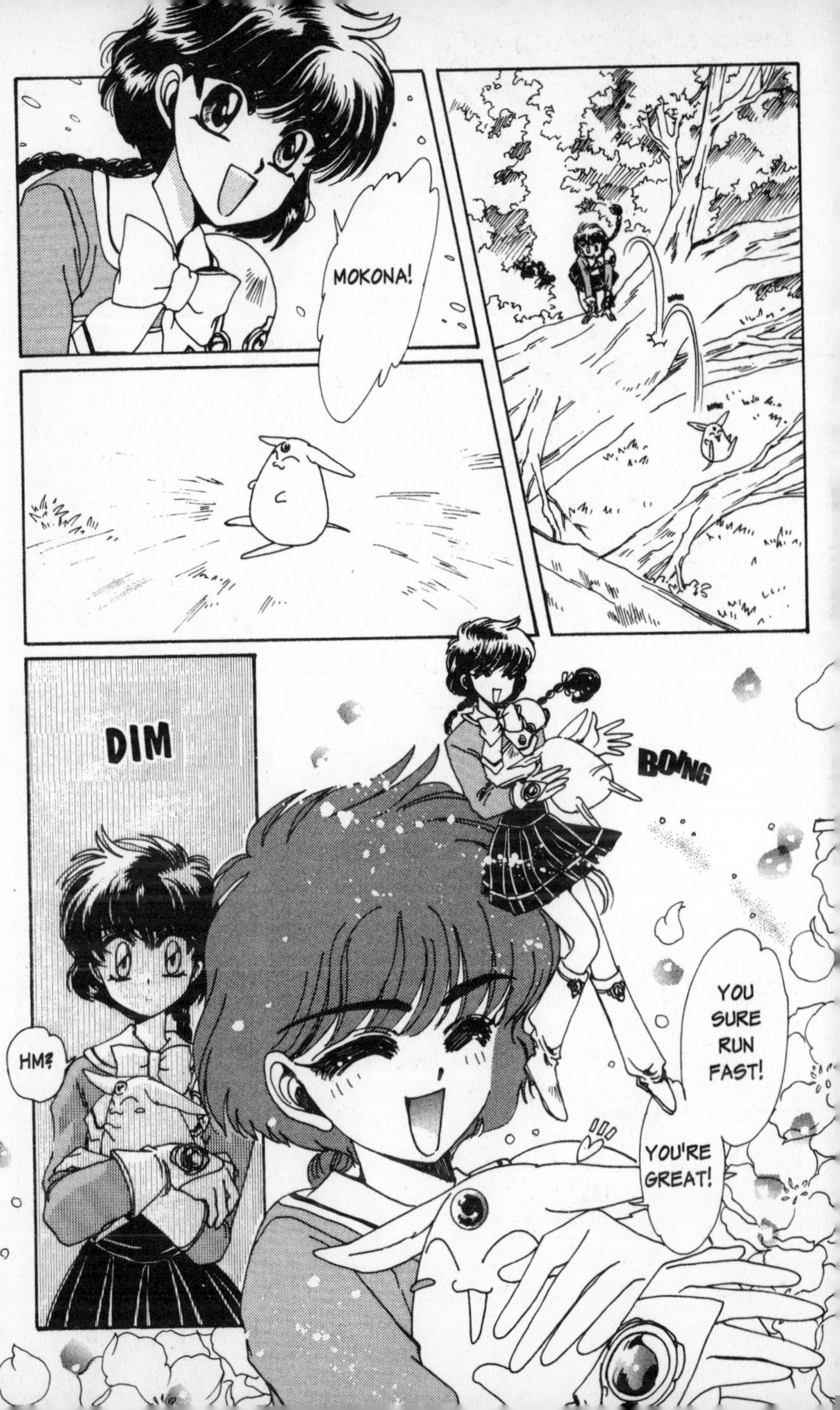
MOKONA!
BOING
YOU SURE RUN FAST!
YOU'RE GREAT!
DIM
HM?

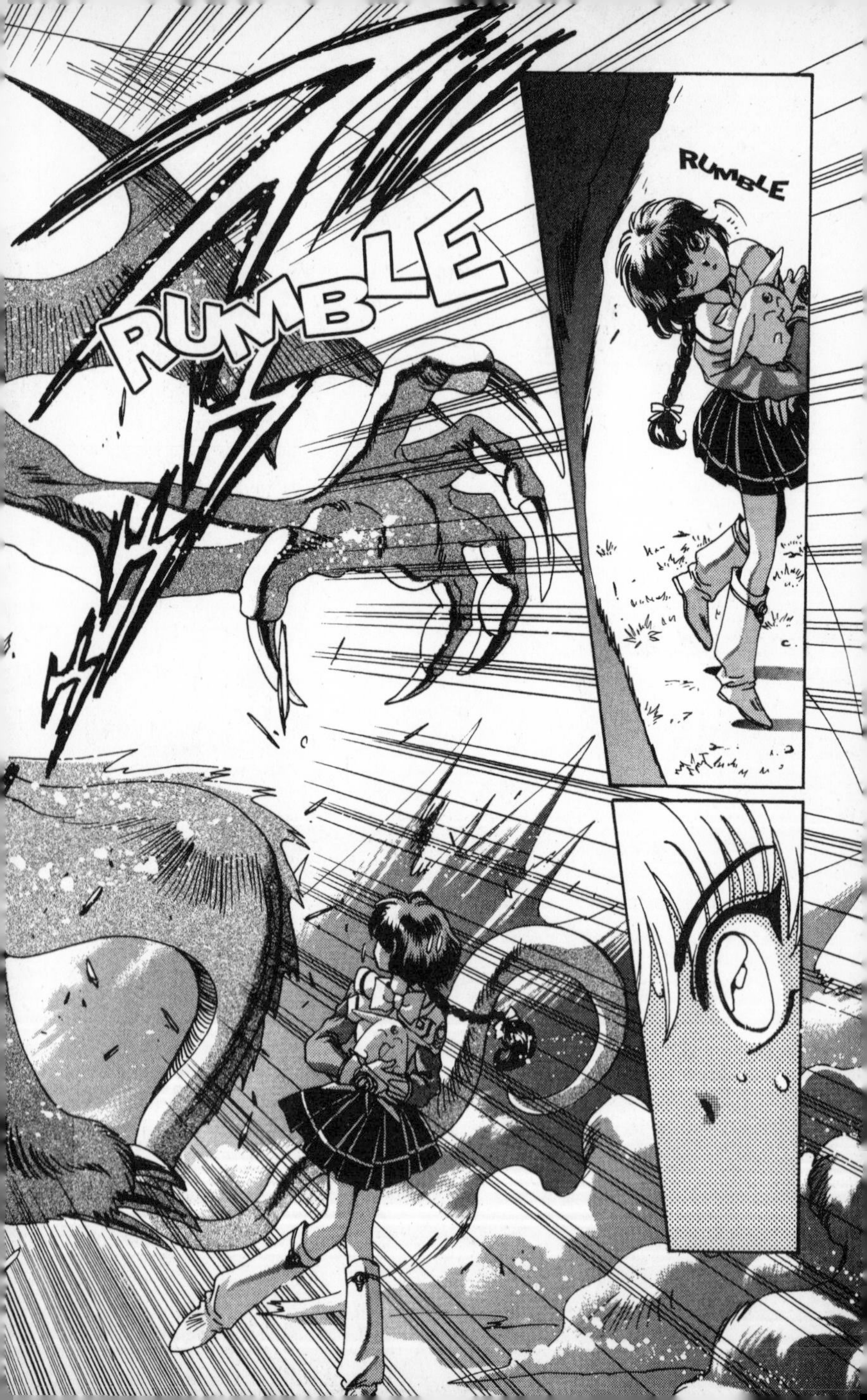
RUMBLE
RUMBLE

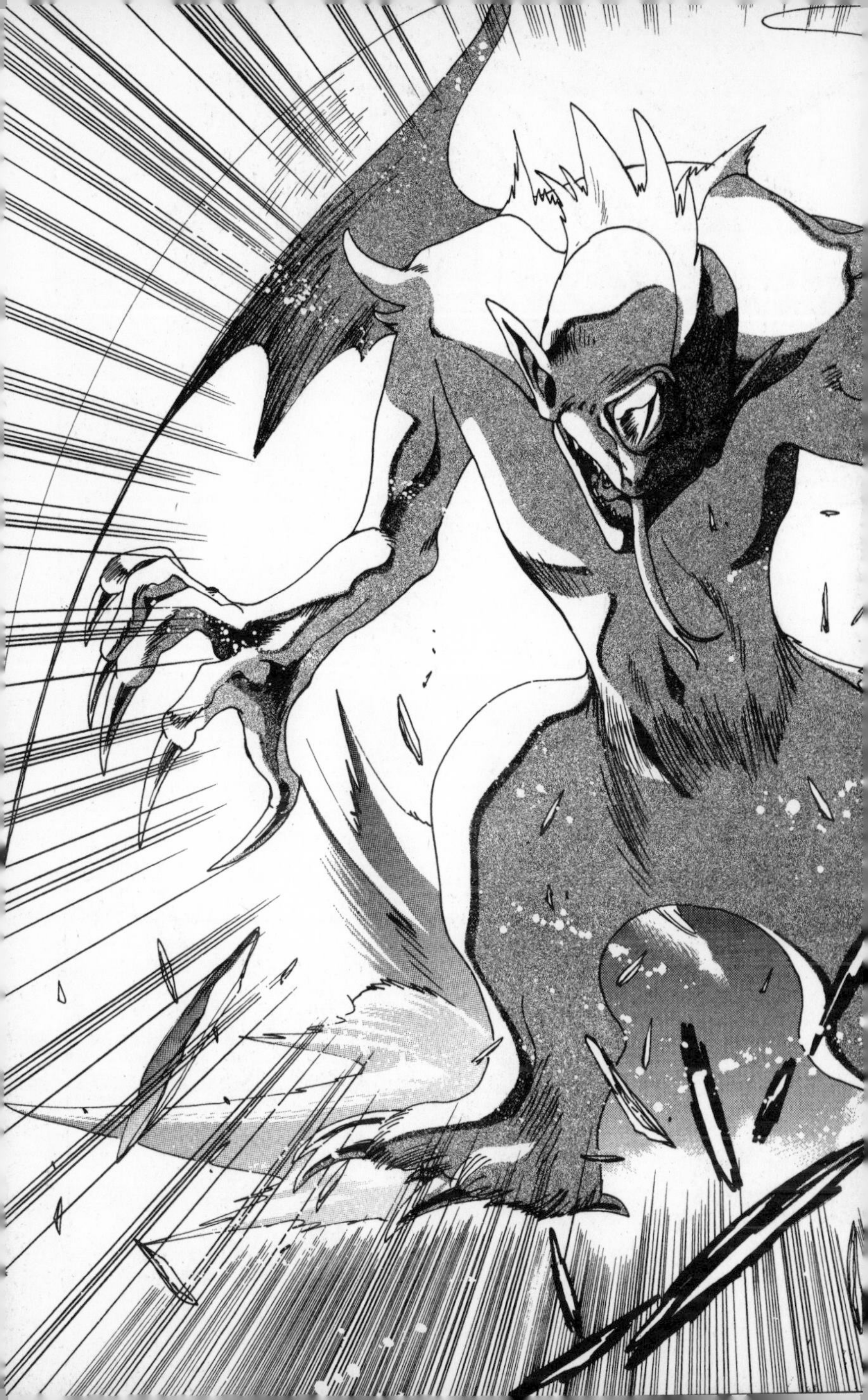

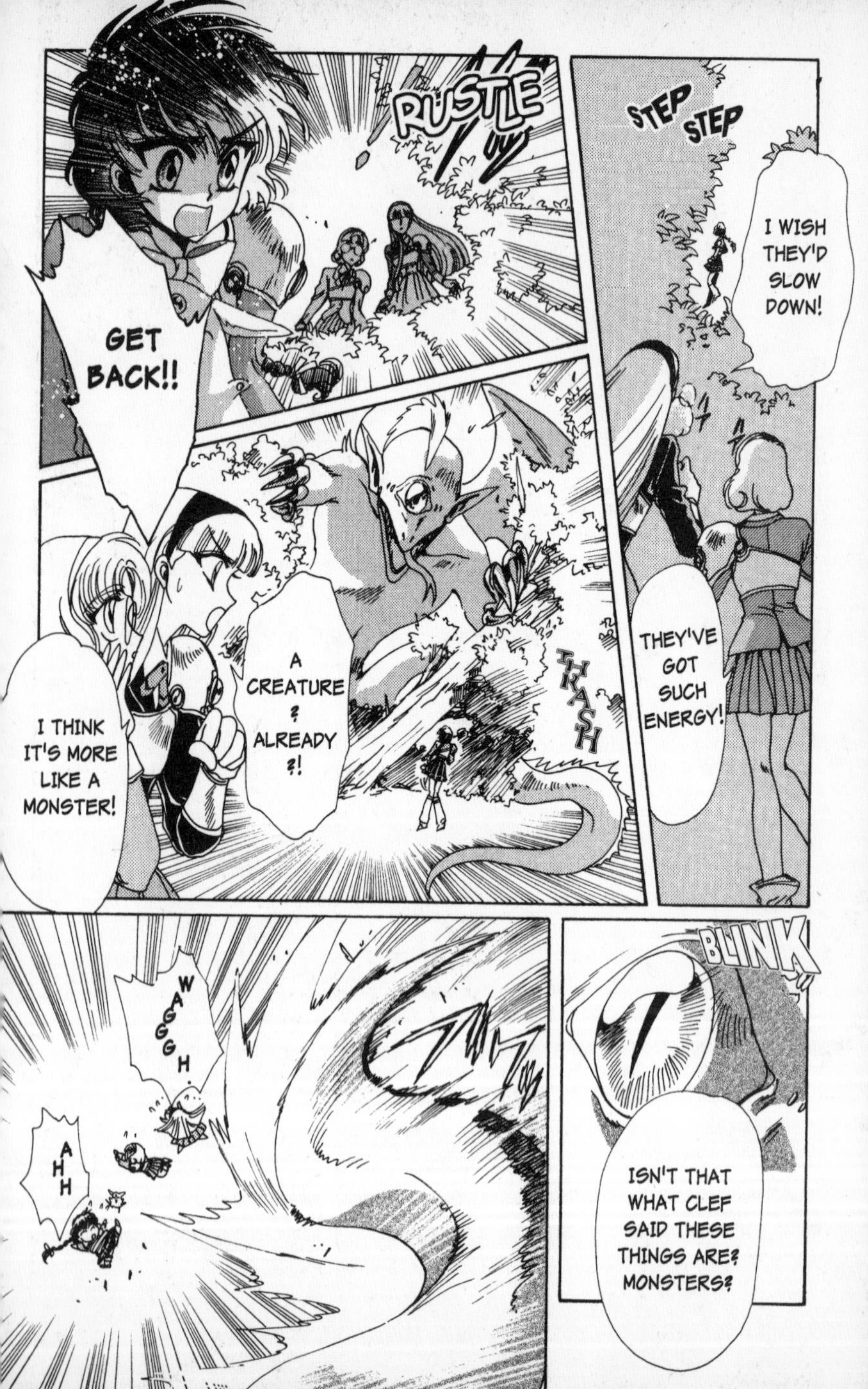
STEP STEP
I WISH THEY'D SLOW DOWN!
THEY'VE GOT SUCH ENERGY!
RUSTLE
GET BACK!!
A CREATURE? ALREADY?!
THRASH
I THINK IT'S MORE LIKE A MONSTER!
BLINK
ISN'T THAT WHAT CLEF SAID THESE THINGS ARE? MONSTERS?
WAAGGH
AHH

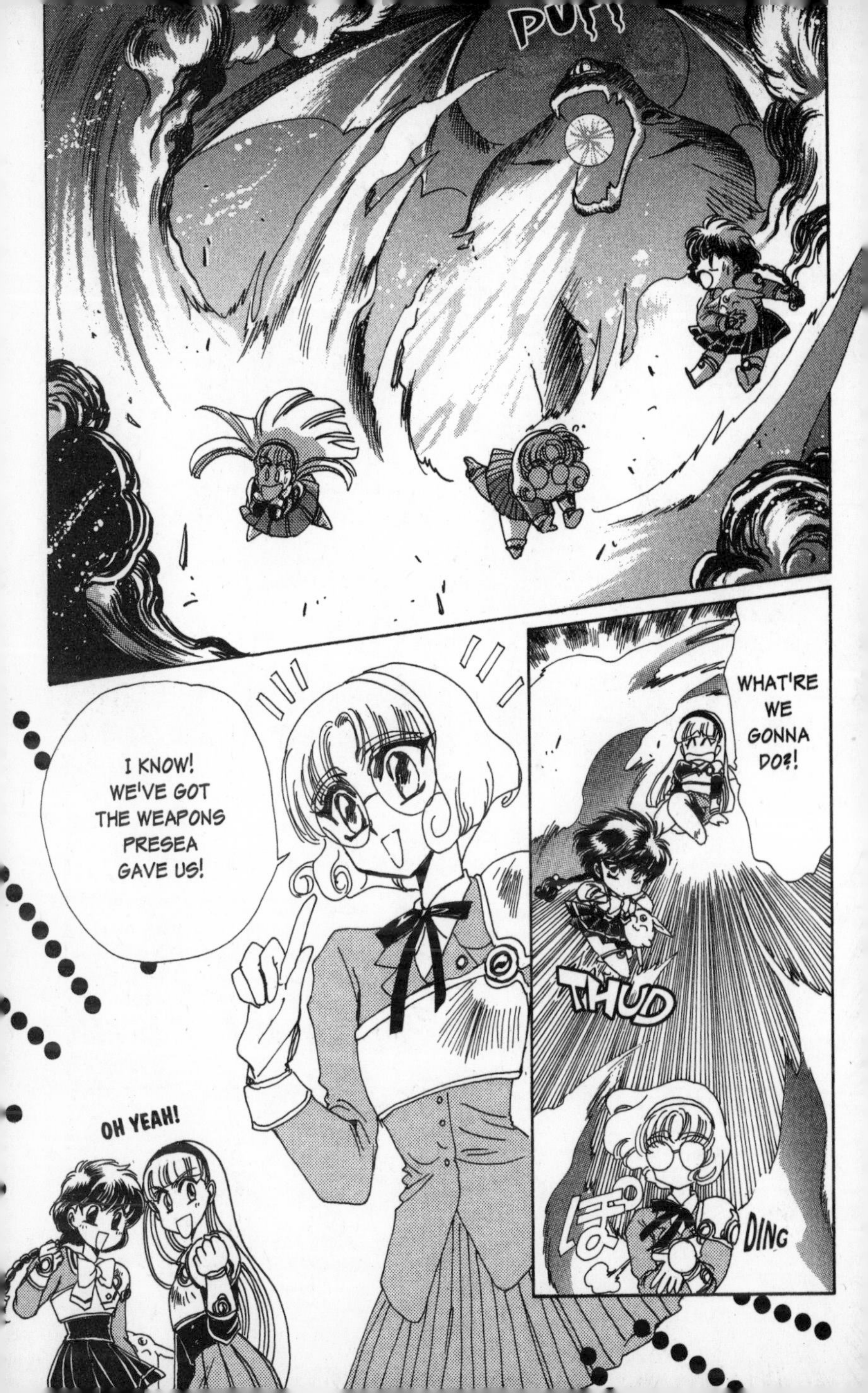
WHAT'RE WE GONNA DO?!
THUD
ぽっ
DING
I KNOW! WE'VE GOT THE WEAPONS PRESEA GAVE US!
OH YEAH!

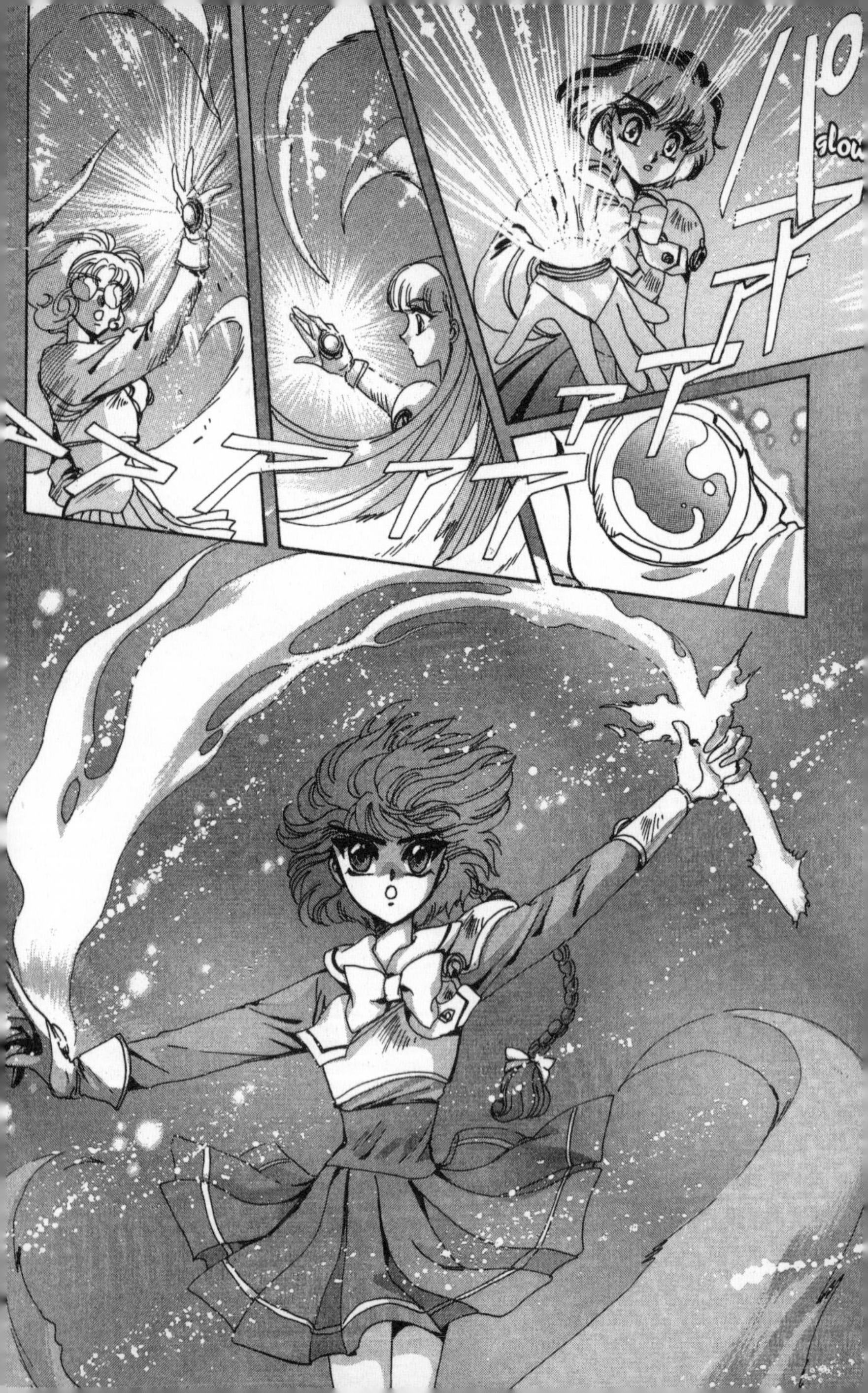

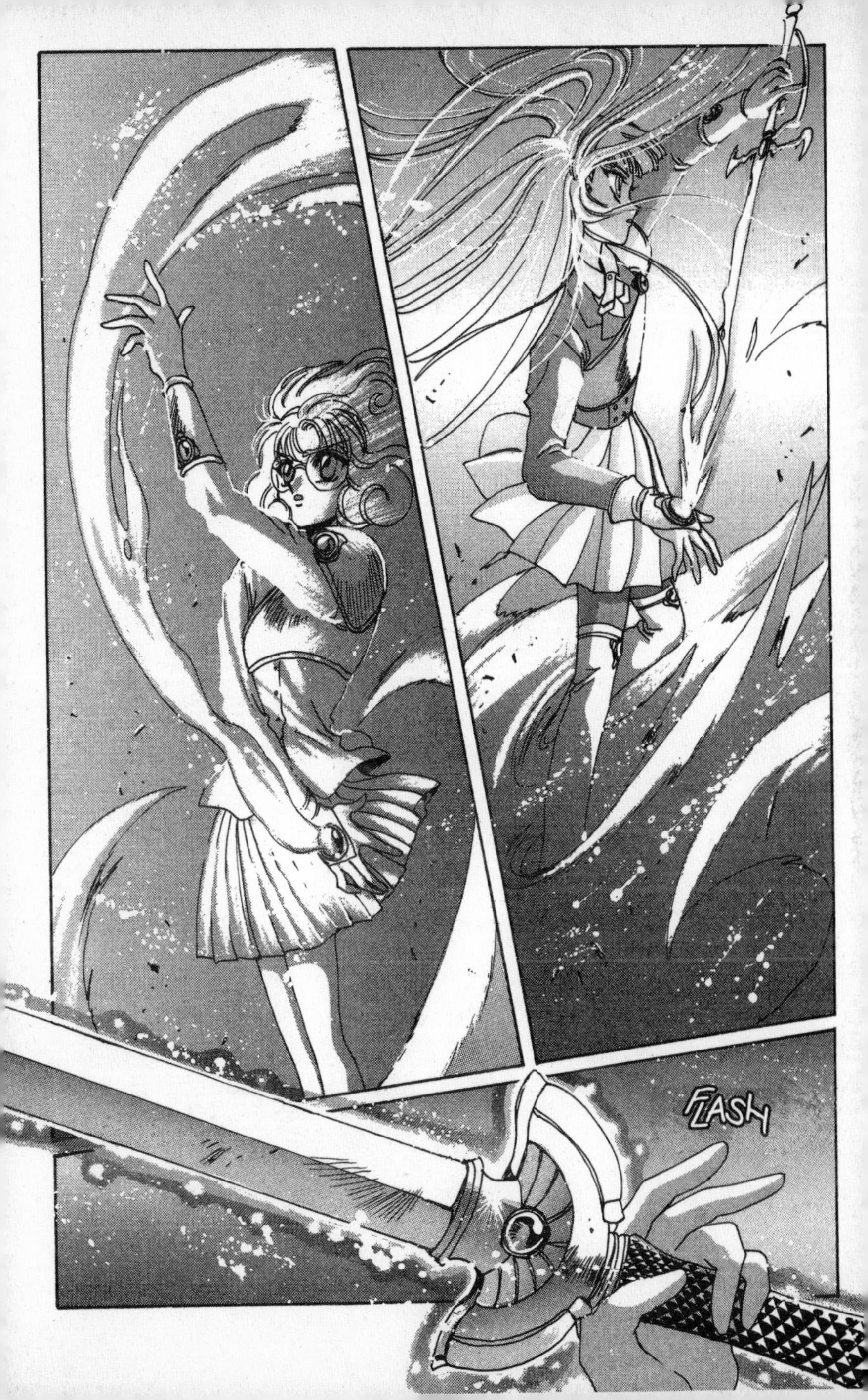
FLASH

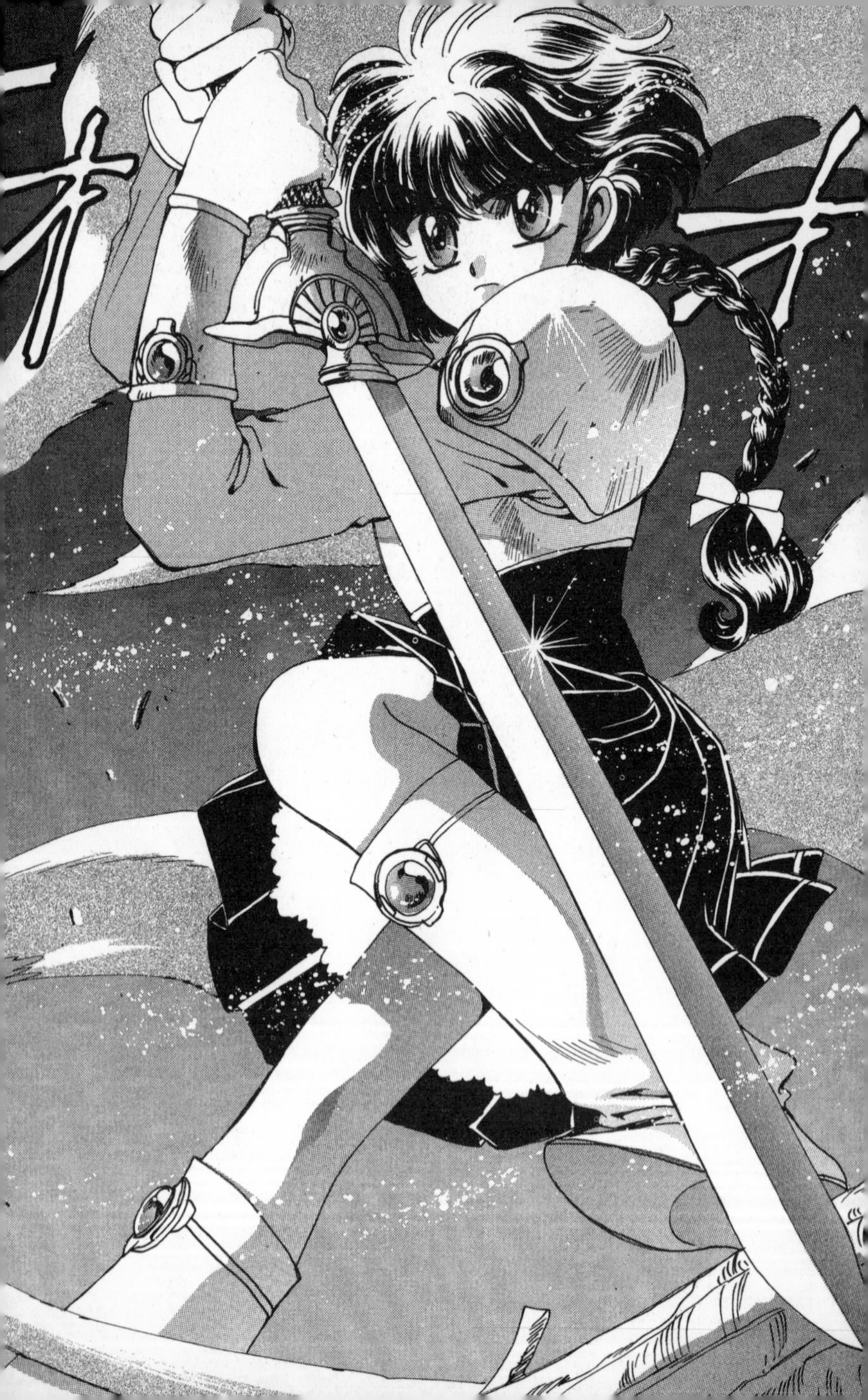

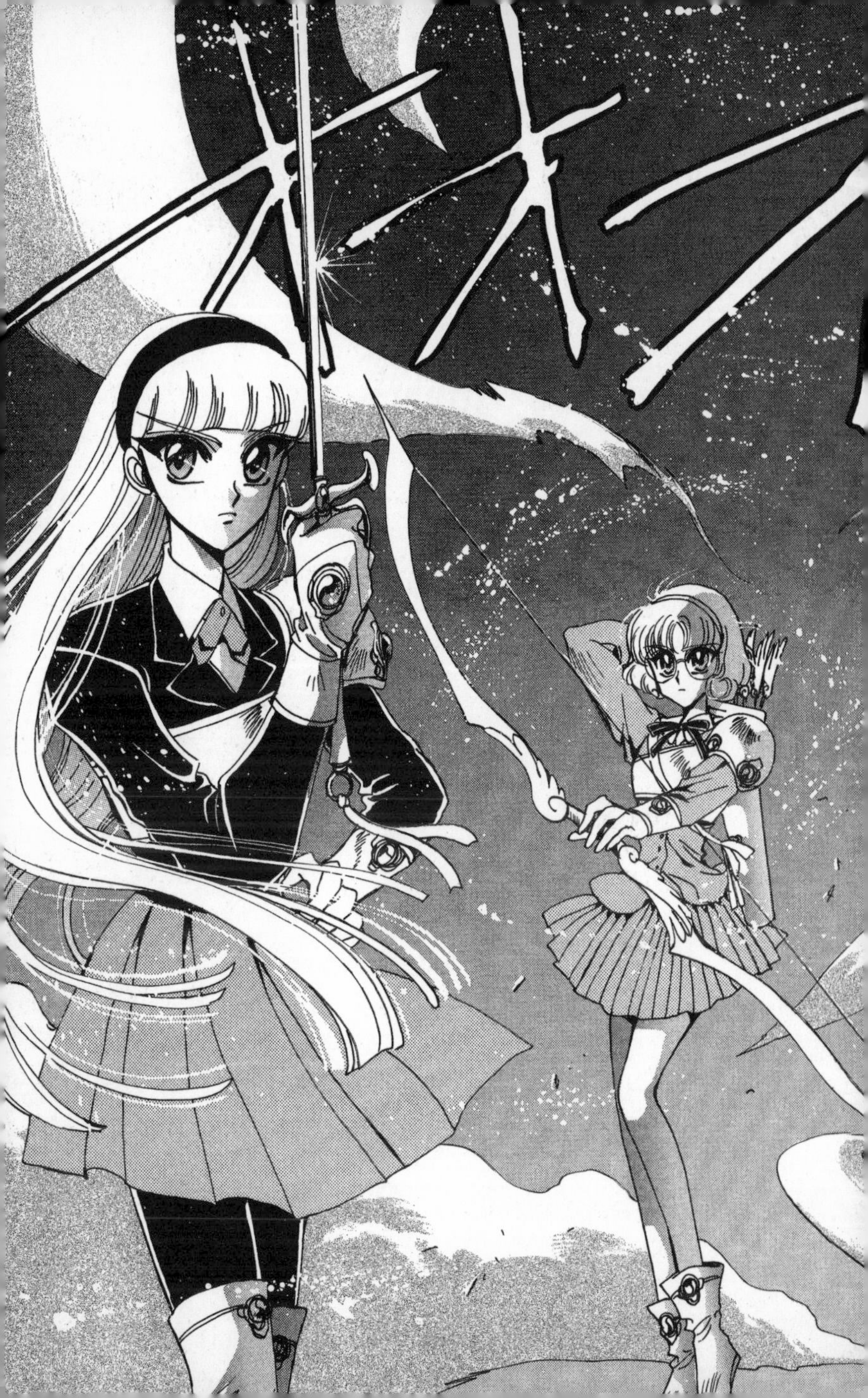

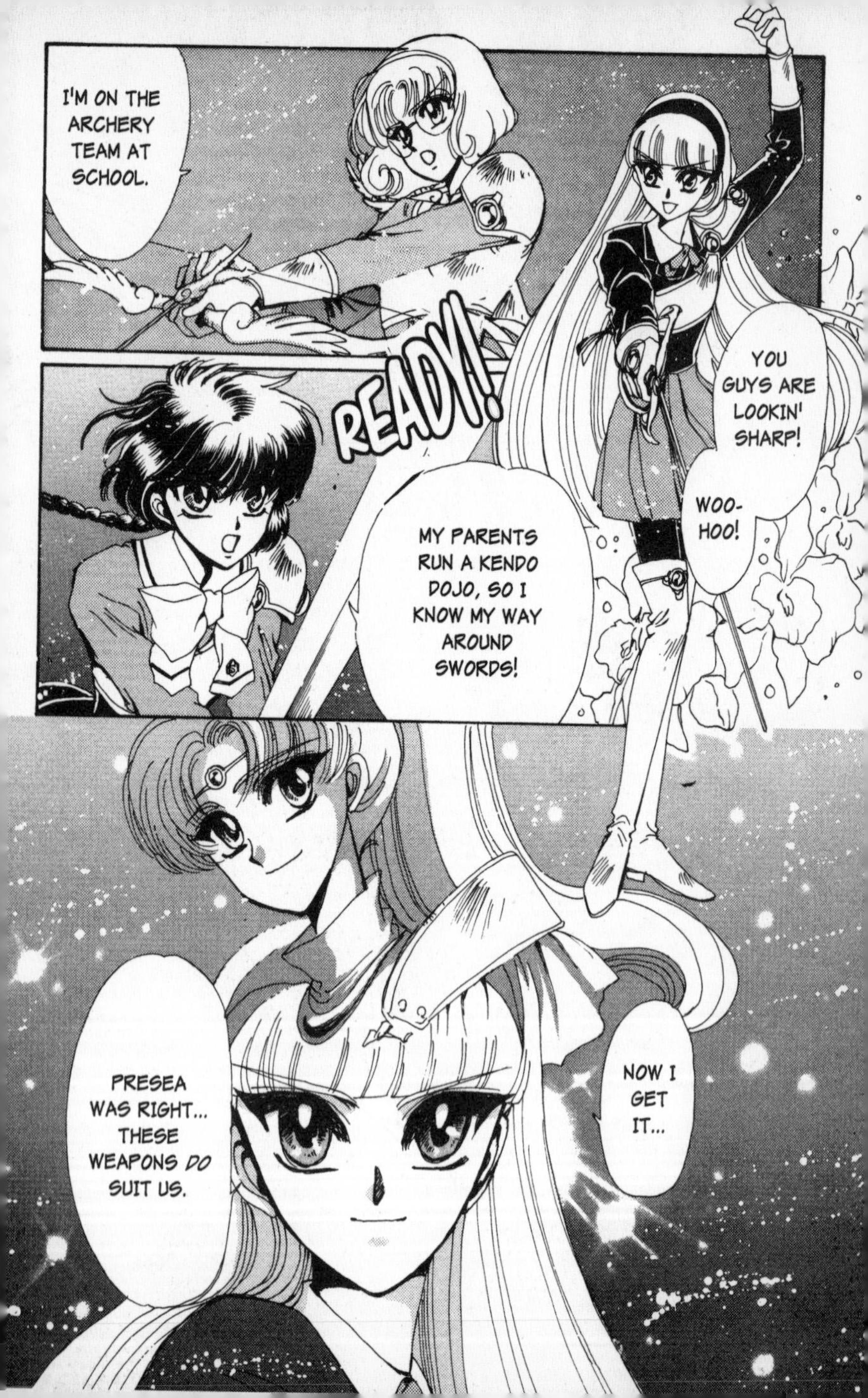
YOU GUYS ARE LOOKIN' SHARP!
WOO-HOO!
I'M ON THE ARCHERY TEAM AT SCHOOL.
READY!
MY PARENTS RUN A KENDO DOJO, SO I KNOW MY WAY AROUND SWORDS!
NOW I GET IT...
PRESEA WAS RIGHT... THESE WEAPONS *DO* SUIT US.

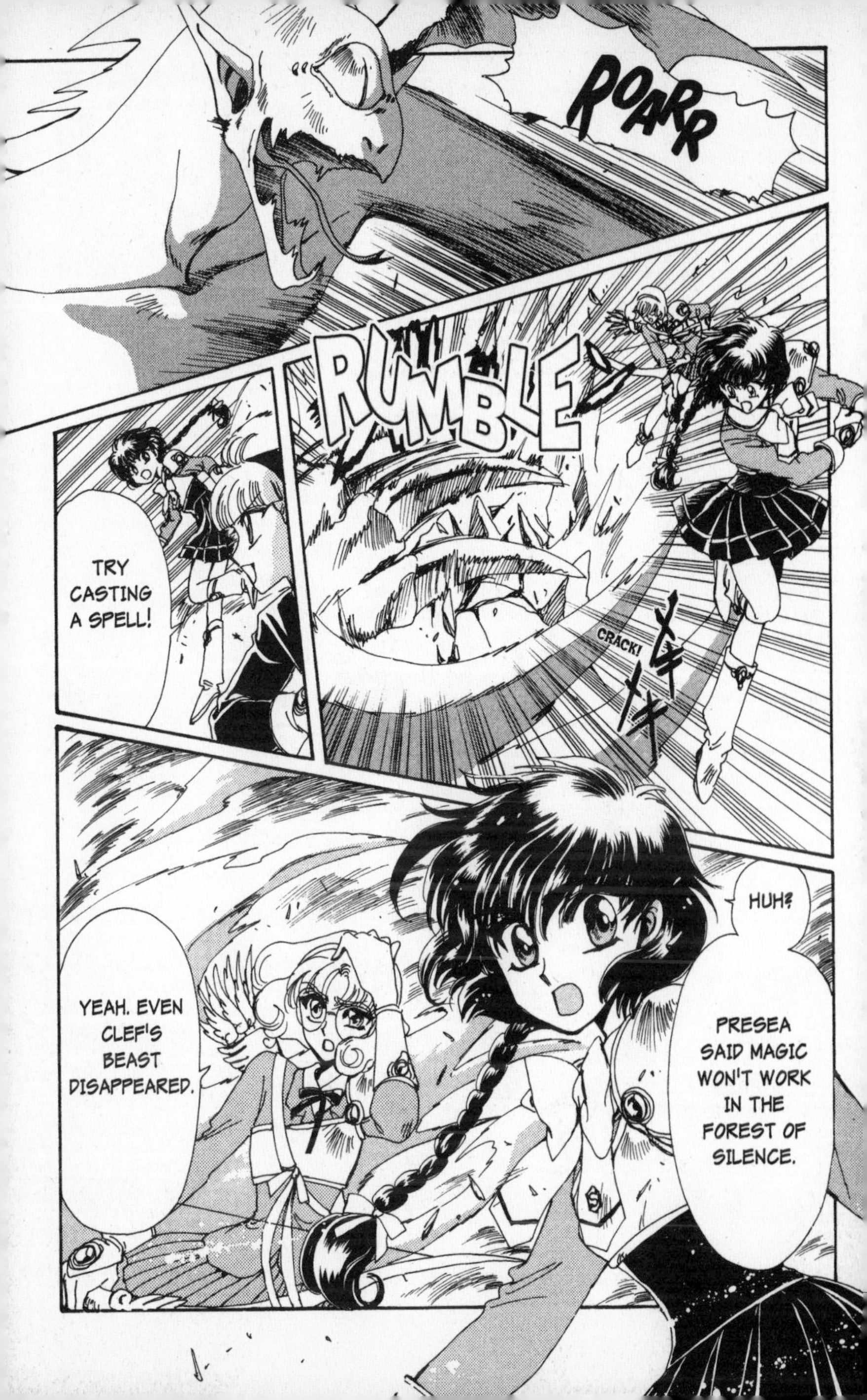

ROARR
RUMBLE
CRACK!
TRY CASTING A SPELL!
HUH?
PRESEA SAID MAGIC WON'T WORK IN THE FOREST OF SILENCE.
YEAH. EVEN CLEF'S BEAST DISAPPEARED.

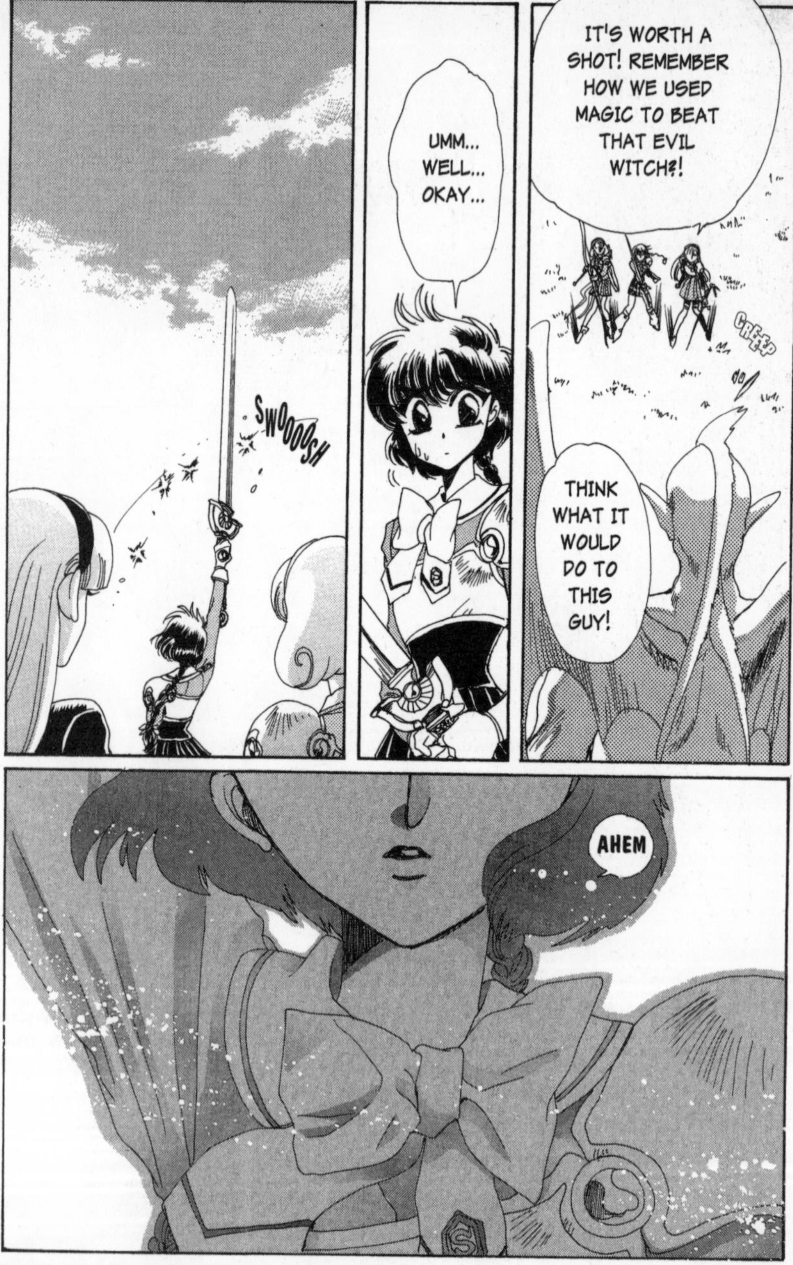
IT'S WORTH A SHOT! REMEMBER HOW WE USED MAGIC TO BEAT THAT EVIL WITCH?!
CREEEP
THINK WHAT IT WOULD DO TO THIS GUY!
UMM... WELL... OKAY...
SWOOOOSH
AHEM

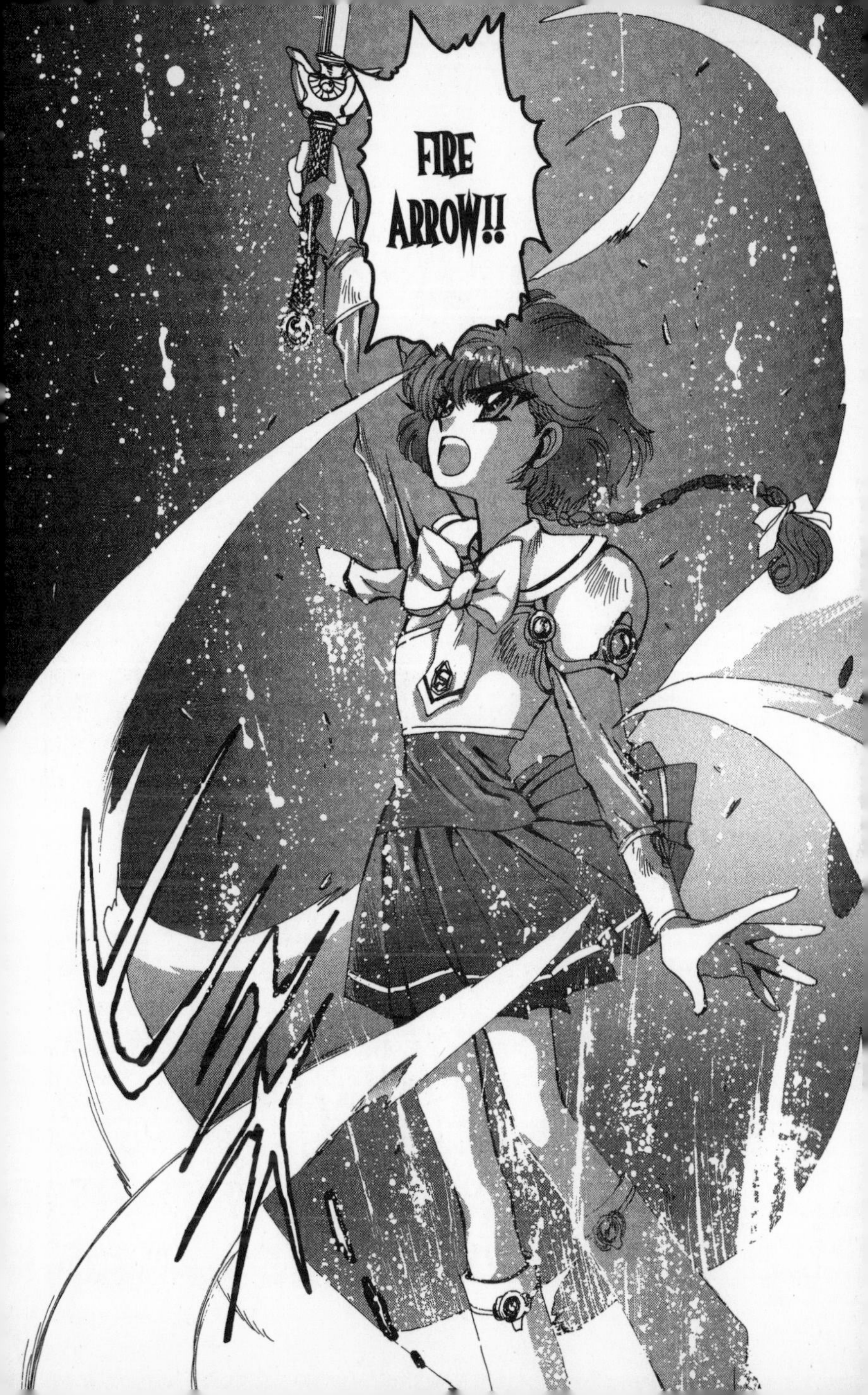
FIRE ARROW!!

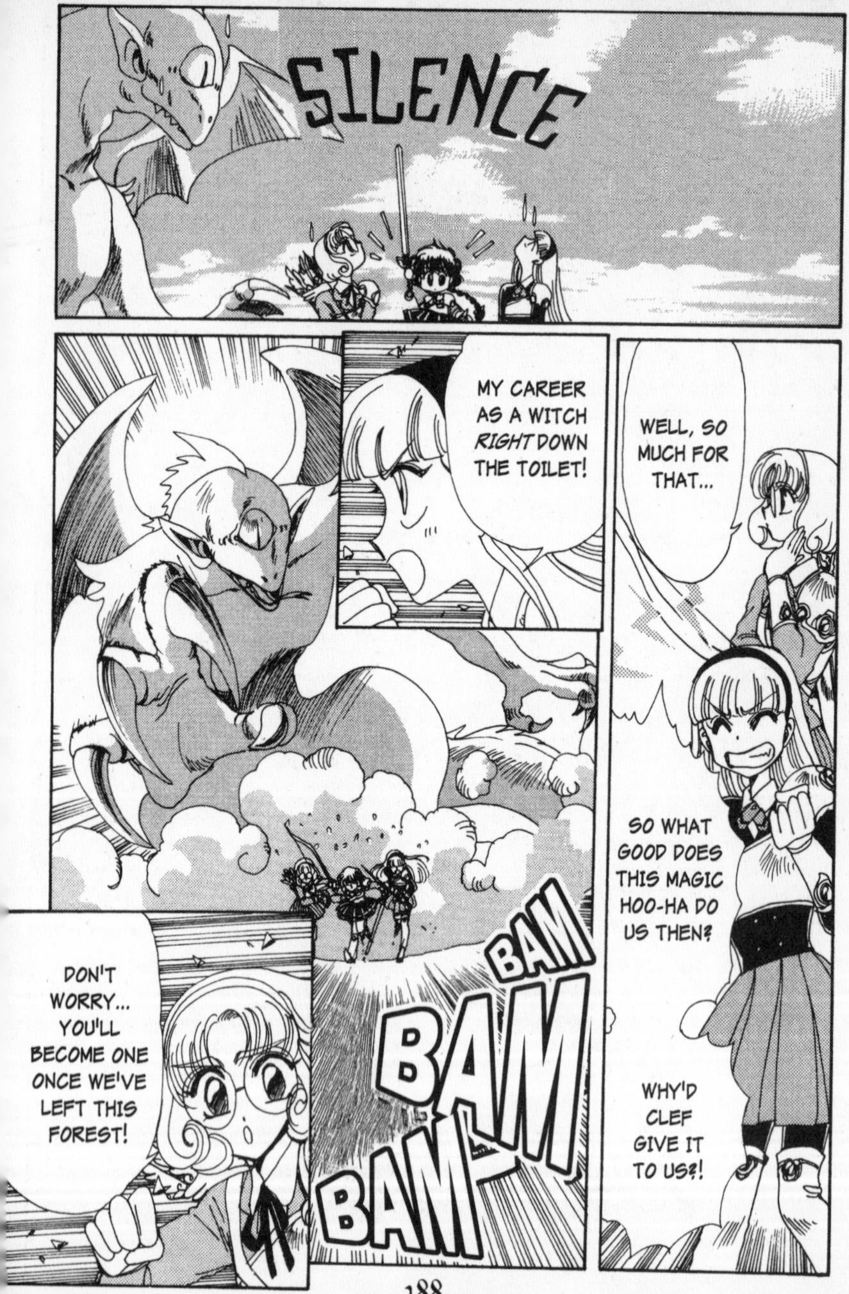
SILENCE
WELL, SO MUCH FOR THAT...
SO WHAT GOOD DOES THIS MAGIC HOO-HA DO US THEN?
WHY'D CLEF GIVE IT TO US?!
MY CAREER AS A WITCH *RIGHT* DOWN THE TOILET!
BAM BAM BAM
DON'T WORRY... YOU'LL BECOME ONE ONCE WE'VE LEFT THIS FOREST!

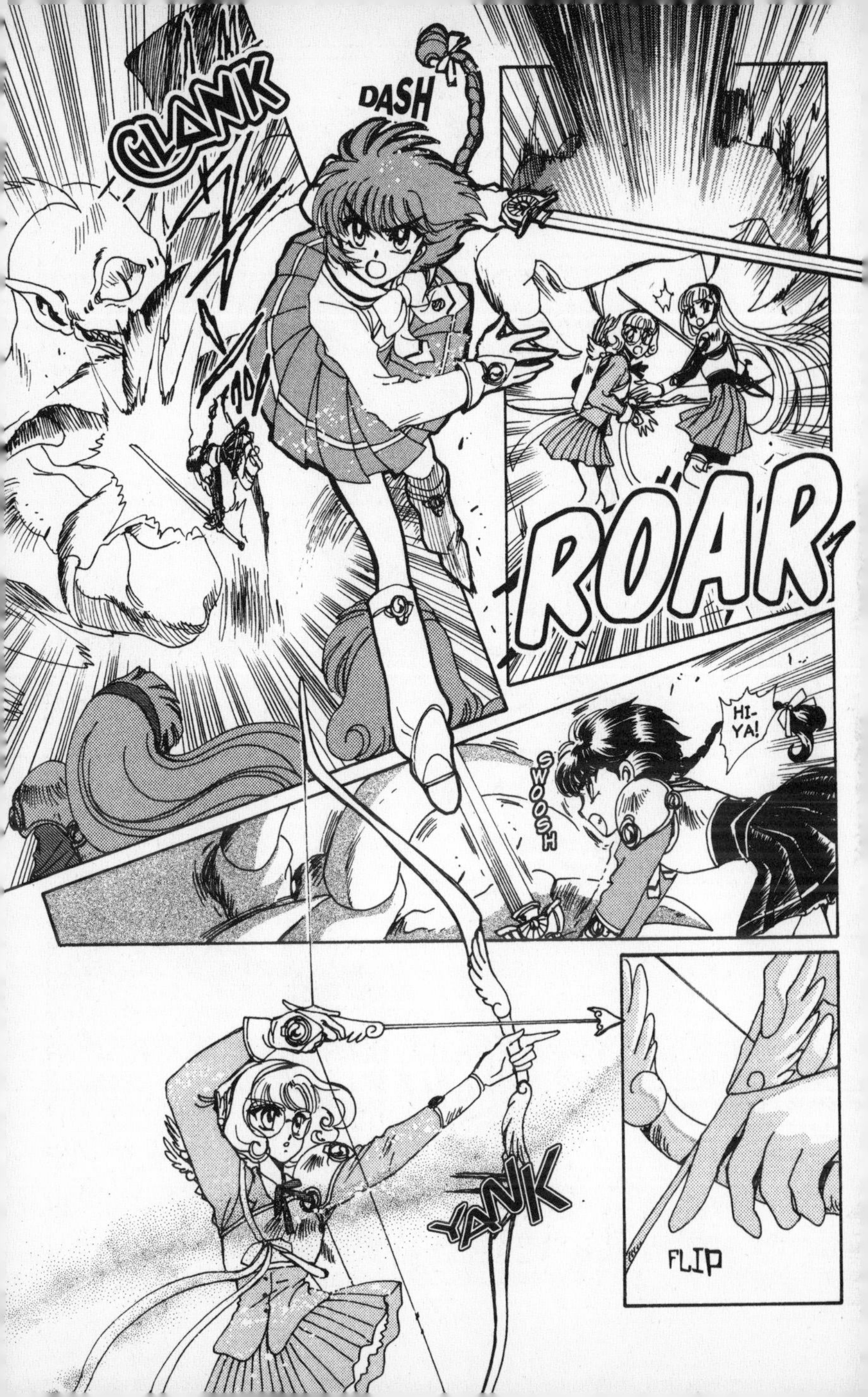
ROAR
DASH
CLANK
HI-YA!
SWOOSH
FLIP
YANK

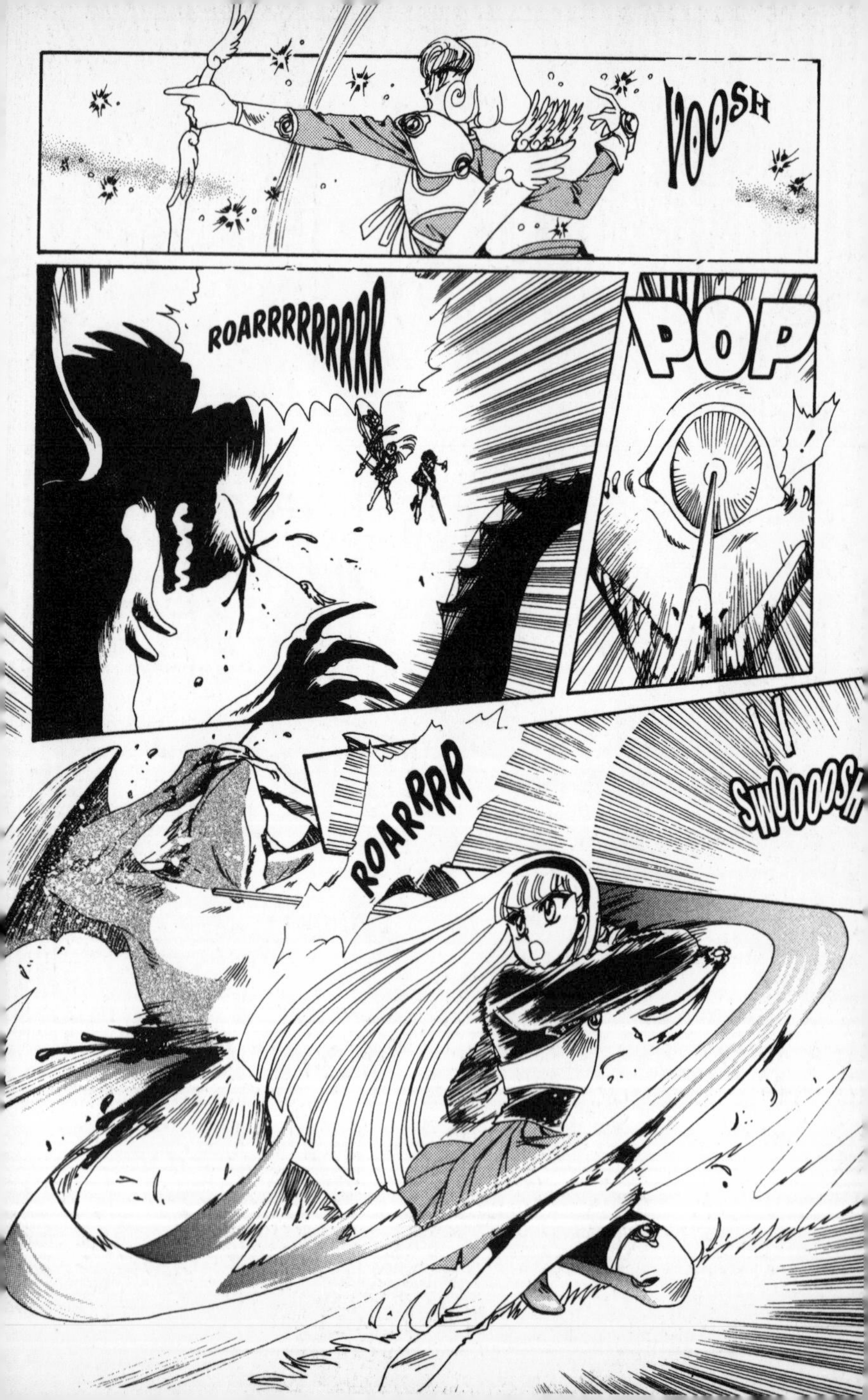
VOOSH
POP
ROARRRRRRRRR
SWOOOOSH
ROARRRR

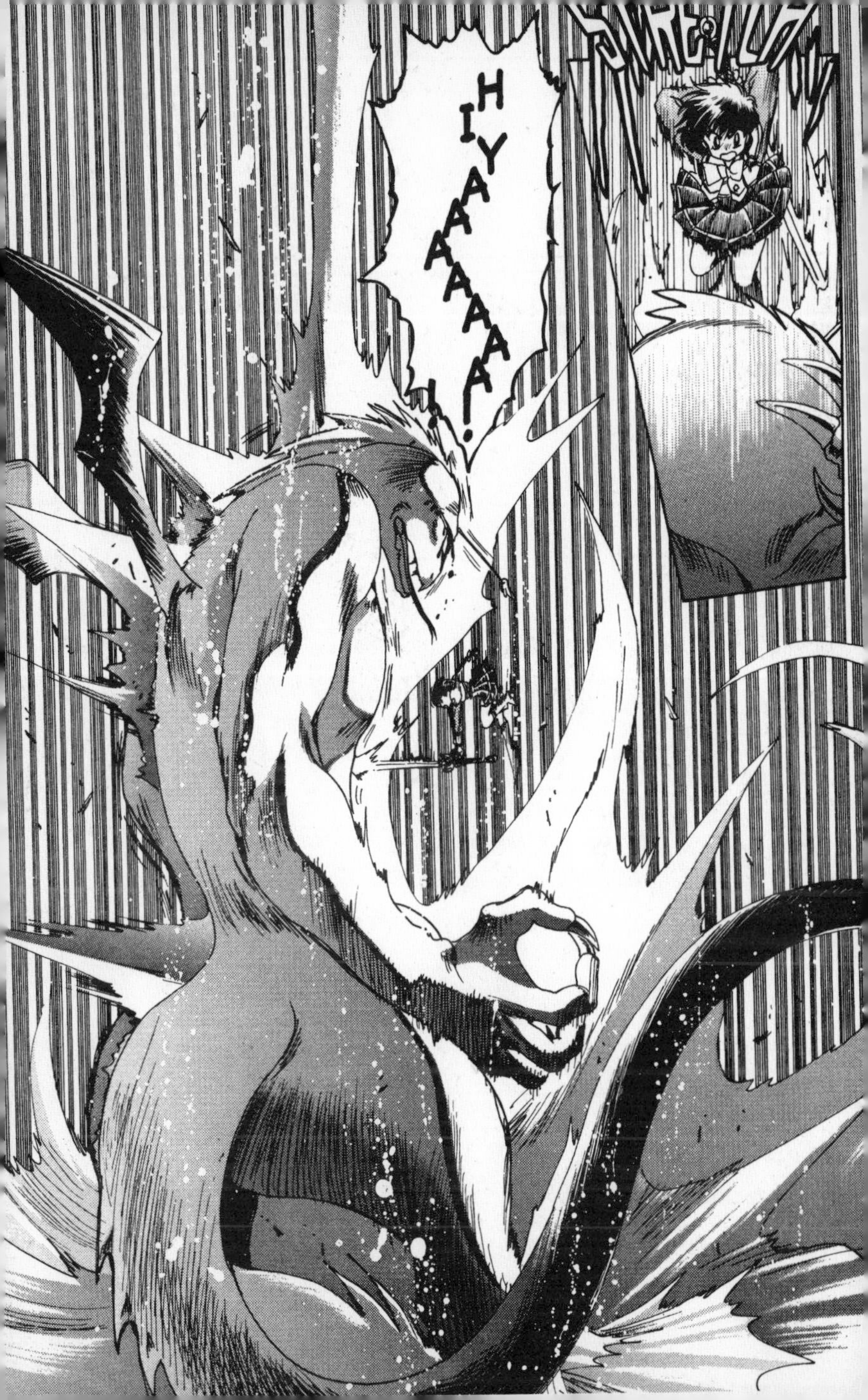
HIYAAAAAAA!!

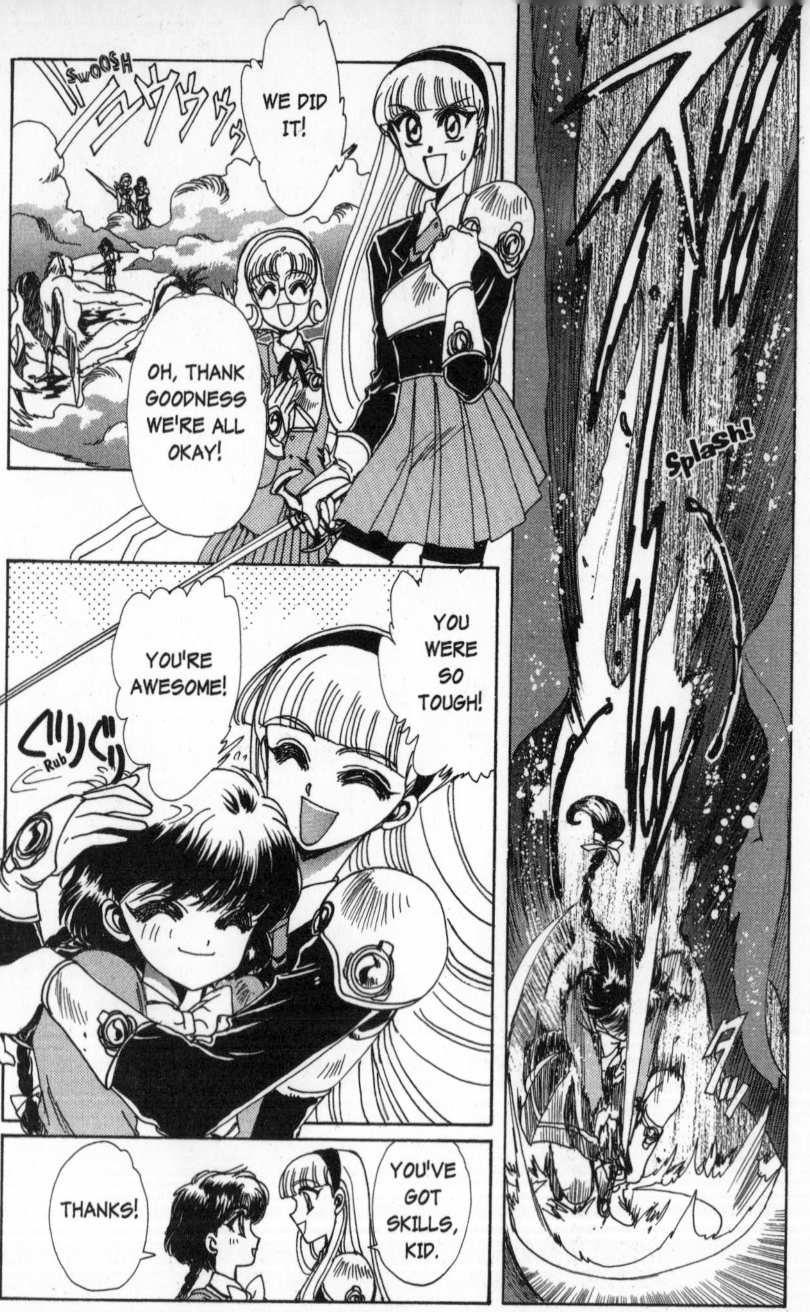
Splash!
SWOOSH
WE DID IT!
OH, THANK GOODNESS WE'RE ALL OKAY!
YOU WERE SO TOUGH!
YOU'RE AWESOME!
Rub
YOU'VE GOT SKILLS, KID.
THANKS!

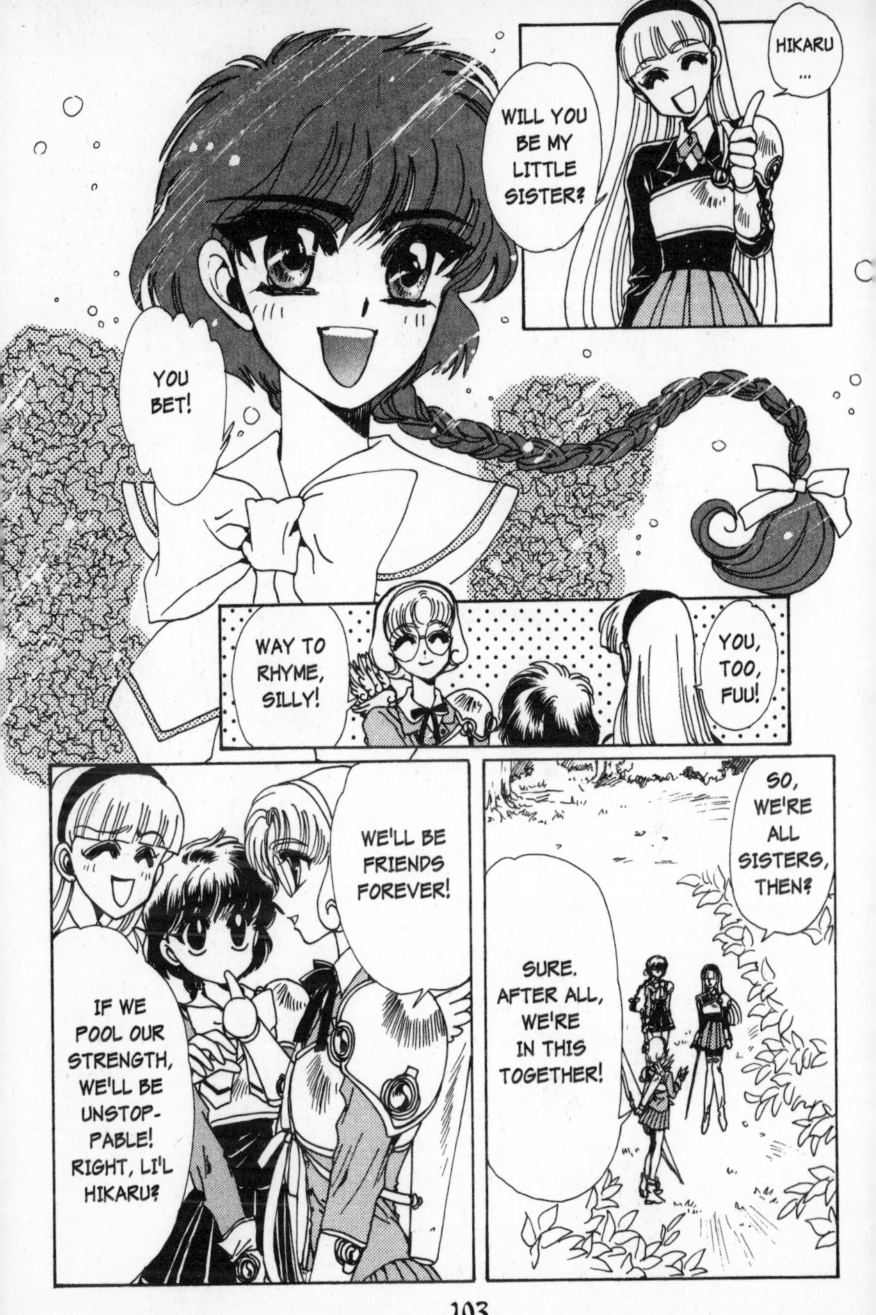
HIKARU ...
WILL YOU BE MY LITTLE SISTER?
YOU BET!
YOU, TOO, FUU!
WAY TO RHYME, SILLY!
SO, WE'RE ALL SISTERS, THEN?
SURE. AFTER ALL, WE'RE IN THIS TOGETHER!
WE'LL BE FRIENDS FOREVER!
IF WE POOL OUR STRENGTH, WE'LL BE UNSTOP-PABLE! RIGHT, LI'L HIKARU?

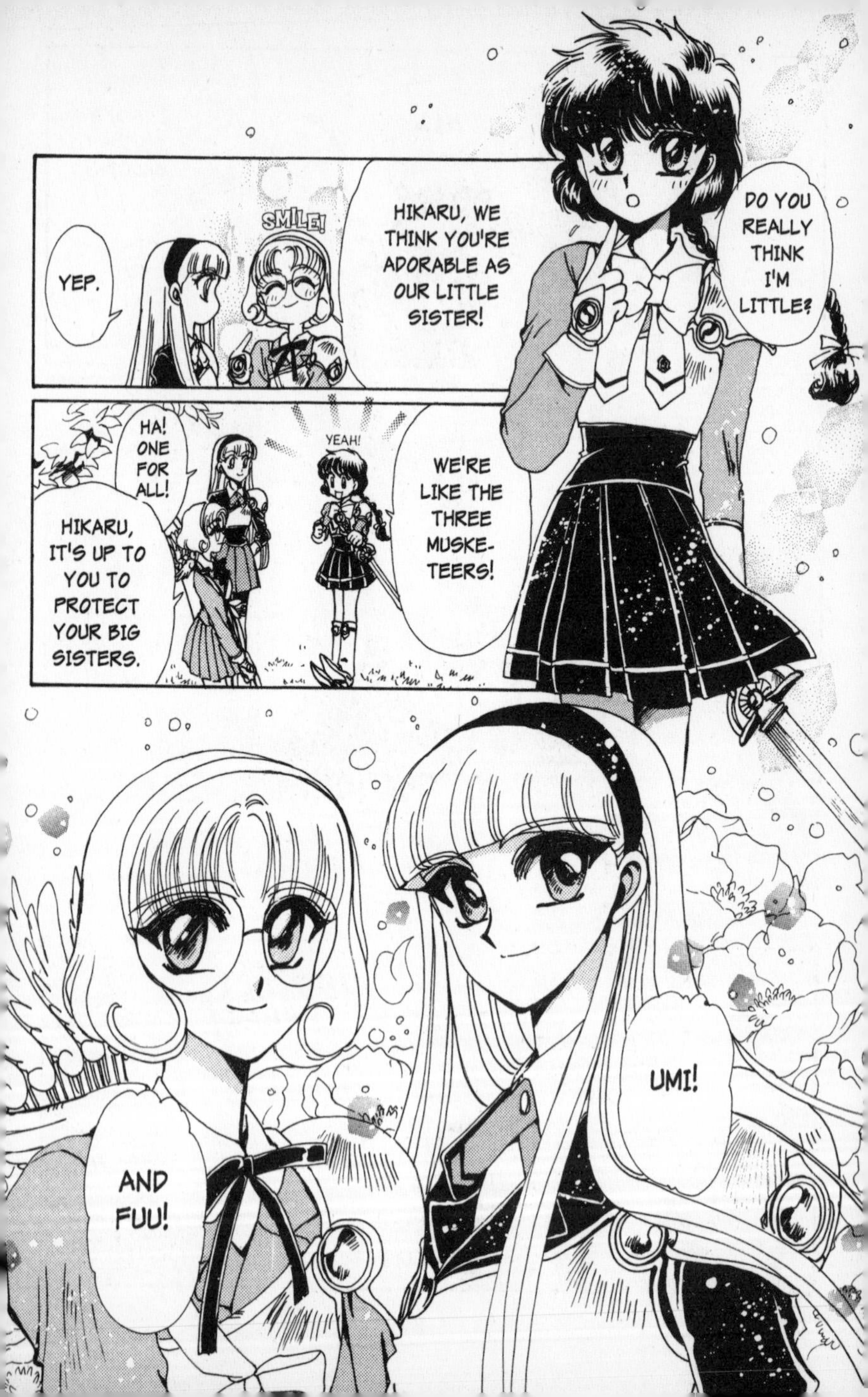
DO YOU REALLY THINK I'M LITTLE?
HIKARU, WE THINK YOU'RE ADORABLE AS OUR LITTLE SISTER!
SMILE!
YEP.
WE'RE LIKE THE THREE MUSKETEERS!
YEAH!
HA! ONE FOR ALL!
HIKARU, IT'S UP TO YOU TO PROTECT YOUR BIG SISTERS.
UMI!
AND FUU!

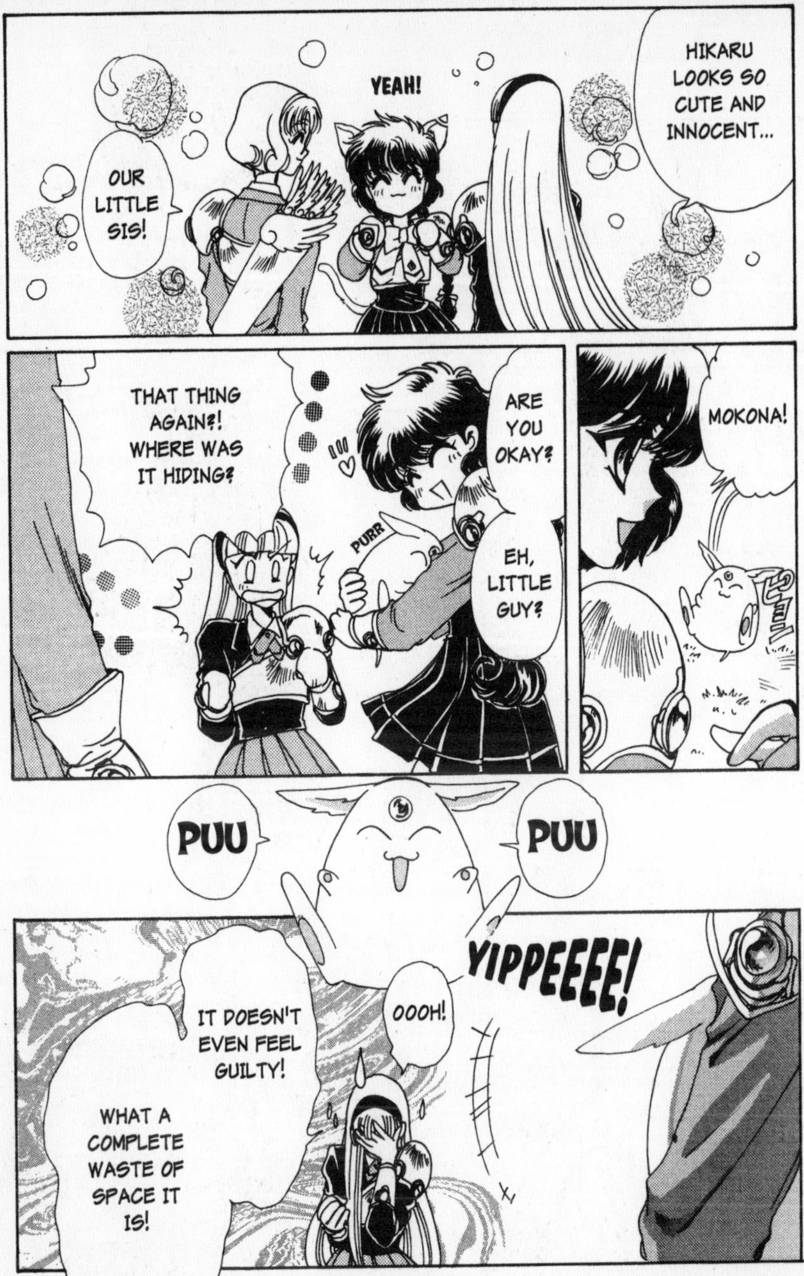
HIKARU LOOKS SO CUTE AND INNOCENT...
YEAH!
OUR LITTLE SIS!
MOKONA!
ARE YOU OKAY?
EH, LITTLE GUY?
PURR
THAT THING AGAIN?! WHERE WAS IT HIDING?
PUU
PUU
YIPPEEEE!
OOOH!
IT DOESN'T EVEN FEEL GUILTY!
WHAT A COMPLETE WASTE OF SPACE IT IS!

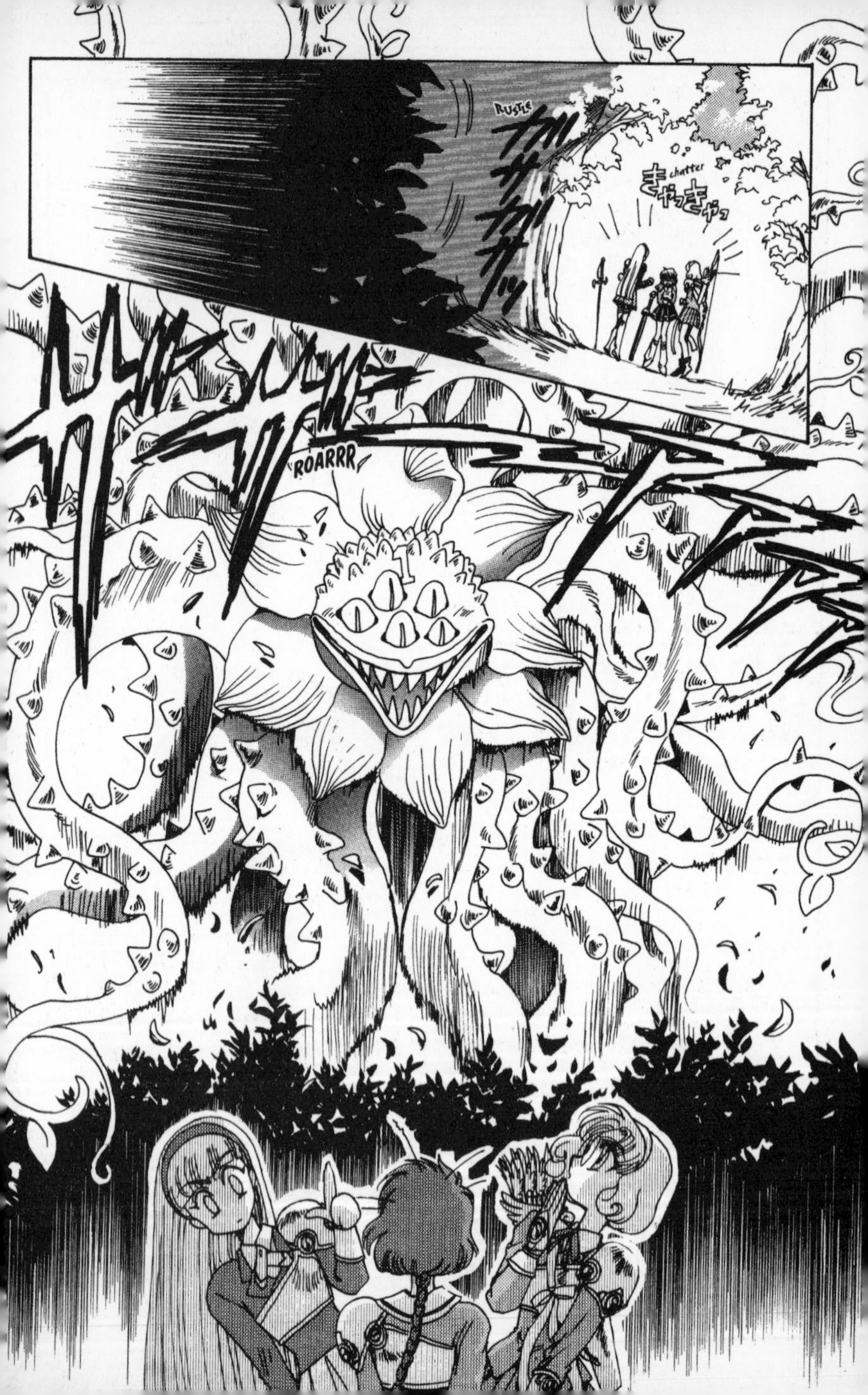
RUSTLE
chatter きゃっきゃっ
ROARRR

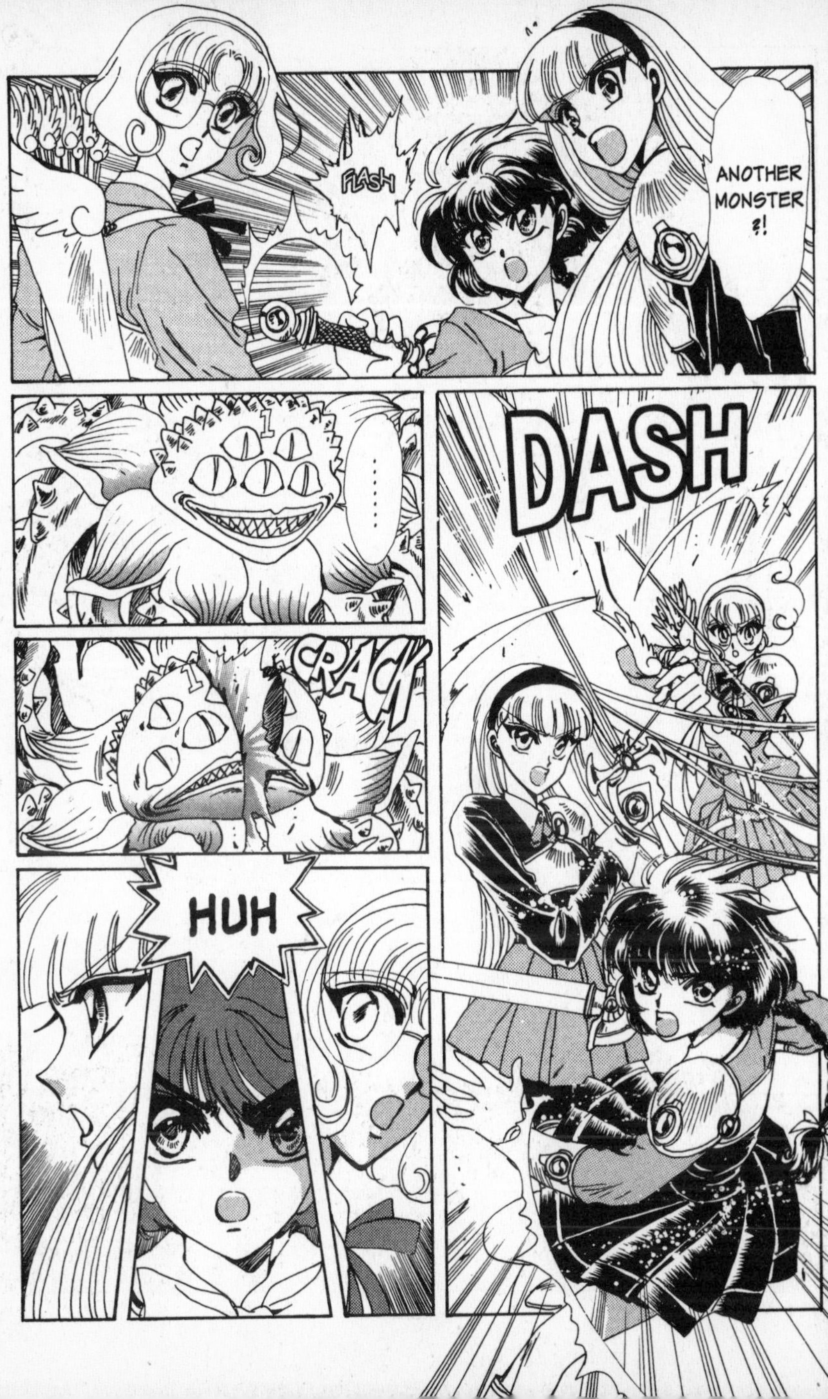
ANOTHER MONSTER ?!
FLASH
DASH
......
CRACK
HUH

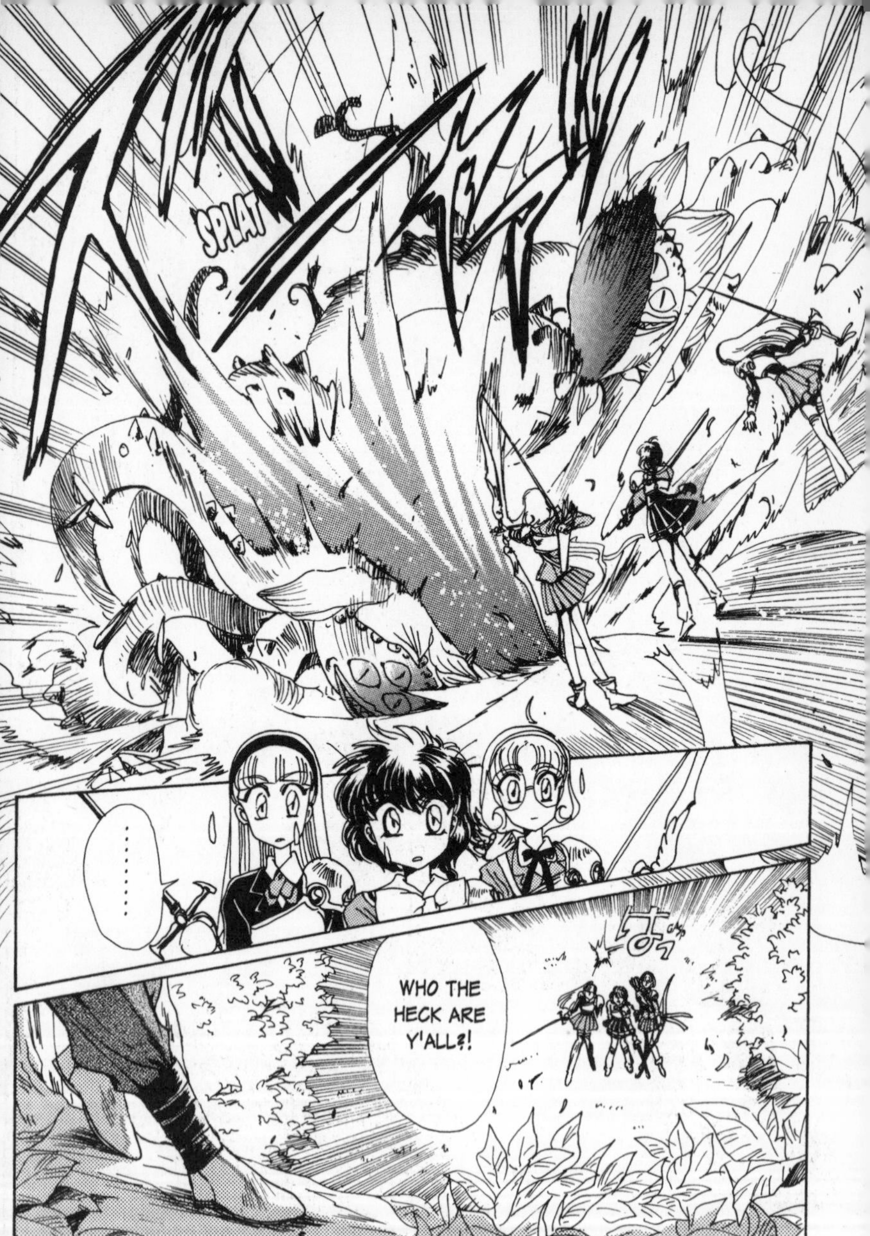
SPLAT
......
WHO THE HECK ARE Y'ALL?!

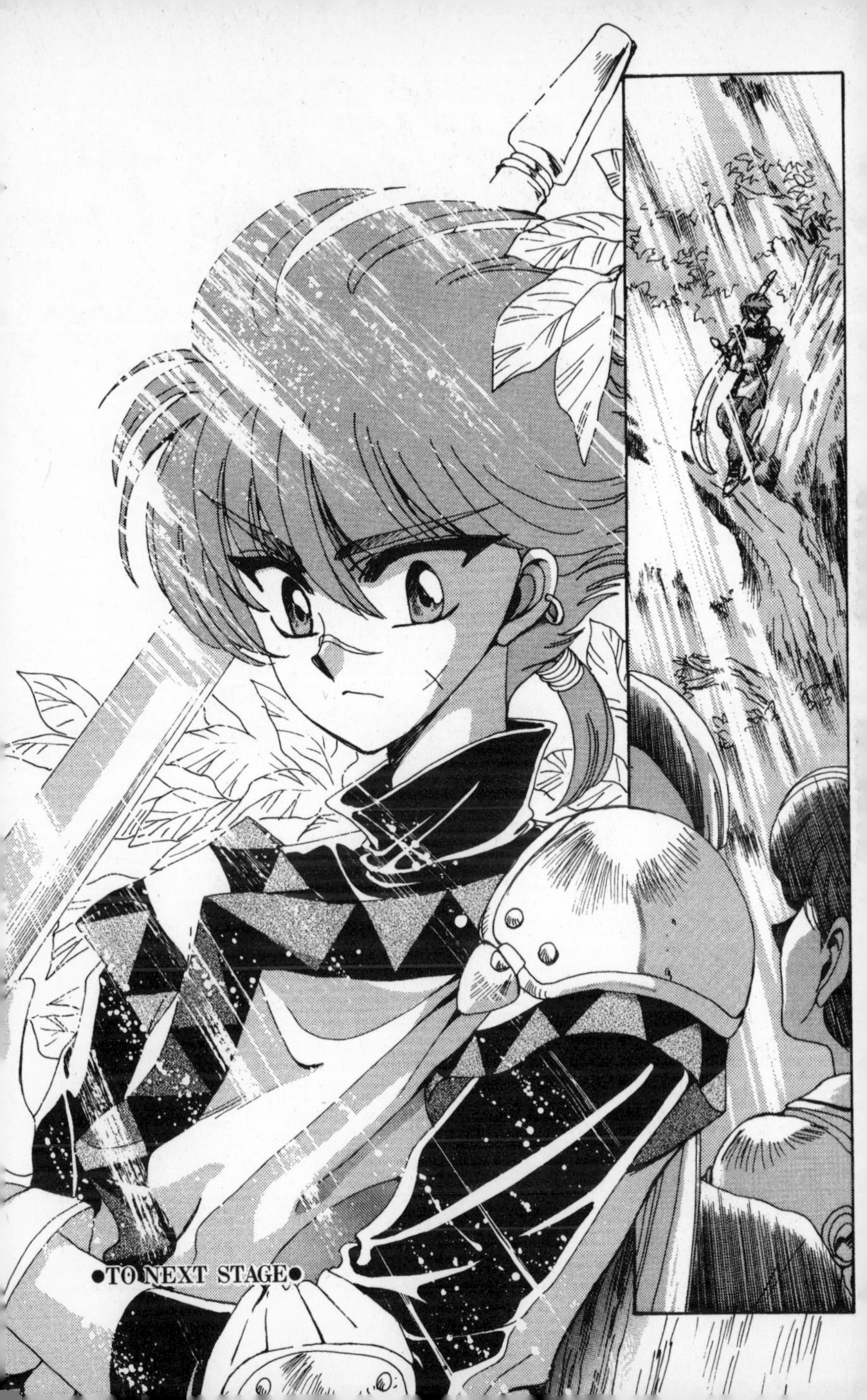
●TO NEXT STAGE●

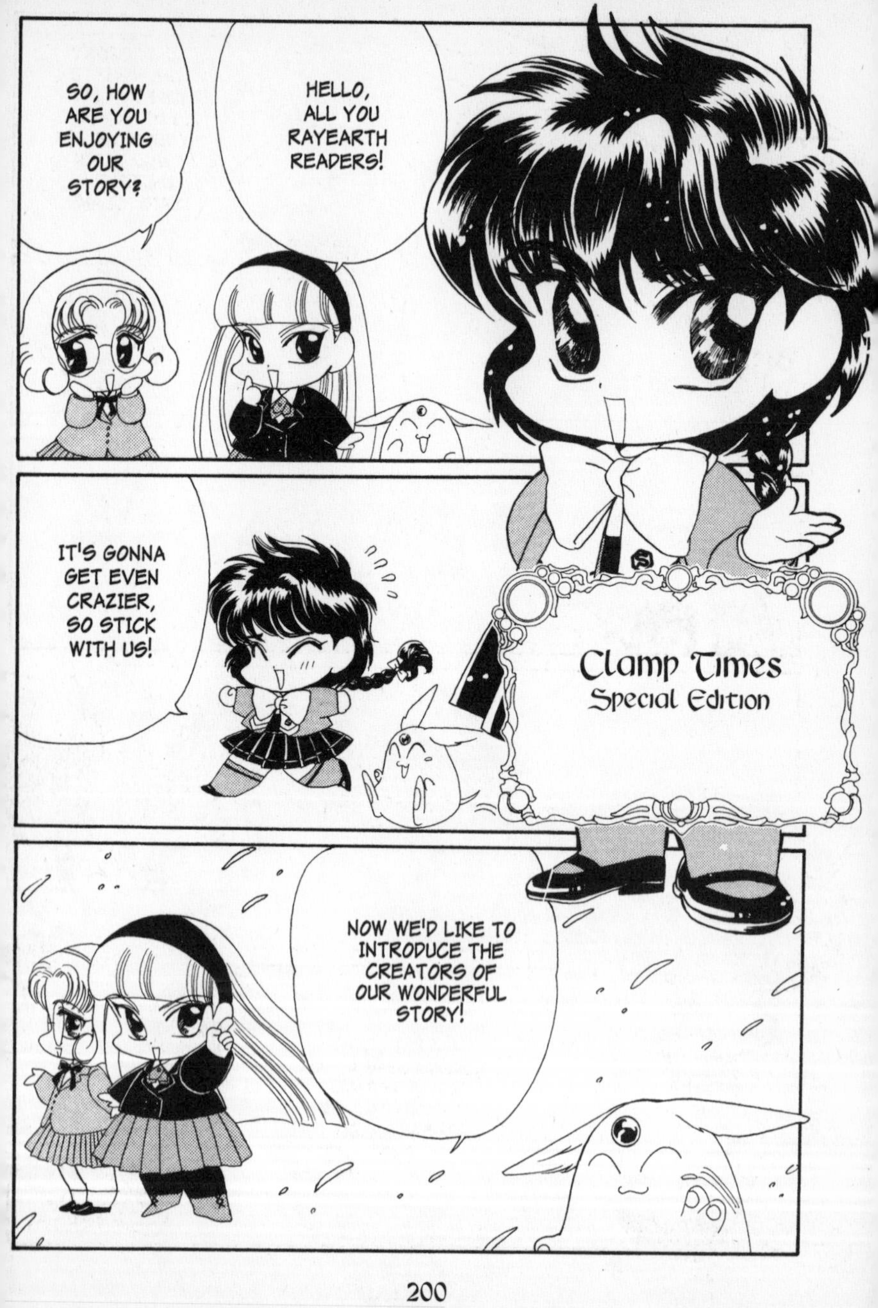
Clamp Times
Special Edition
HELLO, ALL YOU RAYEARTH READERS!
SO, HOW ARE YOU ENJOYING OUR STORY?
IT'S GONNA GET EVEN CRAZIER, SO STICK WITH US!
NOW WE'D LIKE TO INTRODUCE THE CREATORS OF OUR WONDERFUL STORY!

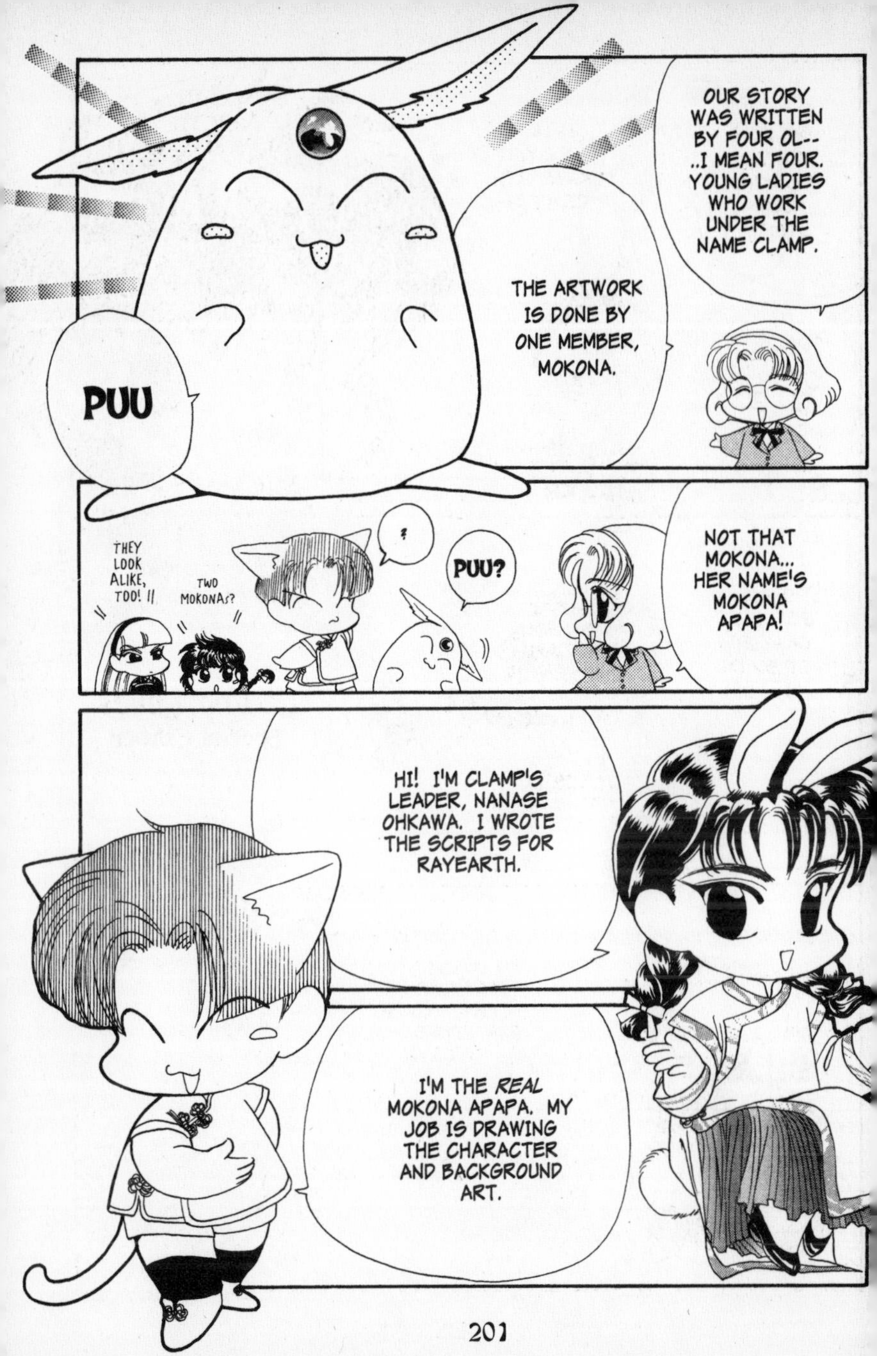
OUR STORY WAS WRITTEN BY FOUR OL-- ..I MEAN FOUR. YOUNG LADIES WHO WORK UNDER THE NAME CLAMP.
THE ARTWORK IS DONE BY ONE MEMBER, MOKONA.
PUU
NOT THAT MOKONA... HER NAME'S MOKONA APAPA!
PUU?
?
TWO MOKONAs?
THEY LOOK ALIKE, TOO!
HI! I'M CLAMP'S LEADER, NANASE OHKAWA. I WROTE THE SCRIPTS FOR RAYEARTH.
I'M THE *REAL* MOKONA APAPA. MY JOB IS DRAWING THE CHARACTER AND BACKGROUND ART.

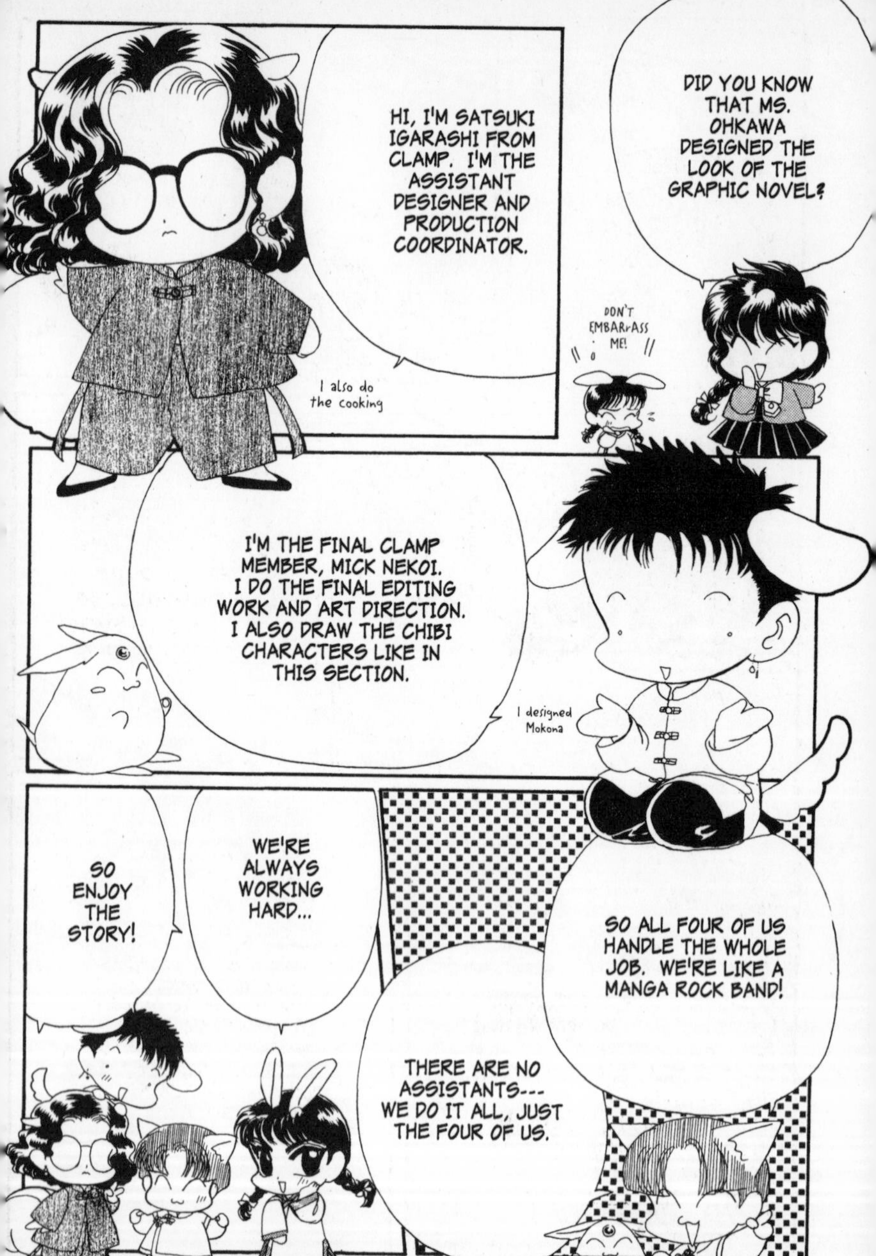
DID YOU KNOW THAT MS. OHKAWA DESIGNED THE LOOK OF THE GRAPHIC NOVEL?
DON'T EMBARrASS ME!
HI, I'M SATSUKI IGARASHI FROM CLAMP. I'M THE ASSISTANT DESIGNER AND PRODUCTION COORDINATOR.
I also do the cooking
I'M THE FINAL CLAMP MEMBER, MICK NEKOI. I DO THE FINAL EDITING WORK AND ART DIRECTION. I ALSO DRAW THE CHIBI CHARACTERS LIKE IN THIS SECTION.
I designed Mokona
SO ALL FOUR OF US HANDLE THE WHOLE JOB. WE'RE LIKE A MANGA ROCK BAND!
THERE ARE NO ASSISTANTS--- WE DO IT ALL, JUST THE FOUR OF US.
WE'RE ALWAYS WORKING HARD...
SO ENJOY THE STORY!

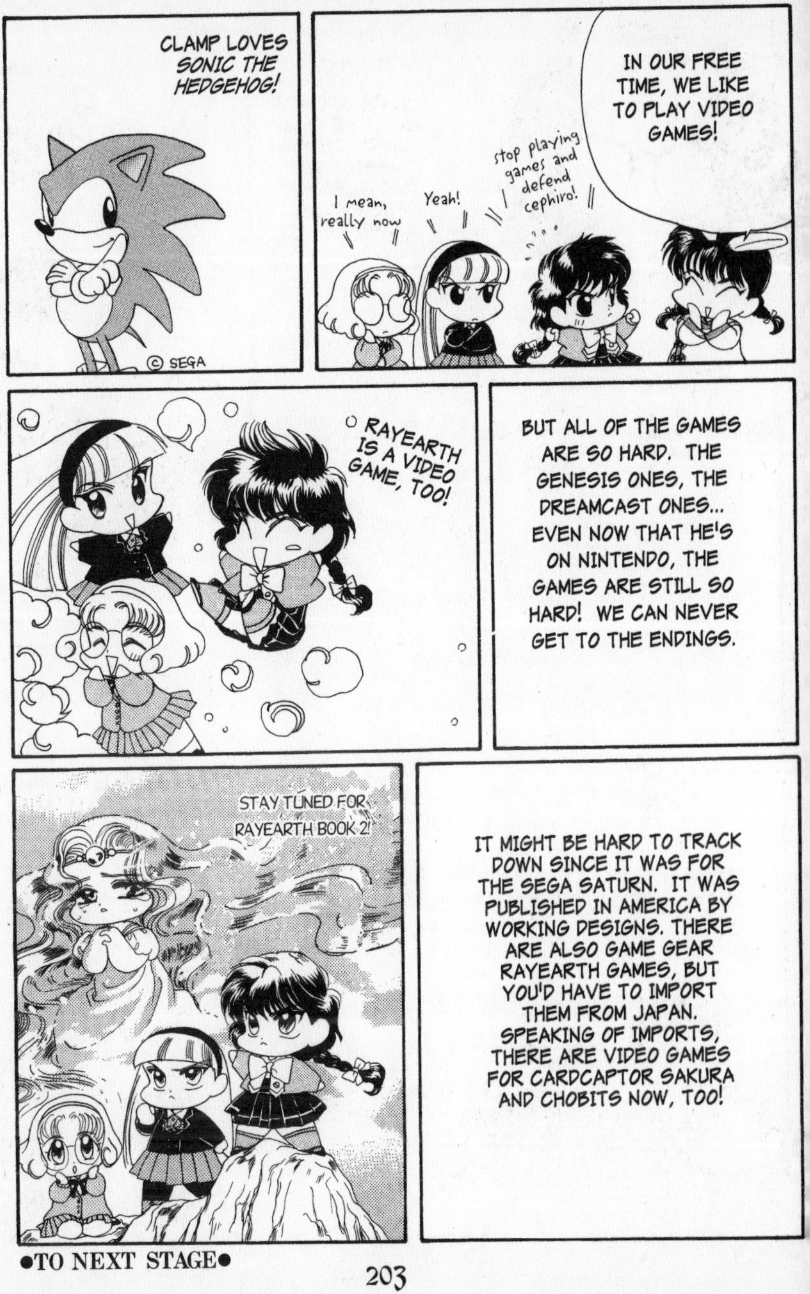
IN OUR FREE TIME, WE LIKE TO PLAY VIDEO GAMES!
stop playing games and defend cephiro!
Yeah!
I mean, really now
CLAMP LOVES SONIC THE HEDGEHOG!
© SEGA
BUT ALL OF THE GAMES ARE SO HARD. THE GENESIS ONES, THE DREAMCAST ONES... EVEN NOW THAT HE'S ON NINTENDO, THE GAMES ARE STILL SO HARD! WE CAN NEVER GET TO THE ENDINGS.
RAYEARTH IS A VIDEO GAME, TOO!
IT MIGHT BE HARD TO TRACK DOWN SINCE IT WAS FOR THE SEGA SATURN. IT WAS PUBLISHED IN AMERICA BY WORKING DESIGNS. THERE ARE ALSO GAME GEAR RAYEARTH GAMES, BUT YOU'D HAVE TO IMPORT THEM FROM JAPAN. SPEAKING OF IMPORTS, THERE ARE VIDEO GAMES FOR CARDCAPTOR SAKURA AND CHOBITS NOW, TOO!
STAY TUNED FOR RAYEARTH BOOK 2!

•TO NEXT STAGE•

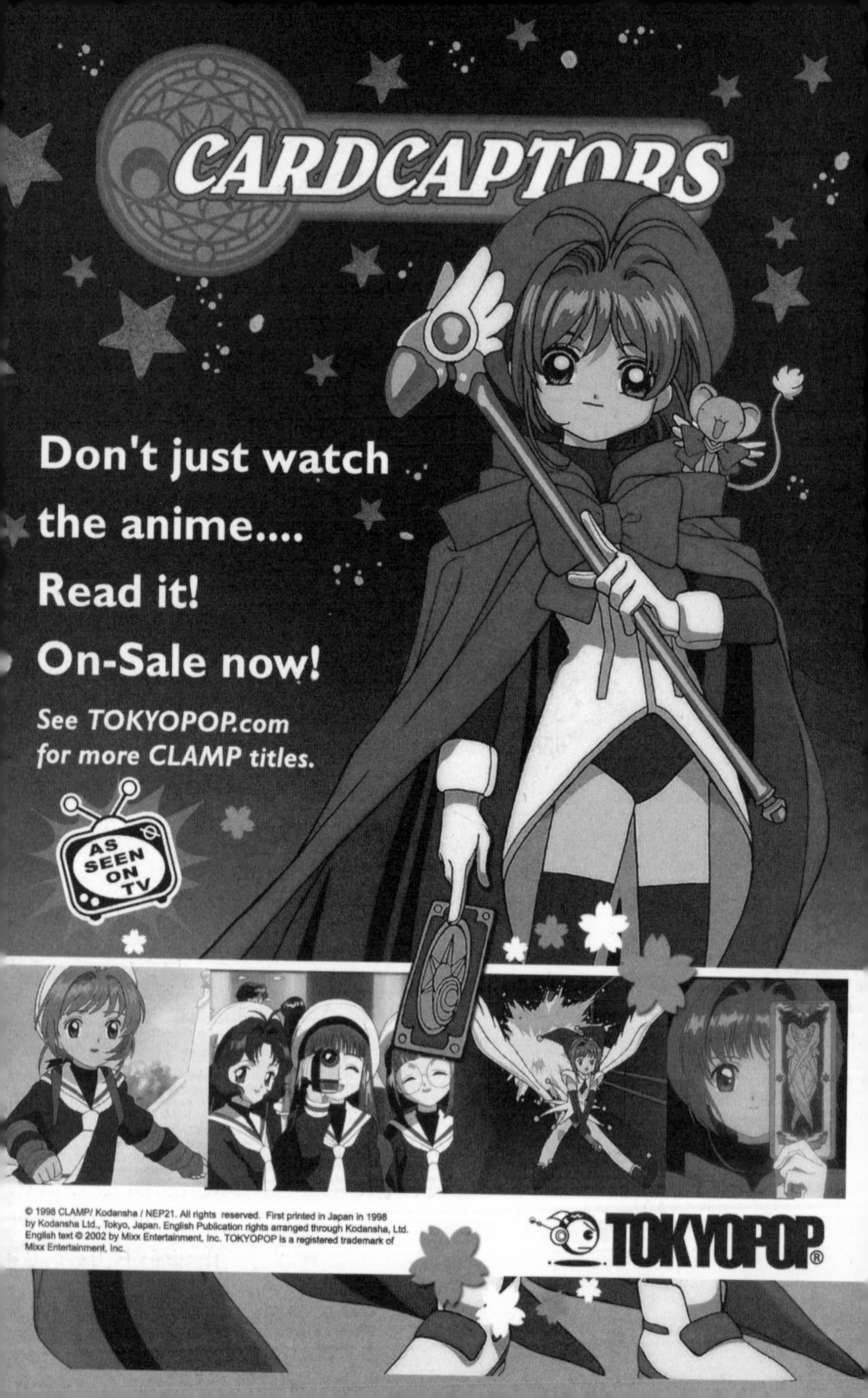
CARDCAPTORS
Don't just watch the anime.... Read it! On-Sale now!
See TOKYOPOP.com for more CLAMP titles.
AS SEEN ON TV
© 1998 CLAMP/ Kodansha / NEP21. All rights reserved. First printed in Japan in 1998 by Kodansha Ltd., Tokyo, Japan. English Publication rights arranged through Kodansha, Ltd. English text © 2002 by Mixx Entertainment, Inc. TOKYOPOP is a registered trademark of Mixx Entertainment, Inc.
TOKYOPOP®

Meet Misaki, the Prodigy.

A lightning-fast fighting doll.
An insane mentor.
A pinky promise to be the best.

The new manga from CLAMP, creators of Cardcaptor Sakura.

Volume 1 & 2 available now!

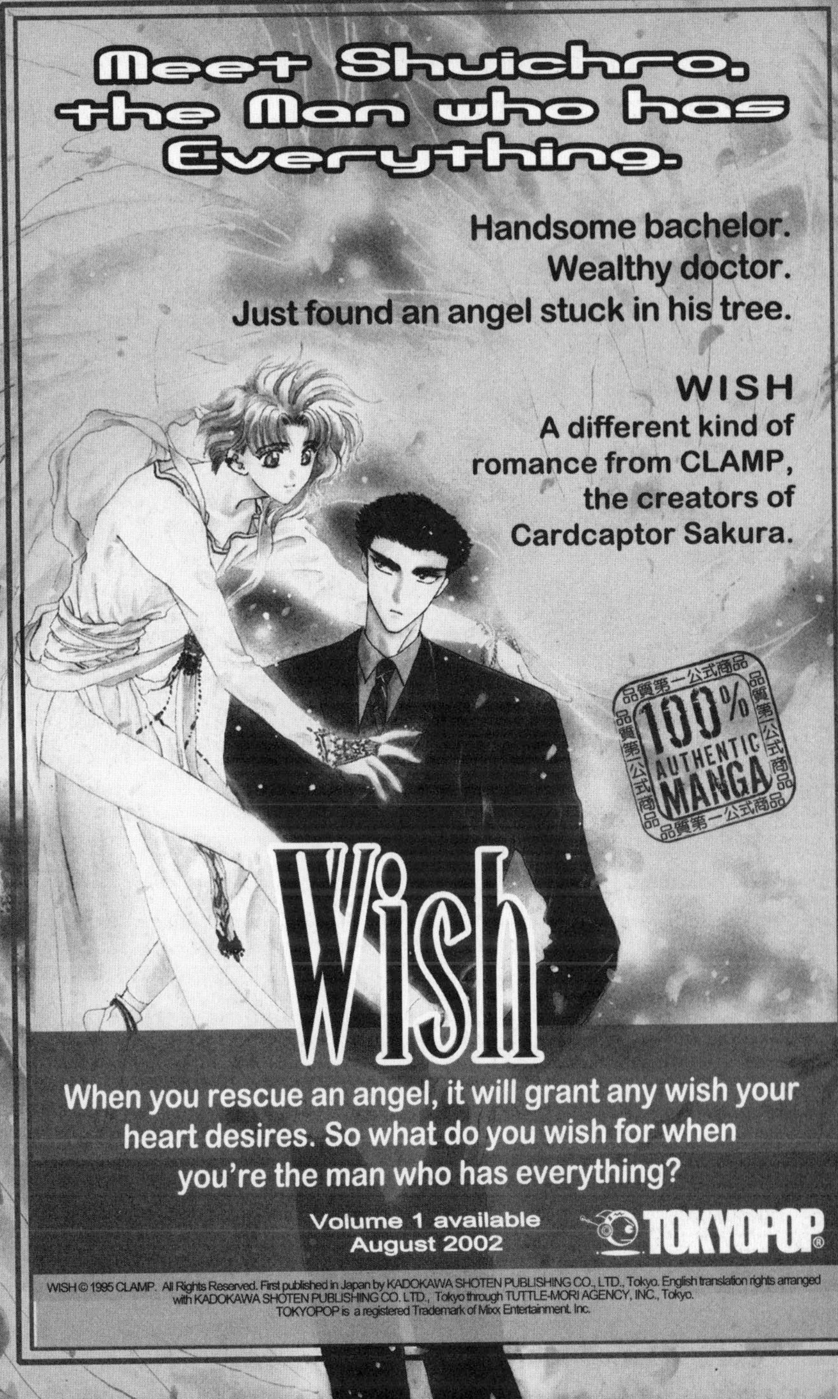
Meet Shuichro, the Man who has Everything.
Handsome bachelor. Wealthy doctor. Just found an angel stuck in his tree.
WISH
A different kind of romance from CLAMP, the creators of Cardcaptor Sakura.
100% AUTHENTIC MANGA
Wish
When you rescue an angel, it will grant any wish your heart desires. So what do you wish for when you're the man who has everything?
Volume 1 available August 2002
TOKYOPOP®
WISH © 1995 CLAMP. All Rights Reserved. First published in Japan by KADOKAWA SHOTEN PUBLISHING CO., LTD., Tokyo. English translation rights arranged with KADOKAWA SHOTEN PUBLISHING CO. LTD., Tokyo through TUTTLE-MORI AGENCY, INC., Tokyo.
TOKYOPOP is a registered Trademark of Mixx Entertainment Inc.

STOP!

This is the back of the book.
You wouldn't want to spoil a great ending!

This book is printed "manga-style," in the authentic Japanese right-to-left format. Since none of the artwork has been flipped or altered, readers get to experience the story just as the creator intended. You've been asking for it, so TOKYOPOP® delivered: authentic, hot-off-the-press, and far more fun!

DIRECTIONS

If this is your first time reading manga-style, here's a quick guide to help you understand how it works.

It's easy... just start in the top right panel and follow the numbers. Have fun, and look for more 100% authentic manga from TOKYOPOP®!